Raising Capital

Third Edition

Raising Capital

Get the Money You Need to Grow Your Business

Third Edition

Andrew J. Sherman

⋏MACOM

American Management Association
New York • Atlanta • Brussels • Chicago • Mexico City • San Francisco
Shanghai • Tokyo • Toronto • Washington, D. C.

Bulk discounts available. For details visit:
www.amacombooks.org/go/specialsales
Or contact special sales:
Phone: 800-250-5308
E-mail: specialsls@amanet.org
View all the AMACOM titles at www.amacombooks.org

This publication is designed to provide accurate and authoritative information in regard to the subject matter covered. It is sold with the understanding that the publisher is not engaged in rendering legal, accounting, or other professional service. If legal advice or other expert assistance is required, the services of a competent professional person should be sought.

Library of Congress Cataloging-in-Publication Data

Sherman, Andrew J.
Raising capital : get the money you need to grow your business / Andrew J. Sherman. — 3rd ed.

    p. cm.
Includes bibliographical references and index.
ISBN: 978-0-8144-1703-4 (hardc)
ISBN: 978-0-8144-3901-2 (pbk)
ISBN: 978-0-8144-1704-1 (ebook)

1.   New business enterprises—United States—Finance.   2.   Venture capital—United States. I. Title.
HG4027.6.S534   2012
658.15'224—dc23

                                        2011051128

About AMA

American Management Association (www.amanet.org) is a world leader in talent development, advancing the skills of individuals to drive business success. Our mission is to support the goals of individuals and organizations through a complete range of products and services, including classroom and virtual seminars, webcasts, webinars, podcasts, conferences, corporate and government solutions, business books and research. AMA's approach to improving performance combines experiential learning—learning through doing—with opportunities for ongoing professional growth at every step of one's career journey.

Printing number

18   19   20   PC/LSCC   10   9   8   7   6   5   4

For my wife Judy and my children, Matthew and Jennifer; they are my never-ending source of support and inspiration.

Contents

Preface to the Third Edition

When updating a preface to a new edition of a book, many authors update a few statistics, change a few key data points and relay on the sage advice that appeared in the previous edition opening words. And I must admit that as my deadline for submission reared in the summer of 2011, I was tempted to do the same. But in a world that had completely changed in the seven years since the publishing of the second edition, that would be unfair, even borderline unethical to you, the reader, the visionary, the entrepreneur about to begin your quest for capital.

So here it is, an all-new, all-fresh preface to the third edition. Other than my favorite John May quote at the end, not a single word is the same. Why did the preface need a complete overhaul and not just a few cosmetic changes? Well, let's take a look as to how the capital markets and capital formation trends have changed since 2005:

- After one of our nation's deepest recessions in 2008 to 2010, there was already talk of a second "tech bubble" by 2011 (as was feared and then realized in 2001) as social networking, gaming and technology companies such as Groupon, Living Social, Zynga, Airbnb, 4Square, Twitter and Jawbone, fetched multi-billion dollar valuations (based at the latest price paid by recent investors), while LinkedIn, Zillow, and Pandora completed their initial public offerings and the king of the buzz, Facebook, was flirting with a $100 billion dollar valuation (who says history doesn't repeat itself every ten years???).

- Investors of all types insisting on greater controls and covenants tied to specific real or perceived weaknesses in the entrepreneur's business plan or model
- Investors engaged in a paradigm shift between "betting on the come" (BOTC) style investing vs. show me some success and traction first approach
- Uptick in the tension and growing gulf between the vision defined strategic path of the CEO and the executives and demands of investors
- Wider, deeper, slower (and more personal) due diligence in an era of distrust between lenders and sources of capital triggered by Enron, WorldCom, Madoff, Stamford, the mortgage meltdown, the great recession of 2008-2010, etc.
- Communications and disclosure has also been more critical on a post-investment basis to maintain that trust as "who knows what when" evolves into a critical strategic governance issue (e.g., is information shared as a "light switch" or as a gradual "dimmer dial"?)
- A significant increase in "cross-border" investment transactions, which means that in addition to the typical gaps between investors and entrepreneurs, oversight, language and legal gaps also need to be bridged
- The lines between what is private and what is public blur as new models and securities markets emerge inspired by companies such as SecondMarket and Share Post
- In the public markets, the presences of quarterly reporting are chipping away at company's commitments to long-term investment and innovations – the unintended consequences of public disclosure
- With Sarbanes-Oxley celebrating its eighth (8th) birthday, smaller public companies continue to struggle with the costs of compliance, choosing to go private or be acquired — these same companies are having a hard time attracting high quality outside directors as the cost-benefit analysis becomes harder and harder to justify
- Social networking and Web 2.0 has inspired new investing models and resources for entrepreneurs as crowdfunding, peer-to-peer lending, sophisticated online barter networks and investor-entrepreneur matching services are more robust and accessible
- The total capital costs required by many start-ups have dropped significantly (I remember when a website cost at least $1 million to build

properly) and many entrepreneurs are bootstrapping and delaying, deferring, or avoiding capital formation completely or at least until that can demonstrate sustainable customers, revenues, market penetration and even profitability before seeking outside investors

- The lines between venture capital (VC) and private equity (PE) have not only blurred but actually have become downright competitive. Typically, PE buys companies outright, builds them and sells them for a profit. VC firms invest in a minority stake in earlier stage enterprises, coach them to success and work towards a higher valuation. But both seem to be eyeing each other's lunch. VC's are taking control positions in early-stage enterprises and actively managing and running them and PE's seem willing to take minority stakes in companies and grow them side-by-side with existing management teams and ownership groups. Silver Lake, a PE firm, bought Skype®, cleaned it up a bit and sold it to Microsoft. That same week in July of 2011, Silver Lake teamed with Kohlberg Kravis Roberts (KKR) to buy GoDaddy® for over $2 billion dollars – companies like Skype and GoDaddy were traditionally the domain of larger venture capital firms.

- The amount of investor dollars being thrown at entrepreneurs building "killer apps" for the rapidly growing mobile market has taken off like a rocket ship. Some applications, like Airbnb, which helps people rent rooms in their homes and Scvngr, which is a Groupon model for gamers, make some sense, but The Melt, also just raised $15 million from prominent venture capital from Sequoia Capital (who, interestingly, had declared venture capital dead in 2008 in a widely distributed an compelling PowerPoint presentation that went viral), is a mobile application that sells grilled cheese sandwiches (who knew? Even I can make a great grilled cheese sandwich for $15 million dollars!).

- Web 1.0 (1995 to 2002) featured big investments being provided to the companies that helped us all get on to the internet (AOL, Yahoo, Netscape, Google, Amazon, eBay, DoubleClick, etc. and other "on-ramp" companies) and Web 2.0 (2008-date) has featured by investments in the companies that help us stay connected as passengers on the internet highway (social, local, mobile, real-time connectors such as Facebook, LinkedIn, Groupon, LivingSocial, Zynga, Twitter, etc.) – the truly visionary investors are already focused on Web 3.0 (2012-____?)

where advanced communication, cloud-driven data storage, holography and 3-D, voice commands, robotics, ultra-fast processors, and multiple types of biometrics will rule the road.

- Although the excitement about social networking pervades, some companies have quietly gone public and grown like wildfire, yielding billions for their investors in some pretty traditional industries, such as PriceLine (travel), Netflix (movie rental), OpenTable (restaurant reservations), and some of the "hottest" initial public offerings (IPOs) of late 2011 included traditional industries such as: Dunkin' Donuts (food services), C&J Energy (hydraulic fracturing services to extract oil and gas), ADS Tactical (government procurement management services), Teavana (purveyor of premium loose teas), Tangoe (a communications software company) Chef's Warehouse (specialty foods distributor), Skullcandy (audio equipment), and American Midstream Partners (a natural gas pipeline and processing partnership).

- The gap between the "haves" and the "have-nots" when it comes to truly motivated and passionate workers continues to grow. While employees at Zynga play poker at breaks at its progressive, high energy offices in San Francisco and the teams at Google go up to the mountain during mandated innovation sessions, a disturbing chunk of the U.S. workforce is either underemployed or strongly disengaged in their jobs, significantly affecting productivity, customer service and innovation levels of their employers. Many feel stuck in "dead-end" jobs because the weaker economy has forced a lack of mobility and a narrow band of new internal or external opportunities. While our politicians and policy makers fret and debate as to how to solve our nation's nine percent unemployment rate, a much broader problem is standing in the way of our country's advancement and ability to compete, innovate and grow–the underemployment rate of nearly 25%! Almost one-fourth of our nation's workers are under-challenged, under-appreciate, under-motivated and under-paid, not exactly creating ideal workplace conditions and culture inside companies across America. Leaders and board members need to be acutely aware of this disturbing trend and development strategies and systems to empower their teams. A recent study by Mercer of nearly 30,000 workers in 17 countries, including 2400 US workers, indicates that one out of every two employees is either planning to leave his or her organization or is "mentally missing in action" on the job. The report mirrors last year's Gallup study demonstrating that a whopping 71% of America's employees are either disengaged or actively disengaged at work. And if that's not disturbing enough, the economic impact of the "actively disengaged" worker segment alone- those with one foot out the door, who are also poisoning the well along the way- costs America $350 billion per year in lost productivity.

- Larger companies need to "take a page from the playbook" of these venture-backed companies to create passion and engagement in their workplace if we are ever going to get the economy fully kick-started again and review competition in the global marketplace.

- The number of organizations, universities, economic development councils, non-profits and other groups that have been formed to support entrepreneurship and capital formation make me bullish for our nation's future – the efforts of organizations that have been in existence for many years, such as Entrepreneurs Organization (www.www. eonetwork.org), SCORE (www.score.org), the SBDC program (www. wsbdc.org), NCIIA (www.nciia.org), are being augmented by newer and online organizations and social networks which woven as a fabric, make our country stronger, such as Venture Hacks/AngelList, Startup Tribe, and many of the regional and local web communities that match investors and entrepreneurs. We even have primetime television shows such as Shark Tank and TechStars providing guidance and insights on the capital formation process.

- The dividend ratio (e.g., the percentage of earnings paid to shareholders relative to cash preserved in the company's treasury) hit the lowest in the summer of 2011 than it had been since 1936. Why were so many public companies hoarding their cash–estimated in the aggregate at well over two trillion dollars–saving deployment for a rainy day – when the economy so desperately needed that capital to create new jobs, stimulate new revenues, seed new innovations and penetrate new markets to drive shareholder valve? Surely it was not to earn interest on its money market holdings at a time of historically-low interest rates! In fact, many companies borrowed more cash and then sat on it in order to take advantage of these low borrowing costs. The volatility of the global economy, the failure to properly integrate certain large mergers, the uncertainty of the political situation of so many countries around the globe have caused CFOs of large companies to be tentative and nervous when it comes to putting capital to work. And stagnated capital leads to a stagnated economy – one that is neither growing or declining, but feels almost frozen in time without progress. You don't need to be a trained economist to understand why the GDP growth estimates are in the unimpressive low single digits for the future, while many developing countries such as China, India and even places like Ethiopia and Colombia are growing at rates well into the teens. Dormant capital cannot sit idle indefinitely without shareholder revolt. Hopefully, the floodgates will open soon and the ripple effects will be felt by a wide swath of the U.S. population.

- In August of 2011, the S&P rating agency downgraded the United States credit rating to AA + from AAA for the first time since 1936. The political fighting and inability to reign in our nation's debt has the world capital markets wondering out loud about our ability to govern and comparison to situations in Ireland, Italy, Spain and Greece were already being made.

So, what's the bottom line? What's the take-away lesson and concrete advice that can be gleaned from all of these trends and observations? First, there will always be a limited number of truly entrepreneurial, game changing companies who are blessed with remarkable upsides. Capital market trends and investor confidence and psychology will dictate whether those few truly exceptional companies fetch $10 billion dollar valuations or $100 billion dollar valuations. Cycles vary from time to time as to how high and how far these high flyers can soar. And there will always be the "also-rans", the "wanna-bes," the "Johnny-come-latelys," the "copycats," the "rose-colored glasses dreamers," the "tinkerers," the "business-model lacking geeks," and the "stubborn asses," who will only raise capital during a genuine short-lived hysteria from unsophisticated investors with a bursting of the bubble just around the corner.

Raising Capital was written in 2000, the second edition in 2005, and the third edition in 2012 dedicated to everyone else in between these two extremes. This third edition is dedicated to the incremental innovators, the passionate leaders, the determined entrepreneurs, the engaged employees, the visionary angels and early-stage investors, the inspirational academics teaching entrepreneurship, the nurturing organizations that support entrepreneurs, the government leaders who understand how to craft policies that support, not deter, entrepreneurship, and the professional advisors who become the mentors and sounding boards for millions of entrepreneurs each year. This book is for all of the entrepreneurial leaders who are committed to the notion that capital formation is a process, not an event, with best practices, norms, rules and documents that govern and guide that process and who are committed to raising capital the right way and then treating their investors with the integrity and respect they deserve. As we will explore in the pages that follow, the characteristics that all types of investor find compelling have really never changed – a clear vision (and ability to articulate it to others), a willingness to listen, an ability to adapt, a strong and functional team, a well-defined marketplace, traction and momentum in the implementation of the business plan, a durable and sustainable business model, proof of concept supported by willing and happy customers, a product or service that people want and need at the right price, a motivated and engaged workforce, an ability to penetrate global markets, loyal distributor channels and a steady and calm hand when inevitable potholes and speed bumps arise along the road to success. If you want to raise capital in these volatile and unpredictable markets, you need to demonstrate that your team and business plan are truly exceptional in one or more of these critical areas.

As my old friend and author John May (**Every Business Needs An Angel**) has often cautioned "It is not enough these days to build a better mousetrap, you now need to demonstrate that you have built a team with a passion for murdering mice." Well said.

So, let's take a journey together on the pages ahead to develop as many tools for your capital formation strategic toolkit as you are willing to learn to use.

Andrew J. Sherman
Bethesda, Maryland
Fall 2011

ACKNOWLEDGMENTS

The strategies, concepts, issues and best practices, discussed in this book are the result of over thirty (30) years' experience in serving as a strategic and legal advisor to emerging growth and established companies on capital formation, business planning and corporate financial and governance matters. It would be impossible to thank all of the people with whom I have had the pleasure of working along the way. The support and loyalty of my many domestic and international clients as well as my esteemed colleagues at Jones Day, including Steve Brogan, Mary Ellen Powers, Andrew Kramer, John Majoras, Greg Shumaker, Michael Shumaker, David Neuville, John Welch, Robert Profusek and Alan Schaeffer who all deserve special mention.

There are certain individuals whose time, hard work, support, and research for this book deserve special mention. I want to thank my colleague Alex Badillo for his review of chapters 6, 11 and 12 as well as Georgetown University Law Center student Aaron Horn for his significant research support and assistance. We have a dynamic and talented group of global lawyers at Jones Day focused in the areas of mergers and acquisitions and capital markets transactions and I am honored to be part of the team. I owe special thanks to my assistant, Jo Lynch, who often serves as my right arm, and for her organizational skills and patience.

Bob Nirkind of AMACOM Books was there as always to provide moral and logistical support in pulling this entire project together. He is an excellent orchestrator, editor and sounding board. I also want to thank Jim Bessent at AMACOM for his skillful copy editing.

Last, but certainly not least, I am grateful to my wife, Judy, and to my son Matthew, and daughter, Jennifer, who once again sacrificed time with me so that I could complete this manuscript. I couldn't ask for a more supportive family.

Raising Capital

Third Edition

Chapter 1

Capital-Formation Strategies and Trends

After more than three decades of being an entrepreneur, serving as a legal and strategic advisor to entrepreneurs and growing companies, and speaking and writing on entrepreneurial finance, I have found one recurring theme running through all these businesses: *Capital is the lifeblood of a growing business.* In an environment in which cash is king, no entrepreneur I have ever met or worked with seems to have enough of it. The irony is that the creativity that entrepreneurs typically show when they are starting and building their businesses seems to fall apart when it comes to the business planning and capital-formation process. Most entrepreneurs start their search for capital without really understanding the process and, to paraphrase the old country

1

song, waste a lot of time and resources "lookin' for love [money] in all the wrong places."

Not only is capital the lifeblood of a growing business, but it is also the lifeblood of our economy. When its flow stalls, our progress stalls. And when small and entrepreneurial companies cannot gain access to capital at affordable costs, we all suffer. According to recent Small Business Administration (SBA) statistics, smaller companies make up 99.7 percent of all employer firms, pay 44 percent of total U.S. payroll, and have generated 64 percent of net new jobs over the past 15 years. When small companies do not have the access to the resources they need in order to grow, our nation cannot grow. If entrepreneurial leaders are too concerned with what new crisis, burdensome regulation, budget deficit, tax hike, or economic downturn may await them to make any new hiring, growth, or capital investment decisions, we are destined to be in a perpetual recession. Healthy credit and equity markets are vital to our country's ability to foster and commercialize innovation, penetrate new markets, seize new opportunities, create new jobs, offer raises and promotions, and compete on a global basis. The economic downturn of 2007 to 2009 put a dent in everyone's pocketbook, but for smaller and entrepreneurial companies, it robbed them of the critical fuel that they needed to keep the engines of the economy moving forward. Payrolls were slashed, creativity was halted, inventories were reduced, capital investment decisions were delayed, and motivation in the workforce was virtually nonexistent.

I wrote *Raising Capital* to help entrepreneurs and their advisors navigate the often murky waters of entrepreneurial finance and explore all of the traditional and nontraditional sources of capital that may be available to a growing business. I'm assuming that you, the reader, are the entrepreneur—the owner of a business that's looking for new money. So, wherever possible, I'll address you directly, as if you were a client sitting across the desk from me. My goal is to provide you with pragmatic guidance based on years of experience and a view from the trenches so that you'll end up with a thorough understanding of *how* and *where* companies at various growth stages are successfully raising capital. This will include traditional sources of capital, such as "angels" and private placements; the narrower options of venture capital and initial public offerings; and the more aggressive and newer alternatives such as joint ventures, vendor financing, and raising capital via the Internet. The more likely the option, as demonstrated by the Capital-Formation "Reality Check" Strategic

Pyramid in Figure 1-1, the more time I'll devote to it. Look at the figure as an outline—it'll make more sense as you read further.

Figure 1-1.	**The Capital-Formation "Reality Check" Strategic Pyramid.**

1. *Your own money and other resources (credit cards, home equity loans, savings, 401(k) loans, and so on).* This is a necessary precursor for most venture investors. (Why should we give you money if you're not taking a risk?)

2. *The money and other resources of your family, friends, key employees, and other such people.* This is based on trust and relationships.

3. *Small Business Administration loans, microloans, or general small-business commercial lending.* This is very common, but it requires collateral (something that is tough to provide in intangible-driven businesses).

4. *Angels (wealthy families, cashed-out entrepreneurs, and other such people).* These can be found by networking or by computer. You need to separate smaller angels from superangels. This is a rapidly growing sector of the venture-investment market.

5. *Bands of angels that are already assembled.* These include syndicates, investor groups, private investor networks, pledge funds, and so on. Find out what's out there in your region and get busy networking.

6. *Private placement memoranda (PPM) under Regulation D.* This involves groups of angels that you assemble. You need to understand federal and/or state securities laws, have a good hit list, and know the needs of your targeted group.

7. *Larger-scale commercial loans.* To get these, you'll need a track record, a good loan proposal, a banking relationship, and some collateral.

8. *Informal venture capital (VC).* This includes strategic alliances, Fortune 1000 corporate venture capital, global investors, and so on. These investors are synergy-driven; they are more patient and more strategic. Make sure you get what was promised.

9. *Early-stage venture capital or seed capital funds.* These make up a small portion (less than 15 percent) of all VC funds. It is a very competitive, very focused niche—the investors are typically more patient and have less aggressive return on investment (ROI) needs.

10. *Institutional venture capital market.* This is usually second- or third-round money. You'll need a track record or to be in a very hot industry. These investors see hundreds of deals and make only a handful each year.

11. *Big-time venture capital.* Large-scale institutional VC deals (fourth- or fifth-round level—for a pre-IPO or merger and acquisition deal).

12. *Initial public offerings (IPOs).* The grand prize of capital formation.

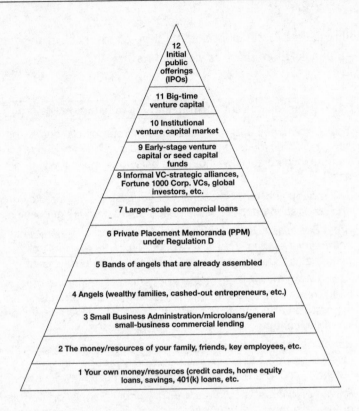

Understanding the Natural Tension Between Investor and Entrepreneur

Virtually all capital-formation strategies (or, simply put, ways of raising money) revolve around balancing four critical factors: *risk, reward, control,* and *capital.* You and your sources of venture funds will each have your own ideas as to how these factors should be weighted and balanced, as shown in Figure 1-2. Once a meeting of the minds takes place on these key elements, you'll be able to do the deal.

Risk. The venture investors want to mitigate their risk, which you can do with a strong management team, a well-written business plan, and the leadership to execute the plan.

Reward. Each type of venture investor may want a different reward. Your objective is to preserve your right to a significant share of the growth in your company's value and any subsequent proceeds from the sale or public offering of your business.

Figure 1-2. | **Balancing Competing Interests in a Financial Transaction.**

THE DEAL
(Meeting of the
minds/compromise)

INVESTOR WANTS/NEEDS
Maximum return
Mitigate risk/downside protection
Input on future and growth of the
    business/control

ENTREPRENEUR WANTS/NEEDS
Maximum capital/valuation
Avoid dilution/control
Affordable cost of capital

COMMON OBJECTIVES
Growth in the value of the business
Additional rounds of $ at more
    favorable valuations
Mutually beneficial exit strategy

Control. It's often said that the art of venture investing is "structuring the deal to have 20 percent of the equity with 80 percent of the control." But control is an elusive goal that's often overemphasized by entrepreneurs. Venture investors have many tools to help them exercise control and mitigate risk, depending on their philosophy and their lawyers' creativity. Only you can dictate which levels and types of controls may be acceptable. Remember that higher-risk deals are likely to come with higher degrees of control.

Capital. Negotiations with venture investors often focus on how much capital will be provided, when it will be provided, what types of securities will be purchased and at what valuation, what special rights will attach to the securities, and what mandatory returns will be built into the securities. You need to think about how much capital you *really* need, *when* you really need it, and whether there are any alternative ways of obtaining these resources.

Another way to look at how these four components must be balanced is to consider the natural tension between investors and entrepreneurs in arriving at a mutually acceptable deal structure.

Virtually all equity and convertible-debt deals, regardless of the source of capital or stage of the company's growth, require a balancing of this risk/reward/control/capital matrix. The better prepared you are by fully understanding this process and determining how to balance these four factors, the more likely it is that you will strike a balance that meets your needs and objectives.

Throughout this book, I'll discuss the key characteristics that all investors look for before they commit their capital. Regardless of the state of the economy or what industries may be in or out of favor at any given time, there are certain key components of a company that must be in place and be demonstrated to the prospective source of capital in a clear and concise manner.

These components (discussed in later chapters) include a focused and realistic business plan (which is based on a viable, defensible business and revenue model); a strong and balanced management team that has an impressive individual and group track record; wide and deep targeted markets that are rich with customers who want and need (and can afford) the company's products and services; and some sustainable competitive advantage that can be supported by real barriers to entry, particularly barriers that are created by proprietary products or brands owned exclusively by the company. Finally, there should be some sizzle to go with the steak; this may include excited and loyal customers and employees, favorable media coverage, nervous competitors who are genuinely concerned that you may be changing the industry, and a clearly defined exit strategy that allows your investors to be rewarded within a reasonable period of time for taking the risks of investment.

Understanding the Private Equity Markets

In many ways, the private equity markets mimic the conditions of the public stock market, much the way a little brother copies the mannerisms of an admired big brother. When the public markets have raised the bar to access, as they have done pretty consistently since the dot-com meltdown, the private equity markets also raise the bar to access. When the bar is raised, Darwinian principles begin to apply strongly. It is survival of the fittest. The "fittest" companies are those with the strongest management teams, the largest potential markets, the most loyal and established customers, the most defendable market positions, and the clearest path to profitability. It has often been explained as the "state of the capital markets" snowman, as diagrammed in Figure 1-3.

Understanding the Different Types of Investors

Most investors fall into at least one of three categories: *emotional investors*, who invest in you out of love or because they have a relationship with you; *strategic investors*, who invest in the synergies offered by your business (based primarily on some nonfinancial objective, such as access to research and development, or a vendor-customer relationship, although financial return may

Figure 1-3.   **The State of the Capital Markets Snowman.**

Normal Private Equity Conditions
(Ex. 1994 to1997, 2004)

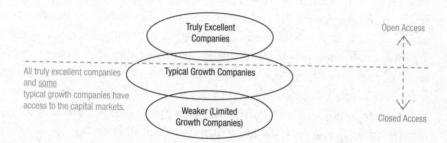

Truly Excellent
Companies

Open Access

All truly excellent companies
and <u>some</u>
typical growth companies have
access to the capital markets.

Typical Growth Companies

Weaker (Limited
Growth Companies)

Closed Access

Weak Capital Market Conditions
(Ex. 2000 to 2002)

Open Access

Only the "best of the best" in
favored industry sectors get
access to the private equity
markets (and even those face
much tougher terms and
conditions).

Truly Excellent
Companies

Typical Growth Companies

Closed Access

Weaker (Limited
Growth Companies)

Abnormally Exuberant Market Conditions
(Ex. 1998 to 2000)

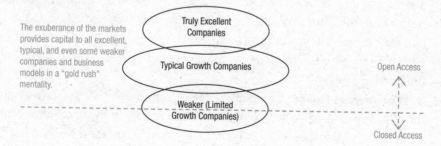

Truly Excellent
Companies

The exuberance of the markets
provides capital to all excellent,
typical, and even some weaker
companies and business
models in a "gold rush"
mentality.

Typical Growth Companies

Open Access

Weaker (Limited
Growth Companies)

Closed Access

still be a factor); and *financial investors*, whose primary or exclusive motivation is a return on capital and who invest in the financial rewards that your business plan (if properly executed) will produce. Your approach, plan, and deal terms may vary depending on the type of investor you're dealing with, so it's important for you to understand the investor and his objectives well in advance. Then your goal is to meet those objectives without compromising the long-term best interests of your company and its current shareholders. Achieving that goal is challenging, but it can be easier than you might think *if* your team of advisors has extensive experience in meeting everyone's objectives to get deals done properly and fairly. The more preparation, creativity, and pragmatism your team shows, the more likely it is that the deal will get done on a timely and affordable basis.

Understanding the Different Sources of Capital

There are many different sources of capital—each with its own requirements and investment goals—discussed in this book. They fall into two main categories: debt financing, which essentially means that you borrow money and repay it with interest; and equity financing, where money is invested in your business in exchange for part ownership.

Sources of Debt Financing

Commercial Banks. Smaller companies are much more likely to obtain an attentive audience from a commercial loan officer after the start-up phase has been completed. In determining whether to "extend debt financing" (essentially, make a loan), bankers look first at your general credit rating, your collateral, and your ability to repay. Bankers also closely examine the nature of your business, your management team, your competition, industry trends, and the way you plan to use the proceeds. A well-drafted loan proposal and business plan will go a long way toward demonstrating your company's creditworthiness to a prospective lender.

Commercial Finance Companies. Many companies that get turned down for a loan from a bank turn to a commercial finance company. These companies usually charge considerably higher rates than institutional lenders, but they might provide lower rates if you sign up for the other services they offer for fees, such as payroll and accounts receivable management. Because they are subject to fewer federal and state regulations, commercial finance companies generally have more flexible lending policies and more of a stomach for risk than traditional commercial banks. However, the commercial finance companies are just as likely as commercial banks to mitigate their risk—in their case, through higher interest rates and more stringent collateral requirements for loans to undeveloped companies.

Leasing Companies. If you need money to purchase assets for your business, leasing offers an alternative to traditional debt financing. Rather than borrowing money to purchase equipment, you rent the assets instead.

Leases typically take one of two forms. *Operating leases* usually provide you with both the asset you would be borrowing money to purchase and a service contract over a period of time, which is usually significantly less than the actual useful life of the asset. That means lower monthly payments. If negotiated properly, the operating lease will contain a clause that gives you the right to cancel the lease with little or no penalty. The cancellation clause provides you with flexibility in the event that sales decline or the leased equipment becomes obsolete. *Capital leases* differ from operating leases in that they usually don't include any maintenance services, and they involve your use of the equipment over the asset's full useful life.

State and Local Government Lending Programs. Many state and local governments provide direct capital or related assistance through support services or even loan guarantees to small and growing companies in an effort to foster economic development. The amount and terms of the financing will usually be regulated by the statutes authorizing the creation of the state or local development agency.

Trade Credit and Consortiums. Many growing companies overlook an obvious source of capital or credit when they are exploring their financing alternatives—their suppliers and customers. Suppliers have a vested interest in the long-term growth and development of their customer base and may be willing to extend favorable trade credit terms or even provide direct financing to help fuel a good customer's growth. The same principles apply to the customers of a growing company who rely on the company as a key supplier of resources.

An emerging trend in customer-related financing is the consortium. Under this arrangement, a select number of key customers finance the development of a particular product or project in exchange for the right of first refusal or an exclusive territory for the distribution of the finished product. Carefully examine applicable federal and state antitrust laws before organizing a consortium.

Sources of Equity Capital

Private Investors. Many early-stage companies receive their initial equity capital from private investors, either individually or as a small group. These investors are called "angels" or "bands of angels," and they are a rapidly growing sector of the private equity market.

Institutional Venture Capital Firms. Perhaps the best-known source of equity capital for entrepreneurs in recent years is the traditional venture capital firm. These formally organized pools of venture capital helped create Silicon Valley and the high-technology industry, which is our nation's fastest-growing sector. But as you will see in Chapter 9, these funds do very few deals each year relative to the total demand for growth capital, so be ready to expand your horizons.

Mergers and Acquisitions. Mergers and acquisitions (M&As) with companies that are rich in cash assets can be a viable source of capital for your growing company. This kind of transaction triggers many legal, structural, and tax issues that you as the seller and your legal counsel must consider. There are more deals than ever among midsize companies as a result of the consolidation impact of technology, the "trickle-down" effect from the megamergers of 2010–2011, and the need for midsize companies to remain competitive in an age dominated by megacompanies and small niche players.

Strategic Investors and Corporate Venture Capitalists. Many large corporations, such as Intel, Nokia, Dell, and ABB, have established venture capital firms as operating subsidiaries that look for investment opportunities (typically within their core industries) to achieve not only financial returns, but also strategic objectives, such as access to the technology that your company may have developed or unique talents on your team. According to 2011 data from the National Venture Capital Association (NVCA), corporate venture capital funds invested nearly $600 million in start-up and early-stage companies in the first quarter of 2011, a growing and significant portion of all venture capital invested in the United States.

Overseas Investors. A wide variety of overseas investors, foreign stock exchanges, banks, and leasing companies, especially those from rapid-growth economies such as China, India, Germany, and Saudi Arabia, are quite interested in financing transactions with U.S.–based companies. Be sure to consider both cultural and management-style differences and governance and contractual laws carefully before you engage in any international financing transaction.

Intermediaries. Many growing companies begin their search for capital with the assistance of an intermediary, such as an investment banker, broker, merchant banker, or financial consultant. These companies and individuals aren't direct suppliers of equity capital but often will assist the growing company in arranging financing through commercial lenders, insurance companies, personal funds, or other institutional sources. Investment bankers will also arrange for equity investment by private investors, usually in anticipation of a public offering of the company's securities.

Goliaths Committed to Helping Davids. At the peak of the credit crunch and equity market meltdown in 2007–2009, many larger companies, such as IBM, AT&T, Wal-Mart, Cisco, Microsoft, and GE, stepped up to the plate with a series of financing programs, procurement set-asides, preferred vendor terms, and other training and support programs to bolster small and entrepreneurial companies. For example, the IBM International Foundation awarded a $10 million grant to support a "one-stop shopping" procurement site that would enable smaller companies to be suppliers to IBM and has invited many other large companies to join it in the procurement process. Organizations like the Women's Business Enterprise National Council (WBENC) and WE Connect have boards packed with representatives of large companies that help certify women-owned businesses around the country and around the globe as being qualified for supplier diversity initiatives and opportunities.

My favorite headline consistent with this trend was in the July 20, 2011, issue of the *New York Times*, which read "Google Looks for the Next Google." Itself a start-up only a few short years ago, Google now enjoys a stock price that is typically north of $600 and a market capitalization of more than $200 billion. Google Ventures has set aside $200 million to invest in start-ups and early-stage companies that offer exponential growth potential. Google is not just putting its money to work, but also offering portfolio companies access to critical knowledge (including access to Google's 29,000 creative-thinking employees), channels, infrastructure and office space at the Googleplex, technology, and best practices to help them drive success. In deciding which companies are ripe for investment, Google has (of course) developed a proprietary algorithm to help it screen and filter candidates and their business plans.

Google is not alone. Amazon.com has also been an active investor in start-up companies. Facebook and Zynga, well capitalized by private investors, are also making investments in earlier-stage social media companies that can help propel their own growth. Intel Capital invested more than $327 million in 2010 and was on track to exceed $500 million in 2011 as of the date of publication of this third edition. Even struggling AOL and Yahoo! are actively looking for deal flow for strategic investments that will help keep them competitive.

Common Mistakes Entrepreneurs Make in the Search for Capital

- Preparing inadequately. Today's capital markets require you to get inside the head of the typical investor and deliver a business plan and a business model that meet her key concerns. You must build an infrastructure that can be responsive to rapid growth (a scalable business) in an underserved niche within the market. You will be expected to demonstrate that you can ramp up quickly and that you have a team that really understands the target industry. You want to show that your company can generate a sustainable and durable revenue stream and will become profitable in a reasonable period of time.
- Letting the search resemble a shotgun instead of a rifle (the search must be focused on the most likely sources).
- Misjudging the amount of time it will take to close a deal.
- Falling in love with your business plan. (This creates stubbornness, inflexibility, and defensiveness—all deal killers.)
- Spending too much time raising the money and not enough time managing the business along the way.
- Failing to understand (and meet) the investor's *real* needs and objectives.
- Taking your projections too seriously.
- Confusing product development with the need for real sales and real customers.
- Failing to recognize that the strength of the management team is what really matters to investors.
- Providing business plans that are four inches thick (size *does* matter, and shorter is better). Be prepared to have multiple presentations in different lengths—the one-pager, the two-pager, and the full plan.
- Not understanding that most investors are very, very busy and hate to have their time wasted. Keep it simple, and get to the point in your presentations.
- Providing business plans that are more exhibits than analysis.

- Forgetting that timing is everything. Don't raise money at the last minute. It will already be too late, and the cost of desperation is very high. The best time to raise money is when you can afford to be patient.
- Being so afraid of sharing your idea that you don't tell anyone about it. You can't sell if you don't tell.
- Being price wise and investor foolish. It's not just about getting the best financial deal, it's also about learning what other strategic benefits the investor brings to the table.
- Not recognizing that valuation of small companies is an art, not a science. Be ready to negotiate as best you can, depending on your negotiating leverage.
- Believing that ownership equals control. An investor can have 10 percent of the ownership and 90 percent of the control (or vice versa), depending on how the deal is negotiated and structured.

How Much Money Do You *Really* Need?

One mistake that entrepreneurs often make in their search for capital is to raise too little or too much of it. They often lose credibility if, during a presentation to prospective investors, it becomes clear that they have misbudgeted or misjudged their *actual* capital needs or have failed to explore ways to obtain the resources other than buying them. I'll cover the latter point in more detail in Chapter 5, when we look at bootstrapping strategies. The problem of misbudgeting is problematic—if you ask for too little and have to go back to the well, the cost of capital will usually be much higher and the process more painful the second time. However, if you ask for too much (even though some experts say you can never have too much capital in an early-stage enterprise), you may turn off a prospective investor. Worse, you may cause greater dilution of your ownership than was really necessary.

Consider Staged Investment

One way in which investors protect against "overinvesting" is to invest capital in stages instead of in a lump sum. These stages (or *tranches*) are often tied to specific business-plan milestones or performance objectives, such as revenues and profits, obtaining customers, recruiting team members, and achieving regulatory approvals. Breaking the investment into tranches protects the investors against capital mismanagement and waste, and protects you against premature dilution or loss of capital. You may be inclined to request that all the necessary capital be invested as a lump sum (to reduce the chances that future conditions will get in the way of receiving all the money that you need), but bear in mind that there may be some real advantages to being patient and allowing for a staged investment.

Capital-Formation Strategies

There are many choices available to a small but growing company that's looking to raise capital, but basically your choices are limited to two flavors: *debt* and *equity*. Defining your *optimal capital structure*—the proper balance between the two—is a challenge, as is finding those sources of capital at affordable rates. What's considered affordable varies, depending on whether you're pursuing debt or equity. Affordability in the debt context refers to the term, the interest rate, the amortization, and the penalties for nonpayment. In the context of equity, affordability refers to worth (known as valuation), dilution of the shares or control held by the current owners, and any special terms or preferences, such as mandatory dividends or redemption rights.

Your first available option is to issue securities. There are essentially three types: debt securities, equity securities, and hybrid (or convertible) securities. Each has certain characteristics, variable features, and attendant costs.

Debt Securities

When you authorize the issuance of a debt security, it is usually in the form of a *bond*, a *note*, or a *debenture*. Typically, a bond is an obligation secured by a mortgage on some of the company's property. Debentures and notes are unsecured and therefore are issued on the strength of the company's reputation, projected earnings, and growth potential. (They usually carry a higher rate of interest.)

The terms of the debt security and the earnings, or yield, to the holder will be determined by an evaluation of the level of risk and the likelihood of default. Growing companies that lack a high bond or credit rating will often be faced with restrictive clauses, or covenants, in the debenture purchase agreement or in the actual terms of the bond; these govern your activities during the term of the instrument. For example, the covenants might restrict management's ability to get raises or bonuses, or might require you to maintain a certain debt-to-equity ratio at all times. You and your attorney should assess the direct and indirect costs of these terms and covenants before you choose this option.

Equity Securities

Equity securities include *common stock, preferred stock,* and *warrants and options.* Each type provides a different set of rights, preferences, and potential rates of return in exchange for the capital contributed to the company. The typical growing company (whose value to an investor usually depends on intangible assets, such as patents, trade secrets, goodwill, and projected earnings) will issue equity securities before incurring additional debt. This is because it lacks the assets necessary to secure the debt, and because additional debt is likely to increase the company's failure risk to unacceptable levels.

Common Stock. An offering of common stock and the related dilution of interest in the company is often traumatic for owners of growing companies that operate as closely held corporations. The need for additional capital to allow for growth, combined with the lack of readily available personal savings or corporate retained earnings, leads to a realignment of the capital structure and a redistribution of ownership and control. Although an offering of common stock is generally costly and entails a surrender of some ownership and control, it does provide you with an increased equity base and a more secure foundation on which to grow, and it increases your chances of getting loans in the future.

Preferred Stock. Broadly speaking, preferred stock is an equity security that shares some characteristics with debt securities. Holders of preferred stock are entitled to receive dividends at a fixed or adjustable rate of return (like holders of a debt instrument) before dividends are distributed to holders of the common stock. Owners of preferred shares also participate in the distribution of assets in the event of liquidation ahead of the holders of common stock. The preferred stock may carry certain rights regarding voting and convertibility to common stock. The shares may also have antidilution or preemptive rights, or redemption privileges that may be exercised by either the company or the shareholder. Although your fixed dividend payments are not tax-deductible (as interest payments would be) and company ownership is still diluted, preferred stock offers a balance between risk and reward because you need not return the principal invested (unless there are provisions for redemption). In addition, preferred stock's return on investment is limited to a fixed rate of return (unless there are provisions for convertibility into common stock), and their holders' claims are subordinated to the claims of creditors and bondholders in the event of the liquidation of the company. The use of convertible preferred stock is especially popular with venture capitalists.

Warrants and Options. These give the holder the right to buy a stated number of shares of common or preferred stock at a specified price within a specified period of time. If that right isn't exercised, it lapses. If the stock's price rises above the option price, the holder can essentially purchase the stock at a discount, thereby participating in the company's growth.

Convertible Securities

Convertible securities (in their most typical form) are similar to warrants and options in that they provide the holder with an option to convert the security—such as a convertible note or convertible preferred stock—into common stock. The incentive is usually the same as for the exercise of a warrant: The conversion price (the price the company will receive for the common stock upon conversion) is more favorable than the current rate of return provided by the convertible security. Convertible securities offer your company several distinct advantages, including the opportunity to sell debt securities at lower interest rates and with fewer restrictive covenants (in exchange for the investor's having a chance to participate in the company's success if it meets its projections and objectives).

The Due Diligence Process

Another significant component of the capital-formation process is the due diligence that the venture investor and its legal and financial advisors will conduct. The due diligence process is designed to reduce the investors' risk by educating them as fully as possible about the problems, liabilities, key challenges, trends, and other factors that will affect your ability to implement and surpass your business plans. Venture investors need to understand the potential consequences of the problems and challenges facing your company *before* they commit their capital. This is a basic principle of federal and state securities laws known as the "informed investor" provision. The due diligence process involves a legal, financial, and strategic review of all of your documents, operating history, contractual relationships, and organizational structure. You and your team must organize the necessary documents, and the venture investor and its team must be prepared to conduct a detailed analysis of the documents and ask all the right questions.

When done properly, due diligence can be tedious, frustrating, time-consuming, and costly. Venture investors expect entrepreneurs to become defensive, evasive, and impatient during the due diligence phase of the transaction. This is because most entrepreneurs (and you're probably one of them) don't enjoy having their business plans and every step of their history put under the microscope and questioned, especially for an extended period of time and by a party whose purpose is to search for skeletons in the closet. Nonetheless, from your perspective, the key to this process is to be *prepared* and to be *cooperative*. If you're disorganized and defensive when the due diligence team arrives, you give the team a reason to recommend to the source of capital that it not make the deal. It's in your best interest to have a basic understanding of the art and science of the due diligence process.

The Art and Science of Due Diligence

Due diligence is usually divided into two parts that are handled by separate teams: the financial and strategic part, handled by the venture investor's accountants and management, and the legal part, conducted by the venture investor's counsel. Throughout the process, the two teams compare notes on open issues and on potential risks and problems. Business due diligence focuses on the strategic and financial issues surrounding the deal, such as confirmation of your past financial performance and the future potential of your business plan; confirmation of the operating, production, and distribution synergies; and the economies of scale to be achieved; this involves the acquisition and gathering of the information necessary for financing the transaction. Legal due diligence focuses on any potential legal problems that may serve as impediments to the transaction and outlines how the documents should be structured.

From the investor's perspective, effective due diligence is both an art and a science. The *art* is the experience to know which questions to ask and how and when to ask them, and the ability to create feelings of both trust and fear in you and your team. (This encourages full and complete disclosure.) In this sense, the due diligence team is on a "search and destroy" mission, looking for potential problems and liabilities (the search) and finding ways either to resolve these problems prior to closing (destroy) or to ensure that the risks are allocated fairly and openly among the parties after closing.

The *science* involves preparing comprehensive and customized checklists of the specific questions that will be presented to you, maintaining a methodical system to organize and analyze the documents and data that you provide, and being in a position to quantitatively assess the risks raised by the problems that the advisors to the prospective investor or source of capital uncover (see Figure 1-4 for typical questions asked by venture capitalists).

| Figure 1-4. | Ten Questions All Venture Investors Ask Entrepreneurs. |

NOTE: The answers to these questions determine *whether* the deal gets done and *how* it gets done.

1. How much can I make?
2. How much can I lose?*
3. What is my exit strategy from this deal?
4. Who else says this deal is viable?
5. Does the founder (and others) already have resources at risk?
6. What other value (beyond money) can I bring to the table?
7. Can I trust this management team?
8. Is this company's target market large, growing (not stagnant or shrinking), and reachable?
9. Does the company have (or will it have) a sustainable competitive advantage, as a result of either operational effectiveness, its strategic positioning, or its intellectual capital or other barriers to entry?
10. Is the company's business, revenue, and profit model credible, verifiable, efficient, and sustainable?

---

* Many entrepreneurs wrongly think that the answer to this question is equal to the amount of the investment, but the potential losses or costs to the investor are much more, and include potential liability costs, opportunity costs, reputational costs, favors/chits used, time costs, commitments to follow-on capital, and other such factors.

In business due diligence, venture investors will be on the lookout for issues that are commonly found in an early-stage company. These typically include undervaluation of inventories, overdue tax liabilities, inadequate management information systems, related-party transactions (especially in small, closely held companies), an unhealthy reliance on a few key customers or suppliers, aging accounts receivable, unrecorded liabilities (for example, warranty claims, vacation pay, claims, or sales returns and allowances), and an immediate need for significant expenditures as a result of obsolete equipment, inventory, or computer systems. Each of these problems poses different risks and costs for the venture investor, which must be weighed against the benefits to be gained from the transaction.

Due diligence must be a cooperative and patient process between you and the venture investor and your respective teams. Attempts to hide or manipulate key data will only lead to problems for you down the road. Material misrepresentations or omissions can (and often do) lead to postclosing litigation, which is expensive and time-consuming for both parties. It's also common for entrepreneurs to neglect the human element of due diligence. I can remember working on deals where the lawyers were sent into a dark room in a corner of the building, without any support or even coffee. In other cases, we were treated like royalty, with full access to support staff, computers, telephones, food, and beverages. It is only human for the investor's counsel to be a little more cooperative in the negotiations when the entrepreneur was helpful and allowed counsel to do the job at hand.

Key Best Practices Affecting Capital Formation in the New Millennium

- *Don't underestimate the power of trust, relationships, strategic introductions to the sources of capital, integrity, and a strong advisory team (the "people issues").* Even in today's high-tech world, capital formation is still very much a process that is driven by *people*, not by financial formulas, especially in the private equity markets.

- *Don't waste precious time and resources on a capital-formation strategy that is neither realistic nor affordable (from a cost-of-capital perspective).* Match your deal and its likely rate of return with the Capital-Formation "Reality Check" Strategic Pyramid (see Figure 1-1). Nobody likes to have his time wasted—especially not wealthy or sophisticated venture investors. Take the time to understand the targeted investor's motivation, deal criteria, industry focus (where applicable), required rates of return, and strategic objectives. Your likelihood of raising money will be directly related to your understanding of the investor's needs and your ability to meet them (without sacrificing your own needs and objectives). This will often require some creative deal structuring and out-of-the-box thinking.

- *There's no room here for whiners.* You'll find a rough-and-tumble ride in these roller-coaster capital markets, but the stronger companies will survive it. There's a lot of capital out there right now, and if you deserve to get it, you probably will—but you must be persistent, creative, and focused, and have a well-prepared business plan.

- *What really makes an excellent business plan?* There are dozens of books, software programs, and suggested outlines out there; in my opinion, they are all worthless. There is no one right way to prepare a business plan. *An effective business plan tells a great story and draws the reader in.* The investor will then want to learn more, which leads to a meeting that significantly increases your chances and reduces the possibility that your plan will wind up in the circular file. Nobody tells that story better than you! Tailor your plan to the targeted reader.

- *Due diligence is a two-way street.* As the sources of capital learn more about you, try to learn more about them. What is their investment track record? What deals have they done recently? How are they structured? Why? What additional value do they bring to the table? How many of their investments have gone public? Talk to the founders of one of the companies in which they have invested. Are they happy? Do they have any regrets? What would they do differently? Was follow-up capital available, if needed?

- *An effective capital-formation strategy is part preparation, part presentation, and part sizzle.* Having these three parts in harmony will allow your business plan to rise to the top of a very deep pile.

- *Raising money is not a substitute for making money.* You can raise multiple rounds of capital, but at some point you must start producing revenues, profits, and returns to your investors. Most venture investors are impatient—they're looking to date, not necessarily to marry.

  You've got to stay focused on your core business during the distracting and time-consuming capital-formation process. Many entrepreneurs neglect their companies in their efforts to raise money—only to find that there's no company left by the time they get a commitment and negotiate the deal.

- *Timing is everything.* Try to have a capital-formation plan that allows you to raise capital when you need it the least, as this will enhance your valuation and your negotiating posture. Patience is critical. An experienced venture investor can detect desperation at first whiff and may structure the investment accordingly. Your perceived anxiety can—and will—come back to haunt you later as you regret the rough terms that you agreed to when you didn't have the time or ability to say no or explore alternatives.

- *Seasoned investors will judge you by the team that you assemble.* Hire great people and high-profile advisors. Piggyback on their strength, advice, and credibility in the market. Put together a broad blend of talent on a team that has a track record but isn't too bullheaded to listen to the suggestions or requirements of the venture investors. The team members must have visible passion, commitment, and an ability to communicate their vision and objectives. Demonstrate to the investor that your team can be functional and productive without the need for babysitting or "adult supervision."

- *Capital formation is not an activity for the dispassionate and uncommitted.* To succeed in your quest, you need high energy and an ability to demonstrate your commitment. Show that you have some "skin in the game" by sharing the sacrifices that you have made and that you are prepared to keep making to ensure that the company will succeed.
- *It's a lot easier to start the process with the door halfway open.* Figure out ways to leverage the Rolodexes and relationships of your management team and your outside advisors, such as your lawyers and your accountants. If you hire the right advisors, they will already have working relationships with the key sources of capital.
- *Have fun.* Too many entrepreneurs approach the capital-formation process with fears, insecurities, and doubts, and assume that the end result will be very painful. This is the exciting world of entrepreneurial finance, not torture. Relish the process and welcome the challenge. After all, what could be more exciting than inviting others to participate in your future success?
- *Be honest with your investors and yourself!*

Are You Really, *Really* Ready to Raise Capital?

Before we turn to other topics in the chapters ahead, there is one more critical preliminary area that we need to discuss honestly and candidly. Are you really, *really* ready for the fiduciary, ethical, moral, legal, and psychological responsibilities of having third-party investors? Are you truly ready to be transparent, attentive, responsive, and respectful and to assume the role of a steward with an obligation to protect and build the assets of the company for the benefit of *all* shareholders? Are you ready to be accountable for your mistakes in judgment and your errors in decision making?

Some entrepreneurs should avoid seeking money from investors or even commercial lenders at any cost. They are either not ready or not mentally

prepared or wired to accept and embrace these responsibilities and obligations. We rarely talk about the complex emotional and psychological aspects
of capital formation, but these are critical elements of the process. You must
be mentally ready to raise capital and be open to the criticism, responsibility,
human dynamics, and relationship management skills that legally and morally
come with the territory when you take money from others. People invest in
people whom they can trust and who they are confident can drive growth and
implement the business plan. Trust must be a two-way street. Entrepreneurs
must also trust and respect each of their investors, whether the investor is your
Aunt Tillie or Kleiner Perkins. Some entrepreneurs are truly better off without
any investors, some can handle these obligations only with regard to family
and friends, and some are ready for emotional relationships with angel or
private placement memorandum investors; however, relatively few are really
ready for the rough-and-tumble dynamics of life with an institutional investor.
Know yourself. Be honest with yourself concerning your maverick tendencies;
you are not doing yourself or your investors any favors by trying to force-feed
a square set of relationship expectations and norms into a round hole.

Sophisticated investors know that there is a difference between a loose can-
non and a heat-seeking missile. They know which types of teams are workable
and coachable and which types of teams will be rebellious mavericks. They
know that you are a high-energy, high-emotion, high-anxiety person in the first
place, or you would not have chosen the entrepreneurial path. Venture investors
seek to separate those entrepreneurs who can be part of something great from
those who are too manic or too disorganized to ever truly build a fantastic enterprise. You need to demonstrate that balance of emotions to investors as a matter
of due diligence, but, even more important, you need to be self-actualized and
conduct an honest self-assessment first, to be sure that you are fully ready for
commitment, collaboration, decision by consensus, accountability, and transparency, and that you are convinced that this *is* who you truly are. If it is not,
then skip to bootstrapping in Chapter 5.

Many entrepreneurs mistakenly go into a meeting overfocused on their
own needs and plans when they are seeking capital. Here is a revelation: *"It's
not about you, it's about them!"* Your investment thesis and your business plan
need to meet *their* criteria, *their* investment needs, *their* emotional needs, and
their risk analysis. Your job is to get your investors as comfortable as possible
with you, your team, and your vision, while remaining true to and in touch

with your own emotions, fears, uncertainties, and doubts. Walk a mile in their shoes. How does your plan or proposal fit into their current portfolio? How does it meet their needs or solve their problems or challenges, especially when you are meeting with strategic sources of capital? They will also want to be assured of the health and strength of your business marriage (for example, the strength of your relationship with co-founders, where applicable) before committing to an investment. Are your visions aligned? Are you ready to bring in third-party investors and accept the obligations that come with it? Do you understand how your methodologies for solving problems and your decision-making paradigm will change? Are you ready for a shift from executive-driven decision making "on the fly" to more reason-bound decision making for more significant decisions and problems?

It is also important to understand how you will react to the typical controls in a term sheet (honest self-assessment). Do you understand and embrace what it truly means to have a fiduciary duty and a stewardship role to protect the best interests of minority shareholders? In venture investing, due diligence is both strategic and personal. Is there an alignment of your core values, beliefs, moral fiber, and goals with those of your investors? Do you understand investors' expectations in an era of transparency and distrust? Do you recognize the emotional aspects of angel investing, the delicate balance between love/friendship and money with family, friends, and fools (FFF) investors, or the dynamics of a business marriage with one or more co-founders or early team members? Can you embrace your fear, uncertainty, and doubt about having investors and raising capital? What makes you the happiest? Describe your lifestyle, hobbies, interests, and so on. Are these activities aligned with the best interests of the investors? Can you live your life in a fishbowl?

Always remember that the capital formation process is *both* quantitative and qualitative. Investors will *always* be interested in the key acronyms, such as IRR (internal rate of return), EBITDA (earnings before interest, taxes, depreciation, and amortization), and ROI (return on investment), but some newer acronyms may be just as important in the evaluation process when making final decisions on investments, such as CITY (can I trust you?), SMTM (show me the market), WSIGAD (why should I give a damn?), and CYTP (can your team perform?). As veteran entrepreneur and angel investor Devin Schain is famous for saying, "Numbers follow, they don't lead." Well said, my friend.

Chapter 2

Selecting the Best Legal Structure for Growth

Now you've got an idea of the basic kinds of equity and debt strategies that you might use in your search for capital. But before you start looking for money, you should decide on the best business format for you, even if you're already in business. Choosing the appropriate legal structure—proprietorship, partnership, corporation, or limited liability company—or changing the structure that you currently have is a complex issue because of the inherent tax consequences and liabilities of the owner(s), and because the structure selected will determine what capital-formation options are available to you. Many factors will affect your choice, including the number of owners involved, the need for management flexibility, and the level of interaction with the public. This chapter will give you an overview and comparison of the basic business formats to consider, both at the outset of a new venture and periodically throughout your company's growth.

Proprietorship

A sole proprietorship is the simplest business form: an unincorporated company that is owned and operated by one person who directly and personally owns the assets used in the company. To establish a sole proprietorship, you need only whatever licenses are required in your line of work—there are no annual fees required to maintain ownership. All profits and losses flow directly to you and appear on your federal tax returns. In lieu of social security taxes that are paid equally by an employer and an employee, your company's net earnings are subject to self-employment tax. Generally, any payments for personal coverage under hospitalization, life insurance, or medical plans can't be deducted as a business expense, but payments for employee coverage are deductible. You may establish a retirement plan and deduct contributions as an adjustment to total gross income, but not as a deduction from income.

The biggest advantages of a proprietorship are that you maintain exclusive control, it's simple (compared with other forms of ownership), there are lower start-up costs, and you are not taxed as both an individual and a business (commonly referred to as *double taxation*).

The primary *disadvantage* is that, as the proprietor, you are personally responsible for all business liabilities, and therefore, creditors may force you to use your personal assets to satisfy the company's debts. (However, insurance may be available that will limit your liability for business debts.) Another significant drawback that becomes relevant if you want to raise capital is that the proprietorship structure significantly limits the range of available money-raising strategies because there's no way to share equity, and you'll need to personally guarantee any debt.

The proprietorship may seem to be the most appropriate structure for a typical "mom-and-pop" operation, but if the business fails, you and your family could face disaster. For most small businesses, it's better to choose a form of ownership that provides for limited personal liability.

Partnership

In a partnership, the assets used in the company are generally jointly owned by two or more parties, and the parties agree to share the profits, losses, assets, and liabilities in proportion to their equity in the partnership, unless specified otherwise in the partnership agreement. You can create a partnership with either a written or an oral agreement, but a written agreement is preferable.

General Partnership

In a general partnership, any or all of the individual partners may be liable for the debts and obligations of the partnership. For example, if three general partners form a business that later runs into financial difficulty, and only one of the three has sufficient personal assets to satisfy creditors, then that partner will be responsible for 100 percent of the obligations (not a prorated share based on her actual ownership of the company). Whether she will later seek reimbursement from the other partners doesn't affect her obligations to third-party creditors. There are no formal officers; your partnership agreement assigns the management functions.

General partnerships are typically found in professions that are service-oriented (such as law, accounting, and medicine) and not capital-intensive. Many states require that you file a certificate of partnership or similar document; failure to do so may prevent your partnership from making use of the courts of the state in which it conducts business. Although the partnership must file a tax return, the individual partners (not the partnership itself) pay in proportion to their ownership as reported on the annual K-1 return filed with the IRS. Income and expenses flow through to the partners in accordance with the partnership agreement, and the applicable payroll taxes must be paid directly.

The primary advantages of this arrangement are that you have a high degree of flexibility, that profits and losses can be shared disproportionately and flow through directly to the partners, and that you avoid double taxation.

A general partnership's biggest drawback is that each partner bears unlimited personal liability. Also, the partnership technically terminates whenever one partner withdraws, which heightens the impact of the entry and exit of any partner. And once again, you're limited in your money-raising strategies: Either the partnership takes out a loan that the partners personally guarantee, or you raise equity capital by admitting a new general partner. Most investors in a partnership prefer a limited partnership (discussed next) because of the controlled liability that it offers and because they probably won't have to be involved in day-to-day operations.

Limited Partnership

A limited partnership (often referred to as an LP) includes not only the general partners, but also one or more partners who are not bound by the obligations of the partnership. A general partner usually forms an LP to secure additional capital or to spread risk without forming a corporation. The general partners are still personally liable for all partnership debts, but each limited partner's liability is based on his capital contribution to the partnership. All management functions concerning the day-to-day operations of the business are delegated to the general partner. The limited partners may not exercise any significant management control, or—by law—they may jeopardize their limited-liability status.

LPs are common in real estate development, oil and gas exploration, and motion-picture ventures. Nearly every state requires that you file a formal certificate of limited partnership before the LP is valid. If the partnership isn't legally formed, the limited partners' liability is the same as that of the general partner.

The primary advantage of this structure (from a capital-formation perspective) is that the limited partners' potential liability is limited to the extent of their capital contribution, making them more willing to invest. The primary disadvantage is the general partner's unlimited liability.

Corporation

In a corporation, a legal entity (as opposed to individuals) owns the assets of the business and is liable for the debts. A corporation offers the greatest flexibility in raising money from venture investors and is the structure that investors find most comfortable. For federal income tax purposes, the distinguishing characteristics of a corporation include:

Continuity of life. All state corporation laws provide that a corporation will continue to exist until articles of dissolution are filed, even if the owners (shareholders) die, go bankrupt, retire, or give up their interest in the company.

Limited liability. A shareholder isn't *personally* liable for corporate debt or claims against the corporation, except in special circumstances, such as the misuse of the corporation to perpetrate a fraud.

Free transferability of interest. Shareholders may generally sell all or part of their interest to any buyer without the consent of the other shareholders. *Centralized management.* The board of directors (elected by the shareholders) has the authority to make independent business decisions on behalf of the corporation.

The details of forming a corporation vary from state to state; however, virtually every state requires that you file articles (or a certificate) of incorporation. Once you choose the state in which you'd like to incorporate, you'll have to meet a number of registration requirements in order to obtain (and *maintain*) corporate status and to enjoy the protections that the state affords corporations. Observing all the legal formalities will help protect shareholders from personal liability.

General Characteristics of a Corporation

A corporation is owned by its shareholders, who may be individuals, partnerships, trusts, or even other corporations (except for S corporations, to be discussed next, there is no limit to the number of shareholders a corporation may have). The corporate entity is separate and distinct from its shareholders, and the shareholders' personal assets aren't available to satisfy corporate obligations. The corporation's creditors may look only to the corporation's assets for payment, a protection commonly referred to as the *corporate veil.* If a corporation is involved in a number of lines of business, separate corporate subsidiaries (corporations owned by another corporation) may be created to protect the assets of one business activity from the liabilities of the other(s).

Management responsibility is vested in the company's board of directors, which is responsible for overall policy decisions as well as the company's general direction and business plan. The board appoints officers to manage the day-to-day operations.

Unlike a partnership, a corporation is a tax-paying entity; federal and state tax returns are filed, and taxes are paid on the profit of the corporation (unless the corporation elects an S status, as discussed in the next section). Losses are not passed through to the shareholders, but may be carried forward as an offset against the corporation's future income. The board may elect to distribute after-tax profits to the shareholders as dividends; the shareholders are then taxed on these dividends at their individual rates (known as *double taxation*).

The document that determines the mechanical aspects of the corporation's governance is known as the *bylaws*. The bylaws may not exceed the scope of the articles of incorporation or the authority set forth in the state's statute.

Subchapter S Corporations

If your corporation meets certain IRS requirements, you can choose "S" status, which affects how the corporation is taxed on the federal level. An S corporation must have no more than 75 shareholders, who (with very few exceptions) must be both individuals and U.S. residents, and the corporation cannot have two classes of stock with different financial interests. The management responsibility is the same as in a regular corporation (which is taxed under Subchapter C of the Internal Revenue Code), but the S corporation doesn't pay federal tax on its income. Rather, the profits and losses are passed through to the shareholders and are declared on the individuals' tax returns. The main reason to elect S corporation status is that you avoid the double taxation inherent in a Subchapter C corporation.

Managing the Corporation: Duties and Responsibilities

For all types of corporations, the acts and decisions of the board of directors must be made in good faith and for the corporation's benefit. The directors' legal obligations fall into three broad categories: the duty of care, the duty of loyalty, and the duty of fairness.

    Duty of care. The directors must carry out their duties in good faith with diligence, care, and skill in the best interests of the corporation. Each director must actively gather the information needed to make informed decisions regarding company affairs. In doing so, the board member is entitled to rely primarily on the data provided by the corporation's officers and professional advisors, provided that she has no knowledge of any irregularity or inaccuracy in the information. I've seen cases in which board members were held personally responsible for misinformed or dishonest decisions made "in bad faith," such as failing to properly direct the corporation or knowingly authorizing a wrongful act.

    Duty of loyalty. Each director must exercise his powers in the interests of the corporation and not in his own interest or that of another person or organization. The duty of loyalty has a number of specific applications: The director must avoid any conflicts of interest in dealings with the corporation and must not personally usurp what is more appropriately an opportunity or business transaction to be offered to the corporation. For example, suppose an officer or director of the company was in a meeting on the company's behalf and a great opportunity to obtain the distribution rights for an exciting new technology was offered. It would be a breach of this duty for him to try to obtain those rights for himself and not first offer them to the corporation.

Duty of fairness. The last duty that a director has to the corporation is that of fairness. For example, questions may arise if a director of the company owns the building leased by the corporate headquarters and is seeking a significant rent increase. It would certainly be a breach of this duty to allow that director to vote on this proposal. The central legal concern here is that the director may be treating the corporation unfairly in the transaction because her self-interest could cloud her duty of loyalty to the company.

When a transaction between an officer or director and the company is challenged by a shareholder, the officer or director has the burden of demonstrating the propriety and fairness of the transaction. If any component of the transaction involves a substantive conflict of interest or conduct that may amount to fraud, then the courts might rescind the transaction in question. In order for the director's dealings with the corporation to be upheld, the "interested" director will have to demonstrate that the transaction was approved or ratified by a disinterested majority of the company's board of directors.

To meet the duties of care, loyalty, and fairness to the corporation, follow these general guidelines:

Know the principles of corporate law. Work with your attorney to develop written guidelines on the basic principles of corporate law as they apply to the duties of officers and directors. Keep the board informed about recent cases or changes in the law.

Work closely with your corporate attorney. Do this as a general rule. If the board or any director is in doubt about whether a proposed action is in the corporation's best interests, consult your attorney immediately—not after the deal is done.

Keep good records. Keep careful minutes of all meetings and comprehensive records of the information on which the board bases its decisions.

Be prepared to show financial data, business valuations, market research, opinion letters, and related documentation in case a shareholder challenges an action as being "uninformed." Well-prepared minutes also serve a variety of other purposes, such as written proof of the directors' analysis and appraisal of a situation, proof that parent and subsidiary operations are being conducted at arm's length, or proof that an officer had the authority to engage in the transaction that is being questioned.

Be selective in choosing candidates for the board of directors. Avoid the nomination of someone whose name lends credibility, but who is unlikely to attend meetings or have any real input into the management and direction of the company. I have found that choosing such people only invites claims by shareholders of corporate mismanagement. Similarly, don't accept an invitation to sit on another company's board unless you're ready to accept the responsibilities that go with it.

Focus on the best interests of all shareholders. In threatened takeover situations, be careful to make decisions that will be in the best interests of all shareholders, not just the board and the officers. Any steps taken to protect the economic interests of the officers and directors (such as lucrative "golden parachute" contracts that ensure a costly exit) must be reasonable in relation to the actual degree of harm to the company.

Avoid conflicts of interest. Any board member who independently supplies goods and services to the corporation should not participate in board discussions or votes regarding his dealings with the corporation. This will help avoid conflict-of-interest claims. Proposed actions must be approved by the "disinterested" members of the board after the material facts of the transaction are disclosed and the nature and extent of the board member's involvement is known.

Assess possible conflicts of interest. Periodically issue questionnaires to officers and directors regarding their recent transactions with the company to assess possible conflicts of interest. Use a more detailed questionnaire with incoming board members and newly appointed officers. Always circulate these questionnaires among board members prior to any securities issuances (such as a private placement or a public offering).

Provide directors with information. Provide directors with all appropriate background and financial information relating to proposed board actions well in advance of a board meeting. An agenda, proper notice, and a mutually convenient time, place, and date will ensure good attendance and compliance with applicable statutes.

A meeting of the board of directors is not valid unless a quorum is present. The number of directors needed to constitute a quorum may be fixed by the articles or bylaws, but it is generally a majority of board members.

Handle board members' objections properly. Board members who object to a proposed action or resolution should either vote in the negative and ask that such a vote be recorded in the minutes, or abstain from voting and promptly file a written dissent with the secretary of the corporation.

The advantages of the corporate form of ownership include limited liability for owners and the ability to continue the business easily, even if there's a change in the shareholders. However, a corporation can also be more expensive to form and maintain than a proprietorship or a partnership, primarily because of the filing and annual fees imposed by state agencies.

Limited Liability Company

The limited liability company (LLC), which has grown in popularity in recent years, is touted by many as the business structure of the future and lends itself to a wide variety of capital-formation options. The concept, developed in Germany and popular in Europe and Latin America for many decades, was introduced in the United States in 1977 by the state of Wyoming. The LLC received its strongest endorsement in 1988, when the IRS stated that for federal tax purposes, an LLC would be treated as a partnership, not a corporation, provided that it met certain requirements (discussed later). This encouraged virtually all states to pass legislation recognizing LLCs. The flexibility, security, and tax savings of an LLC can be significant, and the structure lends itself to the management and structural flexibility that's needed for just about all capital-formation strategies.

You should structure your LLC so that it qualifies as a partnership under federal tax laws, which means that it must lack at least two of the corporate characteristics—continuity of life, limited liability, free transferability of interest, and centralized management. Some states have adopted "bulletproof" statutes, which provide that an LLC formed in that state will *automatically* lack at least two of the four characteristics and will always qualify as a partnership. The majority of states, however, have "flexible" statutes that allow LLCs to include some or all of the corporate characteristics, with the attendant risk that if the LLC has too many corporate characteristics, it will be taxed as a corporation.

Flexibility for Owners

If you establish an LLC, you'll have tremendous flexibility in structuring its economic and management arrangements. The owners of the LLC, who are referred to as members, may elect to manage the LLC themselves or may designate one or more managers (who may or may not be members) to manage the business and operations of the LLC. Capital contributions to the LLC may be in the form of cash, property, or services, and the profits and losses may be allocated among the members in any manner they choose as long as it complies with tax laws. As with a corporation, you may create multiple classes of membership, including a "preferred" level that mimics the types of equity that venture investors prefer to purchase.

Forming the LLC

Most states allow any legal entity to be a member of an LLC. However, most statutes require that an LLC be formed by two or more people or entities that sign and verify the articles of organization filed with the secretary of state. To issue a certificate of organization, most states require that you file only the barest of information, such as:

- The name of the LLC
- Its duration (not to exceed 30 years)
- The purpose of the organization
- The address of the principal place of business and the registered agent (who has been designated to receive official documents)
- The amount of cash invested and the description and value of any other property contributed to the LLC
- Any additional contributions that may be required in the future
- A reservation of the right to admit additional members and a statement of the terms on which they can be admitted
- A reservation of the right to continue the business and the vote necessary to achieve continuation
- Whether there will be a centralized management team

The most important documents in the formation of an LLC are your operating agreement, which is essentially a substitute for the corporate bylaws, and the member control agreement, which is essentially a substitute for the shareholder agreement or the partnership agreement.

Advantages of an LLC

- Members of an LLC enjoy the same protection from personal liability that the officers and shareholders of a corporation do.
- The LLC itself does not pay federal income tax. If properly structured, it will be classified as a partnership for tax purposes and be exempt from state income or excise tax. It allocates taxable income to its members, who pay at their personal rates (which avoids double taxation). The members can write off the LLC's losses to the extent of their tax basis in the LLC, including their share of the company's debts. In contrast, shareholders in an S corporation can write off losses only to the extent that such losses exceed the money that they have contributed to the company in the form of capital stock and loans.
- Management authority can be delegated either to specific members or to professional managers who are not members of the LLC.
- Once the operating agreement is formed, there are few other formalities like those that corporations must follow, such as holding annual meetings or issuing stock certificates.
- There are no restrictions on the number or type of owners (unlike an S corporation).
- There are no restrictions on multiple classes of stock (unlike an S corporation).
- Distributions of property can be made by LLCs without the realization of taxable gain (unlike an S corporation).

Disadvantages of an LLC

- In most states, the death or withdrawal of a member will trigger the dissolution of the LLC. However, under most operating agreements, members may elect to continue the company's operation. That's what usually happens.
- A member who is also a manager may be required to treat her share of

the income as self-employment income subject to additional taxes to fund social security and Medicare.

- In some states, an LLC doesn't qualify for state tax credits or sales and property tax exemptions for which corporations qualify.

Evaluating Your Selected Legal Structure

Once you've selected the best structure, as your company grows, periodically evaluate whether the structure still suits your company's needs. You might want to change the structure because of:

- The need to raise additional capital for business expansion
- A change in tax laws
- Increased risk resulting from additional dealings with creditors, suppliers, or consumers
- A shift in the business plan that affects the distribution and use of earnings and profits
- An opportunity to develop a new technology, either in conjunction with others or under the umbrella of a separate but related subsidiary or a research and development partnership
- The retirement, death, or departure of a founder
- The need to attract and retain additional top management personnel
- Mergers, acquisitions, spin-offs, or an initial public offering planned for the near future

These situations arise as a business grows and evolves, as shown in the example in Figure 2-1. In this example, a small retail business starts out as a sole proprietorship. Once the store is open and running, the owner decides to share ownership with a key employee, so the business becomes a general partnership. Eventually the owners need to remodel, so they bring in a passive investor to help with the cost; the business is now a limited partnership. Let's say sales increase, prompting the hiring of new employees. The two general partners and the limited partner incorporate to better protect the assets of *all* the partners against claims of and liabilities to third-party creditors, but they choose to become an S corporation to preserve their "pass-through" tax status. When they open a second store, their attorney advises the three owners to form two additional corporations, one as a parent "holding company" and one for the operations of the new store. This prevents creditors of one store from trying

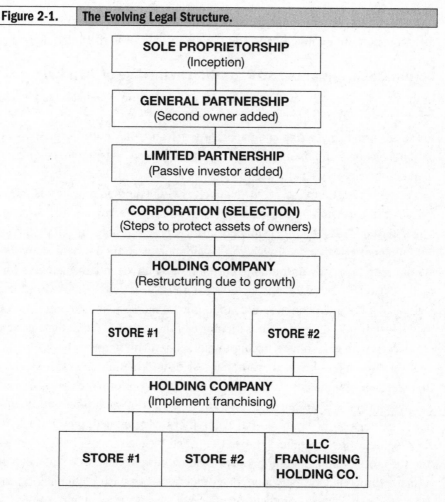

Figure 2-1.   The Evolving Legal Structure.

SOLE PROPRIETORSHIP
(Inception)

GENERAL PARTNERSHIP
(Second owner added)

LIMITED PARTNERSHIP
(Passive investor added)

CORPORATION (SELECTION)
(Steps to protect assets of owners)

HOLDING COMPANY
(Restructuring due to growth)

STORE #1   STORE #2

HOLDING COMPANY
(Implement franchising)

STORE #1   STORE #2   LLC FRANCHISING HOLDING CO.

to proceed against the assets of the other store. This structure also becomes helpful when a fourth individual is offered shares in the second store—to raise capital—but not equity ownership in the first store. Finally, two years later, the owners consider growth through franchising, and they form an LLC to handle the franchise operations. An LLC will also better insulate the assets of the two company-owned stores from possible claims down the road by a disgruntled franchisee.

Making the best business-structure decision *early* could create savings for you and avoid the unnecessary expense of converting to another structure down the road. For these reasons, if you are just starting a new business venture, consult with qualified legal and tax advisors prior to making a decision.

Corporate Governance and Reporting in the Age of Scrutiny

In the early 2000s, we saw the collapse of Enron, Arthur Andersen, and World-Com, and investigations at AOL Time Warner, Tyco, Qwest, Global Crossing, ImClone, and many other companies. As a result, the public's trust in our corporate leaders and financial markets—by employees, shareholders, or bond-holders—had been virtually destroyed.

In response, Congress acted relatively swiftly (and some say hastily) by passing the Sarbanes-Oxley Act, which was signed into law on July 30, 2002. The SEC, the NYSE, the Department of Justice, Nasdaq, state attorney generals, and others also responded quickly to create more accountability to shareholders and employees by and among corporate executives, board members, and their advisors. Central themes included more objectivity on the part of board members; more independence and autonomy for auditors; more control over financial reporting; stiffer penalties for abuse of the laws and regulations pertaining to corporate governance, accounting practices, and financial reporting; and new rules to ensure fair and prompt access to information and current events that affect the company's current status and future performance.

These events led to an age of scrutiny—an era of *validation* and *verification*. The roles of the board and its committees were refined, reexamined, and retooled. Now, best practices, procedures, and protocols have been rewritten, and the costs of implementation have become burdensome and expensive. Internal controls and systems have been redesigned to ensure compliance with the rules, and managers are held accountable for enforcement and results. The CEO's job description has come to read, "Forget the gravy; where's the beef?" and includes less pay, fewer perks, and less power in exchange for more performance and less tolerance for error or abuse. CEOs now live in an era that features more accountability and shorter tenure. The collapse of the financial markets, the failure of Lehman Brothers, the housing market meltdown, the Stanford and Madoff scandals, the federal debt debate, and the S&P downgrade, all of which took place between the publication of the second and third editions of this book, have not in any way eased these concerns. Leadership and good governance are more important than ever, especially in an era of distrust. Investors must have confidence that company leaders will be guided by strong ethical and moral values, integrity, transparency, fairness, and respect for their fiduciary obligations to minority shareholders.

The Impact on Privately Held Companies

Why do privately held and emerging-growth companies need to be aware of the requirements of Sarbanes-Oxley? There are a few reasons:

1. There has been a "trickle-down" effect of requirements for *accountability* and *responsibility* in corporate America that affects board members and executives of companies of all sizes as shareholders look for better, more informed leadership.

2. Some of the provisions of Sarbanes-Oxley apply to private companies. Section 802, for instance, forbids the illegal destruction of documents before litigation.

3. If a private company plans a strategy that includes an IPO or a merger, it is best to be prepared prior to the offering. This includes having governance practices, accounting reports, and financial systems as close to the requirements of Sarbanes-Oxley as possible in order to avoid any problems in these areas that could serve as impediments to closing (be ready for a high level of due diligence questions in M&A that focus on governance practices and dig deeper into financial, compensation, and accounting issues).

Corporate Governance Best Practices Audit

A natural place to begin the review and analysis of corporate governance practices is a legal audit that focuses on ensuring that systems and internal processes are in place to comply with all laws and regulations. The legal audit should include recommendations for improvement and provide a series of compliance training programs for officers, directors, and managers with significant financial or reporting responsibilities.

Among the topics and questions to be examined and discussed during the corporate governance best practices audit are:

- The size and composition of the board and the relationship of its composition to the performance of the company. There is a definite trend toward smaller boards with higher ratios of outside directors.
- The independence and objectivity of the audit committee, which must meet Sarbanes-Oxley requirements.

- The knowledge, skills, and discipline of the compensation committee.
- The overall structure of executive compensation and stock option plans. Pay for performance, fairness issues, linking reward with the meeting of strategic objectives, the reduction of excessive perquisites, the board's ability and willingness to stand up to the CEO, and other such matters are all issues that require examination.
- Internal control processes to ensure that the board is fully and promptly informed, is adequately performing its oversight role, has systems in place to manage and mitigate enterprise-level risks, and is addressing "red flags" in a timely and proper manner. It is critical to have a written statement of corporate governance policy in place.
- How closely and effectively the board monitors the integrity and accuracy of the company's financial statements and reports (without micromanaging the process).
- The compensation system for the board members and the extent to which board members' compensation influences their objectivity. For example, are directors required to own (or not) a specific amount of company stock?
- The transparency of communications with shareholders and the financial markets. Are the requirements of Regulation FD being met?
- The effectiveness of the board's strategic and business planning skills. Have clear goals been set for the executive management team? How well is the team implementing these goals, and how closely is its performance being monitored?
- The risk management procedures that are in place. The audit should include a comprehensive review of the officer and director liability insurance policies as well as other types of risk management, such as information/data security, physical security, and so on.
- The succession plans that are in place for both the board and the executive management.
- How well the skills of the various board members match up with the company's current medium-term (and long-term) strategy. Have changes in the company's business model caused shifts in its focus, triggering a need for new directors with a different set of skills? What procedures are in place for replacing directors whose skills now may be obsolete?

- Any proactive steps that the board is taking to maximize shareholder value, such as the leveraging of existing intellectual assets.
- Whether the board has a nominating committee. Are its policies and criteria clearly articulated? If so, how closely are these policies followed? What due diligence is done on prospective candidates (and vice versa)?
- Whether there is a performance review process for board members. Why or why not? If so, how effective have these reviews been in improving the performance of individual members or the overall board?
- Whether board meetings are held both with and without the CEO present to encourage candor and objectivity. Who selects and appoints committee members? The board? The CEO? Do the bylaws allow for a nonexecutive chairman? If so, have the differences in the responsibilities of the chairman and the CEO been clearly articulated? Is there good chemistry between the chairman and the CEO? Why or why not? Are periodic meetings of only the independent directors held?
- The frequency of board meetings. Who sets the agenda? How effective are the meetings? Are there minimal attendance standards? How often do the committees meet? How many committees are in place, and how well do they function? Are they adequately reporting to the entire board? Are lines of authority between the committees and the entire board clearly established?
- Any contingency plan that the board has in place should the company become financially distressed. Does the board understand that its fiduciary responsibilities may extend to other types of stakeholders, such as creditors and vendors, as workout plans and strategies are being developed?
- Whether the board has a formal orientation program for new members. If so, when was it last updated?
- Whether the composition of the board reflects gender, ethnic, and racial diversity. How many international members are there on the board? What is the average age of board members?

A corporate governance process must be put in place for *both* privately and publicly held companies that upholds the *integrity* of the company's leadership in the eyes of shareholders and employees, that creates *truly informed board members* who have the power to act based on timely and accurate information, and that *protects the authority and fosters the courage* of the board to take whatever actions are necessary to fulfill its fiduciary obligations. In reexamining the roles, functions, and responsibilities of board members, it is no longer sufficient for directors to merely make a periodic meaningful contribution to the strategic direction of the company; rather, they must now be *proactive* as defenders of the best interests of the shareholders and of the employees, participants, and beneficiaries of pensions, 401(k), and stock option plans. Board members and corporate leaders should assume that their meetings will be in "rooms with glass walls" and that their actions will be examined under a microscope.

Establishing Effective Boards of Directors and Advisory Boards

The quality of an entrepreneurial company's executive and management team and the staff members selected by that team are critical to your growing company's long-term success and to meeting its growth objectives. But whom can the senior management team typically turn to for advice and guidance? Who provides the general policy and direction to the company's executives concerning which specific growth plan is built and executed? For most growing companies, the answer is twofold: (1) a formal *board of directors* and (2) an informal *advisory board* (or a series of advisory boards for specific purposes).

These two boards are often confused, but they actually play very different roles and have very different responsibilities. The board of directors is required under virtually all applicable state corporate laws and has very specific fiduciary duties with regard to the shareholders of the corporation, as described later. The basic governance structure is that the shareholders elect the directors, who in turn appoint the officers. It is the role of the directors to set broad goals and policy objectives for the company that will benefit and protect the interests of the shareholders, and it is incumbent upon the officers to develop and implement plans to meet these goals and objectives. A strong director has broad-based business experience, strong industry knowledge, a useful Rolodex, adequate time to devote to truly understanding the company's key challenges and weaknesses, and the objectivity to challenge decisions made by the management team; she is a good listener and sounding board for the team and has generally been well trained by the university of hard knocks. A good director does not easily get discouraged if the company goes off course, nor does she view the world through rose-colored glasses. Board members should take their fiduciary and stewardship responsibilities very seriously, especially in this post–Sarbanes-Oxley and post-Madoff era; should not be too casual when it comes to critical tasks, such as preparation for and attendance at board meetings; and must not take confidentiality lightly or pursue what appears to be a personal agenda. Each board member and the board as a whole must be constantly guided by questions such as: "What is in the best interest of our shareholders?" and "How can we efficiently and creatively drive shareholder value?"

On the other hand, an advisory board is not required or governed by state corporate laws, does not owe the same levels of fiduciary duties to the shareholders (and hence cannot generally be held as responsible for its acts or recommendations), and can be much more informal with regard to the number of meetings and the agendas for meetings. A single advisory board can be assembled for general purposes, or a series of advisory boards can be set up for very specific purposes, such as technical review, marketing strategy, recruitment and compensation, or research and development. An advisory board can also be an excellent way to get a second opinion on certain matters without interrupting existing relationships.

Leaders of growing companies will often set up an advisory board in connection with the capital formation process in order to demonstrate to prospective investors in the business plan that the officers of the company have access to a credible and objective source of advice and contacts, without filling up precious board of directors seats. The board of directors seats are usually initially set aside for co-founders and investors, and many prospective advisory board members may be reluctant to accept the responsibility that comes with a board of directors seat, especially at the outset of the relationship. Of course, the "showcase value" of putting together a bunch of names of people who barely know you and who will never show up for any meetings dilutes the credibility that you sought to establish when you appointed the advisory board. Prospective investors will put varying weights on the strength and composition of the advisory board in making their final investment decisions and will often want direct access to the advisory board members as part of their due diligence process and to ascertain the depth of their commitment.

One critical difference between a board of directors and an advisory board is the management's ability to accept or ignore the recommendations of any advisory board, a flexibility that it does not have when a mandate comes down from the board of directors. Also, because members of the advisory board do not owe the same duties to the company and its shareholders, they can be used in mediating disputes among the officers or between the officers and the directors. They can also be used to identify potential board of directors candidates or be a recruiting ground for eventual seats on the board.

Since the rules governing the advisory board are not set forth in a corporate law statute, it is critical that you be very clear concerning your expectations of each advisory board member, and also how they will be compensated for their efforts. The best way to capture these objectives and rewards is to prepare a description of the rules and duties of advisory board members.

In the early stages of the company's development, the rewards to advisory board members should be structured in a fashion that encourages a long-term commitment and provides for their being proactive, not merely reactive, contributors to the company's growth plans. Governance challenges will evolve as the company grows and evolves, as set forth in Figure 2-2.

Figure 2-2.	Governance Models.

A. The Early Days

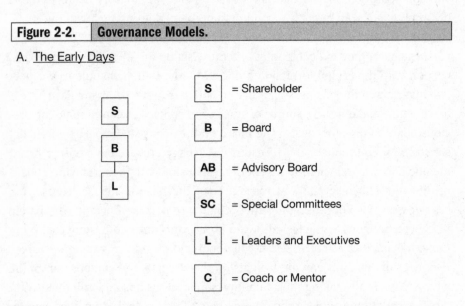

The founding shareholder is chief cook mâitre d' and bottle washer from a governance perspective. This person wears the hats of the shareholder, board member, and leader all at the same time and must learn to segregate decision making and record keeping according to applicable state corporate laws and liability protection best practices.

B. Initial Growth Phase

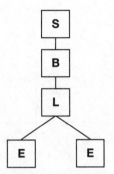

In the initial growth phase, there is now a wider pool of shareholders, which may include some owners, such as angel investors, who are not actively involved in the day-to-day operations of the company. The board is likely to be expanded from one to three or five. There are a few more executives reporting to the founder now that the company is growing, and some delegation of control must be entrusted to the management team.

C. Rapid Growth Phase

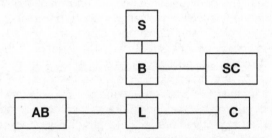

The shareholders may have now increased to include a venture capital firm or even a corporate strategic investor. Communications with all shareholders and transparency in governance is now critical. Decision making must be well documented and strongly substantiated. The board has probably appointed members to several key committees, including audit (to oversee finance), compensation (to oversee recruiting and HR), and nomination (to ensure board diversity, good governance, and board member pipelines). The leaders of the company may have one or more executive coaches or mentors/consultants and may be members of peer networks, associations, and industry groups, such as the Entrepreneurs Organization (EO; www.eonetwork.org), based in Alexandria, Virginia, for advice and guidance. One or more advisory boards may have been put in place to augment the governance at the formal board of directors level and to be a sounding board to the leadership on a wide variety of strategic planning and operational matters.

D. Established Company

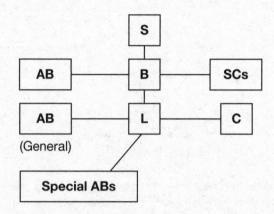

The shareholders may now include both voting and nonvoting shareholders as well as nonvested employees who have option plans. The board continues to increase in size and in the number of committees, including an executive committee. The board may also now have its own special advisory board and teams of special advisors giving it guidance and drawing on a variety of matters, trends, and best practices. The company's leadership and management team is likely to have evolved into a financial organizational chart, presiding over a number of operating divisions, regional and global operations, and new subsidiaries (which will require their own governance structures). The leaders of the company may now have a variety of general advisory boards (in areas such as scientific/technical, customer/vendor, innovation, corporate social responsibility [CSR], diversity, and so on) that augment its interaction with the general advisory board as well as its interaction with outside lawyers, accountants, and consultants. The company may also be involved in joint ventures or other structures where separate governance practices and leadership teams must be put in place.

Chapter 3

The Role Your Business Plan Plays

Entrepreneurs and owners of businesses at all stages of growth know that effective business planning is critical to a company's long-term success and its ability to raise capital. As a result, much has been written by bankers, accountants, consultants, and academicians on the preparation of a business plan. Yet it seems that the more information there is, the more confused people get about what a business plan should include. There's no one "right answer." A business plan should tell a compelling story, make an argument, and conservatively predict the future, and companies have different stories to tell, different arguments to make, and different futures to predict. It has been said that failing to plan is planning to fail. Opportunity clearly favors the prepared mind.

Business planning is the process of setting goals, explaining objectives, and then mapping out a plan for how the company's management team will achieve these goals and objectives. In essence, a business plan is the articulation of *why* your idea is a valuable opportunity, what resources it will require, who will provide the vision and leadership to execute the plan, and how you will reach your goals. It proves the key underlying premises of the business model and offers the readers insights into your game plan for mitigating and managing risk. It will also answer these questions:

- Who are we?
- What do we do?
- What is our business model? In other words, how do we make money? What problem do we solve? Who are our customers?
- How do our customers pay us?
- How far along is our business?
- What do we need?
- What business are we really in?
- What need are we meeting?
- Who is on our team?
- How do we know that our solution works?
- Who else is offering this solution right now? Who may be offering the same or a similar solution in the near future? (The ability to identify and anticipate the competitors that are likely to appear in the future is a critical business planning skill.)
- What advantages do we have over other providers of the solution?
- How do our targeted customers make their buying decisions?
- How do we get them to try us?
- How do we get them to come back?
- What is the cost of attracting them?
- What will it cost to keep them happy?

There are, always have been, and always will be only four things that any experienced investor really cares about, and these should always be answered in a business plan:

1. Who are the team members (internal and external)? Do they know how to get things done?

2. How do you make money? What is the product, the opportunity, the price, the customer, and the competition?

3. What bad stuff can happen? What factors outside your control could mess things up? What's your fallback plan?

4. How much money do you need? How much do you *really* need? For what? Are there alternative ways to acquire these resources? How creative or frugal is the plan? What is the upside? How ugly is the downside? How soon will you come back to us looking for more money? What is our exit strategy (and don't just say "IPO" like everyone else)?

Do You Really Need a Business Plan?

Some members of the business and academic communities challenge the idea that an entrepreneur really needs a business plan. They claim that preparing one is a waste of time because the marketplace moves so rapidly. This is like asking a pilot to fly without navigation equipment, or a ship's captain to set sail without a nautical map—it's a bad idea. There are many reasons to prepare a business plan, including the following:

- To explain—to yourself and others—why a viable opportunity exists
- To provide a roadmap for the future direction of the business
- To hold the founders accountable for meeting their performance goals and to demonstrate that you have put together a capable and balanced management team that is able to execute the strategy and implement the business plan
- To provide a schedule and a time frame for meeting key milestones
- To identify what resources will be needed to accomplish objectives and *when* they will be needed
- To mitigate the risks of future business failure by identifying potential bottlenecks and problems that will affect the growth of the company and offering possible solutions
- To provide internal financial controls and direction
- To provide a channel for communication between you and the outside investors
- To provide an analysis of what your company does "faster, better, and cheaper" than its competitors
- To provide an analysis to demonstrate that you have both a sustainable revenue model and a sustainable competitive advantage
- To educate and motivate key employees, reward their performance, and serve as a recruitment tool for new employees
- To prevent litigation with investors by providing disclosures of the potential risks and challenges faced by the company
- To determine the feasibility and viability of the business and to identify the fatal flaws in the assumptions underlying your business model (don't wear rose-colored glasses—deal with the problems head on!)
- To analyze the marketplace to determine to what extent you enjoy the advantage of being first with your idea ("first mover advantage" analysis)
- For technology or Web 2.0/social networking businesses, to identify how and why your technology or social networking application solves problems or cures market inefficiencies

Interesting Perspectives on Business Planning

"[Alice saw] the Cheshire Cat sitting on a bough of a tree…. 'Would you tell me, please, which way I ought to go from here?' 'That depends a good deal on where you want to get to,' said the Cat. 'I don't much care where–' said Alice. 'Then it doesn't matter which way you go,' said the Cat. '–so long as I get somewhere,' Alice added…. 'Oh, you're sure to do that,' said the Cat."   —Lewis Carroll, *Alice's Adventures in Wonderland*

"But then again there is no greater example of a work of fiction then a business plan. As an entrepreneur you write it, then you spend your life trying to turn it into a work of non-fiction."   —A conversation with Sam Calagione, founder of Dogfish Head Craft Brewery

"Planning without action is futile; action without planning is fatal"   —Unknown

"Having no plan is like sailing the seven seas without a compass, digging a ditch without a shovel, or hunting for pirate's treasure without an 'x' marks the spot. Without one, you're better off heading down to the horse races and betting on the 'Win Three.' A plan helps keep you on schedule, makes it easier to recognize success and failure, helps pump you up when things aren't going so well, and most importantly, provides an essential focus—a beacon of light in an ocean full of treachery. In fact, a plan not only acts as your road map for success (a metaphor that's been beaten to death), it is your vehicle for prosperity, or if you prefer, your own personal prescription for greatness.   —Peter J. Patsula, "Supercharging Promising Projects with a Plan of Action"

"If you go to work on your goals, your goals will go to work on you. If you go to work on your plan, your plan will go to work on you. Whatever good things we build end up building us."   —Jim Rohn

"There's no shortage of remarkable ideas; what's missing is the will to execute them."   —Seth Godin

"Plan your work…then work your plan.   —Norman Vincent Peale, *Inspiring Messages for Daily Living*

"If you don't know where you are going, then you'll be lost when you get there"   —Yogi Berra

That thing about, "If we build it, they will come" works only in the movies. The business plan must answer several questions: How crowded is the market? What vehicles will you use to sell the customer *your* product or service? Why is this the best vehicle, and what will it cost? What market research have you done to ensure that anyone *wants* to buy this product or service? Does your company truly modify the way business is being done in your industry (as a change agent), or is your product or service more of a fad or a trend? Nobody has a crystal ball to predict what will work and what won't—neither the most savvy investor nor the most experienced entrepreneur. The better the analysis, the better the chances that most of the goals set forth in the business plan will be achieved.

Your business plan explains how and why you selected this path, what resources you'll need for your journey, and what you hope to achieve along the way—but there is no guarantee that you'll reach your goals. (Note: Christopher Columbus disappointed several investors who backed his early missions before he "discovered" America, and things are no different now from what they were in 1492!) A well-written business plan doesn't *oversell* the good, *undersell* the bad, or *ignore* the ugly. It is essentially a plan to manage the risk involved in starting a new venture. Business plans should be written in a manner that acknowledges that growth and success are moving targets and anticipates as many future events or circumstances that will affect the company's objectives as possible. Business planning is a fluid and dynamic process, so when the target stops moving, the game is over.

Before exploring the different kinds of financing that are available, you should thoroughly understand the fundamentals of preparing a plan, because regardless of what kind of capital you're raising—or how—any lender, underwriter, venture capitalist, or private investor will expect you and your management team to be able to prepare a meaningful business plan. The plan will have to address specific financial questions, such as:

- What market problems and financial opportunities have you identified?
- What services, products, and projects are you planning in order to exploit these opportunities or solve these problems?
- How much capital will you need to obtain the resources necessary to bring these projects to fruition?
- Exactly how will you allocate the capital? How will this infusion of capital increase sales, profits, and the overall value of the company?
- How will you meet your debt-service obligations and provide a meaningful return on investment to your investors and lenders?
- How much equity in the company are you offering to investors? How is it being valued?
- What "exit strategies" will be available to the equity investors?

When preparing a business plan for capital-formation purposes, one of the key goals is to use the plan to work for the blessing of a local market influencer, such as an angel or venture capitalist, who will champion your plan, put some initial money into the company, and, most important, show your plan to others who have the money and the resources to help the company achieve its objectives. Using the plan to convince this first penguin to jump through the ice is an important market validator that will build credibility and excitement for the company and its business model. Another key aspect of building a business plan for use in the capital markets is to answer a critical question about *empowerment*. The question that the plan must answer is, "How will the money you seek to raise enable and empower the management team to achieve objectives that it has been unable to achieve to date?" This shows your initial champion and others that you have really thought through the capital-formation process and are not just raising money for the sake of raising money.

Business plans are used by both start-up companies and operating companies. For example, a company that has been operating for 15 or more years will need to draft a business plan in order to raise the necessary capital to reach the next stage in its development. Regardless of your company's age, you should prepare your plan with the help of a financial consultant, an investment banker, your internal management team, your attorneys, and your accountants.

One commonly asked question is, how long should my business plan be? The latest thinking is that an entrepreneur with a growing company should have three versions—the two-pager, the ten-pager and the thirty (or so)–pager. The two-pager is for the initial introduction to targeted investors; it is about the same length as the description of your business that you could give in a 30-second elevator ride (it's often referred to as the "elevator speech"). It devotes about two sentences to each of the key topics described in the outline that follows. The ten-pager expands the depth of the discussion of the topics to about two paragraphs per topic and is often used as a presentation tool in the second or third round of meetings with targeted investors. Finally, the thirty (or so)–pager is the detailed strategic game plan that describes exactly how the company will meet its growth objectives; it devotes about two or three pages to each of the key topics. See Figure 3-1 to make sure your business plan is aligned with the needs of the target readership.

The Mechanics of Preparing a Business Plan

You've probably guessed that I don't believe in using a generic approach to preparing a business plan. But what would a book on new-venture financing

Figure 3-1. | **The Business Planning Paradox: Where Do You Fit?**

- Business Plan weak
- Capital markets trending downward
- Industry trends neutral

- Capital markets strong
- Industry trends positive
- Business Plan strong

- Business Plan weak
- Capital markets weak
- Industry trends negative

- Business Plan strong
- Industry trends moderate
- Capital markets neutral

V I A B I L I T Y

STRENGTH

be without at least *one* suggested outline? I stress that it is only an outline, not a rigid format that should be followed section by section or line by line.

I.   **Executive Summary**
   A.   Brief history
   B.   Mission statement (why you are in this business)
   C.   Discussion of your revenue and your business model
   D.   Overview of your products and services
   E.   Background of your management team (summary)
   F.   Key features of your market
   G.   Summary of the company's financial performance to date (where applicable)
   H.   How much money you need to raise and why

II.   **The Company: An Overview**
   A.   Organizational and management structure
   B.   Operational and management policies
   C.   Description of products and services (both current and anticipated)
   D.   Overview of trends in the industry and marketplace in which you compete (or plan to compete)
   E.   Key strengths and weaknesses of the company

III. Products and Services: An Extended Discussion
A. Key products and services currently offered
B. Proprietary features, strengths, and weaknesses of each
C. Anticipated products and services (how future product development and research will be affected by the financing you seek)

IV. Market Analysis
A. Extended description of the markets in which you compete (size, trends, growth, and so on)
B. Analysis of key competitors and likely future competitors (and how your business model will change or evolve in order to face the new competitors)
C. Description and analysis of key customers and clients (current and anticipated)
D. Market research supporting current and anticipated product lines
E. Analysis of barriers to entry and your sustainable competitive advantage

V. Marketing and Advertising Strategy
A. Strategies for reaching current and anticipated customers or clients
B. Pricing policies and strategies
C. Advertising and public relations plans and strategic alliances

VI. Financial Plan and Strategies
A. Summary of financial performance for the past three to five years
B. Current financial condition (include recent income statements and balance sheets as attachments)
C. Projected financial condition (present forecasts for three to five years)
D. Extended discussion of working budgets and how capital will be allocated and used consistent with these budgets

VII. Suggested Exhibits and Attachments
   A. Résumés of key members of the management team
   B. Organizational chart
   C. Timelines for completion of goals and objectives
   D. Copies of key documents and contracts
   E. Copies of recent media coverage
   F. Pictures of key products or advertising materials for services offered
   G. List of customer and professional references

Screens, Filters, and Tools to Assess the Viability and Predictability of Your Business and Strategic Plans

There is a wide variety of screens, filters, and tools that you can use to test the viability of your business plan. It is best to apply protocols to your plan objectively prior to meeting with suppliers of capital. Rest assured that any sophisticated lender or investor will apply these basic tools, as well as some of their own screening criteria, to the analysis of your plan before investing in your company.

Key Analytical Tools

Scenario Analysis

- Predict the likelihood of outcomes and consequences of a proposed macro strategy or transaction.
- The process involves analyzing possible future events by considering possible outcomes or scenarios to improve decision making and identify risks.
- The goal is to present alternative future outcomes and the key *variables* that will influence those outcomes (controllable vs. noncontrollable events, wild cards, predictable vs. unpredictable events, events involving human error/emotion/turfmanship, logistics, and so on) and the *consequences* of each outcome for the stakeholders and the ecosystem.
- The likelihood or probability of each outcome and its consequences will influence the shaping of the future strategies and actions as the outcomes are monitored following implementation.
- All relevant variables (legal, political, social, economic, ethical/moral,

competitive marketplace, environmental, and so on) influencing the likelihood of each outcome should be considered.

- Look for alignments and disconnects between proposed strategies or transactions and the external variables that may influence the outcomes of these strategies or transactions (for example, is the proposed strategy or transaction aligned with or disconnected from current trends; historical performance; due diligence results; fear, uncertainty, and doubt issues; and so on).
- Gather empirical, experimental, qualitative, and quantitative data to perform your analysis, but also trust your gut feelings and instincts.
- Build a scenario analysis–driven model for evaluating a proposed business plan, strategy, or proposed transaction or investment; this involves identifying the key "drivers" or "linkages" that will influence the answers to basic forecasting or budgeting or risk analysis questions such as:
  - What would be the impact on divisional gross margin if we changed the product mix as follows:
    - _____?
    - Or _____?
    - Or _____?
  - If our regional office in Paris could do X _____, how would that influence Y _____ or Z_____?
  - If we reduced headcount costs in Asia by 27 percent, what would the consequences be for sales, morale, legal risks, future recruitment, competitive perceptions, and so on?
- For scenario analysis to be complete and most accurate and productive, each player must think outside her typical silo's perspectives, basis, and training, and there should be diversity of experiences and viewpoints on the teams in order to mitigate risks, reduce surprises, and avoid being blind-sided.
- Scenario analysis is a tool, not a crutch for predicting the outcomes or consequences of proposed strategies, transactions, or investments of resources—it is not a substitute for careful monitoring of relationships, transactions, or decisions, and teams should "expect the unexpected (for example, the most probable outcome is not necessarily the most likely outcome).

Situational Analysis

- What are the *specific* consequences or variables that will influence this micro plan or transaction
- Drill down to the micro-level variables that will influence a specific situation, plan, transaction, or market entry.
- Key variables include:
  - Core and secondary or supporting product or service features
  - Competitive analysis—direct and indirect
  - Channel analysis—how will products or services reach the marketplace?
  - Environmental factors—specific economic or sociological factors in this market that influence outcomes
  - The legal and regulatory environment and challenges to compliance or enforcement
  - SWOT analysis on the particular market, transaction, or relationship
  - Demographics and social trends in this target marketplace
  - Norms, culture, beliefs, superstitions, values, habits, and fears of the consumers being targeted
  - Likely risks of bribery, corruption, not invented here issues, nepotism, or protectionism or localism in the target market
  - Topographical and other physical characteristics of the target market (and their impact on distribution and logistics)
  - Governmental, public, private, or nongovernmental organizations; trade associations; chambers of commerce; professional societies; business groups; community or civic groups; churches; and other organizations that may influence the ecosystem
- Characteristics of the population in the target micro market, including:
  - Educational levels
  - Cultural characteristics
  - Lifestyles and living standards
  - Primary occupations
  - Life expectancy and most common health challenges
  - Income levels
  - Consumption patterns
  - Transportation logistics

- Access to technology and the Internet
- Communities and their distinguishing characteristics
- Mobility and rates of inflow and outflow of citizens
- Services available
- Any other aspect of society that may be useful in assessing factors such as attitudes, motivation, and so on.
- Avoid the personal biases or beliefs of the person conducting the situational analysis—*focus, focus, focus* on the situations of the target market itself.
- Situational analysis is akin to a soldier studying the terrain before battle or a golfer playing a practice round on a course before the tournament begins—achieving familiarity with the circumstances influencing the specific market in order to increase the chances of success and decrease or mitigate the risk of failure or defeat.

Risk Analysis

- Predict the legal, financial, reputational, ethical, political, and opportunity cost risks of a proposed action/inaction, market entry, transaction, or decision.
- What are the legal, financial, reputational, political, ethical, or opportunity cost risks of a(n):
  - Decision?
  - Nondecision?
  - Strategy?
  - Plan?
  - Change in course?
  - Transaction?
  - Relationship?
  - Market entry?
  - Organizational structure?
- Risk management plans focus on continuity of business operations and impact analysis on future company plans or strategies.
- Costs and consequences range from minimal business interruptions to direct operational impact (for 24 or more hours) to disastrous impact.
- Costs can be tangible (quantitative and measurable) or intangible (reputation, trust, brand, and so on).

- Cost and impact may vary from department to department on business function and by division or region.
- Risk analysis is typically "bucketized" into:
  - Human threats (workplace violence, negligence, accidents, human error, strikes, vandalism, terrorism)
  - Natural disasters (flooding, fire, hurricanes, tsunami, snowstorms, spoilage, and other weather events)
  - Political threats (government overthrow, price freezes, war, civil disorder, and so on)
  - Financial threats (embezzlement, capital markets, large-scale fraud, currency, taxes, and so on)
  - Environmental disasters (chemical spills, hazardous waste, explosions, biological contamination, and so on)
  - Technology threats (power failures, hacking, social media, system or server failures, computer crime, telephone breakdown, and so on)
- Risk analysis can take many forms and focus on a wide variety of variables. Key risk analysis questions are:
  - What direct and indirect risks does this new strategy, plan, initiative, project, relationship, channel, or market entry pose?
  - What is the magnitude (severity) of the possible adverse consequences?
  - How vulnerable are we to these threats? Have we conducted a thorough business impact analysis?
  - What is the likelihood (probability) of occurrence of each adverse consequence?
  - Who will be responsible if these risks manifest themselves into reality?
  - What is our game plan for managing, mitigating, and monitoring these risks?

Common Business-Planning Myths

MYTH 1: Business plans are only for start-up companies.

REALITY: Companies at all stages of development need to prepare business plans, either for a specific project or for general expansion financing, mergers or acquisitions, or to set milestones to measure the company's performance.

MYTH 2: Business plans should be as detailed and slick as possible. The more money you spend preparing the plan, the better your chances of getting financing.

REALITY: Sophisticated investors don't have time to review hundreds of pages of text. Your plan must be concise and well written, focusing on the lender's or investor's principal areas of concern. Avoid overly technical descriptions of your company's processes or operations. Investors will commit funds based on the quality and clarity of the document, not its thickness. Although business plans ought to have a professional look, a very expensive binder or presentation often demonstrates inefficient resource management.

MYTH 3: Business plans should emphasize ideas and concepts, not people.

REALITY: Many entrepreneurs fear that if the success of a company depends too heavily on any specific person, an investor will shy away. Although this is partially true, an experienced venture capitalist ultimately prefers to invest in a company that has great people and only a good concept, rather than one that has a great concept and a weak management team. Ultimately, lenders and investors will commit funds based on the strength of your management team. *There should also be a section that explains to investors and others how the business plan matches with your "life plan." In other words, how does the achievement of the company's goals and objectives fit with the founders' personal goals and objectives?*

MYTH 4: Business plans should be prepared only by the founding entrepreneur(s).

REALITY: Most entrepreneurs are highly skilled in a particular profession or area of management, but that doesn't necessarily mean that they can prepare a business plan in the form to which prospective lenders or investors are accustomed. Ideally, the plan should be developed by a team of your managers and reviewed by *qualified* experts, such as accountants, attorneys, and the board of directors. The business plan should never be prepared solely by outside advisors without input from internal management. A venture capitalist will quickly recognize a "cooked" plan, or one that reflects the views and efforts of professional advisors rather than those who are responsible for running the company.

MYTH 5: Business plans should be distributed as widely as possible.

REALITY: The business plan will inevitably contain information that is proprietary and confidential, so you should control its distribution and keep careful records of who has copies. The cover sheet should have a conspicuously positioned notice of proprietary information and a management disclaimer reminding the reader that these are only the company's plans (the success of which cannot be assured). Carefully consider all applicable federal and state securities laws if you intend to use the business plan as a financing proposal. However, it should not be used in lieu of a formal private-placement memorandum, which is discussed in Chapter 6. Finally, some institutional investors will consider investments only in certain kinds of companies or industries. Research these criteria before sending a business plan, so that you save both the time and resources of all concerned parties.

Characteristics of Successful Entrepreneurial Teams

The characteristics of successful entrepreneurial teams (which you should attempt to demonstrate and support in your business plan) include:

1. Balance
   b. Complementary talents
   c. Dreamer/schemer/reamer
   d. Ability to wear multiple hats
2. Truly shared objectives and core values with a genuine sense of teamwork
3. Legal agreements in place to protect the company and its founders
4. Communication channels that foster open dialogue, room for disagreement, and methods for resolving conflicts
5. Accountability and judgment
6. Egos parked at door
7. A track record of having done something together successfully
8. Integrity, trust, fairness, and respect
9. Strong, cooperative work ethic
10. Commitment to the long-term success of the company

MYTH 6: A business plan should follow a specified format, regardless of the industry in which the company operates.

REALITY: While it may be true that all companies face certain common challenges in the areas of marketing, management, administration, and finance, companies that are at different stages of growth and operating in different industries will require very different topics in their business plans. The plan for a start-up manufacturing company may be far more concerned with financing of the plant, equipment, patents, inventory, and production schedules than that for an established service-oriented company, which may be more focused on personnel, marketing costs, and the protection of trade secrets and goodwill.

MYTH 7: Optimism should prevail over realism.

REALITY: The business plan should demonstrate your enthusiasm and generate excitement in the reader, but it still has to be credible and accurate. Investors want—and need—to know all the company's strengths and weaknesses. In fact, a realistic discussion of the company's problems, along with a reasonable plan for solving them, will have a positive impact on the prospective investor. The unstated rules of the game are that investors would rather have you identify your own "warts" and explain them than leave the problems for them to discover. Generally, investors feel more comfortable investing in someone who has learned from previous business failures than in someone who has never managed a company before. Finally, any budgets, sales projections, company valuations, or related forecasts should be well annotated with accompanying footnotes, for both legal and business reasons. Unrealistic or unsubstantiated financial projections and budgets will reveal inexperience or lack of attention to detail. They can even lead to litigation by disgruntled investors if there are wide disparities between your representations and reality.

MYTH 8: A well-written business plan should contain an executive summary that is written before the full text of the document is prepared.

REALITY: Institutional investors see hundreds of business plans every month and can devote only a few minutes to each one. The executive summary (generally one to three pages long) will be the first (and possibly the last) impression you make. If you don't capture the reader's attention in these first few minutes, she is unlikely to read further. The executive summary should contain all the information that will be critical to the investment decision, such as the nature of the company and its founders, the amount of money you're seeking, the allocation of the proceeds (how you'll use the money), and a summary *first* (before the main components have been drafted). It's more effective—and ensures consistency—to prepare the main body of the plan, then the executive summary. The executive summary is then a true preview of the plan's details.

MYTH 9: Business plans are written only when a company needs to raise capital.

REALITY: Although most business plans are written in connection with the search for money, a well-written business plan will serve a variety of purposes for the company and its management team. It can be a roadmap for growth; a realistic self-appraisal of the company's progress to date and its projected goals and objectives; and a foundation for a more detailed strategic and growth management plan (especially after you've received the proposed financing).

MYTH 10: The business plan should showcase the company's proprietary products and services.

REALITY: Most investors are not interested in a business plan that merely demonstrates that you have built a better mousetrap. Many entrepreneurs (who are also investors) fall in love with their proprietary product creations and fail to recognize that investors want to commit capital to successful *companies*, not just successful *products*. If the business plan overemphasizes the product without demonstrating that a long-term, sustainable business can be built around that product, then it will fail to attract sophisticated investors.

Figure 3-2 offers guidelines for drafting a business plan.

Some Final Thoughts on Business Planning

Write your business plan with the wants, needs, perspectives, and priorities of your audience firmly in mind! Conduct due diligence in advance of the meeting so that you know what is truly important to your investors—which may vary depending on whether the investor is an angel, a venture capitalist, or a strategic investor. The business plan is less about you and your story or needs than it is about meeting the investor's objectives and investment parameters. One way to assemble a list of potential strategic investors (and have a great presentation ready to go) is to ask a simple strategic question: *"If my company were to be wildly successful, who else would benefit?" "Who is rooting for me to succeed?"* These are the sources of capital or other resources that have a genuine stake in your success and may be motivated (or even compelled) to have a vested interest in that success.

Figure 3-2.	Business Plan Drafting.

EXAMPLES OF SAMPLE SECTIONS AND COMMON MISTAKES ON COMPETITION

Unacceptable
1. **We are unique** and we have no competition.
2. **We have a lot of competition,** but if we can capture only one percent of the marketplace... (Avoid the "myth" of "if we can just get 1%...)
3. **We will smash the competition to bits** by recruiting engineers with at least ten years experience. (This does not explain *how* and *why* the years of experience are important to the targeted customer, how or why the customer uses this data to make purchasing decisions, or why an engineer with eight years experience is inadequate. How or why is this a problem? How or why does it matter to the customer? How are you sure?)

Acceptable
1. **We have identified** the following companies as competitors
   _____ [WHO?]
   because_____ [WHY?].
   Our strengths are _____ [HOW AND WHY ARE YOU BETTER, IF AT ALL?], and our weaknesses _____ [WHERE ARE YOU VULNER-ABLE AND WHY?]. [COMPETITIVE ANALYSIS] [ENTRY BARRIERS?]
2. **Our primary strategies** to distinguish ourselves from our competitors include
   _____ [EXPLAIN THE STRATEGY]. These strategies present the following risks and opportunities _____
   [DISCUSS]. Our feedback plan would be to _____

Better Than Acceptable
The information in "Acceptable" above, plus a distinction between direct and indirect competition; a more detailed analysis of key competitors (including relevant trends, historical information, or reasonable forecasting); a discussion of competitors that you will face (or will no longer face) in the future as you grow, and why; an analysis of the feasibility of turning enemies into allies; the competitive forces in your initial and forecasted trading areas (for example, whether you have a local, regional, national, or global focus); and how your targeted consumers make buying decisions. (Note: One common business-planning trap is to focus

on how *you* perceive the competition instead of looking at the world through the customer's eyes, as set forth below.)

ON COSTS, PRICING, AND PROFITS

Unacceptable
We think we will be able to buy our widgets at price *x*, resell them at price *y,* and then retire in comfort with all of the *z*.

Acceptable
We have certain challenges in acquiring raw materials at the following price ranges due to _____. Our other costs of goods sold will include _____ and _____. Our preliminary market research indicates a consumer price of _____ based on _____, leaving us a margin of _____ based on _____ [BASED ON WHAT?], which, given our administrative costs, will result in _____.

Better Than Acceptable
All of "Acceptable" above, plus: We recognize that there are many tangible and intangible factors influencing a customer's buying decision. We will not be driven by price alone, but will look at decision factors such as convenience (like 800-Flowers), quality of service (Nordstrom), speed (Jiffy Lube, McDonald's), reliability (Timex, Maytag), consistent customer experience (Southwest Airlines, Federal Express, Starbucks) even if not the highest quality (Taco Bell), and the pleasantness of the transaction (Saturn). We will strive to shape and manage our customer's expectations by _____ and emphasize these factors as they relate to our pricing strategy. (Note: if you will be driven by price alone, you will have to state how you plan to replicate the operational efficiency that companies such as Wal-Mart, Syms, Dell Computer, and Charles Schwab have demonstrated.)

Chapter 4

Start-Up Financing

Raising capital at any stage of a company's growth is challenging and requires creativity and tenacity, but these hurdles are especially difficult to conquer at the earliest stages of an enterprise's development, when the business model is still under consturction and the track record for success is minimal or non-existent. In this chapter, we'll take a look at *where* and *how* to raise capital at the seed level—when you're first organizing your business, or when it is in its earliest stages of growth.

In the chapters that follow, we'll look at funding strategies that are commonly used after a business has gotten past the start-up phase and has established a steady flow of customers and a reliable revenue stream, even if the company is not yet profitable. These include alternatives to raising capital in the early stages, private placements (a more organized and expanded method of angel financing for moderate-growth companies), commercial debt financing (once the business has assets in place to serve as collateral for the loan), and ways to acquire resources that you would have purchased if you had raised capital. Later in the book, we'll explore growth-financing strategies, such as seeking institutional venture capital (for rapidly growing companies that offer exceptional potential returns on investment) or raising capital by taking your company public with an initial public offering (IPO). Then we'll offer some creative alternatives to traditional financing as ways to grow your business. The main thing to understand is that no one plan fits all: The strategies that are available to—and useful for—a particular company depend mainly on that company's stage of development and the nature of its business. What works for a start-up retailer may not work for a 10-year-old manufacturer, and neither of those strategies may work for an early-stage technology or social networking business!

At the seed level, you are looking for capital to acquire the initial resources that you need to launch the enterprise, attract and hire employees, conduct research and development, acquire computer systems, and build initial inventory. The lines have blurred among what was once a relatively clear-cut demarcation between seed investors, angels, and venture capital (VC) funds. We now have microangels, crowdfunding, superangels, micro-VC funds, "normal" VC funds, and mega-VC funds, whose typical investment size and style start bleeding into the private equity fund area. Other funds are laser-targeted on a particular industry, region, or situation [such as management buyouts (MBOs) or turnarounds]. Start-up funding has even become the topic of a reality television show, *Shark Tank* (www.abc.go.com/shows/shark-tank.com), where hopeful entrepreneurs are given an opportunity to present their business plans to five self-made millionaires who may invest in their companies, and TechStars (www.techstars.org), where entrepreneurs compete for capital resources and support. During the first season of the show on Bloomberg television, a wide variety of concepts were presented, ranging from a plus-sized women's clothing line to a children's medicine dispenser to a mobile application that helps mitigate college sports recruiting violations. Clearly, early-stage investing is still motivated by two parts cash and one part love and passion and faith, since many of the ventures can and will fail and the investors hope to get as much emotional reward from investing as they do financial return.

I'm devoting the rest of this chapter to the likely sources of seed and early-stage capital described in Figure 4-1. Although this stage of your business is characterized by frustration, struggles, setbacks, and delays, if you are creative and aggressive in your search, there are many sources of cost-effective seed capital available that will let you maintain control and majority ownership of the business.

Figure 4-1.	Matching Capital Needs to Likely Sources.	
Stage of Growth	**Amount Probably Needed**	**Most Likely and Affordable Source of Capital**
Seed/Early-Stage	$25,000 to $500,000 (depending on type of business)	**(a) Founder/Team:** Personal savings, credit cards, home equity line of credit, 401(k) and retirement account/pension/life insurance borrowing. (It is critical to demonstrate to investors in future rounds of capital that you have risked your own assets and have some "skin in the game.") **(b) External investors:** Family and friends, angels, vendors, customers, key employees, Small Business Administration (SBA) loan and loan guaranty programs, third-party loan guaranties, severance and downsizing payments, liquidation of stocks and bonds, networking, university and private incubator programs, venture-investor clubs, advances on inheritances, ACE-Net and other Internet/database angel/investor matching services, foundation grants, and economic development agencies.
Growth Stage	$500,000 to $3 million (depending on rate and method of growth)	Private placements, superangels, bands of angels, institutional venture capital, commercial lenders, venture leasing companies, strategic alliances and joint ventures, corporate venture capitalists, small business investment companies or minority enterprise small business investment companies.

Stage of Growth	Amount Probably Needed	Most Likely and Affordable Source of Capital
Mezzanine/Bridge	**$1 million to $5 million** (financing at this level is usually tied to a near-term initial public offering)	Merchant banks, investment bankers, private equity funds, institutional international investors, commercial banks, small securities offerings (via Internet)
Harvest	**$2 million to $20 million** (depending on exit strategy and founder's personal goals)	• Initial public offerings • Creative exit strategies (franchising, licensing, and so on) • Mergers and acquisitions

Financing the Business with Your Own Resources

The combination of your own financial investment and time investment ("sweat equity") is a prerequisite to obtaining capital from third-party sources. The capital markets expect you to put your own funds at risk before you ask others to risk investing in your business. This is often called the "straight-face test" because you are able to look a venture investor in the eye and demonstrate your own commitment to the new enterprise and your belief in its potential. If you have co-founders, all of you are expected to make this type of commitment. This is true even if the level of personal investment varies because of differences in the partners' financial circumstances or the degree to which a particular individual contributes a particular skill, recipe, knowledge, or relationship—the intangible, nonfinancial aspect of contribution.

Your initial capital may come from savings, 401(k) plan loans (where permitted) or withdrawals, home equity loans, a severance package in connection with downsizing, credit cards, or other sources as set forth here. Of course, this also violates the OPM (other people's money) rule: Wherever possible, use other people's money to invest in a risk enterprise. But in the world of new-venture financing, the OPM rule usually goes out the window unless you're a veteran entrepreneur with an established track record and can demand that others risk their capital without your investing your own funds in the enterprise.

If I Don't Have a Rich Uncle, Where Can I Get the Initial Seed Capital?

Traditionally, entrepreneurs have used their own savings and credit (credit cards, home equity lines of credit, and other such sources) to finance the pre-launch expenses and initial seed investment for their companies. If you don't have liquidity in your personal or retirement savings, you may be able to borrow against your 401(k) account, pension, or life insurance policies.

Only you can dictate what portion of your life savings you're willing to risk, and prudence should dictate some level of conservatism, which may vary depending on both your immediate cash needs and your short- to medium-term goals and needs. An individual with limited savings and two children nearing college age should be very careful with his savings and may want to reconsider whether this is the right time to launch a business venture at all. Conversely, a young couple with toddlers and one working spouse may decide that this is a perfect time to use their savings to launch a business. They know that they have a steady source of income from the working spouse and plenty of time to replenish their savings if the business venture is unsuccessful.

Family, Friends, and Fools

After exhausting the portion of your life savings and available credit lines that you have determined is appropriate to finance the start of your business, the next most likely source of capital is usually those who love and trust you, or the three "Fs"—family, friends, and fools. Whether they're looking for an equity investment or a formal or informal loan, entrepreneurs often turn to old friends and family members, who typically provide capital on the basis of a relationship rather than on the basis of financial rewards.

If your family is anything like mine, however, you may want to reconsider this strategy. You will have to be prepared to provide business-plan updates at family dinners and to be reminded weekly of "who helped you get started." The benefits of this inexpensive capital may be outweighed by the costs in terms of family dynamics and by the complex emotions of guilt, despair, and frustration if the business fails and the family investment is lost.

Turning to old friends for money may also be unwise, particularly when the friend is investing in your new business based on trust and can't really afford to lose the money if things go south. Business loans and investments have ruined a lot of long-standing relationships over the years. The catch-22, of course, is that if things go very well, then your family and friends wind up arguing with you because you didn't give them a chance to participate. Again, you know your friends and family and their tolerance for risk, and only you can decide whether it will be advisable or appropriate to approach them for seed and early-stage capital.

If you decide to solicit friends and family as a source of capital, you must be very open and honest about the risks and rewards of the enterprise—and the risks are likely to be much more significant than the rewards in the early stages of the business. Make sure that they know that this is *not* like investing in the public stock market, where public reporting, a track record, and the availability of liquidity protect against downside risk. You should also put the terms of the investment arrangements in writing to formalize the transaction and to avoid confusion about the rights and responsibilities of the parties.

Family Business Offices

Many wealthy families have set up formal business offices, with financial managers handling investments, the review of proposals, reporting to family members, and related tasks. Different family business offices (or FBOs) will have different processes for evaluating prospective investments. Some are quite formal and are operated as quasi-venture capital funds with essentially one investor (the family), and others are very informal, with no clear-cut strategy or focus, or even a web site. Many FBOs will co-invest in or "piggyback" on transactions that are being considered by local angel groups or venture capitalists, and many rely heavily on their personal networks to generate deal flow. As of the fall of 2011, it was estimated that there are more than 3,000 FBOs in America; some may be U.S. offices of families abroad, and there may be many others that do not formally report their operations. Most of these FBOs are focused on wealth management and venture investment, *not* on running the underlying family business. Most of them have $100 million or more under management, and their investments include real estate, stocks and bonds, precious metals, and venture capital–style investments, either on a stand-alone or a syndicated basis.

Heaven on Earth—Finding an Angel Investor

Once you've demonstrated that your own funds are at risk and that you have exhausted your "emotional investors" (family, friends, coworkers, and others who love and trust you), it's time to begin your quest for an angel. If flying with angels isn't your cup of tea, then pay close attention to the other likely sources of seed and early-stage capital that are discussed later in the chapter.

The term *angel* originated on Broadway, where wealthy investors provided funds to aspiring directors to finance the production of a new musical or drama. The motivation for these investments included financial reward, but they were mainly driven by a love for the theater and the chance to develop friendships with aspiring actors, playwrights, and producers. The point was that these investors provided high-risk capital and were motivated by something more than money. Even today, playwrights, artists, producers, and musicians often rely on the altruism of others to advance their projects or careers; likewise, an aspiring entrepreneur must rely on something other than financial reward as an impetus for an investment. Your focus in meeting and presenting to angels must be more on what makes this *person* motivated to invest than on what internal rate of return (IRR) will be attractive to her wallet.

Beyond Broadway, angel investing has become a critical source of financing for seed and early-stage companies. From Arthur Rock in the early 1960s, whose angel dollars and capital-formation efforts helped launch companies such as Intel and Apple Computer, to cashed-out entrepreneurs such as Lotus founder Mitch Kapor, whose angel investments include RealNetworks and UUNET, to new-economy multimillionaires and Internet pioneers like Ted Leonsis of America Online, thousands of modern-day angels have played a key role in the launch, development, and financing of scores of early-stage companies, as well as provided mentoring and assistance to thousands of entrepreneurs. Some active entrepreneurs play the dual role of angel and active CEO, such as Tim O'Shaughnessy, who is the leader of Living Social and an angel investor in start-up 410 Labs, based in Baltimore. Interestingly, the investors in Living Social included former AOL CEO Steve Case. As of the date of publication, Living Social had raised $630 million in venture capital and was in the process of filing for its initial public offering (IPO).

Angels come in different shapes and sizes and often invest for very different reasons. Some are motivated by something much larger than financial return—a good thing, since it is hard to convince someone with a net worth of $125 million that *your* deal will make him rich. There are "checkbook angels," usually friends, neighbors, and others, who typically invest $5,000 to $25,000 on a passive basis, hoping to get in early on the next Yahoo!. Then there are "capital-A" angels, who typically invest $50,000 to $250,000 on a more active basis and who may insist on having some advisory or mentoring role as a condition of their commitment. Finally, there are the "superangels," the cashed-out multimillionaires and even billionaires who have the capacity and the guts to invest $500,000 to $2 million in an early-stage enterprise in a deal that may look more like a venture capital transaction (from a legal paperwork and control perspective) than like a deal made in heaven!

The recession led to a contraction in the angel investor market, but it has since started to spring back, and it remains a continually increasing source of seed funding. In 2008, angel investment dollars had decreased 26.2 percent from 2007 levels, signaling that these investors were significantly more cautious than they had been in prior years. In 2009, the contraction slowed, but continued, with an 8.3 percent decrease in the amount invested from 2008. Thankfully, this trend came to a halt in 2010, and the market began to rebound, with $20.1 billion in investments (a 14 percent increase over 2009).

The Importance of Angels

Although the business media tend to focus on the activities of the institutional venture capital firms, the amount of money that is invested in growing businesses by angels or private investors each year is much, much greater. Researchers at the Center for Venture Research at the University of New Hampshire estimate that 265,000 active angel investors are investing some $20 billion annually in 60,000 ventures. In contrast, institutional venture capital funding was estimated to be $10 billion—or half of that amount—in 2008. Angel investors have become a critical source of seed capital at a time when venture capital funds are leaning toward later-stage investments. The amount of money managed by venture capital (VC) firms has grown dramatically, from $2.3 billion in 1986 to more than $60 billion in over 800 VC firms in 2003, according to a study. By 2009, there were 2,624 reported venture capital financings, raising a total of $24.9 billion. But the number of ventures under management remains small because it takes as much time to research and manage a small investment as a large one. Thus, the average first-round investment by a venture capital firm is now about $5.6 million, eliminating many entrepreneurs who are looking for investments of as little as $50,000. The enormous success of the venture capital industry has opened a window of opportunity for angels or private investors looking for start-ups in which to invest.

Angels Versus Venture Capitalists

Before the second half of the twentieth century, American private equity investing was dominated by families and individual placements in emerging-growth opportunities. Wealthy families and individual investors provided start-up capital for companies such as Xerox and Eastern Airlines. The birth of the venture capital industry is generally considered to be the formation in 1946 of the first pooled and professionally managed fund, American Research & Development (ARD). As a limited partnership, ARD and other early funds offered a passive, diversified approach for investors in earlier-stage private companies.

Over the last 40 years, the VC fund model has become a centerpiece of the alternative-asset arena. Venture firms have grown larger, with more funds coming from large institutions, pension funds (which were permitted to make a limited amount of venture capital investments when the "prudent man" rules were revised in the 1980s), corporations, and endowments. Today only 20 percent of institutional venture capital is derived from individuals and families. Paid professionals—general partners of these limited-partnership vehicles—have taken over responsibility for searching, researching, negotiating, closing, monitoring, and developing exits for these types of investments.

Angel investing has grown significantly in recent years as the baby boomers near retirement with significant wealth. Angels also include cashed-out entrepreneurs who may have feathered their nests by selling their business or taking it public. Some angels provide capital to entrepreneurs as a type of quasi-philanthropy, a way to give something back to their communities by fostering local economic growth. Others are savvy private investors who are also helping entrepreneurs launch new businesses along the way. It is critical for an entrepreneur who is seeking angel investment to understand the angel's needs and motivations, then take steps to meet these needs. Maybe you're the son or daughter that the angel never had; maybe you remind her of herself when she was younger; or perhaps she just wants someone to coach. Maybe the angel has retired and needs to get out of the house and feel useful; maybe she has expertise and relationships that she wants to share; or maybe she's just bullish on your industry and is looking for a way to participate. It's your job to discover the reason and structure your relationship accordingly.

The size of the investments that angels make varies depending on the type of investor, but angels typically invest anywhere from as little as $50,000 to more than $1,500,000. Since the recession, the amount invested by venture capital firms has fallen, leaving an increasingly large gap for angel investors to fill. However, it is important to understand that getting angel investing for your first round of financing (or "first sequence") has become increasingly difficult. This is not because the amount of money invested by angels has dropped in the past several years (although it has), it is because fewer angels are investing in first-sequence rounds of financing. In fact, first-sequence financing represented 45 percent of all angel investments in 2008, but this figure dropped to 30 percent in 2010. This drop has been attributed to a variety of causes: the need to increase investments in existing portfolio companies to keep them afloat, a cautiousness resulting from the recession, and the fact that more and more start-ups require less initial capital than before and have been finding more creative ways to get started. For entrepreneurs who are in search of angel investors for early-stage seed capital, there is an increasing need to be more competitive and prepared in seeking it out.

Profile of a "Typical" Angel

Generalizations about a group as diverse as the informal investor population are hazardous. Nevertheless, the data reveal a number of interesting characteristics. Despite the pitfalls, and as a starting point for discussion and further research, the following profile of the mythical "typical" angel is offered:

- Age 47
- Postgraduate degree, often technical
- Previous management experience with start-up ventures
- Invests between $50,000 and $100,000 in any one venture
- Invests approximately every two years
- Participates with other financially sophisticated individuals
- Prefers to invest in start-up and early-stage situations
- Willing to finance technology-based inventors when the technology and markets are familiar
- Limited interest in financing established, moderate-growth small firms
- Strong preference for manufacturing ventures, high technology in particular
- Invests close to home—within 300 miles and usually within 50 miles
- Maintains an active professional relationship with portfolio ventures, typically in a consulting role or by serving on the board of directors
- Not especially interested in diversification or tax-sheltered income as an investment objective

- Expects to liquidate an investment in five to ten years
- Looks for compound annual rates of return on individual investments, ranging from more than 50 percent from inventors to 20 percent from established firms
- Looks for minimum portfolio returns of about 20 percent
- Often will accept limitations on financial returns or accept higher risks in exchange for nonfinancial rewards
- Learns of investment opportunities primarily from friends and business associates
- Would like to look at more investment opportunities than the present informal system permits

The characteristics of different types of angels are given in Figure 4-2, and some of their perspectives on what they are looking for are given in Figure 4-3. Almost half of all known angel groups have banded together to form a trade association called the Angel Capital Association (ACA). In 2009, the 5,632

Figure 4-2.	Types of Angels.

1. **Enthusiasts.** (Older, more established investors, successful and with a short work schedule)
   - Invest $10,000 to $100,000.
   - Satisfied with making the deal.

2. **Professionals.** (Have another profession; invest in companies in their field because of knowledge and comfort factor)
   - Invest $25,000 to $200,000.
   - Paranoid investors—want to be hired by the company.
   - Main goal is to increase personal wealth.
   - Devote a lot of capital to risky, unproven ventures.
   - Instrumental in helping entrepreneurs past the family stage.
   - Both entrepreneur and angel need to complete their due diligence.

3. **Micromanagers.** (Serious, business savvy, built their own success)
   - Sense of self-entitlement because of successful ventures.
   - Like to share strategies and gain a seat on the board.
   - Invest $100,000 to $1 million if they "believe".

4. **Corporate.** (Most were senior managers at Fortune 500 companies)
   - Took early retirement or were laid off.
   - Main goal is profitability of investment.
   - Possess a minimum of $1 million capital and invest up to $200,000.

5. **Entrepreneurial.** (Currently own personal successful businesses)
   - More willing to take risk because of business and entrepreneurial attitude.
   - Enjoy personal fulfillment from helping fellow entrepreneurs in their ventures.
   - Devote from $200,000 to $500,000.
   - $20.1 billion invested in 2010, up from $17.6 billion in 2009.
   - 62,000 ventures funded in 2010, up from 57,000 in 2009.
   - 18.4 percent yield rate—abnormally high.

Figure 4-3.	What Do Angels Really Want?

Here are some interesting perspectives from well-known angel investors:

"Angels are a unique blend of sophisticated private investor and mentor to entrepreneurs. They never have to write a check—they do it because it is in their blood and temperament to help entrepreneurs to create something new out of the ether. An angel looks at passion, drive, vision, the ability to network along with desire, as much as patents and finished product and cost of good sold. The higher the goal, the more we angels strive to become the 'systems integrators' of the new and innovative. We look for something compelling and special—in that we see hundreds of plans and invest in only several a year. Entrepreneurs should strive to exude confidence, passion, and drive—we are backing the jockey, not the horse, as the old saying goes."

—John May, New Vantage Partners, quoted in *Every Business Needs an Angel*

"I look for companies that solve problems in intelligent and friction-free ways and which break traditional boundaries."

—Ashton Kutcher, Hollywood actor and angel investor

"We're in a golden age of start-up innovation because the cost of starting a company has crashed through the floor. I want to see companies that leverage these efficiencies."

—Mitch Kapor, founder, Lotus Development

"I love hearing about other people's dreams. Tell me about your dreams and, like Pavlov's dog, I begin to salivate. Encouraging (and funding) people's dreams makes me happy, and I am good at it!"

—Whitney Johnson, Rose Park Advisors, columnist and angel investor angel investors who were participants in the ACA made 947 investments in 512 companies, providing $228.8 million to start-up ventures. The ACA member survey provides the basic demographics of its angel groups, reporting that:

- The average angel group invests in 3.8 companies.
- The average angel group investment is $241,528 per round.
- The median age of a group is three years.
- The average age of the investors in the group is 47.
- The average size of a group is 47.6 members, with a median of 37 members.

With that said, the ACA estimates that 17.5 percent of angel group members invest individually in each deal that is done as a group. More than 50 angel groups have formed nationwide as private, seed-round investing has begun to regain its popularity. Angels have a greater tendency to be drawn by the potential equity returns of funding new technology companies. As of the end of 2010, more than a million accredited angels have a total of $20 billion invested in more than 30,000 technology start-ups.

Finding an Angel

While you can find individual angels through referral from an accountant or attorney, angels are increasingly participating in a variety of networks.

Nonprofit angel networks. There are more than 50 loose-knit organizations nationwide through which investors learn about opportunities, attend programs on investing, and develop a sense of community. These networks are usually run by nonprofit entities, have tax-exempt status, and are oriented toward economic development. The greatest benefits come from community building among investors and creating a more efficient marketplace in which entrepreneurs can approach sources of capital.

Pledge funds. A more recent phenomenon involves pools of funds in which investors (anywhere from a handful to dozens) pledge a specific amount of money, to be invested in private equity transactions that are selected and managed by the group. Sometimes the group has a centralized paid staff; sometimes it is led and organized by a lead investor. These groups set legally rigorous standards, are focused, and are designed to profit from multiple transactions.

The club approach. In this model, investors place a set amount of money into a "club" account that is used like a venture fund to make investments that have been found and voted on by club members. These clubs can be staffed or unstaffed. More money can be accumulated than an individual can afford, and a more diversified fund can be created. Group dynamics are involved because each member must review potential opportunities in order to decide to "vote" for or against a deal.

CEO angels. In this situation, a small venture fund, usually a limited partnership, is created by investors drawn from a specific business community. They provide assistance as well as capital to chosen companies, which are usually from the same field. Members of the group may take on general partnership responsibilities, or professional managers can be employed. This model is very similar to the traditional venture capital model, except that the investments are more focused and the limited partners are more active in helping to find opportunities and providing hands-on assistance to the companies chosen.

Active angels. In this model, angels propose to play a more active role in the growing company once funds are committed. Some angels in this model are really looking for full- or almost full-time employment with the companies in which they invest.

Hybrid Approaches to Angel Investing

The growth of social networking has inspired some hybrid approaches to angel investing. For example, the founders of Venture Hacks (www.venturehacks.com) launched AngelList.com in early 2010, with the support of the Kauffman Foundation, and by July of 2011, the entrepreneur-angel social networking site had claimed responsibility for 8,000 introductions, 400 investments, and 8 acquisitions, and that is just one type of data that gets reported by the community (http://angel.co/). Investors have included some of the world's top venture capital firms and angel investors, including Kleiner Perkins and Andreessen Horowitz, Mitch Kapor and Dave Morin. Fast-growth start-ups such as Uber, Yipit, Wanderfly, BranchOut, and many more have been successfully matched up with their ideal investors on this web site, which serves as a cross between the dating service Match.com and the social networking phenomena Facebook and LinkedIn.

Another hybrid model is Lightbank (www.lightbank.com), which looks a bit like a hybrid of a venture accelerator, an angel group, and a traditional venture-capital firm. The Lightbank team, led by veteran entrepreneurs Eric Lefkofsky (the co-founder of Groupon) and Brad Keywell, has launched 5 companies, invested in more than 20 start-ups, and raised more than $1.2 billion to invest in more companies. Lightbank provides strategic expertise, access to its networks, and technology support and infrastructure to its portfolio companies. It looks for start-ups with great teams, disruptive technologies, and large, addressable target markets. Interested entrepreneurs apply online to demonstrate that they have a game-changing idea for investment consideration by initially answering a few simple (but insightful) questions:

- What is your brilliant idea?
- Who are your people?
- Why should we be interested?
- How are we going to make money together?
- Where can we reach you?

You can also submit an attachment (such as PowerPoint slides, an executive summary, or a business plan) of up to 10 MB to support your business model and communicate your vision. If your idea makes it through the initial screens and filters, you'll be invited to Chicago to pitch the team in person and possibly play them at Ping-Pong. Really.

Asking an Angel to Dance

From a practical perspective, it's just as important for you to perform due diligence and prequalify your prospective funding sources as it is for the angel to scrutinize your business plans and evaluate your management. In addition to the regional or national angel networks mentioned earlier, there are a number of online resources that can direct entrepreneurs to private investors. You should also attend venture and trade fairs and forums (see Figure 4-4). Networking through friends and associates—getting out there and talking to as many people as possible—is still the best way to find an angel. Remember, dancing is, in the end, a person-to-person activity.

You can also find potential angels through networking in business and venture groups, private investor clubs (which usually have organized monthly presentations by entrepreneurs to potential prequalified angels), venture capital networks, incubators, industry trade associations, university and fraternity/sorority alumni

| Figure 4-4. | Where to Find an Angel. |

ANGEL FUNDS AND CLUBS

Active Angel Investors
c/o New Vantage Group
402 Maple AVE West
Vienna, VA 22180
(703) 255-4934
www.activeangelinvestors.
com/index.htm

Mid-Atlantic Angel Group
www.magfund.com

ARC Angel Fund
885 3rd Avenue, 20th Floor
New York, NY 10022
www.arcangelfund.com

AngelList.com
http://angel.co

ANGEL NETWORKS

Angel Investment Network
www.
midwestinvestmentnetwork.
com

Investor's Circle
165 11th Street
San Francisco, CA 94103
(415) 255-6844
www.investorscircle.net

Minority Angel Investor Network
Building 100 Innovation Center
Suite 200
S. 13th ST & Constitution AVE
The Navy Yard
Philadelphia, PA 19112
(215) 564-6857
www.
minorityangelinvestornetwork.
com

Rain Source Capital
1600 University Avenue West
Suite 401
St. Paul, MN 55104
(651) 632-2140
www.rainsourcecapital.com

ONLINE RESOURCES AND SERVICES
A wealth of information about angels, or informal private equity, exists on the Web. Here are a few of the most comprehensive resources.

Venture Funding Network
www.venturefundingnetwork.
com

Mid-Atlantic Venture Association
www.mava.org

The Angels' Forum
www.angelsforum.com

SBIC Program
www.sba.gov/content/sbic-program-0

Technology Capital Network at MIT
www.thecapitalnetwork.org

Angelsoft
www.angelsoft.net
Go BIG Network
www.gobignetwork.com

FundingUniverse
www.fundinguniverse.com

TheFunded
www.thefunded.com

Angel Capital Association
www.angelcapitalassociation.
org

VENTURE FORUMS

Baltimore-Washington Venture Group
c/o Dingman Center for Entrepreneurship
The Robert H. Smith School of Business
University of Maryland
College Park, MD 20742-1815
(301) 404-2144
www.rhsmith.umd.edu/
Dingman

Charlottesville Venture Group
P.O. Box 4547
Charlottesville, VA 22905
(434) 231-5255
www.cville-venture.org

Florida Venture Forum
2121 Ponce de Leon BLVD
Suite 720
Coral Gables, FL 33134
(305) 446-5060
www.floridaventureforum.org

New York Venture Group
347 West 57th Street
Suite 4C
New York, NY 10019
www.unifx.com/nyvg.html

VENTURE FAIRS

Angel Venture Fair
held at: 140 South Broad Street
Philadelphia, PA 19102
(215) 563-6500
www.angelventurefair.com

Mid-Atlantic Venture Fair
c/o Mid-Atlantic Venture
Association (MAVA)
1600 Tysons BLVD
Suite 575
McLean, VA 22102
(703) 506-9300
www.mava.org

The Gathering of Angels
#4 Hawthorne Circle

Santa Fe, NM 87506
(505) 982-3050
www.gatheringofangels.com

**MATCHING SERVICES AND
ONLINE BROKER-DEALERS**

**Garage Technology
Ventures**
502 Waverley ST
Suite 300

Palo Alto, CA 94301
(650) 838-0811
www.garage.com

**Virginia Center for
Innovative Technology**
www.cit.org

meetings, social and country clubs, and virtually any other place where semiretired and cashed-out entrepreneurs may hang out. Angels may invest alone or as a group through clubs and networks ("bands of angels"), and while many won't individually consider a deal that requires more than $50,000, a growing number of very-high-net-worth individuals ("superangels") will invest $500,000 or more of their own money and help you identify other potential investors. These superangels also bring respect and credibility to a new business because others respect their expertise and industry knowledge.

As I mentioned earlier, you've got to do your own due diligence on each angel you consider. Remember that the relationship is akin to that with a spouse or parent—so you have to be sure that you can get along personally with the individual. You'll also need to define your nonfinancial expectations and have a meeting of the minds on these issues. A good angel offers you (and your business) a lot more than money, and you need to reach an agreement regarding how much of the angel's time will be available for advice, coaching, and mentoring, and also what doors the angel is expected to open on your behalf. Ideally, your angel should have a diverse (and current) network, deep industry experience, and significant company-building experience, in addition to being a source of seed capital. The angel-entrepreneur relationships that don't work out over the years often fail because of misunderstandings about the nonfinancial aspects of the relationship.

Angels or Devils—You Be the Judge

In the rough-and-tumble world of new-venture investing, one common myth is that angels—because they invest in part for nonfinancial reasons—are somehow kinder and gentler in the way they structure deals. While it may be true that few angels want seven inches of legal documents to govern their deals, they also will not tolerate a cocktail-napkin or handshake deal. They didn't amass their wealth by being pushovers, and the same holds true in their venture investing. Be prepared for some tough one-on-one negotiating over risk, control, and rewards with a sophisticated angel who has a first-rate advisory team. These high-paid advisors usually view their mission as protecting their wealthy client from bad deals or transactions that haven't been carefully thought out or properly structured. For more information on the advantages and disadvantages of attracting an angel investor, see *Every Business Needs an Angel* by John May and Cal Simmons (Random House, 2001).

Understanding Angel Investment Club Criteria

Each angel investment club has its own processes and criteria for the decision-making process, and some of these vary by region. Set forth here are the "10 investment commandments" of the California-based The Angels' Forum (www.angelsforum.com), which made its first investment in 1998 and remains an active investment club today.[1]

1. *Management:* Thou shalt invest in good management that demonstrates an ability to execute the business plan rapidly, provide sound cash management, raise additional cash, lead the organization, and adjust the business plan where necessary. Thou shalt seek leaders with industry expertise who are driven and charismatic.

2. *Board of Directors:* Thou shalt invest only in companies where the majority of the board is composed of strong outsiders, who possess solid business experience in the industry and/or in the stage of the company. Said directors shall push the company to execute the business plan rapidly within cash constraints and shall have also have the ability to recognize the need for a CEO change and act swiftly in implementing it. Thou shalt seek Directors with good contacts for initial customers and/or raising capital.

3. *Business Plan:* Thou shalt seek business plans that effectively address the technology, customer acquisition, and competitive challenges, to establish the business with realistic gross margins, unit volume, and return on capital invested.

---

[1] Copyright © 2003, The Angels' Forum Management Company, LLC. All rights reserved. Used with permission

4. *Access to Capital:* Thou shalt identify and establish relationship with sources of capital with a history of investing in like kinds of businesses in the amounts needed for the company. Thou shalt work with these co-investors for the betterment of the company and all investors.

5. *Product Need:* Thou shalt invest in companies that have an in-depth knowledge of their customers' usage habits and needs (through to the end user). Thou shalt forsake all those "nice to have" products or services and save thy resources for "must haves."

6. *Sustainable Differentiation:* Thou shalt invest in companies that have advantages such as patents, first-mover position, world-class technologists, proprietary processes, and/or key customers under contract.

7. *Market Size and Trajectory:* Thou shalt invest in companies that have large and/or rapidly growing markets or can realistically create such markets. Thou shalt invest in companies with a low risk of market loss to alternative technologies.

8. *Technology Risk:* Thou shalt have sufficient technical expertise at the table, or through thy trusted contacts, to evaluate all product and technology claims before committing thy resources.

9. *Investment Execution Risk:* Thou shalt have established the ability to influence key company decisions, create and link milestones to capital rounds, and seek early customer learning, as through use of prototypes. Thou shalt receive a fair valuation on thy investments and not release investment funds until the full round is raised. Thou shalt stay involved and work with companies to assist—aggressively if necessary—in their success. Thou shalt invest only in those companies that provide a clear exit strategy for thy investment.

10. *Investment Evaluation Risk:* Thou shalt ask tough questions of the company, listen to the market, and discuss the company with other investors. Thou shalt always speak the truth with thy fellow Members and be loyal in voicing any opposition or apprehensions, now and forever and ever.

Other Sources of Seed and Early-Stage Capital

Let's assume that your personal funds or credit lines are limited, either your friends and family have no money or you don't want to ask them for it, and angel investors are not for you—what alternatives do you have? There's still hope for finding money at the early stages. In fact, over the past several years, there has been something of a groundswell in the creative financing area: With options such as microloans, incubators, accelerators, and crowdfunding, there are a variety of ways to finance your project with nontraditional sources of capital. In the realm of high-probability/low-cost capital-formation options, consider the following creative sources.

Incubators

Often it is very difficult for a company to meet the initial capital requirements that come with starting up. In these cases, what is called an *incubator* can prove to be very helpful. Many angel investors and cashed-out entrepreneurs look to and start up business incubators to find potential investments and mentoring opportunities. These types of organizations are interested in getting a firm past the often tough start-up phase that so many businesses fail to survive. They can help to defray or eliminate some of the initial costs that many start-up firms face. It is for these reasons that about 87 percent of the firms that have gone through a business incubator stay in business once they graduate, according to the University of Michigan.

There are a number of areas in which incubators typically provide assistance to young firms. The first of these is physical office and storage space. Most entrepreneurs do not have the space to run a business efficiently from their home or place of residence, but buying or renting space from which to operate the business can be too costly and make the venture seem unattractive to many potential entrepreneurs. It is not uncommon for an incubator to provide flexible space and leases at very low rates to the new firm.

Entrepreneurs of start-up firms may also receive support in several other ways. Discounts on fee-based support services like fax and copy machine access, bookkeeping, telephone answering, secretarial assistance, meeting rooms, and libraries can help tremendously in reducing the cost of a new venture. These services involve many key day-to-day tasks that must be completed to ensure that the company can run smoothly. While these services can be vital to a firm's survival, many entrepreneurs who are not affiliated with an incubator may choose to attempt to do them on their own or forgo them completely to avoid the costs.

Employee-focused services are also a common part of many businesses' cost structures. Providing health insurance, life insurance, and other such services can be quite costly to the firm. Incubators can frequently get group rates for many of these services that can bring down their price and make them affordable to the business owner.

In addition to providing their own money, incubators can help entrepreneurs find additional funding. Insight into how and where money can be obtained on terms favorable to the entrepreneur is a main reason many individuals contact an incubator. Incubators also tend to know many wealthy individuals or angel investors who may express an interest in investing in the venture.

Incubators can provide much more than money to a firm. They offer business advice on many levels. They have had a hand in growing many businesses, and they are very knowledgeable about the challenges that often arise. They have lots of experience to share with entrepreneurs on how to grow their business, make it self-sustainable, and make it profitable. The voice of experience can be just as valuable as the services and capital that an incubator brings to the firm, if not more so.

As a result of years of helping small businesses grow, incubators are able to build up an impressive list of contacts. An incubator can introduce the entrepreneur to a large number of individuals who may be beneficial to the company. People who are well versed in a specific industry, can provide technical assistance, create and maintain strong supply chains, provide funding, and offer any number of value-adding insights can help a start-up take off.

Information on a number of business incubators is given in Figure 4-5.

University and Private Incubators

Many universities have established business incubators, both to foster entrepreneurship and to assist in the "birthing" of new businesses and ideas. These incubators offer shared resources, on-site advisors, cooperative research and development, and the natural synergies of having entrepreneurs with different ideas all at the same venue. A more recent trend is the "private incubator," often established by cashed-out entrepreneurs who offer their expertise as well as the physical facilities to foster business growth and development.

Advantages of Business Incubators

- Greatly increase the likelihood of survival for start-up firms
- Create jobs in the community, helping to retain individuals who might otherwise leave the area because of lack of job opportunities

Figure 4-5. | **Incubator Resources.**

Alabama Business Incubation Network (ABIN)
1020 Ninth Avenue, SW
Bessemer, AL 35022
(205) 481-2101
E-mail: bessemerincubator@yahoo.com

Arkansas Business Incubator Manager Association
c/o GENESIS Technology Incubator
1 University of Arkansas Engineering
Research Center
Fayetteville, AR 72701
(501) 575-7227

Colorado Business Incubator Association (CBIA)
c/o Alcott Administrative Services
2738 S. Newton Street
Denver, CO 80236
(303) 934-9117

Illinois Small Business Development Center
c/o Illinois Department of Commerce and Economic Opportunity
500 E. Monroe
Springfield, IL 62701
(309) 837-4684
www.commerce.state.il.us/dceo

Louisiana Business Incubator Association (LBIA)
7117 Florida BLVD
Baton Rouge, LA 70806
(225) 218-1100
www.lbia.org

Maryland Business Incubation Association
c/o Maryland Technology Development Center
9700 Great Seneca Highway
Rockville, MD 20850
(240) 832-3612
www.mdbusinessincubation.org

Mississippi Business Incubator Association
c/o Mississippi Development Authority
P.O. Box 849
Jackson, MS 39205
(601) 359-3593
E-mail: jbrandon@mississipi.org

National Business Incubation Association (NBIA)
20 East Circle DR #37198
Athens, OH 45701
(740) 593-4331
www.nbia.org

Business Incubator Association of New York State, Inc.
P.O. Box 95
Albany, NY 12201
(518) 689-0553
http://bianys.com

Oklahoma Business Incubator Association
c/o Pioneer Technology Center Business Incubator
900 N. Stiles AVE
Oklahoma City, OK 73104
(405) 377-2220
(405) 809-3553

www.okbia.org
E-mail: bonniec@pioneertech.org

Pennsylvania Incubator Association (PIA)
c/o Corry Industrial Center
1524 Enterprise RD
Corry, PA 16407
(814) 664-3884
E-mail: rnovo@corryidc.org

Texas Business Incubator Association
9600 Long Point Road
Suite 150
Houston, TX 77055
(713) 932-7495
www.tbiaonline.org

Wisconsin Business Incubator Association
2320 Renaissance BLVD
Sturtevant, WI 53177
(262) 898-7524
www.wbiastate.org

- Target low- to moderate-income groups
- Place fledgling businesses together, allowing tenants to participate in joint problem solving, support others facing similar problems, exchange information, and discuss mutual commercial interests

Disadvantages of Business Incubators

- Require long start-up time (but the community can be working with entrepreneurs during the start-up period to provide business planning and assistance)
- Carry high start-up cost
- Demand a continual operating budget
- May never become self-supportive
- Most businesses started in an incubator do not grow to be large businesses
- Existing businesses may not be supportive because of fear of competition

Accelerators

After the dot-com bubble burst, the incubator model lost popularity, and many incubators disappeared between 2003 and 2009. Over the past few years, however, an alternative form of incubator has begun to pop up: the accelerator. While sharing some characteristics with incubators, accelerators are a new utility used to achieve business growth and have proved fruitful for several start-ups. Accelerators typically provide start-ups with mentoring, expertise, a small amount of financing (typically about $20,000), and connections to angel and venture capital in exchange for equity (typically about 7 percent). Unlike incubators, accelerators are not conducive to allowing a business to grow slowly. They are usually based on a boot-camp model to get businesses going in a few months. Many companies that are chosen to take part in an accelerator are successful in finding further rounds of financing through the venture capital connections that they made during the program.

Many established businesses have a desire for rapid growth. After a certain point in their life, however, most firms experience a growth slowdown. While some companies are satisfied with their position in the market, others want to jump-start their growth. Some angel investors and angel investor groups provide business accelerators that cater to these companies. Many angels who are not affiliated with the accelerators will also look to them for potential investment opportunities. With the help of an accelerator, a firm can get its growth onto the fast track to a degree that it was not previously able to achieve.

Business accelerators differ from incubators in that they are much more focused on in-depth technical training, software, marketing, and Web presence. In addition, accelerator programs are typically for-profit, whereas incubators are mostly nonprofit organizations. Companies will choose a business accelerator when the most basic functions of a business are intact and there is a need for more of an emphasis on communication technologies and the development of an Internet presence.

In-depth technical training is important to many accelerator programs. Business owners and key employees are taught the skills they need to be able to use and maintain complicated software and develop technologies to maintain a competitive edge. Database, bookkeeping, and inventory tracking software are just some examples of technology that businesses need to be able to use to accelerate their growth.

Marketing is another aspect of most accelerator programs. If a business wants to increase the number of units it sells or increase its customer base, marketing is an obvious choice. A business accelerator will teach firms how to identify their target market and who is most likely to buy their product. It can even help a firm discover how to break into other markets and demographics. Companies will learn how to improve their sales skills and leverage affordable marketing tools to achieve the greatest impact.

Web presence is one thing that has been proven to stimulate business growth in the past. A larger presence on the Internet leads to more exposure in an increasingly digital business landscape. Use of the Internet can streamline many sales and marketing functions. Simple programs such as Facebook and LinkedIn can be used to increase sales calls, while more complex but easy-to-use ordering systems allow customers to make purchases faster and more easily.

While business accelerators can be very useful in getting a business on the fast track, they do have some drawbacks. Most accelerator programs are a service in exchange for fees. If the company does not derive more value from the accelerator program than it puts in, then its participation in the accelerator could be detrimental to it.

Also, businesses in accelerator programs are looking to grow and increase sales. While most of these companies are in stable financial positions, some may have seen the growth and increased sales promised by most accelerators as the only way for the company to survive. It is possible that these companies are in the red and are merely looking for a way to save a sinking ship.

Companies in accelerator programs may also have an inexperienced management team that has difficulty dealing with high growth. Even though this is what accelerator groups are set up to help with, not all accelerators are created equal. The quality of the accelerator program itself should be evaluated to determine the expectations for the health of the companies coming out of it.

Unexpected growth should not always be considered a drawback. Accelerator programs prep businesses to grow. Most of the time, these companies will be ready to take on the increase in growth with little interruption to their normal business activities. If a business is growing rapidly and cannot handle the growth, an angel investor with experience in the industry may be the best thing for the company. The investor should be able to determine whether the company needs help in handling growth and whether he can help before he provides the firm with any money.

Figure 4-6 provides information on a number of business accelerators.

Advantages of Business Accelerators

- Provides expertise, (typically) facilities, and shares the intellectual resources of several other entrepreneurs in the program
- Gives funding to help grow the business and living expenses for the entrepreneurs during the start-up phase
- Allows entrepreneurs to make connections with investors for future rounds of financing

Disadvantages of Business Accelerators

- Must sacrifice equity, so a careful cost-benefit analysis must be completed to discover whether the capital being infused and the other resources offered are really worth the ownership stake that is being given up, or whether there is a cheaper way to achieve business growth
- Typically have to relocate to the site of the accelerator if there isn't one in your area
- Usually must give up other responsibilities to focus on the program
- Not all accelerators are created equal—thoroughly investigate the programs available before you choose one

Figure 4-6.	Business Accelerators and Incubators.

Y Combinator
320 Pioneer Way
Mountain View, CA 94041
www.ycombinator.com

Launch Pad Ignition
643 Magazine ST
Suite 102
New Orleans, LA 70130
www.launchpadignition.com

SPARK Business Accelerator
201 S. Division
Suite 430
Ann Arbor, MI 48104
www.annarborusa.org/business-accelerator

SproutBox
Bloomington, IN
http://sproutbox.com

TechStars
Locations: Boston, Boulder, Seattle, NYC
www.techstars.com

Dreamit Ventures
PMB 263
North Bryn Mawr AVE
Bryn Mawr, PA 19010
www.dreamitventures.com

Capital Factory
Austin, TX
www.capitalfactory.com

MassChallenge, Inc.
One Marina Park Drive, 14th Floor
Boston, MA 02210
(888) 782-7820
http://masschallenge.org

NYC SeedStart
Six MetroTech Center
Brooklyn, NY 11201
(707) 469-3669
www.nycseedstart.com

American Family Insurance Business Accelerator Business Program
www.amfambusinessaccelerator.com

IBM SmartCamp
(Multiple locations)
www.ibm.com/ie/smarterplanet/smartcamp

Excelerate Labs
820 West Jackson BLVD
Suite 700
Chicago, IL 60661
www.exceleratelabs.com

Houston Tech Center
410 Pierce ST
Houston, TX 77002
www.houstontech.org

Launchpad LA
Los Angeles, CA
www.launchpad.la

Jumpstart Foundry
Nashville, TN
http://jumpstartfoundry.com

OCTANe LaunchPad
Orange County, CA
www.octaneoc.org/home/launchpad

Gangplank
260 South Arizona AVE
Chandler, AZ 85225
http://gangplankhq.com

AlphaLab
2325 East Carson ST
Pittsburgh, PA 15203
www.alphalab.org

Portland Ten
Portland, OR
www.portlandten.com

Betaspring
One Davol Square
Providence, RI 02903
http://betaspring.com

Silicon Valley Association of Startup Entrepreneurs Seed Program
Redwood City, CA
www.svase.org

The Startup Project
San Francisco, CA
www.startupproject.org

Berkeley Ventures
727 Allston Way
Berkeley, CA 94710
www.berkeleyventures.com

Tech Wildcatters
2700 Fairmount ST
Dallas, TX 75204
http://techwildcatters.com

Bizdom U
Detroit, MI
www.bizdom.com

NEXTSTART
135 South Main ST
Suite 600
Greenville, SC 29601
www.nextstart.org

The Awesome Inc.
Experience
348 East Main ST
Lexington, KY 40507
www.awesomeinc.org/the-awesome-experience

Lightspeed Venture
Partners Summer
2200 Sand Hill RD
Menlo Park, CA 94025

www.lightspeedvp.com/summerfellowships

Startup Utah
Utah
www.startuputah.com

LaunchBox Digital
Washington, DC
www.launchboxdigital.com

BetaFish
Wilmington, DE
http://betafishde.tumblr.com

The Founder Institute
(Multiple locations)
www.founderinstitute.com

Peer-to-Peer Lending, Microloans, and Crowdfunding

The financial crisis has had at least one interesting side effect: the rise of alternative and increasingly creative forms of financing. During the economic recession, and continuing to today, credit and other traditional forms of start-up financing became more difficult to obtain. As a result, entrepreneurs began looking to newer, less-traditional forms of raising capital that cut out the financial intermediaries (banks, for instance) that are typically present in the process.

Peer-to-peer (also known as person-to-person or P2P) lending is a process of borrowing directly from individuals; in most instances, the lender and the borrower never meet. There are a variety of ways this happens, but generally, the process is relatively simple: The borrower registers on one of the many peer-to-peer web sites (see Figure 4-7) and is then matched up with a number of lenders who are interested in investing based on the borrower and the interest rate, among other things. The P2P industry has been growing rapidly over the past few years: In 2005, there was $118 million in outstanding P2P loans; by 2011, that number had reached more than $500 million. P2P web sites make a profit by charging the borrowers an interest rate (usually 2 to 5 percent) on top of what the lenders require. The overall success rate of getting a loan through a P2P process is about 10 percent. Certain web sites, such as Kiva, specialize in small loans (or microloans) for entrepreneurs.

In addition to the peer-to-peer phenomenon, there are several institutions that specialize in providing microloans to entrepreneurs. The U.S. Small Business Administration (SBA), for instance, has a microloan program under which eligible entrepreneurs can borrow up to $50,000 to finance their business. Most of the entrepreneurs that take advantage of this program borrow about $13,000 for start-up costs, such as inventory, overhead, and the like. Microfinancing

Figure 4-7.	Crowdsourcing and P2P Resources.	

PEER-TO-PEER LENDING	MICROFINANCE AND MENTORING	CROWDFUNDING
Lending Club www.lendingclub.com	**ACCION USA** 115 East 23rd Street, 7th Floor New York, NY 10010 (212) 387-0377 www.accionusa.org	**Startup Addict** www.startupaddict.com
Prosper www.prosper.com	**Small Business Administration** Microloan Program 409 3rd ST, SW Washington, DC 20416 (704) 344-6640	**ProFounder** www.profounder.com
Peer-Lend www.peer-lend.com	**Kiva** Kiva Microfunds 3180 18th Street, Suite 201 San Francisco, CA 94110 (828) 479-5482 www.kiva.org	**Kickstarter** www.kickstarter.com
Microloan www.microloan.com	**Startup America Partnership** www.startupamericapartnership.org	**Indie GoGo** www.indiegogo.com
	Samuel Adams Brewing the American Dream (888) 661-2337 www.samueladams.com/btad	

has become more popular recently because new ventures are requiring less financing than in previous years. In fact, according to data gathered by the Panel Study of Entrepreneurial Dynamics (PSED), solo entrepreneurs have had median start-up costs of only $6,000, while team ventures have had expected start-up costs of about $20,000. Besides financial institutions and governmental entities that provide microloans, many businesses have programs to help fund start-ups with smaller loans. Samuel Adams, for instance, has teamed up with ACCION USA (a provider of microloans) to create the Brewing the American Dream program. The Brewing the American Dream program provides loans of from $500 to $25,000 to fund entrepreneurs in the food and beverage industry. In addition to the loan, the program also provides business education seminars and "speed coaching" events to help the business owner turn the loan into a successful venture.

In the same vein, one creative funding source that has evolved in recent years is crowdfunding. Crowdfunding (or crowd financing), like P2P, involves getting individuals to pool their resources to finance a project without a typical financial intermediary. Unlike P2P, however, the lenders (also known as "crowdfunders" or "backers") often do not engage in crowdfunding strictly for financial gain. In fact, the "lenders" often actually act more like donors. In a typical transaction, an entrepreneur can go onto a crowdfunding web site, propose the amount needed for the project, and, if the amount pledged is met by backers, receive the funds. Usually, the backers receive something in return, like a product from the business (a DVD or CD from the film or album produced, for instance) but not their money back, if the project is funded, so the funds are not donations in the strict sense. In fact, studies show that for the majority of backers, the reward is the main motivator of their monetary pledge. Crowdfunding sites generally make a profit by taking a small percentage (about 5 percent) from the projects funded before the money goes to the entrepreneur.

While crowdfunding has mainly been the domain of the entertainment industry, many for-profit and nonprofit new ventures in other industries have been making headway and successfully funding projects via crowdfunding. For instance, BeerBankroll (a member-managed brewery and pub) received $2.5 million using crowdfunding. While this is an atypical example, it goes to show that creative forms of financing can be useful for financing entrepreneurial ventures—subject to certain caveats. For more information on the process, look at some of the leading web sites that facilitate the process, such as Kickstarter (www.kickstarter.com), IndieGoGo (www.indiegogo.com), and Sellaband (www.sellaband.com); some also use Facebook and Twitter to manage their own campaigns, as well as the resources in Figure 4-7.

Advantages of Peer-to-Peer Lending and Crowdfunding

- Eliminates the use of banks and other financial intermediaries.
- May provide lower interest rates than traditional forms of borrowing (and no monetary repayment or interest is typically expected in the case of crowdfunding).
- Provides alternative forms of financing.
- The borrower can appeal to the lenders/backers on a personal level and tell her "story" to convince them to invest.
- Much of the red tape and paperwork required for a traditional bank loan can be avoided.
- Funds are typically dispersed to the borrower quickly, usually within 10 days.
- Entrepreneurs can raise funds without sacrificing equity.

Disadvantages of Peer-to-Peer Lending and Crowdfunding

- Most loan requests are not met—the funding success rate is about 10 percent in the case of P2P.
- The borrower still has to pay a percentage fee to the P2P company (and give a reward in the case of crowdfunding).
- During the recession, many borrowers defaulted, making lenders in the P2P arena more cautious.
- The regulatory future of P2P is uncertain: The SEC has determined that the promissory notes issued to lenders by P2P companies are "securities" and subject to federal regulation, and both the SEC and the Consumer Financial Protection Bureau (created under Dodd-Frank) are in the process of determining how the P2P industry should be regulated.
- Crowdfunding may also run afoul of securities regulations, depending on the structure of the transaction.
- The equivalent of the entrepreneur's business plan is released to the general public.
- The entrepreneur will not receive the advice, involvement, and expertise that other types of investors (such as angels or VCs) may provide.
- Lenders and backers will not be involved in future rounds of financing, and the amount that entrepreneurs can raise in the initial funding is limited.
- In the case of crowdfunding, there are tax implications—the amount received in exchange for the gift is "income" and is taxed accordingly.

As of the final printing of this third edition (early 2012), Congress and the SEC were still holding hearings and formulating guidelines as to how crowdfunding would be regulated as a strategy for private enterprises.

Economic Development Agencies

The U.S. Department of Commerce's Economic Development Administration (EDA) was established by Congress to generate jobs, help retain existing jobs, and stimulate industrial and commercial growth in economically distressed areas of the country. EDA assistance is available to rural and urban areas of the nation that are experiencing high unemployment, low income, or sudden and severe economic distress. The EDA works in partnership with state and local governments, regional economic development districts, public and private nonprofit organizations, and Native American tribes. EDA programs include public works, urban development, economic adjustment, research and evaluation, economic development districts, local technical assistance, national technical assistance, trade adjustment assistance, university centers, and redevelopment centers (see Figure 4-8).

Customer Financing

No one (besides you) is more interested in your success than your customers, and they may be willing to provide funds or other resources to facilitate your launch. In addition to equity, your customers may want some type of partial or full exclusivity for a given product or service, and they can play an expanded role in influencing how the product will be offered, distributed, or packaged. For example, a group of retailers may be interested in an early-stage software company

Figure 4-8.	Economic Development Contacts and Resources.

Brownfield's Home Page
U.S. Environmental
Protection Agency
www. epa.gov/brownfields

Bureau of the Census
U.S. Department of
Commerce
www.census.gov

Bureau of Labor Statistics
U.S. Department of Labor
www.Stats.bls.gov

Center of Excellence for
Sustainable
Development
U.S. Department of Energy
www.smartcommunities.ncat.org

Economic Development
Administration
U.S. Department of
Commerce
1401 Constitution AVE, NW

Suite 7800
Washington, DC 20230
(202) 482-5081
www.eda.gov

Environmental Justice Home
Page
U.S. Environmental
Protection Agency
www.epa.gov/
environmentaljustice

International Economic
Development Council
www.iedconline.org

National Association of
Development Organizations
www.nado.org

National Governors
Association
www.nga.org

Northeast-Midwest Institute
www.nemw.org

Office of Solid Waste and
Emergency Response Home
Page
U.S. Environmental
Protection Agency
www.epa.gov/aboutepa/
oswer.html

Rural Development
U.S. Department of
Agriculture
www.rurdev.usda.gov

Trade Adjustment
Assistance Program
www.taacenters.org

University Economic
Development
Association
http://universityeda.org

U.S. Environmental
Protection Agency Home
Page
www.epa.gov

whose product, once finished, could streamline their inventory-management systems. In some cases, the customers may form a consortium or buying group to invest in the company. Customers with a vested interest in a business are likely to stay long-term, offer free expertise, and lead to new customer referrals.

An alternative to an equity investment would be for the customers to prepay for the product or service in exchange for a discount or other benefits. These customer-financing arrangements can be especially useful if the business requires large up-front development costs, such as companies in the software industry, where targeted licensees/customers could provide early-stage financing in exchange for perpetual, royalty-free, and unlimited rights of use of the end product.

Vendor Financing

This form of early-stage financing is fast becoming one of the most popular methods that small businesses use to acquire the resources they need in order to grow. Statistics from the Equipment Leasing and Finance Association, based in Washington, D.C., show that vendor financing leapt from a seldom-used sales option to a $13 billion a year industry between 1992 and 1998, and by 2010 the equipment leasing and vendor financing industry had reached $518 billion (www.elfaonline.org).

Vendor financing can be obtained through companies of all sizes, from small suppliers to large corporations. The firms listed in Figure 4-9 are finance companies owned by major manufacturers. The trade associations listed in the figure can provide information about vendor financing and help you find a vendor that meets your needs.

Usually business owners select the equipment or supplies that they need and then apply for financing through a vendor that offers such arrangements. Some businesses work in reverse, first locating a vendor that offers financing and then selecting equipment from that vendor. Most vendors will prepare the documents in-house, even though financing is a transaction separate from the lease or purchase of the equipment and may be handled by an outside company.

Vendors may also be a useful source for other resources that you would otherwise be raising money to obtain, such as research and development, advertising and promotion, and even customer referrals. Typically, larger vendors in a wide variety of industries offer formal programs, have large budgets for customer support and services, or focus on smaller, emerging-growth companies that may mature into larger customers. Talk to your largest vendors, and shop competitively for the

Figure 4-9.	Vendor Financing Resources.	

Canon Financial Services
(office equipment)
(800) 815-4000
www.cfs.canon.com

Equipment Leasing and
Finance Association
(all types of equipment)
(202) 238-3400
www.elfaonline.org

GE Capital
(all types of equipment)
(800) 553-7287
www.gecapital.com

HP Financial Services
(high-tech equipment)
(888) 215-8868
www8.hp.com/us/en/hp-
financial-services/index.html

IBM Global Financing
(IBM products and services)
(877) 426-2223
www-03.ibm.com/financing/
us/index.html

IKON Financial Services
(office products)
(610) 296-8000

www.ikon.com

John Deere Financial
(agricultural and construction
equipment)
(800) 356-9033
www.deere.com/en_US/jdc/

Oracle Credit Corp.
(computers and software)
(650) 506-7000
www.oracle.com

products and services that they may be in a position to offer. You'll be pleasantly surprised at how many larger companies have targeted the small-business customer as a high priority and have resources ready to offer you at little or no cost.

Additional Resources:

Ante, Spencer E. "These Angels Go Where Others Fear to Tread." *BusinessWeek* 4133 (2009): 44–48. EBSCO, Academic Search Premier; accessed April 27, 2010.

"Business Incubation." *Small Business Notes*. http://www.smallbusinessnotes. com/starting/busincubation.html; accessed April 25, 2010.

Cameron, Chris. "'Super Angel' Firm Maples Investments Rebrands as FLOODGATE." Web log post. *ReadWriteWeb*, Microsoft BizSpark, March 24, 2010. http://www.readwriteweb.com/start/2010/03/super-angel-maples-investments-rebrands-floodgate.php; accessed April 25, 2010.

Cook, John. "Ten-Year VC Returns Slump, with More Bad News on the Horizon." *Puget Sound Business Journal*, October 27, 2009. http://www.techflash. com/seattle/2009/10/10-year_venture_capital_returns_hit_a_big_slump. html; accessed April 25, 2010.

Gelles, Jeff. "Innovators Meet Investors at Angel Venture Fair." *Philadelphia Inquirer*, April 7, 2010. http://www.philly.com/inquirer/business/20100407_ Innovators_meet_investors_at_Angel_Venture_Fair.html; accessed April 24, 2010.

Hardy, Quentin. "Where Angels Dare to Tread." *Forbes* 170, no. 9 (2002): 303–304. EBSCO, Academic Search Premier; accessed April 24, 2010.

Ibrahim, Darian. "The (Not So) Puzzling Behavior of Angel Investors." February 2008. angelcapitalassociation.org; accessed April 22, 2010.

Lajoie, Scott. "Cities of Angels." *Forbes* 165, no. 8 (2000): 146–150. EBSCO, Academic Search Premier; accessed April 25, 2010.

May, John. "Angel Investing: State of the Art 2010." BMGT 365. Lecture at Robert H. Smith School of Business, University of Maryland, Gaithersburg, March 9, 2010.

Ricadela, Aaron. "VCs Aim to Out-Angel the Angels." *BusinessWeek Online* (2007): 9. EBSCO, Academic Search Premier; accessed April 27, 2010.

Rose, David. "Current Trends in Angel Investing." EBSCO, Academic Search Premier. http://search.ebscohost.com.proxy-um.researchport.umd.edu/login.aspx?direct = true&db = bth&AN = 19557191&loginpage = Login.asp&site = ehost-live; accessed April 22, 2010.

Shane, Scott. *The Importance of Angel Investing in Financing the Growth of Entrepreneurial Ventures*. Working paper no. 331, Small Business Administration Office of Advocacy, Shaker Heights, Ohio, 2008.

Sohl, Jeffrey. "The Angel Investor Market in 2009: Holding Steady but Changes in Seed and Startup Investment." March 31, 2010. http://www.unh.edu/news/docs/2009angelanalysis.pdf; accessed April 24, 2010.

Spors, Kelly. "Angel Groups Spread Their Wings Beyond Tech." smSmallBiz.com, October 2007. http://www.smsmallbiz.com/capital/Angel_Groups_Spread_Their_Wings_Beyond_Tech.html; accessed April 24, 2010.

University of Michigan, NBIA, Ohio University, and Southern Technology Council. *Business Incubation Works*. Athens, Ohio: National Business Incubation Association, 1997.

Washington, Isobel. "Business Accelerator vs. Business Incubator." *EHow*. http://www.ehow.com/facts_5903618_business-accelerator-vs_-business-incubator.html; accessed April 25, 2010.

Wiltbank, Robert, and Warren Boeker. "Returns to Angel Investors in Groups." angelcapitalassociation.org, November 2007. http://www.angelcapitalassociation.org/data/Documents/Resources/AngelGroupResarch/1d%20-%20Resources%20-%20Research/6%20RSCH_-_ACEF_-_Returns_to_Angel_Investor_in_Groups.pdf; accessed April 18, 2010.

Chapter **5**

The Art and Science of Bootstrapping

Bootstrapping is the art of learning to do more with less. During the prelaunch phase of your business (and for some time after the launch), raising capital may be difficult, so bootstrapping becomes a substitute for—or addition to—your capital-formation strategies. It's not about writing 200-page business plans, power lunching with venture capitalists, or triple-mortgaging your home to pay legal and accounting fees. An entrepreneur who operates with the mind-set of bootstrap management understands that all resources are scarce and that cash must be cherished. "Cash is king" becomes the mantra. Figure 5-1 lists other key aspects of bootstrapping, and Figure 5-2 gives the traits of veteran bootstrappers. This chapter covers all the traits of a bootstrapper and the business techniques that he would use. You may find that you fit the profile!

Entrepreneurs across America have started successful businesses on a wing and a prayer, along with one special ingredient: an understanding of the art of bootstrapping. Indeed, the Federal Reserve estimates that more than 70 percent of all start-up companies use bootstrapping techniques in order to launch their business; the National Federation of Independent Business estimates that just over 25 percent of all small companies in the United States were started with $500 or less, and that less than 15 percent of the annual *Inc.* 500 companies had venture capital or formal institutional investment.

Figure 5-1.	Key Aspects of Bootstrapping.

- Learn to do more with less.
- Buy (or lease) only what you need today—delay it if you can.
- Find another way to get access to what you would otherwise buy or lease.
- Understand the difference between wants and needs.
- Focus on income-producing or market-expanding expenditures only.
- Control costs.
- Remember that there is *always* a way to get it done; your resourcefulness, creativity, and tenacity are your only limits.
- Reduce your *personal* cost of living.

Figure 5-2.	Profile of a Veteran Bootstrapper.

- *Leaves no stone unturned* in her search for the capital and resources necessary to grow the company.
- *Displays excellent cash flow management skills*—has perfected the art of getting paid early and disbursing late, but stays within legal and moral boundaries.
- *Uses the word* we *instead of* I when describing his business, even if it is a sole proprietorship.
- *Manages her personal affairs in a modest and conservative fashion*—drives an older but functional car and lives in a reasonable house, for example.
- *Is not likely to be seen in fancy restaurants*—is not afraid to eat tuna fish sandwiches three days in a row if necessary.

- *Is not likely to be seen in fancy clothes*—is not afraid to wear the same suit three days in a row if necessary.
- *Knows that bootstrapping leaves little room for error*—growing the company with very thin resources means that if there is one major misstep, the game is over.
- *Is always willing to be the last to get paid* and to make personal sacrifices for the good of his company—is not afraid to miss three paychecks in a row if necessary.
- *Makes friends with local commercial bankers and other sources of capital* early in the development of his business (a variation on the adage that "the best time to borrow money is when you don't need it" holds that the best time to make friends with bankers is when you don't have to).
- *Earns frequent-flyer miles while shopping* at discount warehouse clubs, then uses them for business trips, not family vacations.
- *Reads* The Life and Times of the Spartan Warrior *in none of her spare time.*
- *Looks for opportunities to leverage someone else's expense* to save her costs.
- *Is not likely to devote large amounts of time and resources* to business-planning and capital-formation efforts because this is time and energy that is needed to run and grow the business creatively.

Imagine building one of the most recognized brands in the winemaking industry with a few hundred dollars. That's exactly how Ernest and Julio Gallo started in 1933 in a rented warehouse in Modesto, California. They were turned down for a loan by several banks, so they convinced local farmers to provide them with grapes and defer payment until the wine was sold. They also convinced manufacturers of crushing and fermenting equipment to sell to them on 90-day terms. Instead of hiring expensive consultants, they learned to make wine by using the resources of the local library. The company started by these two bootstrappers had worldwide revenue of more than $3 billion in 2009.

And they are not alone. Household names such as Domino's Pizza, Hallmark Cards, Black & Decker, Dell Computer, Apple, Nike, Subway, Five Guys, and many of today's social network rock stars were started by bootstrapping entrepreneurs with less than $1,000. (See the sidebar "Great American Bootstrapping Stories.") These companies are living proof that necessity is truly the mother of invention. They all learned how to survive on a shoestring budget— by being creative and aggressive, and by carefully monitoring their cash flow. Thousands of companies each year start with just hundreds of dollars and manage to survive. But many others die because they try to grow too big too fast or, worse, because they successfully raise capital and then squander it.

Let's assume that your company is like most early-stage businesses and could really use $100,000 for growth and expansion (or for survival). Instead of focusing on *how* and *where* this money can be raised, the bootstrapper will ask, "What would we actually do with the money, and are there other ways to obtain those resources?"

Twelve Proven Bootstrapping Techniques and Strategies

1. *Launch Your Company Without Delay.* Bootstrappers tend to move quickly to launch their businesses. They choose a product or service that their target market will be ready to accept, without the need for extensive research and development or excessive advertising and promotional budgets. They might mimic the business model of a competitor to avoid having to educate the target consumer. They focus on projects that will generate cash flow immediately without being concerned about the company's long-term best interests (knowing that there will be no long term if they don't get past the short term). They may supplement their income by remaining in their current full-time jobs at the outset or by doing some part-time consulting to help pay their living expenses. They squelch their desire to recruit a "blue-chip" management team in order to avoid a top-heavy payroll. Bootstrappers focus on building and strengthening loyal customer relationships as early in the development of the business as possible, because they know that referrals from satisfied customers are the cheapest and best form of advertising. They use social networking and Web 2.0 tools and platforms cost-effectively to create "buzz" and plant the seeds for consumer demand even before the product or service is ready to launch. They resist the desire to grow their business quickly, which is the kiss of death for many entrepreneurs. They keep a low profile to avoid showing up on their competitors' radar screens until they have built their foundation, which also means keeping their entrepreneurial egos in check.

2. *Focus on Cash Flow.* The experienced bootstrapper knows that there is always a way to find the necessary resources: The only real limits are an entrepreneur's resourcefulness, creativity, and tenacity. The veteran

bootstrapper will also keep her staff focused on those activities that produce income or expand market share, and try to direct all expenditures to these areas as well. The bootstrapper will lead by example, not only by having a spartan personal lifestyle, but also by continuously asking the staff whether a given project is helping to create cash flow and whether a specific expense could be postponed. A positive cash flow is an indicator of entrepreneurial happiness. And the entrepreneurial credo "Happiness is a positive cash flow" is possible only if everyone is dedicated to getting beneficial terms from suppliers and receiving timely payments from customers, within reasonable moral and financial boundaries.

The bootstrapper understands that raising capital is secondary to producing profitable and durable income streams—that raising money is not a substitute for *making* money—and that managing expenses doesn't mean trimming the expense account from $5,000 per month to $3,000 per month. Set achieving and maintaining profitability as your goal from day one, with a focus on positive cash flow. Positive cash flow is also a sign of a happy and loyal customer base who demonstrate their satisfaction through the act of paying their bills on time. These are exactly the characteristics that a venture investor will look for in the company down the road. The smart bootstrapper knows that having too much capital can actually destroy an otherwise viable company—that when the belly is too full, there is no room left for the fire. A fancy office, bloated staff, big houses and cars, hefty expense accounts, and big-name investors don't create an atmosphere of prudence and conservation.

3. *Be Frugal, but Not Cheap.* There's a big difference between being frugal and being cheap. The bootstrapper must distinguish between costs that can be avoided, like lavish office space, and those that are necessary to build a foundation for growth, such as the proper computer systems. Being cheap with your employees and vendors is shortsighted and will have long-term negative implications. Being frugal means being creative concerning how and when employees will be motivated and rewarded. For example, a bowling party and home barbecue can be more fun and far less expensive than a staff retreat at a fancy resort. The same goes for entertaining customers and clients. Lavish meals

Great American Bootstrapping Stories

Apple Computer Inc. Steve Jobs and partner Steve Wozniak sold a Volkswagen van and a Hewlett-Packard programmable calculator to raise $1,350 in seed capital; they built the first Apple I PC in Atari employee Jobs's garage in 1976.

Black & Decker Corp. Started for $1,200 in 1910, the $5 billion tool manufacturer ensured its success in 1916, when its founding partners realized that there was greater demand for electric drills than for their original products, which included a milk-bottle-cap machine.

Clorox Co. In May 1913, five men from Oakland, California, pooled $100 apiece and started Clorox. The group had virtually no experience in bleach-making chemistry, but it suspected that the brine found in the salt ponds of San Francisco Bay could be converted into bleach using a process of electrolysis that others had developed. Within six months, the group raised an additional $3,000 in personal funds to build a physical plant for producing a powerful bleach agent for commercial use. A public offering the next year raised $75,000. Struggling to make payroll and bring in revenues, general manager (and early investor) William Murray had the plant chemists develop a less concentrated bleach formula for household use. Murray's wife, Annie, who took over the family grocery store, gave free samples to her customers, and the new product quickly became popular as a laundry aid and disinfectant.

Coca-Cola Co. A 53-year-old Atlanta pharmacist, John S. Pemberton, invented a soft drink in his backyard in May 1886. In 1891, Asa Chandler, a fellow druggist, bought the company for $2,300. In 2009, the company's market capitalization was $220 billion.

Dell Computer Corp. Putting little money down, Michael Dell started selling computers made to order from standard components from his dorm room in 1983. When his sales grew as high as $80,000 a month, he dropped out and put all his energy into the business. In 2009, Dell's sales were more than $134 billion.

Domino's Pizza, Inc. Tom Monaghan didn't finish college, but he stayed long enough to learn that undergrads eat a lot. In 1960, he bought a small pizzeria with his brother for $900 and expanded according to a simple strategy: locate stores near campuses or army bases, and deliver within half an hour.

Eastman Kodak Co. George Eastman's first private investor, Henry Alvah Strong, owned a profitable buggy-whip factory. In 1880, he put up $5,000 to capitalize Eastman, who still held a job as a bank clerk. Eastman's first Kodak $25 camera debuted in 1888.

E. & J. Gallo Winery The famous fraternal winemakers (who invested $923 in savings and borrowed $5,000 to launch their business) had no business or winemaking experience when they rented their first warehouse, in Modesto, California, in 1933. They learned winemaking by studying pamphlets at the local library.

Hewlett-Packard Co. The first big client of HP (started for $538 in 1938) was fellow bootstrapper Walt Disney, who needed sound equipment for the production of *Fantasia* in 1940.

Lands' End Inc. Legend has it that founder Gary Comer was so poor in 1963 that he couldn't order a reprint of his first catalog after he discovered a typo. Hence, the perennially misplaced apostrophe.

The Limited Inc. The Limited was founded in 1963 by 26-year-old H. Leslie Wexner. Wexner had worked at his family's retail store, but left after a disagreement with his father. With a loan of $5,000 from his aunt, he opened one small retail women's clothing store in a strip mall in Columbus, Ohio. Wexner had studied his father's books and discovered the problem that would become his opportunity: Formal and business clothing took too much time to sell. His father's cash was unnecessarily tied up in inventory. Casual clothing provided a slimmer margin, but it sold more quickly. Higher margins, Wexner decided, weren't as important as healthy cash flow—especially if your lack of capital meant that you couldn't afford much inventory in the first place. The cash-flow-is-king approach worked. Today the Limited operates more than 5,600 stores in the United States (including Lane Bryant, Abercrombie & Fitch, Express, Victoria's Secret, Structure, Henri Bendel, and Bath & Body Works stores).

Marriott International Inc. J. Willard "Bill" Marriott, his fiancée, and a partner started a nine-seat A&W soda fountain with $3,000 on May 20, 1927. They demonstrated a knack for hospitality and clever marketing from the beginning, attracting a day-one crowd by playing a radio that continuously updated patrons on the progress of Lindbergh's first trans-Atlantic flight.

Microsoft Corp. Harvard dropout Bill Gates and his high school sidekick Paul Allen moved into an Albuquerque hotel room in 1975. There they started Microsoft, writing the programming language for the first commercially available microcomputer.

Nike Inc. In the early 1960s, Philip Knight and his college track coach, William Bowerman, sold imported Japanese sneakers from the trunk of a station wagon. Start-up costs totaled $1,000. In fiscal 2009, the swoosh's sales exceeded $19.2 billion worldwide.

Roadway Express Inc. Brothers Galen and Carroll Roush and their brother-in-law Charles D. Morrison started Roadway in 1930, with each man contributing $800 in start-up capital. Roadway Express began with 10 owner-operated trucks and terminals in Akron, Chicago, and Kansas City. At first, all the tiny company could get were less-than-truckload shipments, which ran up their costs per truck. The Roushes tried hard to get full-truckload shipments, and the company grew. But real success didn't come until the late 1940s, when the founders realized that their bootstrapping-induced early niche was their meal ticket. Less-than-truckload shipments (LTLs) were moneymakers despite their higher costs, because Roadway could charge higher rates for them. With that discovery, the three founders made LTLs their primary focus. Now the second-biggest trucking company, Roadway's revenues exceeded $8 billion a year in 2009 as part of the YRC Worldwide trucking conglomerate.

United Parcel Service Inc. In 1907, two Seattle teenagers pooled their cash, came up with $100, and began a message- and parcel-delivery service for local merchants. In 1999, the company completed one of the largest IPOs in history.

Wm. Wrigley Jr. Co. William Wrigley Jr., a young soap salesman, started selling baking soda in Chicago in 1891. To entice new customers, he threw in two packages of chewing gum with every sale. Guess what the customers were more excited about? In 2010, Wrigley was acquired by global candy and consumer goods company Mars, based in McLean, Virginia.

will be forgotten long before the memories of a Sunday afternoon at a baseball game with a client's family will be.

4. *Leverage Your Assets.* The bootstrapper understands the importance of growth strategies like franchising, licensing, joint ventures, and establishing strategic and interdependent relationships that can facilitate business growth, yet conserve cash. In many ways, franchising and licensing are the ultimate bootstrapping strategies because they allow you to leverage intangible assets and conserve scarce resources—you get to avoid directly spending the money on what you were otherwise going to buy, and you get access to the resources needed and still share in the financial rewards. For example, assume that you have spent most of your available cash and time developing a certain type of technology, but you lack the capital for advertising and promotion. Rather than trying to raise the capital, you might find a willing licensee who would gain access to the use and further development of the technology in exchange for an initial license fee and ongoing royalty payments. You could use these up-front license payments for other cash flow needs. As an example, a client of mine recently successfully launched an Internet business and received exposure to millions of potential customers by structuring a series of strategic marketing alliances with affinity groups whose members were his exact target customers—at a fraction of what the company would have spent for traditional advertising to send a message to that many potential customers in such a short period of time.

5. *Trade Equity for Services.* The effective bootstrapper also understands the concept of "equity for services." As long as you stay within the securities laws, it's possible to conserve cash by paying lawyers, accountants, architects, designers, advertising agencies, consultants, investment bankers, and other suppliers with the company's stock. When service providers are part owners, they may have a greater sense of loyalty and a higher level of commitment to the project. You may want to create multiple classes of stock or build in certain redemption features to allow the company to eventually repurchase the shares at a predetermined price or using a predetermined formula. It's also possible to use options or warrants that can be exercised only in specific circumstances (such as an initial public offering). If you offer shares to

your lawyers or accountants, be aware of potential conflicts of interest and respect their views if they feel that, for ethical reasons, payment in the form of company stock is not appropriate.

6. *Be a Junkyard Dog.* The bootstrapper understands the meaning of the phrase "one man's trash is another man's treasure." More than one successful entrepreneur has built a business by searching through junkyards, trash containers, and rummage sales to find the equipment and supplies that he needs to start and grow the company. If sifting through trash on a Saturday night is not your cup of tea, at the very least be on the lookout for someone else's underutilized resources. Let's say you need access to specialized computer equipment or a licensed commercial kitchen for research and development. Instead of building your own from scratch, approach others who may allow you to use their resources during off-peak hours (even if it's the middle of the night) at low (or no) rental rates or in exchange for equity.

7. *Make the Most of What You've Got.* The true bootstrapper knows how to make the most of his existing resources. Many bootstrappers have referred to it as the art of "stretching a dollar," but there's more to it now than that. For example, one early-stage client of mine lacked the capital to pay bonuses at the end of one year. Fearful of losing key employees and demotivating a hardworking staff, he "negotiated" six weekends at his parents' cabin in the mountains and then bartered some computer services with a local upscale restaurant. Instead of being empty-handed at holiday time, he was able to deliver a series of getaway weekends and complimentary dinners to his loyal team, and everyone agreed to hang on until the next year—when cash bonuses would be paid.

8. *Distinguish Between Perception and Reality.* In today's virtual economy, it seems that people are getting together in person less and less, and instead are communicating via phone, computer and videoconferencing. If the chances of your having a client visit your offices are very low, don't waste resources by paying for a corner office in a high-rise when you could be saving a lot of money on administrative costs. For many bootstrappers, the biggest real estate decision involves choosing among their basement, their kitchen, their garage, and the back of their minivan! Chances are, if you spend the money on nice letterhead,

high-quality business cards, a good voice-mail system, and a creative Web page, your customers will never know that you are sitting on a 20-year-old chair at a card table in your mother's basement. On occasions when you do host a customer meeting, rent a meeting room at a local hotel. Better yet, ask your accountants or your lawyers if you can use their conference room for no charge.

9. *Use the Resources of Others.* Many of my early-stage clients have gotten access to the resources they need by finding companies that aren't using *their* assets 7 days a week, 24 hours a day. For example, in its early days, one growing retail client of mine could not afford the rental rates of large regional malls, but needed access to the customer base and foot traffic that they attracted. He approached existing retail tenants that had underutilized space and set up a kiosk joint venture with them to create a "store within a store" and make better use of their underused 300 square feet. By structuring the deal as a joint venture, he avoided most of the landlord's requirements for approval of a sublease and got access to the customers he needed. Another client wanted to get into a specialized area of home improvement, but could not afford the insurance, licensing, and bonding required, so he partnered with an existing contractor who was more established and already had all of the state's requirements in place. The existing contractor shared revenues and enjoyed the benefits of the start-up company's guerrilla marketing efforts.

10. *Be Creative and Be Prepared to Sacrifice.* Bootstrappers understand that they must be creative and aggressive in their cash-management techniques and in their quest for resources. Yet sometimes the solutions are right in your own backyard, hidden within your existing relationships with customers, suppliers, advisors and consultants, local government agencies, universities, and business networking groups. You must be prepared to demonstrate that you have assumed risk and made personal sacrifices. We live in a country that lauds entrepreneurs and loves underdogs. Everyone wants to help people who are trying to help themselves. If you're asking a customer to pay early, or asking a key vendor to let you pay late, you'll get a better response when you pull up to their office in a $15,000 car and a $250 suit rather than a $60,000 car and a $1,000 suit.

For the great majority of entrepreneurs, the real challenge is not necessarily the process of raising capital, but rather the tenacity and creativity to do without capital. The bootstrapper knows the difference between *wants* (which can be deferred) and *needs* (which must be addressed). Be prepared to reorient your thinking—instead of focusing on raising capital (which often takes three to six months with an uncertain end result), focus on finding resources.

11. *Leverage Your Inventory.* There is a wide variety of products or services that you may need in order to get started that people will provide in exchange for your own inventory, access to your future inventory, or some other benefit, such as "a monthly free dinner for four" to the equipment suppliers who fit out your new restaurant. For example, Ben & Jerry's offered its competitors and its plumbers a free membership in its "Ice Cream for Life" club if they would be willing to make the repairs needed to the gas station that was being converted into the company's first location. And the rest is history. Use barter networks, listings on Craigslist.com and similar sites, and other such approaches to see who may be interested in product or service exchanges.

12. *Don't Give Up.* Many bootstrappers rely on self-confidence, strong co-founder relationships, and a supportive circle of friends and advisors to keep them going in the toughest of times. They know that entrepreneurship is a marathon, not a sprint. Battles will be lost, but what is most important is that the war is won. Commitment, creativity, and resilience are the traits that are most important for getting through the many sleepless nights ahead.

Ten More Tried-and-Tested Bootstrapping Techniques

1. Wear multiple hats in managing your business to save personnel costs.
2. Buy or lease used furniture and equipment, and don't overpay for unnecessary service warranties.
3. Share office space with (or sublease from) a large company that will offer you access to conference rooms, office equipment, and reception or typing services.
4. Apply for several credit cards at once and use the unborrowed portions as your operating line of credit.
5. Hire student interns who are willing to forgo a salary in exchange for

work experience. Better yet, hire a retired executive or family member who may be willing to help out or serve as a mentor just to stay busy. A wonderful resource for this is the SBA's Service Core of Retired Executives program (SCORE).

6. Work hard to maintain customer relationships that encourage customers to pay you early.

7. Commit only to short-term leases and other obligations to maintain maximum flexibility and cost control.

8. Ask major clients to purchase the key equipment that you'll need in order to service their account, then lease it back from them.

9. Offer shares in your company to vendors, landlords, and key employees in lieu of cash, subject to federal and state securities law and acceptable dilution ratios. (Sam Walton did this when starting Wal-Mart, and his former secretaries and office workers are now multimillionaires.)

10. Join a commercial barter exchange and use it to acquire key products and services. In some cities, alternative currencies have even emerged as a type of barter exchange and bootstrapping technique. These local currencies have stimulated economic development in small towns and rural areas that have not yet been affected by the regional gluts of venture capital and where commercial lending dollars are not flowing freely. Many local-currency programs have been sponsored or financed by the E. F. Schumacher Society, whose local success stories include Ithaca Hours (Ithaca, New York), the Sand Dollars (Bolinas, California), Barter Bucks (Indianapolis, Indiana), Great Lakes Hours (Detroit, Michigan), and the Gainesville Hours program (Gainesville, Florida).

Bootstrapping: The Dark Side

There are two key risks with the bootstrapping strategy that every entrepreneur should understand and try to avoid: (1) stepping outside the bounds of integrity and ethics; and (2) knowing when it is okay to ease up on bootstrapping principles a bit.

Some entrepreneurs confuse bootstrapping with questionable business ethics and use it as an excuse for crossing the line. Failing to pay vendors or professional advisors in the name of bootstrapping and helping yourself to resources that don't belong to you are *just plain wrong*. It is fine to negotiate for good prices and longer credit terms, but don't cross the line—it can and will come back to haunt you.

Similarly, some entrepreneurs do not know when or how to ease up on the bootstrapping mindset once the company reaches certain milestones. Even as the company grows, cash flow management and favorable credit terms can (and should always) remain a top priority for the company, but not at the expense of those who supported you in the early days. At some point, your employees, vendors, and professional advisors will expect you to lighten up a bit, or you may sacrifice their support and your own integrity. For example, paying your employees below-market wages or asking for several extra months to pay vendors will be tolerated when the company is struggling to survive, but not when it reaches critical mass and the founders are taking home $500,000 per annum apiece! It is important to treat people fairly and eventually reward those who have been most loyal, patient, and supportive of you during the early stages of the company's life.

Chapter **6**

Private Placements

One financing strategy that is available to early-stage and emerging-growth companies is the private placement offering, which generally refers to an offering of securities by a small or growing company that does not need to be registered with the Securities and Exchange Commission (SEC). A private placement can offer you (as the "offeror" or "issuer") reduced transaction and ongoing costs because it is exempt from many of the extensive registration and reporting requirements imposed by federal and state securities laws. Private placements usually also offer the ability to structure a more focused and dynamic transaction, because they attract a small number of sophisticated investors. These investors may also provide the company with certain strategic benefits and industry knowledge. In addition, a private placement permits more rapid penetration into the capital markets than would a public offering of securities requiring registration with the SEC.

To find out whether a private placement is a sensible strategy for you, you must (1) have a fundamental understanding of the federal and state securities laws affecting private placements (an overview is provided in the next section), (2) be familiar with the basic procedural steps that must be taken before this capital-formation alternative can be pursued, (3) have a good sense of your list of targeted investors, and (4) have a team of qualified legal and accounting professionals to assist you in preparing the private placement offering documents, usually referred to as the private placement memorandum, or PPM. The PPM is essentially an offering of your securities to family, friends, and angels. The biggest difference is that instead of an arm's-length negotiation with one or a few investors, you're now targeting enough investors that a set of offering documents is required under federal and state laws and the terms of the offering will be established by you in advance.

Federal Securities Laws Applicable to Private Placements

Although the SEC generally requires you to file a registration statement before you offer to sell securities in interstate commerce, the Securities Act of 1933 allows some exemptions. The most commonly recognized exemption is a private placement. (I'll cover public offerings in Chapters 11 and 12.)

To qualify for a private placement, you'll have to work with your attorney and an investment banker to structure the transaction so that it falls within one of the categories of available exemptions. The most common is Regulation D, which covers three specific exemptions from the registration provisions under Rules 504, 505, and 506, as set forth in the next sections. You may also want to consider a Small Corporate Offering Registration (SCOR), which I'll describe later in this chapter.

Rule 504

This exemption permits offers and sales of not more than $1,000,000 during any 12-month period by any issuer that is not an investment company, is not a development-stage company that is without a specific business plan or one whose business plan is to engage in the acquisition of an unidentified company or companies, and is not subject to the reporting requirements of the Securities Exchange Act of 1934, which applies to most publicly traded companies.

Rule 504 requires that the terms and conditions of Rule 501 (that is, accredited investors) and clauses (a), (c), and (d) of Rule 502 are met, except that clauses (c) and (d) will not apply under certain conditions that depend largely upon state law. For example, Rule 504 doesn't require you to register a formal disclosure document (also known as a *prospectus*), or even send one to offerees. (However, Regulation D filings do require you to file a Form D—a simple form that summarizes your offering and the basis for the exemption—within 15 days of the first sale.) An offering under Rule 504 is still subject to the general anti-fraud provisions of the Securities Exchange Act. All information that you provide to the prospective investor must be accurate and not misleading in its content or its omissions. Since there's a great deal of information that potential investors must understand and procedures that they'll have to follow, I recommend that you have a prospectus—it will protect you, your management team, and your company against any subsequent claims by disgruntled or confused investors.

Finally, if you're looking to raise capital under Rule 504, be sure to examine applicable state laws very carefully. Although many states have adopted overall securities laws similar to Regulation D, many do not include an exemption similar to Rule 504, and as a result, you may have to prepare a more formal offering memorandum or rely on another exemption.

Rule 505

Many companies select this rule instead of Rule 504 because its requirements are consistent with those of many state securities laws. Rule 505 allows for the sale of up to $5,000,000 of securities in a 12-month period to an unlimited number of accredited investors and up to 35 nonaccredited investors, regardless of their net worth, income, or sophistication. An accredited investor is any person who qualifies for—and must fall into—one or more of the categories that are typically measured based on net worth or annual income requirements. The categories include officers and directors of the company who have policy-making functions and outside investors who meet the income or net worth criteria found in Figure 6-1.

Rule 505 has many of the same filing requirements and restrictions as Rule 504, plus an absolute prohibition on advertising and general solicitation for offerings, and restrictions on which companies may rely on the exemption. This applies to persons who have been subject to certain disciplinary, administrative, civil, or criminal proceedings, or sanctions that involve the company or its predecessors.

Figure 6-1.	Types of Accredited Investors.

As used in Regulation D under the Securities Act of 1933, the following are defined as accredited investors:

- *Any bank as defined in section 3(a)(2) of the Act*, or any savings and loan association or other institution as defined in section 3(a)(5)(A) of the Act whether acting in its individual or fiduciary capacity; any broker or dealer registered pursuant to section 15 of the Securities Exchange Act of 1934; any insurance company as defined in section 2(13) of the Act; any investment company registered under the Investment Company Act of 1940 or a business development company as defined in section 2(a)(48) of that Act; any Small Business Investment Company licensed by the U.S. Small Business Administration under section 301(c) or (d) of the Small Business Investment Act of 1958; any plan established and maintained by a state, its political subdivisions, or any agency or instrumentality of a state or its political subdivisions, for the benefits of its employees, if such plan has total assets in excess of $5,000,000; any employee benefit plan within the meaning of the Employee Retirement Income Security Act of 1974 if the investment decision is made by a plan fiduciary, as defined in section 3(21) of such Act, which is either a bank, savings and loan association, insurance company, or registered investment adviser, or if the employee benefit plan has total assets in excess of $5,000,000 or, if a self-directed plan, with investment decisions made solely by persons that are accredited investors;

- *Any private business development company* as defined in section 202(a)(22) of the Investment Advisers Act of 1940;

- *Any organization described in section 501(c)(3)* of the Internal Revenue Code, corporation, Massachusetts or similar business trust, or partnership, not formed for the specific purpose of acquiring the securities offered, with total assets in excess of $5,000,000;

- *Any director, executive officer*, or general partner of the issuer of the securities being offered or sold, or any director, executive officer, or general partner of a general partner of that issuer;

- *Any natural person whose individual net worth*, or joint net worth with that person's spouse, at the time of his purchase exceeds $1,000,000;

- *Any natural person* who had an individual income in excess of $200,000 in each of the two most recent years or joint income with that person's spouse in excess of $300,000 in each of those years and has a reasonable expectation of reaching the same income level in the current year;

- *Any trust*, with total assets in excess of $5,000,000, not formed for the specific purpose of acquiring the securities offered, whose purchase is directed by a sophisticated person as described in clause (b)(2)(ii) of Rule 506; and

- *Any entity* in which all of the equity owners are accredited investors.

Rule 506

This rule is similar to Rule 505 in that you may sell your securities to an unlimited number of accredited investors and up to 35 nonaccredited investors. For companies that need more than $5,000,000 in capital for growth or to achieve their business-plan objectives, this exemption is the most attractive because it has no dollar limitation. The big difference under Rule 506 is that any nonaccredited investor must be "sophisticated." In this context, a "sophisticated investor" is one who doesn't fall into any of the categories found in Figure 6-1, but whom you believe to "have knowledge and experience in financial and business matters that render him capable of evaluating the merits and understanding the risks posed by the transaction (either acting alone or in conjunction with his 'purchaser representative,' such as a financial adviser or accountant)." The best way to remove any uncertainty over the sophistication or accreditation of a prospective investor is to request that she complete a comprehensive confidential purchaser (or offeree) questionnaire (an example of which is shown in the appendix) before the securities are sold. If only accredited and sophisticated investors participate in the transaction, then Rule 506 eliminates the need to prepare and deliver disclosure documents in any specified format. Here too, an absolute prohibition on advertising and general solicitation exists.

State Securities Laws Applicable to Private Placements

You and your team will have to consider the expense and requirements on both the federal and state levels. Every state has statutes governing securities transactions and securities dealers, and Regulation D was designed to provide uniformity between federal and state securities laws. It has worked in some states, but there's still a long way to go on a national level. Whether or not your offering is exempt under federal laws, registration may still be required in the states where the securities will be sold under applicable "blue sky" laws. (These are laws that require securities issuers to register the offering and provide financial details so that investors have solid information on which to base their decisions. The story goes that a judge once said that a particular offering had as much value as a patch of blue sky.)

There are many levels of review among the different states, ranging from very tough "merit reviews" (which ensure that all offerings of securities are fair and equitable) to very lenient "notice only" filings (which primarily promote full disclosure). Before you distribute offering documents in any state, check the securities laws of that state and be aware of their specific requirements. Although a comprehensive discussion of state securities laws is beyond the scope of this book, you should review these laws to determine:

- Whether the particular limited offering exemption under federal law that you've selected also applies in that state
- Whether presale or postsale registration or notices are required
- Whether special legends or disclosures must be made in the offering documents
- What remedies are available to an investor who has purchased securities from a company that has failed to comply with applicable state laws
- Who may offer securities for sale on behalf of the company

SCOR Offerings. Most states have adopted the Small Corporate Offering Registration (SCOR), which may make the use of Regulation A or Rule 504 of Regulation D a more viable source of growth capital for entrepreneurs and smaller companies. It does this by using Form U-7, a disclosure document in question-and-answer format, which you complete with assistance from your accountant or attorney. The form simplifies and streamlines the disclosure process and reduces your cost of compliance, but you may need to add material disclosures that are not covered by the form.

Preparing the Private Placement Memorandum

Armed with a basic overview of the regulatory issues, you're ready to begin preparing your offering documents. You'll be working with your attorney and your banker to assemble the documents and exhibits that will constitute the *private placement memorandum* (PPM). The PPM describes your company's background, the risks to the investor, and the terms of the securities being sold. You'll also have to determine the exact degree of disclosure that should be included in the document, and there are several factors that affect the type and format of information that must be provided. These include:

- The minimum level of disclosure you must make under federal securities laws (this depends, in part, on the registration exemption that you're using)
- The minimum level of disclosure you must make under an applicable state's securities laws (which depends on the state or states in which an offer or sale of the securities is to be made)

- The sophistication and expectations of the targeted investors (for example, some investors will expect to have a certain amount of information presented in a specific format, regardless of what the law requires)
- The complexity or the nature of the company and the terms of the offering (for example, many entrepreneurial companies should prepare a set of disclosure documents, regardless of whether they are required to do so, in order to avoid liability for misstatements, fraud, or confusion, especially if the nature of the company or the terms of its offering are very complex).

Your attorney must first review each transaction or proposed offering of securities carefully to determine the minimum level of disclosure required under applicable federal and state laws. After that, you should weigh the costs of preparing a more detailed document than may be required against the benefits of the additional protection you'll get from a more comprehensive prospectus. Ultimately, the question will always be, "What is the most cost-effective vehicle for providing the targeted investors with the information that they require and that both applicable law and prudence dictate they must have?" There is no easy answer.

Key Sections of the PPM

The specific disclosure items that you include in your PPM will vary depending on the size of the offering and the nature of the investors (as defined by federal and state securities laws). The text should be descriptive, not persuasive, and it should allow the reader to reach his own conclusions about the merits of the securities being offered by the company. If you are in doubt as to whether a particular piece of information should be disclosed, disclose it. The categories of disclosure items might include the following:

Introductory materials. These introduce the prospective investor to the basic terms of the offering. There should be a cover page that includes a brief statement about the company and its core business, the terms of the offering (often in a summary table format), and all disclosures required by federal and state laws. The cover page should be followed by a summary of the offering, which serves as an integral part of the introductory materials and a cross-reference point for the reader. The third (and final) part of the introductory materials is usually a statement of the investor-suitability standards, which includes a discussion of the federal and state securities laws applicable to the offering and the definitions of an "accredited investor" as applied to the offering.

Description of the company. This is a statement of the company's history and that of its affiliates and predecessors. In addition to the history, this section will include a discussion of the company's principal officers and directors, products and services, management and operating policies, business plan, performance history and goals, competition, industry trends, advertising and marketing strategy, suppliers and distributors, intellectual-property rights, key real and personal property, customer demographics, and any other material information that would be relevant to the investor.

Risk factors. This is usually the most difficult section to write, but it's one of the most important to the prospective investor. Its purpose is to outline all the factors that make the offering risky or speculative. When you are drafting this section, you may be well served by thinking of it as a list of reasons *not* to invest in the company. Of course, the exact risks faced by the investors will depend on the nature of the company and the trends within its industry.

Capitalization of the issuer. This section provides the capital structure of the company both before and after the offering. For the purposes of this section of the PPM, all authorized and outstanding securities must be disclosed (including any convertible debt and all long-term debt).

Management of the company. This section should include the names, ages, special skills or characteristics, and biographical information of each officer, director, or key consultant for at least the last five years. It should detail compensation and stock option arrangements; bonus plans; special contracts or arrangements; and any transactions between the company and individual officers and directors (including loans, self-dealing, and related types of transactions). You should also disclose the role and identity of your legal and accounting firms, and any other experts retained in connection with the offering.

Terms of the offering. This should describe the terms and conditions of the offering, the number of shares to be offered (including the minimum and the maximum) and the price. If the securities are to be offered through underwriters, brokers, or dealers, then the name of each "distributor" must be disclosed, as well as the terms and nature of the relationship between

you and each distributor; the commissions you'll pay; the distributor's obligations; and any special rights, such as the right of a particular underwriter to serve on the board of directors, any indemnification provisions, or
other material terms of the offering. Note: The terms and structure of the
offering should be based on a series of preliminary, informal meetings with
possible investors (without those discussions qualifying as a formal "offer"
as that term is defined by the securities laws). You should also research
current market conditions and recently closed, similarly situated offerings.

Allocation of proceeds. This section gives the principal purposes for
which the net proceeds will be used, and the approximate amount that you
intend to use for each purpose. You need to give careful thought to this section because any material deviation from the use of funds as described in
the PPM could trigger liability. If you don't have an exact breakdown, try
to describe why you're raising additional capital, and what business objectives you expect to pursue with the proceeds.

Dilution. In this section, you should include a discussion of the number of shares outstanding prior to the offering, the price paid for those
shares, the net book value, the effect of the proposed offer on existing
shareholders, and the dilutive effects on new purchasers at the completion of the offering. Often the founding shareholders (and sometimes their
key advisors or the people who will help promote the PPM) acquired their
securities at prices substantially below those in the prospective offering.
As a result, the book value of shares purchased by new investors pursuant
to the offering will be substantially diluted, which may constitute a risk
factor.

Description of securities. This should explain the rights, restrictions,
and special features of the securities being offered, and any applicable provision of the articles of incorporation or bylaws that affect the company's capitalization (such as preemptive rights, total authorized stock, different classes
of shares, or restrictions on the declaration and distribution of dividends).

Financial statements. The financial statements you'll need to provide
will vary depending on the amount of money to be raised, applicable federal and state regulations, the federal exemption used, the qualifications of
the investors, and the company's nature and stage of growth. Provide an
explanation of these financial statements and an analysis of the company's
current and projected financial condition.

Exhibits. Such things as the articles of incorporation and bylaws, key contracts or leases, brochures, news articles, marketing reports, and the résumés of the principals may be appended to the PPM.

Subscription Materials

Once the prospective investors and their advisors decide to provide capital to your growing company in accordance with the terms of the PPM, there is a series of documents that must be signed to evidence the investors' desire to "subscribe" to purchase the securities offered by the PPM. The various subscription materials accompanying the PPM serve several purposes. There are two key documents.

Subscription Agreement

This is the contract between the purchaser (investor) and the issuer (you) for the purchase of the securities. (A sample is given in the appendix.) The subscription agreement should contain acknowledgments of:

- The receipt and review by the purchaser of the information given about the offering and the background of the company
- The restricted nature of the securities to be acquired and the fact that the securities are acquired under an exemption from registration
- Any particularly significant suitability requirements (such as the amount of the investor's investment or passive income, investment experience, tax bracket, and so forth) that the issuer feels may be crucial to the purchaser's ability to obtain the benefits of the proposed investment
- An awareness of the risks that are specified in the disclosure statement
- The advisory role of a purchaser representative (if one is used)

The subscription agreement should also contain confirmation by the purchaser of the accuracy and completeness of the information contained in the purchaser questionnaire; the number and price of the securities to be purchased, and the manner of payment; and agreement to any special elections that the company may contemplate (such as S corporation elections, accounting methods, and any relevant tax elections). The subscription agreement often contains an agreement by the prospective purchaser to indemnify you against losses or liabilities resulting from misrepresentations on the part of the purchaser that would void the registration exemption that you're attempting to invoke. The agreement should also contain representations on the part of the purchaser with respect to its authority to execute the agreement.

Purchaser and/or Purchaser Representative Questionnaires

This questionnaire (a sample of which is given in the appendix) are used to obtain information from prospective offerees and their representatives and serve as evidence of your reasonable efforts to substantiate the investors' accreditation or sophistication. It also proves the investors' abilities to fend for themselves and properly evaluate the merits of an offering. A purchaser questionnaire should obtain information regarding the prospective purchaser's background, citizenship, education, employment, and investment and/or business experience. Many wealthy individuals will complain or refuse to fully complete a detailed questionnaire. While you must respect their time and their desire for confidentiality, you must also obtain enough information to protect yourself and the company in the event of a dispute with the investor or an investigation by the SEC.

Compliance Issues

Once the PPM hits the streets, you should implement a tracking system for its distribution. A number should be assigned to each copy of the offering, and the tracking system should include a log of the name and address of each individual who receives a private placement memorandum, the number assigned to that memorandum, and the date the memorandum was sent. You can use this tracking system to control the distribution of the document and ensure compliance with securities laws. Include a checklist to ensure that all documents that need to be signed by the potential purchaser have indeed been signed and returned to you. The system should also track how many individuals—accredited and nonaccredited—you make offers or sales to.

As part of the "marketing process," consider holding a few group meetings or cocktail receptions so that you can interact with your prospective investors. You'll probably want to have some individual meetings to answer questions and clarify terms. But remember, all statements that you make to potential investors at these meetings must be consistent with the information you provided in the private placement memorandum. When you're speaking to a potential purchaser, don't make any claims about the potential earnings of the security being offered. To avoid possible legal problems, remind the potential purchaser that the purchase of securities is a high-risk venture and that you can make no guarantees or even speculations about earnings. Don't engage in individual negotiations with potential securities purchasers—but if you choose to do so, add the results of the negotiations to the PPM as a written amendment. Finally, make sure that all investors receive the same information.

Accepting Subscriptions

Keep in mind that the PPM is nothing more than a memorandum that informs the public that there is a securities offering available. It does not constitute an offer. If a potential investor indicates (by returning the completed subscription materials with a check) that she would like to invest in the company, that constitutes an "offer to buy," but it is not a form of "legal acceptance" unless and until you decide to accept the offer. When you evaluate the completed subscription materials, use a reasonable standard of due diligence. You are responsible for determining that a purchaser meets the suitability requirements set forth in the PPM questionnaire. If you know that a potential purchaser is affluent, but he chooses not to fully disclose his net worth, you should—as a precautionary measure—insist that the potential purchaser provide enough information to demonstrate that he is qualified to make a securities purchase. Please note that the manner in which "net worth" is calculated is defined by law, with the most recent change having been enacted as part of the Dodd-Frank Wall Street Reform and Consumer Protection Act.

Changing or Updating the PPM Before Completion of the Offering

If, after you've distributed the PPM, you find that there are material changes in the way the securities will be offered or there are substantial new developments affecting the company, you should add information on these material changes to the PPM. Such additions should be done either as an amendment or as a completely new private placement memorandum that replaces the previous version. Material changes include a change in the price of the securities, changes in the purchaser-suitability standards, the grant of stock options to the directors or officers of the company, or any other information that might have a material effect on the targeted investor's ability to make an informed investment decision.

After the Closing

As discussed at the beginning of this chapter, Regulation D requires you to file Form D with the SEC within 15 days after the first sale. (See the sample Form D in the appendix.)

It's also critical that you keep your PPM investors informed. You can accomplish this with periodic reports, shareholders' meetings, and a web site, among other things. Maintaining good relationships and communications channels will help reduce the chances of subsequent disputes, keep investors informed (which may be helpful if you have additional capital-formation needs), and build a track record (which the more sophisticated investment bankers will want to see when you seek to raise additional rounds of capital or consider a public offering). Good communication proves that you're sensitive to the need for good shareholder relations and helps you practice to be a public company one day (where these communications will be mandatory and not optional). Your PPM investors may have access to key relationships, have ideas for growth, or want to participate in strategic planning, and all of these offers of assistance, within reason, should be greeted with appreciation and respect.

The Rise of Secondary-Market Private Placements and the Story of SecondMarket

In the early 2000s, a New York–based investment banker named Barry Silbert was working on some of the most complex bankruptcies of the day. Creditors in those bankruptcies were often compensated by receiving restricted stock in the bankrupt companies, and they sought assistance in monetizing the equity from Barry and his colleagues. Barry was in his mid-twenties, and he was struck by the fact that there was no centralized, transparent marketplace in which these illiquid financial assets could be traded. Thus, in late 2004, Barry left his banking position and founded SecondMarket to address the increasing need for liquidity in illiquid assets. The company served as a marketplace for several different financial products, but it quickly became the market leader in one emerging asset class: shares in private companies.

In late 2007, SecondMarket began receiving calls from former Facebook employees who inquired whether it would be possible for them to sell their vested shares through the platform. SecondMarket began conducting due diligence to identify the viability of the market. After speaking with venture capitalists, private company CEOs, and industry leaders, Barry and the SecondMarket team recognized that there was a substantial need for liquidity in the marketplace. High-growth, VC-backed private companies were taking much longer to go public as a result of a number of systemic changes in the capital-formation process in recent years. The proliferation of high-frequency trading, the lack of research and sales support for growth-stage companies, and the cost of Sarbanes-Oxley compliance are some of the factors that had created a hostile environment for growth-stage companies in the public markets. In essence, companies that would have gone public in past decades—those with market capitalizations of less than $1 billion—are no longer able to succeed in the public markets.

SecondMarket recognized the opportunity to help private companies navigate this landscape, and it officially launched its private company market in April 2009. SecondMarket works closely with the private companies, helping them to establish and manage company-controlled liquidity programs. Startups are able to determine who may buy and sell stock, how much stock may be sold, and the frequency of trading activity. By managing the process on SecondMarket, companies can provide their shareholders with interim liquidity. This allows the companies to either use SecondMarket as a "bridge" to an IPO or remain private. It also provides them with an important employee retention and attraction tool.

In 2009, SecondMarket completed more than $100 million in transactions in the shares of private companies such as Facebook, Twitter, and LinkedIn. That number nearly quadrupled in 2010 as the company completed more than $360 million in transactions across several dozen companies.

SecondMarket's technology has also continued to improve. In 2011, the new SecondMarket platform was introduced, bringing "social" aspects to investing by allowing participants to create their own online profiles. The new platform also provides enhanced corporate information on thousands of private companies that were not previously accessible on SecondMarket. Participants can create "trusted" networks of like-minded investors, choose companies to add to their "watch lists," and add their holdings to their profiles. This enables the SecondMarket community to determine which private companies they find particularly interesting, and it also arms the companies with information on investor interest that can help them determine the timing for their liquidity programs. SecondMarket will not facilitate transactions without the support of the companies.

With the lack of sales and research support in the public markets for growth-stage companies, a new market needs to emerge. If it does not, the negative impact on U.S. job growth and American global competitiveness could be significant. SecondMarket just may be able to fill that void and become the new American growth market.

Practical Tips for Ensuring a Successful PPM Offering

Be ready and have a hit list. You certainly don't want to take the time and expense to prepare a PPM if you don't have any clue as to who you should show it to when it's completed. Prepare a list of targeted investors well in advance to make sure that your offering is viable and to help your lawyers evaluate compliance issues. Remember that not everyone on the list will subscribe, so the list should be considerably larger than the number of units that will be offered. Analyze this list to ensure that you have properly determined the size of the units. For example, a $10,000 unit may be attractive to investors, but it may be too small to get you to your final capital targets or may allow an investor who might be otherwise committed to a larger amount to fall back to a $10,000 commitment. Conversely, a $100,000-sized unit may get you to your goal faster, but may also exclude many of the otherwise qualified investors on your hit list.

Make sure the economic terms are attractive. Remember that unlike a venture capital deal, in which the business plan is presented and then a term sheet is negotiated, the PPM offering is not intended to be negotiated at all. Therefore, you must have a good sense of the attractiveness and fairness of the terms of the offering before the distribution of the document. This may mean holding informal preoffering meetings with prospective investors and others in the business community who can act as a sounding board.

Find some sizzle. There should be some special benefits or rights for the investors. For early-stage companies, the only thing that will really appeal to investors is the opportunity to get in on the ground floor of what might be the next Microsoft. Since that won't be the case for every company, your challenge is to find some special benefit or right that will entice investors to invest in your company. You may be surprised to learn that these special benefits may make your offering successful.

Do it right the first time. The adage that "you never get a second chance to make a first impression" definitely applies to PPMs. Investors don't want to see a lot of glitter or waste, but they will expect to see a well-written and properly formatted document without typographical errors or poor grammar. They'll want exhibits and other information that will really help them understand the business and the risks inherent in the offering. They may expect to be invited to a nice reception where they'll have an opportunity to see a product demonstration and interact with the management team.

Don't send to a friend of a friend of a friend. One of the age-old questions with a PPM offering is, "To whom can we send the document, and how well do we have to know them?" Well, remember that the offering is supposed to be private, not public. The offerees should be people with whom you and your team have a preexisting relationship. The document should not be sent to a blind list of the wealthiest people in your area—you know, the kind of list published by a city magazine. There is a gray area in terms of whether "friends of friends" may receive the offering. Use your discretion and consult with counsel if in doubt.

Chapter 7

Commercial Lending

No small or growing company survives and prospers without some type of debt on its balance sheet. Whether it's a small loan from family or friends or a sophisticated term loan and operating line of credit from a regional commercial lender, most companies borrow some amount of capital along their path to growth.

The use of debt in your capital structure (which is commonly known as leverage) will affect both your company's valuation and your overall cost of capital. The proper debt-to-equity ratio for your business will depend on a wide variety of factors, including:

- The impact that your obligation to make payments on the loan will have on the cash flow of your business

- Your costs related to obtaining the capital
- Your need for flexibility in your capital structure so that you can respond to changing economic or market conditions
- Your access to alternative sources of financing
- The nature and extent of your company's assets (tangible or intangible) that are available as collateral
- The level of dilution of ownership and control that your shareholders (and managers) are willing to tolerate
- Certain tax considerations (interest payments are a deductible expense, but dividends are not)

Determining the maximum amount of debt that a smaller growing company will ultimately be able to handle will usually involve balancing the costs of a loan and the risks of defaulting on it against the owners' and managers' desire to maintain control. Many entrepreneurs want to maintain control over their company's affairs, so they'll accept the risk inherent in taking on additional debt. Your ability to make payments must be carefully considered in the company's financial projections.

Another key issue in debt financing is *timing*. It is critical that you start the process of looking for debt capital early and not wait until you are in a real cash flow crunch, because if you wait, you will lose your negotiating leverage and weaken your company's financial position—a major turnoff to most lenders.

If your business plan and your cash flow projections reveal that making loan payments will strain your company's financial condition (or that you don't have sufficient collateral), then you should explore equity alternatives. It's simply not worth driving your company into bankruptcy solely to maintain maximum ownership and control. Remember the saying, 60 percent of *something* is worth a whole lot more than 100 percent of *nothing*.

You should also compare the level of debt financing you are planning to obtain with the typical ratios for businesses in your industry (such as those published by Robert Morris Associates or Dun & Bradstreet). Once you've figured out your optimum debt-to-equity ratio, you can look into the sources of debt financing, and the business and legal issues involved in borrowing funds from a commercial lender.

Also, you need to recognize that the recession has had a profound effect on lending and has made it more difficult for small businesses to obtain loans from traditional sources. In the second quarter of 2008, banks provided 27.2 million loans to small businesses. By September of 2010, that number had fallen by more than 4 million. While lending, like other areas of the economy, has begun to thaw, its melting is proving to be slow. Additionally, small banks devoted 87 percent of their total loan portfolios to small businesses in the past year, while large lenders have lagged behind at only 26 percent. To succeed at obtaining a traditional bank loan in this economy, businesses are going to have to be more organized, patient, and knowledgeable than in times past.

As of the fall of 2011, the state of the commercial lending industry was still in flux. The hope that many small and midsized companies had that 2011 would finally be the year when the credit freeze would thaw had begun to fade. The data from a March 2011 study by the FDIC showed that lending to smaller enterprises (loan size under $1,000,000) had dropped nearly 15 percent from the prior year, so things have only gotten worse, with spigots tightening and lending standards becoming more rigid. In a June 2011 poll of 1,200 entrepreneurs conducted by Pepperdine University, only 17 percent of loan-seeking business with revenues under $5,000,000 actually obtained debt financing. Regulatory pressures on banks to show that they are making smart loans and reducing risk have made it tougher for small businesses to meet the resulting stricter lending criteria, hampering and even sidelining their plans for growth and keeping our economy's growth rate in check.

For midsized and larger companies with assets, the picture is a bit rosier. With interest rates at 50-year historic lows, companies that are able to access the credit markets are doing so at a frenzied pace in order to lock in terms before rates start creeping up, which is predicted by late 2011, once the Federal Reserve ends its $600 billion Treasury bond buying programs and the effects of quantitative easing come to an end. For example, search engine giant Google issued its first-ever bond offering, raising $3 billion at a blended rate of a paltry 2.33 percent on bonds due between 2014 and 2021. Johnson & Johnson raised $3.75 billion and paid 2.15 percent on debt maturing in 2016. Similar offerings were pursued by Texas Instruments, Duke Energy, and Ryder Systems, and issuers with investment-grade securities raised more than $75 billion in the aggregate through May 2011. The presumption from a shareholder value perspective is that these companies will be able to deploy this cash for R&D, M&A, and other expansion projects that are capable of yielding far more than their total borrowing costs.

The Basics of Commercial Lending

Although you should consider all available alternative sources of debt financing (we'll cover them in Chapter 8), traditional bank loans from commercial lenders are the most common source of capital for small, growing companies. The frenzy of mergers and acquisitions by and among large regional banks has made it somewhat more difficult for small-business borrowers to build relationships with a commercial loan officer, who may be more focused on the bigger borrowers and customers. As a result, small-business owners have turned to smaller and neighborhood banks, which may be more receptive to winning their business, but may offer a limited range of services and have smaller lending limitations.

In addition, the recent retraction of traditional lending has spurred trends like peer-to-peer lending, microlending, barter networks, and crowdfunding. One phenomenon that has begun to emerge, especially for midsize businesses, is lending by hedge funds. Where liquidity for businesses has become scarce, hedge funds have found an opportunity to fill the gap in lending. Borrowing from hedge funds, however, has typically resulted in higher interest rates than have historically been available at banks.

Important Questions to Ask When Seeking Debt Capital

- How large a loan do you need?
- How will you use the money?
- Why will this type of capital benefit your business?
- When can you pay it back?
- How will you pay it back?
- Why are you and your company a good credit risk?
- What if the business fails or you can't repay the loan?
- Are you growing too fast or in a manner that will jeopardize your ability to repay?

Understanding the Lender's Perspective

Before you look at the types of loans that are available from commercial banks, it is important that you understand the perspective of the typical commercial loan officer when she analyzes a loan proposal. There's often a lot of confusion and resentment about the relationship between bankers and entrepreneurs. The entrepreneur believes the banker doesn't understand and appreciate his business requirements, while the loan officer may have had bad experiences

What Bankers *Really* Think When They're Evaluating Your Proposal

- *Have you shown sound business judgment in the past?* Have you always had a written plan with a timeline for specific business goals (accompanied by a backup contingency plan)?
- *Have you gone to see your banker only when you were in a tight spot* and needed immediate help? (This indicates a lack of planning.)
- *Do you inform your banker monthly of both good and bad news* (including the steps you have taken to mitigate the effects of the bad)?
- *Do you show your banker that you have proper financial controls in place?*
- *Do you discuss suppliers,* pricing strategies, marketing plans, and sales results?
- *Do you send customer mailings and samples of new products* to your banker?
- *Do you exhibit a clear understanding of your company's assets and liabilities, and the trends in your industry?*
- *Have you invited your banker to visit your business? Do you arrange for him to meet with your employees?*
- *Do you have a strong five-year strategic plan* for your business? Do you update it in a timely manner and share it with your banker?
- *Are you maintaining a strong growth plan* for your business, including its involvement in community projects? Have you considered cosponsoring community causes with your financial institution?
- *Do you invite input from your banker* as part of your future planning activities?
- *Are you actively addressing safety and environmental concerns* within your business?
- *Are you seen as a strong community leader?*
- *Are you willing to provide a guaranty* (as a reflection of your character and commitment)?

with entrepreneurs who expect to borrow more than a million dollars (collateralized only by a dream), or may have had to foreclose on a default by a small business.

So you see why it's in your best interest to understand the lender's perspective. Banks are in the business of selling money, and capital is the principal product in their inventory. Bankers, however, are often personally risk-averse, and the bank has internal controls and regulatory restrictions that affect their risk tolerance. The bank's shareholders and board of directors expect loan officers to take all the steps necessary to minimize the bank's risk in each transaction and obtain the maximum protection against default. As a result, the types of loans available to growing companies, the terms and conditions of those loans, and the steps the bank takes to protect its interest all have a direct relationship to the loan officer's assessment of risk.

The management team assigned to obtain debt financing from a commercial bank must embark on an immediate risk mitigation and risk management program to prepare for negotiating the loan documentation and must have a deep understanding of the lender's internal evaluation power and risk mitigation analysis. See Figures 7-1 and 7-2 for some insights into the internal evaluation process.

Preparing for Debt Financing

Minimizing and managing risk will always have a direct effect on the attractiveness and affordability of traditional debt financing. For a small and growing company, this will mean producing a loan proposal package that demonstrates the presence of a strong management team; an aggressive management program to handle internal control and accounts receivable; financial statements and projections that demonstrate both the ability to meet your repayment obligations

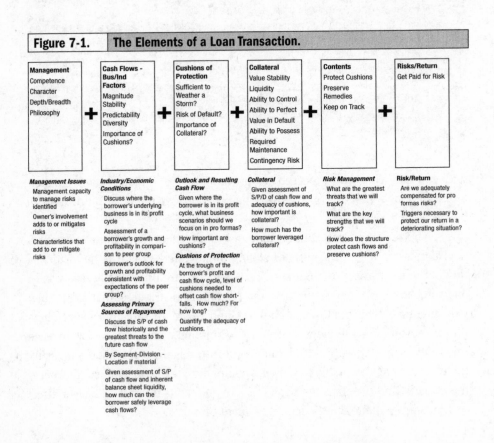

Figure 7-1.   The Elements of a Loan Transaction.

Management	Cash Flows - Bus/Ind Factors	Cushions of Protection	Collateral	Contents	Risks/Return
Competence	Magnitude	Sufficient to Weather a Storm?	Value Stability	Protect Cushions	Get Paid for Risk
Character	Stability		Liquidity	Preserve Remedies	
Depth/Breadth	Predictability	Risk of Default?	Ability to Control	Keep on Track	
Philosophy	Diversity	Importance of Collateral?	Ability to Perfect		
	Importance of Cushions?		Value in Default		
			Ability to Possess		
			Required Maintenance		
			Contingency Risk		

Management Issues

Management capacity to manage risks identified

Owner's involvement adds to or mitigates risks

Characteristics that add to or mitigate risks

Industry/Economic Conditions

Discuss where the borrower's underlying business is in its profit cycle

Assessment of a borrower's growth and profitability in comparison to peer group

Borrower's outlook for growth and profitability consistent with expectations of the peer group?

Assessing Primary Sources of Repayment

Discuss the S/P of cash flow historically and the greatest threats to the future cash flow

By Segment-Division - Location if material

Given assessment of S/P of cash flow and inherent balance sheet liquidity, how much can the borrower safely leverage cash flows?

Outlook and Resulting Cash Flow

Given where the borrower is in its profit cycle, what business scenarios should we focus on in pro formas?

How important are cushions?

Cushions of Protection

At the trough of the borrower's profit and cash flow cycle, level of cushions needed to offset cash flow short-falls. How much? For how long?

Quantify the adequacy of cushions.

Collateral

Given assessment of S/P/D of cash flow and adequacy of cushions, how important is collateral?

How much has the borrower leveraged collateral?

Risk Management

What are the greatest threats that we will track?

What are the key strengths that we will track?

How does the structure protect cash flows and preserve cushions?

Risk/Return

Are we adequately compensated for pro formas risks?

Triggers necessary to protect our return in a deteriorating situation?

Figure 7-2.   Risk Assessment Decision Tree of a Commercial Lender.

Evaluate the Credit Request
Competence
Borrower
Amount
Purpose
Type of Facility
Term/Amortization
Sources of Repayment
Rate/Relationship
Covenants/Controls
Fit with Credit Plan
Borrower's Needs, Desires & Priorities
Competitive Considerations
Does it make sense?
– for borrower
– the bank

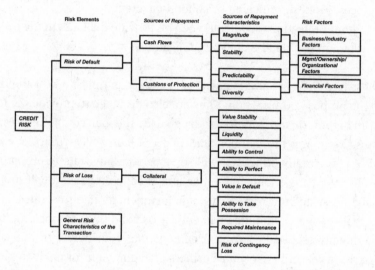

and solid relationships with suppliers, distributors, and employees; and an understanding of industry trends. In addition, many commercial loan officers will apply the traditional test of the four Cs of creditworthiness: *character* (reputation and honesty), *capacity* (business acumen and experience), *capital* (ability to meet debt-service payments), and *collateral* (access to assets that can be liquidated in the event of a default). Loan officers will assess all of these elements to determine your creditworthiness and the relative risk to the bank in making the proposed loan. Loan officers will also assess whether your company and your proposal offer the bank an opportunity to build a long-term banking relationship in which you will need additional services and larger loans down the road. Be sure to help the loan officer understand your long-term needs and your desire to build a relationship as well.

The Loan Proposal

Although the exact elements of a loan package will vary depending on a company's size, industry, and stage of development, most lenders will want the following fundamental questions answered:

- Who are you?
- How much capital do you need and when?
- How will the capital be allocated, and for what specific purposes will it be used?
- How will you service your debt obligations (application and processing fees, interest, principal, or balloon payments)?
- What protection (collateral) can you provide the bank in the event that you are unable to meet your obligations?

These questions are all designed to help the loan officer assess the risk factors in the proposed transaction. They are also designed to provide the loan officer with the information necessary to persuade the loan committee to approve the transaction. You must understand that the loan officer (once she is convinced of your creditworthiness) will serve as your advocate in presenting the proposal to the bank's loan committee and shepherding it through the bank's internal processing procedures. The loan documentation, terms, rates, and covenants that the loan committee will specify as conditions for making the loan will be directly related to how you demonstrate your ability to mitigate and manage risk as described in your business plan and your formal loan proposal.

The loan proposal should include the following categories of information, many of which you can borrow or modify from your business plan (as discussed in Chapter 3):

Summary of the request. This should provide an overview of the company's history, the amount of capital needed, the proposed repayment terms, the intended use of the capital, and the collateral available to secure the loan.

Borrower's history. Give a brief background of your company; its capital structure; its founders; its stage of development and plans for growth; a list of your customers, suppliers, and service providers; your management structure and philosophy; your main products and services; and an overview of any intellectual property that you own or have developed.

Market data. This section should include an overview of trends in your industry; the size of the market; your market share; an assessment of the competition; your sustainable competitive advantages; your marketing, public relations, and advertising strategies; market research studies; and relevant future trends in your industry.

Financial information. Provide multiscenario financial statements (best case/expected case/worst case), federal and state tax returns, company valuations or appraisals of key assets, your current balance sheet, credit references, and a two-year income statement. The role of the capital requested in your plans for growth, an allocation of the loan proceeds, and your ability to repay must be carefully explained, and your discussion of your ability to make your loan repayments on a timely basis must be supported by a three-year projected cash flow statement broken out in a monthly format. Remember that when you present the collateral that might be available to support your loan request, you should not assume that the lender will view the collateral on a dollar-for-dollar basis. For example, real estate valued at $100,000 might be viewed by the lender as representing only between $50,000 and $85,000 (50 to 85 percent) of actual loan collateral value. Other assets, such as equipment, inventory, and accounts receivable, might have a loan collateral value of between 0 and 70 percent in the eyes of the lender.

Schedules and exhibits. As part of the loan proposal, you should also assemble certain key documents, such as agreements with strategic vendors or customers, insurance policies, leases, and employment agreements, to be attached as exhibits. Résumés of your company's principals, recent news articles about the company, a picture of your products or your site, and an organizational chart should also be appended as exhibits to the loan proposal.

Figure 7-3 gives an overview of things that you should *avoid* in preparing your proposal.

Types of Commercial Bank Loans

There are a number of types of loans available from a commercial bank, one or more of which could be tailored to meet your specific requirements. Loans are usually categorized by the term of the loan, the expected use of the proceeds, and the amount of money to be borrowed. The availability of various

Figure 7-3.	The Most Common Reasons Loan Proposals are Rejected.

- Unrealistically low expense forecasts
- Lack of a completed loan proposal
- Inability to take constructive criticism
- Underestimated capital requirements
- Little or no management experience in the underlying industry
- Overstated revenue projections
- Attempts to play one lender against another
- Lack of adequate collateral
- Poor communication skills
- Cash flow projections that do not demonstrate an ability to repay the loan
- Cash flow projections without adequate supporting documentation or explanatory footnotes
- Lack of understanding of the loan proposal and approval process
- Very aggressive growth plans or financial projections

types of loans will depend on both the nature of your industry and the bank's assessment of your creditworthiness. The types of loans traditionally available include the following.

Short-Term Loans. These are ordinarily used for a specific purpose, with the lender's expectation being that the loan will be repaid at the end of the project. For example, a seasonal business may borrow capital in order to build up its inventory in preparation for the peak season; when the season ends, the lender expects to be repaid immediately. Similarly, a short-term loan could be used to cover a period when the company's customers or clients are in arrears; when the accounts receivable are collected, the loan is to be repaid.

A short-term loan is usually made in the form of a promissory note payable on demand. It may be secured by the inventory or accounts receivable that the loan is designed to cover, or it may be unsecured (that is, no collateral is required). Unless a company is a start-up or is operating in a highly volatile industry (increasing the risk in the eyes of the lender), most short-term loans will be unsecured, thereby keeping the loan documentation and the bank's processing time and costs to a minimum.

Lenders generally view short-term loans as "self-liquidating" in that they can be repaid by foreclosing on the current assets that the loan has financed. Because the bank's transaction costs are low, and because it perceives a lower risk during this short period, short-term loans can be easier for a growing business to obtain. Short-term borrowing can also serve as an excellent means of establishing a relationship with a bank and demonstrating your creditworthiness.

Operating Lines of Credit. Lines of credit consist of a specific amount of capital that is made available to a company on an "as needed" basis over a specified period of time. A line of credit may be short-term (60 to 120 days) or intermediate-term (one to three years), renewable or nonrenewable, and at a fixed or a fluctuating rate of interest. Be especially careful to negotiate ceilings on interest rates; to avoid excessive processing, application, and related "up-front" fees (such as origination and commitment fees); and to ensure that repayment schedules won't be an undue strain for you. You should also ensure that your obligations to make payments against the line of credit are consistent with your anticipated cash flow projections.

Intermediate-Term Loans. These loans are usually provided over a three- to five-year period for the purposes of acquiring equipment, fixtures, furniture, and supplies; expanding existing facilities; acquiring another business; or providing working capital. These loans are almost always secured not only by the assets being purchased with the loan proceeds, but also by the company's other assets, such as inventory, accounts receivable, equipment, and real estate. This arrangement usually calls for a loan agreement, which typically includes restrictive covenants that govern the company's operation and management during the term of the loan. The covenants are designed to protect the lender's interests and to ensure that all payments are made on time, before any dividends, employee bonuses, or noncritical expenses are paid.

Long-Term Loans. These are generally extended for specific, highly secured transactions, such as the purchase of real estate or a multiuse business facility. When such a purchase is being made, a lender will consider extending a long-term loan to a small company for 65 to 80 percent of the appraised value of the land or building. (As a general rule, commercial banks don't provide long-term financing to small businesses. The risk of market fluctuations and business failure over a 10- or 20-year term is simply too high for a commercial lender to feel comfortable with such a loan.)

Letters of Credit. These are issued by commercial banks solely in connection with international sales transactions, to expedite the shipping and payment process for those transactions. In a typical letter-of-credit scenario, the seller demands that payment be made in the form of a letter of credit, and the buyer must then make arrangements with its bank to issue the letter of credit. The buyer's bank, often in conjunction with a corresponding bank, will then communicate with the seller of the goods, explaining the documents that it requires (such as a negotiable bill of lading) as a condition for releasing the funds.

It is important to understand that the bank issuing the letter of credit may be liable to the seller for payment if the bill of lading and the related documents are properly presented, *even if* there are problems in the performance of the underlying contract between the buyer and the seller. Any defenses that are available to the buyer relating to the underlying contract are generally not available to the bank that issued the letter of credit. Recently, the *standby letter of credit* has emerged as an indirect method of debt financing that serves as a guaranty of performance. A bank, on behalf of a customer, often issues standby letters of credit to secure payments to a builder, landlord, or supplier. The operative term of such an instrument is *standby* because if the transaction goes as planned, the instrument will never be drawn upon.

Okay, You Have Submitted Your Loan Proposal; Now What?

Once you have submitted your loan proposal, the process that follows should *not* be a mystery, nor should it be indefinite. Here are some key questions to ask your commercial loan officer once the proposal has begun to go through the evaluation process:

- What are the top three strengths and weaknesses in my proposal?
- Does this proposal seem to be a fit with the bank's current lending practices and objectives?
- What problems or challenges do you foresee, and how can we overcome or mitigate these negative factors?
- What key terms or covenants should we anticipate, and why?
- What transaction or closing costs should we anticipate?
- How will the decision be made?
- How long will the process take?
- If we are rejected, will we have another chance to amend our proposal and resubmit? Would that be a waste of time?
- Are there any other lenders or sources of debt capital that you would recommend?

Negotiating the Loan Documents

Negotiating the financing documents requires a delicate balance between the lender's requirements and your needs. The lender will want to protect all of the rights and remedies that may be available to it to mitigate the risk of loan default, while you will want to minimize the level of control the lender exercises and achieve a return on your assets that greatly exceeds your debt-service payments.

Before we examine each document involved in a typical debt financing, you'll need to understand some general rules of loan negotiation:

Interest rates. These will generally be calculated in accordance with prevailing market rates, the degree of risk inherent in the proposed transaction, the extent of any preexisting relationship you may have with the lender, and the cost of administering the loan.

Collateral. You may have to secure the loan by pledging assets that have a value equal to or greater than the proceeds of the loan. Under such circumstances, try to keep certain assets of the business outside the pledge agreement so that they are available to serve as security in the event that you need more money later. Beyond the traditional forms of tangible assets that may be offered to the lender, also consider intangibles (such as assignment of lease rights, key-man insurance, or intellectual property) as candidates for collateral. Naturally, the loss of these assets could be very costly to a firm in the event of default, and they should be pledged only when you're easily able to repay the loan.

Restrictive covenants. These provisions are designed to protect the lender's interests, and the typical loan agreement will contain several kinds.

Affirmative covenants encompass your obligations (and those of your subsidiaries, except as otherwise provided) during the period that the loan is outstanding, and may include the following affirmative acts that you must do:

- Furnish audited financial statements (income and expenses and balance sheets) at regular intervals (usually quarterly and annually, with the annual statement to be prepared and certified by an independent certified public accountant).
- Furnish copies of all financial statements, reports, and returns that are sent to shareholders or to government agencies.
- Provide access to your properties, books of account, and records.

- Keep and maintain proper books of account.
- Comply with all applicable laws, rules, and regulations.
- Maintain your corporate existence (as well as that of any subsidiaries) and all rights and privileges.
- Maintain all property in good order and repair.
- Maintain any agreed-upon dollar amount of net worth (or any agreed-upon ratio of current assets to current liabilities).
- Keep and maintain proper and adequate insurance on all assets.
- Pay and discharge all indebtedness and all taxes as and when they are due.
- Purchase and pay premiums due on life insurance on named key personnel (wherein the company is named as beneficiary).

Negative covenants (generally negotiable) encompass certain actions for which you must obtain the lender's consent; they depend in large part on your company's financial strength and its economic and operational requirements. In general, you must obtain the lender's consent in order to:

- Engage in any business that is not related to your present business.
- Create any mortgage, lien, or other security other than pending security on the property securing the loan.
- Create any mortgage, lien, or other encumbrance, including conditional sales agreements, other title-retention agreements, and lease-purchase agreements, on any property of the company or your subsidiaries (unless excepted).
- Incur any new indebtedness except for trade credit or renewals, extensions, or refunding of any current indebtedness. (Your right to incur indebtedness may be conditioned on compliance with a specified ratio—actual or pro forma—of pretax income to interest expense for a designated period.
- Enter into leases of real or personal property as lessee in excess of a specified aggregate amount. (Your right to make leases may be conditioned on compliance with a specified ratio—actual or pro forma—of pretax income to fixed charges for a designated period.)
- Purchase, redeem, or otherwise acquire (or retire for cash) any of the company's capital stock in excess of a specified amount or for reserves set aside to redeem preferred stock.

- Pay any cash dividends (with stated exceptions), such as those from after-tax earnings earned subsequent to a specified date or in excess of a specified amount.
- Make loans or advances to or investments in any person or entity other than your subsidiaries.
- Merge or consolidate with any other corporation, or sell or lease substantially all of your assets. There may be exceptions in cases where your company is the surviving corporation.
- Permit your net worth or current assets to fall below a specified level.
- Permit capital expenditures that exceed a specified amount (which may be on an annual basis, with or without the right to cumulate).
- Permit officers' and directors' remuneration to exceed a specified level.
- Sell or dispose of all the stock of a subsidiary (subject to permitted exceptions) or permit subsidiaries to incur debt (other than trade debt).

Covenants may be serious impediments to your company's ability to grow and prosper over the long run. Review covenants carefully for consistency with other corporate documents, such as your bylaws and shareholders' agreements. However, given the rapid changes in the area of lender-liability law, some commercial bankers are backing away from the level of control that has traditionally been imposed on a borrower.

Prepayment rights. Regardless of the actual term of the loan, negotiate for the right to prepay the principal of the loan without penalty and without special repayment charges. Many commercial lenders seek to attach prepayment charges that have a fixed rate of interest in order to ensure that they earn a minimum rate of return over the projected life of the loan.

Hidden costs and fees. These might include closing costs, processing fees, filing fees, late charges, attorneys' fees, out-of-pocket-expense reimbursement (couriers, travel, photocopying, and so on), court costs, and auditing or inspection fees in connection with the loan. Another way that commercial lenders earn extra money on a loan is to impose depository restrictions on you, such as a restrictive covenant requiring you to maintain a certain balance in your company's operating account or to use the bank as a depository as a condition to closing on the loan.

Searching for a Business Loan Online

As financial services available on the Internet continue to expand, the areas of small-business and commercial lending have also developed into an active industry. There are a wide variety of lenders, loan aggregators, and related resources available online, including:

- www.smallbusinessloans.com
- www.lendingtree.com
- www.businessfinance.com
- www.wellsfargo.com
- www.sba.gov
- www.eloan.com
- www.paramountmerchantfunding.com
- www.prudential.com
- www.ioucentral.com
- www.rapidadvance.com
- www.merchantloans.com

Understanding the Legal Documents

Anytime you borrow money, you'll have to sign documents delineating the terms of the loan—how much is being borrowed, what collateral you'll be using, what the lender's interest is, and your promise to repay the debt, including guarantees.

The Loan Agreement

The loan agreement sets forth all the terms and conditions of the transaction between you and the lender. The key provisions include the amount, the term, repayment schedules and procedures, special fees, insurance requirements, special conditions to closing, restrictive covenants, the company's representations and warranties (with respect to its status, capacity, ability to repay, title to properties, litigation, and so on), events of default, and remedies available to the lender in the event of default. Your attorney and accountant should review the provisions of the loan agreement and the implications of the covenants carefully. They should also analyze the long-term legal and financial impact of the restrictive covenants. You should negotiate to establish a timetable under which certain covenants will be removed or modified as your ability to repay is clearly demonstrated.

The Security Agreement

The security agreement identifies the collateral you'll pledge in order to secure the loan, usually referencing terms of the loan agreement and the promissory note (especially with respect to restrictions on the use of the collateral and procedures in the event of default). The remedies available to the lender in the event of default range from selling the collateral at a public auction to taking possession of the collateral. The proceeds of any alternative chosen by the lender will be used principally to repay the outstanding balance of the loan. A sample security agreement is given in the appendix.

The Financing Statement

The financing statement records the lender's interests in the collateral and is filed with the state and local corporate and land-records authorities. It's designed to give notice to your company's other potential creditors that a security interest in the collateral specified in the financing statement that will take precedence over any subsequent claim has been granted. Specific rules regarding this document and the priority of competing creditors can be found in your state's version of the Uniform Commercial Code (UCC).

The Promissory Note

The promissory note serves as evidence of your obligation to the lender. Many of its terms are also included in the more comprehensive loan agreement (such as the interest rate, the length of the term, the repayment schedule, your ability to prepay without penalty, the conditions under which the lender may declare default, and the rights and remedies available to the lender upon default). You'll find a sample promissory note in the appendix.

The Guaranty

The guaranty, which you personally execute, serves as further security to mitigate the risk of the transaction to the lender. You and your legal counsel should carefully review and negotiate the conditions of the guaranty, especially with respect to its term, its scope, the rights of the lender in the event of default, and the type of guaranty provided. For example, under certain circumstances, the lender can be forced to exhaust all possible remedies before proceeding against you, or may be limited to proceeding against certain of your assets. Similarly, the extent of the guaranty could be negotiated so that it is reduced annually as your company grows stronger and its ability to meet its repayment schedule becomes more evident.

Although bankers understand and acknowledge an entrepreneur's resistance to providing a personal guaranty, they will often seek this protection from the company's principals to further mitigate their risk. This is especially true if your business is highly leveraged, has operated for fewer than three years, or pays bonuses that absorb most of its profits. Why do lenders usually insist on these protections? The lender's primary goal is to influence management to treat the funds borrowed from the bank prudently. In essence, the guaranty is a psychological tool, designed to keep pressure on the principals of the company to ensure prompt and regular repayment.

Periodic Assessment of Banking Relationships

Recognizing the importance of growing businesses to the economy, many commercial lenders have begun to compete fiercely for the deposits of smaller companies, and while they seem anxious to offer services, they are not as quick to offer loans at affordable rates during recessionary times. It's wise to assess your banking relationship periodically to ensure that you're getting the best rates and services available to businesses of your size within your industry. That doesn't mean that you should discard a long-standing and harmonious banking relationship over a one-percentage-point difference in an interest rate, but it does mean that you shouldn't remain loyal to a bank that doesn't offer a full range of services that meet your needs just because you've "banked there for years." In periodically assessing the relationship, ask yourself:

- When did you last hear from your designated loan officer?
- What was the bank's reaction to your most recent request for another term loan or an increase in your operating line of credit?
- How well does the bank know and understand your industry?
- How strict has the bank been in enforcing loan covenants, restrictions, or late charges?
- What support services has the bank offered you?
- How do the bank's interest rates and loan terms compare with those from other local commercial lenders?
- What is the bank's general reputation in the business community? Has it done anything lately to enhance or damage its reputation?
- Is the bank itself basically operating on a solid financial foundation?

- Is the bank large enough to grow with your financial needs as your business expands and you require additional capital? (This should be considered early in the company's development so that you do not outgrow the relationship just at the time when you need it the most.)
- Does this bank *really* want your company as a customer? What has it done for you lately to demonstrate this?

In this age of "relationship banking," bankers understand that if they have a thorough understanding of your company's operations, they will be in a better position to structure commercial loan arrangements that are capable of satisfying your needs. For example, if your business is seasonal or reflects cyclical economic trends, it may at first blush appear to be a poor candidate for financing, because bankers like consistency and dislike volatility. But if the banker understands the trends within your industry, loans can often be made based on repayment programs that are tied to your company's particular cash flow needs. Conversely, banks that are unfamiliar with your business operations tend to become fair-weather lenders. This lack of understanding perpetuates the myth that bankers are willing to provide funding only when there is little need for it.

Chapter 8

Leasing, Factoring, and Government Programs

Traditional sources of debt financing from commercial banks are not your only choices when you are trying to establish credit and borrow money. Your business—especially if it's in an early stage of its development—simply may not have the collateral or the credit history to qualify for traditional debt financing. This chapter will look at alternative debt strategies and lending services, which include:

> *Leasing.* A leasing company (the lessor) acquires real estate, equipment, or other fixed assets, then executes a contract with a second party (the lessee), who will use the asset. The lessee (that's you) makes fixed

payments to the lessor for a specified period of time. Leasing provides a flexible, creative alternative to purchasing property.

Factoring. Here a business (a factor) buys your receivables, usually at a steep discount. Let's say you have the opportunity to expand, but you don't have enough cash to do so. If you have outstanding receivables from reliable payers, you might be able to find a factor who will give you a percentage of those receivables in cash right away, in exchange for 100 percent of the receivables when they are paid. Factoring is a risk-driven business; depending on the overall conditions in your industry and the relative risks in collecting from the people who owe your business money, factors will discount the value of your receivables by 50 to 95 percent. Factoring is an expedient option when other short-term financing, such as a working-capital loan or a revolving line of credit, is unavailable.

Small Business Administration (SBA) guaranteed loans. These are administered by a federal agency that was created to provide assistance to businesses that lack the access to capital markets (stock and bond markets) enjoyed by larger, more creditworthy corporations.

State and local programs. In an effort to improve their local economies, most states, and many municipalities and counties, sponsor a variety of sources of public funding for certain categories of small businesses. Nearly all states have some form of economic development agency or finance authority that makes loans or offers loan guarantees to small businesses. State commerce departments often have direct or participating loan programs that may be even more attractive than SBA-guaranteed programs. In many regions, there are also specialized programs designed to help women and minorities or to encourage specific industries or policy objectives, such as environmental, alternative energy, biotechnology, or health-care companies. Since programs differ from state to state, it would be impractical to describe them all here. You'll find a few examples of good programs in the appendix. Check with your state and local authorities.

Leasing

Regardless of changes in tax laws and accounting regulations, leasing's greatest appeal continues to be that it permits companies to acquire assets with very little or no down payment. Most rapidly growing companies desperately need the use, but not necessarily the ownership, of certain resources to fuel and maintain their growth. Therefore, leasing offers an alternative to ownership. Monthly lease payments are made in lieu of debt-service payments.

Types of Leases

There are two types of leases: operating leases and finance leases. Most leases for small pieces of office equipment—fax machines, copiers, and so on—are operating leases, in which ownership of the machines reverts to the vendor at the end of the lease term. For tax purposes, operating-lease payments are treated as an operating expense, not a capital investment, and are deducted from your operating revenues immediately. In addition, the lease does not appear as a liability on your balance sheet the way a loan to purchase the same equipment would. That will make it easier for you to borrow money in the future.

Finance leases, also known as full-payout or closed-end leases, require you to purchase the equipment at the end of the lease period at a percentage of the original price or for a nominal amount. Since a finance lease is, in effect, a loan in which ownership of the equipment eventually passes to you, the equipment is treated as a depreciable asset for tax purposes, and the lease will appear on your balance sheet as a liability.

So which option is better for you? The key factors are your cash position, the availability and cost of borrowing, and the potential obsolescence of the equipment. Companies with strong cash positions and good banking relationships are often best served by buying or borrowing equipment that will have a long life. If obsolescence is a concern, a short-term operating lease will bring flexibility. But if cash flow is a problem and the equipment will remain viable for years, a long-term finance lease with a final residual payment will give you the lowest payments plus a purchase option.

Who Should Lease?

Financing new equipment—from computers to phone systems to capital equipment—is a major issue for many business owners. You may want to consider leasing even if you do have the cash to purchase the assets you'll need to grow your business. You may find that by leasing, you can regulate your cash flow more effectively because you have predictable, regular monthly installments, as opposed to a single lump-sum payment. Plus, leasing can help you avoid tying up lines of credit or money that you might want to use for another area of your business.

Advantages and Disadvantages of Leasing

Ownership. The most obvious downside to leasing is that when the lease runs out, you don't own the equipment. Of course, this may also be an advantage, particularly for equipment like computers, where technology changes very quickly.

Total expense. Leasing is almost always more expensive than buying, assuming that you don't need a loan to make the purchase. For example, a three-year lease for a $5,000 computer system (at a typical rate of $40 per month per $1,000) will cost you a total of $7,200.

Finding funds. Lease arrangements are usually more liberal than commercial loans are. While a bank might require two or three years of business records before granting a loan, many leasing companies will evaluate your credit history over shorter terms (six months is fairly typical). That can be a significant advantage for a start-up business.

Cash flow. This is the primary advantage to leasing. It eliminates a large, single expense that may drain your cash flow, freeing funds for other day-to-day needs.

Taxes. Leasing almost always allows you to expense your equipment costs, meaning that your lease payments can be deducted as business expenses. On the other hand, buying may allow you to deduct up to $18,000 worth of equipment in the year it is purchased; anything above that amount has to be depreciated over several years. With the first-year deduction, the real cost of a $5,000 computer system may be only $3,400.

Technology needs. Technology advances at a rapid rate. If you buy a computer or some other type of high-tech equipment outright, in two or three years you may find yourself with outdated equipment that has no discernible resale value. Leasing may allow you to try out new equipment and update your system regularly to stay on top of the technology curve.

The Process

An effective way to organize the process is to send a simple fill-in-the-blanks bid form like the one in Figure 8-1 to several leasing companies that you think might be interested in getting your business. Larger companies do this all the time, and there's no reason you can't do it too. Prospective lessors will still need to do thorough credit checks, but if you have a well-designed bid form, the rest of the process should be greatly streamlined.

Figure 8-1.	Bid Request Form.

TO BE FILLED IN BY THE COMPANY (YOU):

Company name:_____
    1. (For the record, tell lessors the name of the entity that is seeking leasing
       information.)

Product:_____
(Supply the name of the equipment manufacturer and model number.)

Features:_____
(Indicate any additional features that might increase or decrease the resale value.)

Cost to company:_____
(Tell lessors the best price quoted for the equipment listed.)

List price:_____
(What does the equipment list for? This may influence the residual value at the
end of the lease.)

Lease start date:_____
(When do you propose to start making payments? For comparison, you want
everyone on the same schedule.)

Payment frequency:_____
(Specify how you propose to pay—for example, monthly in advance or in arrears.
While leasing companies may have different preferences, you want all bidders to
use the same assumptions.)

Bid due date:_____
(To simplify the process, give everyone the same deadline. As a courtesy, tell lessors, either here or elsewhere on the form, when the winner will by notified.)

Lease term:_____
(Tell lessors how long you intend to use the equipment, recognizing that there
are some standards. If you like, you can ask lessors to price more than one lease
term.)

Notes:_____
_____
_____
_____
_____
_____
_____
_____
_____

_____

_____
_____
_____

(Note here any other considerations you want lessors to be aware of—for instance, that the lease should be structured as an operating lease or a full-payout lease.)

TO BE FILLED IN BY THE BIDDER:

Bidder:_____
(The name of the leasing company submitting the bid.)

Lease rate:_____
(You want lessors to quote you a specific price for the term or terms you ask for.)

Lease Terms

Here are some of the issues to look for when you negotiate your lease or review your lease contract:

Length of the lease. This is often called the term of the lease, and it is usually between 12 and 36 months. The shorter the term, the higher your monthly payments will be. A term of 36 months is typical for a computer lease, although you might want to look at a 24-month lease to keep up with changing technology.

Total cost. Analyze all the charges that you will be accountable for over the entire length of your lease. These include your down payment, monthly payments, a security deposit, any insurance charges, and service or repair costs.

Cancellation clause. This allows you to break your lease, although you will be liable for substantial penalties. If you close your business, change its focus, or no longer need a piece of equipment, you won't be liable for the remaining payments over the entire term of the lease.

Assignment. Find out whether you can assign the lease to another party, and if so, what costs will apply. For example, if you are selling or reorganizing all or part of your company, you want to factor these costs in as part of the transaction.

Modern-equipment substitution. If technology changes rapidly, you might want to consider this option. This allows you to update or exchange your equipment so that you don't get stuck with something that's obsolete.

Service plans. Find out whether your lease comes with an on-site plan, and if so, determine its length. If the lease includes only one year of on-site service, you may need to buy a service contract for the remainder of the lease; if you do not do so, you will be responsible for all repairs after the first year. Also, be sure the contract specifies when the service will be performed (ideally, the next business day after you've notified the lessor of the problem).

When a Lease Is Not a Lease

Read the fine print of any lease you sign. The IRS considers some leases to be capital purchases, which means that you will not be able to deduct your monthly payments. A capital purchase has occurred if under your lease agreement you meet one of the following criteria:

- You have a "bargain buyout" in which you can purchase the machine for a token amount at the end of the lease.
- You are leasing the machine for 75 percent of its useful life.
- The total amount you pay for the equipment during the period of your lease equals more than 90 percent of the fair market value of the machine. Keep in mind that payments include finance charges and sales tax; remember to deduct these charges to find the true price you are paying for the equipment.

Where Do I Find a Lessor?

For a list of lessors that might be interested in your transaction, contact the Equipment Leasing and Finance Association of America, 1825 K Street, NW, Suite 900, Washington, DC 20006, or call (202) 238-3400. Or check the association's web site at www.elfaonline.com.

Factoring

The roots of factoring can be traced back 4,000 years to the time of Hammurabi, when merchants would sell their accounts receivables to a third-party financier at a discount. Modern-day factoring is surprisingly similar. It is simply the process of purchasing accounts receivable, or invoices, from a business at a discount. Factoring provides the business that is selling its receivables with immediate cash and earns investors a desirable rate of return on their money. In modern times, factoring was revived first in the garment industry. Then

World War II came along and created a need for the financing of war materials. Congress subsequently passed the Uniform Commercial Code (UCC), which allows business owners to file a lien on receivables or inventory. Factoring then took root in manufacturing and has expanded into other industries, including distribution, business-to-business services, high tech, and health care.

Factoring's swift growth can be attributed to tougher loan requirements and the difficulties that start-up and growing companies have in obtaining capital. An increasing number of small and midsize companies are turning to it as a cash-management tool. They have learned what big corporations have known all along: Factoring is a viable solution to a need that nearly every business has, and its benefits often outweigh its costs.

If there is a single point of vulnerability in most companies, it's accounts receivable. That's because almost all entrepreneurial companies make the mistake—especially in their early or fast-growth stages—of paying much more attention to making sales than to collecting receivables.

Under the traditional factoring arrangement, a company sells its accounts receivables to a third party in exchange for immediate cash. The third party, or "factor," assumes the risk of collection in exchange for the ability to purchase the accounts receivable at a discount, typically 50 to 95 percent of the face value of the invoices. The amount of the discount is usually determined by how likely it is that the debtors will default and by prevailing interest rates. Once the factor collects the balance, he returns the discount to the company, minus a 3 to 5 percent fee.

Here's how factoring might work: Say your company has $100,000 in accounts receivable, and you want to sell them to raise capital to help expand your business. You might sell the receivables at a 60 percent discount, thus acquiring $40,000 cash immediately. Once the factor has collected all the receivables—and in this example, we'll assume that all of them are collected—you'll receive the remaining $60,000, minus the factor's fee of, say, 5 percent, or $5,000.

Types of Factoring

The example just presented is oversimplified. There are two basic types of factoring agreements: recourse factoring and nonrecourse factoring. In a recourse agreement, you agree to repurchase or pay for any invoices that the factor cannot collect from your customers. The factor still agrees to advance you money and take on the collection responsibility, and he still earns a fee for it. But if the customers don't pay, the invoices are turned back to you for payment. This eliminates any financial risk for the factor. In our example, if the factoring agreement were a recourse agreement and the factor failed to collect $10,000 of the receivables, you would pay the factor the $10,000, and it would be up to you to collect from the customer.

A nonrecourse agreement has no repurchase or repayment provision. In other words, once the factor has purchased the invoice, she owns it, whether it's collectible or not. Returning to our example, if the factor fails to collect that $10,000 from the customers, the factor is out the money; you don't have to pay the factor or try to collect from the customer. To compensate for this additional risk, the factoring fee on a nonrecourse agreement is slightly higher than that on a recourse agreement, typically 10 to 20 percent.

Under a nonrecourse agreement, factors are not obliged to buy every invoice the client presents. They can reject invoices from customers that they deem to be uncreditworthy.

Is Factoring for Your Company?

Factoring can help the following types of companies:

New companies. Early-stage companies often lack the financial track record required for bank financing.

High-growth companies. Factoring can benefit companies that are growing so quickly that traditional loans are unavailable. Fast growth often requires cash. Your cash flow may be negative as your company's receivables and payables expand. A bank may reject a loan application from a fast-growth company because such a company presents a higher risk than a stable-growth company, especially if the receivables are not controlled properly.

Government contractors. Many small and midsize government contractors use factoring to help them navigate through choppy cash flow periods, and factors generally find the "full faith and credit" of the federal government very attractive unless there are performance issues or scope-of-contract disputes.

Turnaround situations. Companies that have had a glitch in their operations can use factoring to reposition themselves.

Seasonal businesses. Factoring can benefit seasonal businesses such as textiles, carpet, electronics, and clothing. Seasonal businesses may have a cash crunch at certain times of the year, which makes them natural candidates for factoring.

Advantages of Factoring

Unlimited capital. Factoring is the only financing source that grows with your sales. It gives you the ability to meet increasing demand, because as your sales increase, more money becomes immediately available to you.

No debt incurred. Factoring is not a loan, so you don't incur any debt. This can make your balance sheet very attractive, which makes it easier for you to obtain other financing or, ultimately, to sell the company.

Elimination of bad debt. The risk of bad debt can be fully assumed by a non-recourse factor, thus eliminating this expense from your income statement.

No loss of business equity. Ownership percentages are unchanged with a factoring arrangement (unlike most venture capital arrangements).

Offers credit terms to your customers. Factoring allows your business to be more competitive by offering credit terms to potential and current customers without the risk of a negative impact on cash flow.

Leverages off your customers' credit. Your company doesn't need to be creditworthy to factor its invoices. In fact, it's not necessary for it to have been in business for three years, or be profitable, or meet any other conventional lender qualifications to factor. If you have a creditworthy customer, you can qualify for a factoring arrangement.

Establishes good credit for your business. Paying your company's bills in a timely manner is less of a challenge when you have improved cash flow. Factoring makes cash immediately available so that you can keep cash flow steady.

Invoice-processing service. You can greatly reduce your cost of processing invoices because the factor handles much of the work. Mailing invoices (addressing envelopes, stuffing them, and paying for postage), posting invoices to a computer system, depositing checks, entering payments on the computer, and producing regular reports can be delegated to the factor.

Professional collections. A good factor can handle collections more professionally and more productively than you can internally. This could translate into further cost savings for your business.

Easy and fast. You don't need tax returns, personal financial statements, business plans, or projections to process a factoring application. Usually, your account is established within about one week of the receipt of signed contracts. Thereafter, accepted invoices are converted to cash within 24 hours. Bureaucracy prohibits banks from processing loans that fast.

Disadvantages of Factoring

Risk of fiscal addiction. If you're not careful, your company can get caught in a vicious cycle. Over time, the cost of factoring may eat away your profits to the point that you need to factor again just to pay for the next month's operations. A cash flow consultant can sometimes help—for example, by figuring out a way to stretch vendors out a bit further or by suggesting a line of credit. These options may eventually enable you to wean your company away from factoring.

Intrusion. Some owners perceive factoring as being intrusive, because the factoring company verifies and monitors the collection of receivables.

Cost. Factored capital tends to be more expensive than bank loans. The commission in a factoring agreement varies, depending on the volume of invoices, the average size of the invoices, and an analysis of your customer list.

What Do Factors Look for?

Companies that are considering factoring should have a variety of creditworthy customers and solid financial statements. Factors often judge the strength of a company by the quality and distribution of its customers. Your company's financial strength and management will be analyzed. Having professionals on your team (such as CPAs, attorneys, and financial consultants) can help you maintain orderly financial statements.

Where Do I Find a Factor?

To find a factoring company, contact the Commercial Finance Association at 370 Seventh AVE, Suite 1801, New York, NY 10001; call (212) 792-9390; or visit the web site at www.cfa.com. The Commercial Finance Association is an international and national trade association for the asset-based financial-services industry, including factors.

A Creative Alternative to Factoring

Traditionally, small and midsize businesses (SMBs) have had fewer options for increasing liquidity than larger companies. While large companies can tap into the commercial paper market, for instance, SMBs rely heavily on institutions like banks, asset-based lenders, and factors to raise capital. With fewer financing options at their disposal, many SMBs end up paying too much for capital, and are forced to sign restrictive liens or personal guarantees to get the money they need. They are more vulnerable than large companies to being underfunded when capital providers deny their applications or, worse, go out of business.

The recent economic downturn exposed the precarious position of SMBs when traditional financial institutions tighten their grip on credit. Since the financial crisis, otherwise healthy businesses have been unable to get the full amount of financing that they need, and have been forced to pay exorbitant rates for what they can get. Government programs meant to spur lending have not been sufficient to overcome those lenders' aversion to risk. The total value of bank loans to small businesses dropped 47 percent from 2007 to 2009, according to the Federal Financial Institutions Examination Council. We are entering a "new normal" of SMB financing, where in order to achieve growth and success, SMBs must look beyond traditional financial institutions to source capital.

In recent years, certain innovative companies have sought to provide businesses with alternative financial solutions. One such company is the *Receivables Exchange*, which was launched in the fall of 2008, on the eve of the financial crisis. The exchange was conceived by its founders, Justin Brownhill and Nicolas Perkin, as a way for businesses to increase their liquidity more flexibly and affordably, an ever-present need that the economic downturn made more pressing. The founders combined the best of factoring with recent advances in technology (specifically, online marketplaces and easier access to lien filings and other credit information) to create an improved, state-of-the-art platform for accounts receivable financing. The company has grown rapidly since its founding, as more and more businesses are seeking alternatives to traditional financing (or capital to supplement existing financing). It grew nearly 500 percent in 2010 alone, and counts thousands of U.S. business-to-business (B2B) companies as its customers, with more joining every day.

The Receivables Exchange is an online marketplace for working-capital financing, where businesses auction their commercial receivables to accredited institutional investors, in real time, to increase their liquidity flexibly and affordably. It's a market-based solution that opens up the sale of receivables to competition from multiple buyers. Businesses with receivables (payments due to them from their customers) post them to an electronic auction platform, and buyers bid to purchase them, with the buyer that comes closest to the set terms winning the auction. This competition drives down the cost of capital for businesses. On average, companies that sell on the exchange get 98 to 99 cents on the dollar for their receivables.

Many businesses that sell to other businesses struggle with their customers stretching out their payment terms. SMBs can use the exchange to access affordable working capital when they need it (in as little as two days), instead of waiting 60 days or more for their customers to pay their invoices. This is important for growing companies that lack sufficient cash flow to fund their operations or acquire new business, and for any company that understands the strategic benefit of a cash cushion.

In addition to speed and affordability, the Receivables Exchange offers companies a great deal more control and flexibility than traditional institutions like banks and factors do. Companies can set the length of their auction and control all of their pricing parameters. They can get cash for a single invoice or all of their invoices, and they can use the exchange as much or as little as they need. Unlike most traditional financial institutions, the exchange does not require personal guarantees or all-asset liens from businesses, and customers are never notified that their receivables are for sale. This, along with the ability to collect early on slow payments, allows SMBs to maintain favorable relationships with their customers, especially larger customers who are used to dictating terms.

Buyers on the exchange are institutional investors such as banks, factors, asset-based lenders, and family offices. They purchase receivables as a short-duration investment with attractive risk-adjusted returns. To facilitate the most affordable pricing, the exchange collects information about the businesses that are seeking capital (called *sellers*), the receivables for sale, and the businesses' customers, and makes that information available to buyers within its secure trading platform. Buyers are able, for instance, to see whether a seller joined the exchange yesterday, or whether it has a long history of selling high-quality receivables. (The vast majority of the receivables sold on the exchange are investment grade.) All of these innovations make the marketplace more affordable for businesses.

The exchange is a new, liquid marketplace serving businesses that historically have had few options for accessing capital. It is open to U.S. B2B businesses with at least $2 million in annual revenue and two years' operating history. Businesses have to apply to sell receivables, a one-time process that is no more arduous than a loan application. Once they are registered to sell on the exchange, they can use it when they need it, and not when they don't. Rather than having to turn over all their receivables—and control over their customer relationships—to a factor, or sign an all-asset lien or personal guarantee with a bank, businesses can auction their receivables as needed, for financing that's virtually on demand.

A transaction begins when a seller chooses to list one or more receivables for sale. Sellers determine the length of the auction and control all the pricing parameters, setting the minimum amount that they are willing to accept for selling their receivable(s) and the maximum fee that they are willing to pay the buyer. Buyers compete against one another, bidding to purchase the receivables that are offered. If the seller's terms are not met, the receivables are not sold. If more than one buyer meets the seller's requirements, then the best bid wins. Sellers also have the option of setting a buyout price for the auction. If a buyer agrees to the buyout price, then the auction closes immediately, and the seller is funded early regardless of the auction end date. All auctions remain open for the time period established by the seller or until the seller's predetermined buyout price is met. When the auction closes, the seller receives its funding the next business day. The transaction is complete when the seller's customer remits payment and the buyer is paid the amount due, which is the advance amount plus any accrued fees; any remaining amount goes back to the seller. If the receivables remain unpaid, the seller is obligated to repurchase them from the buyer.

The Receivables Exchange manages the identity-verification process and registration of buyers and sellers and coordinates payments between the parties electronically. The exchange generates revenue through trading fees on completed transactions, one-time registration fees from sellers, and membership fees from buyers. All transactions are in U.S. dollars.

SBA Programs

The Small Business Administration (SBA) offers a wide range of programs for all types of businesses at various stages of development. These include the 7(a) Loan Guaranty, Microloan, and 504 Certified Development Company (CDC) loans. Figure 8-2 gives a synopsis of each of these programs.

Although the SBA oversees the programs from the agency's Washington, D.C., headquarters, commercial lenders nationwide actually issue the loans and handle the paperwork. To participate in the SBA programs, commercial lenders must be licensed by the SBA.

Figure 8-2.	Synopses of SBA Programs.

7(a) Loan Guaranty

The 7(a) Loan Guaranty Program is one of the SBA's primary lending programs. It provides loans to small businesses that are unable to secure financing on reasonable terms through normal lending channels. The program operates through private-sector lenders that provide loans that are, in turn, guaranteed by the SBA, which has no funds for direct lending or grants.

Specialized 7(a):
Express and Pilot Programs

These programs are designed to offer streamlined and expedited loan procedures for particular groups of borrowers, notably active-duty military personnel, veterans, and borrowers from distressed communities.

Specialized 7(a):
CAPLines

This is an umbrella program designed to help all businesses meet their short-term and cyclical working-capital needs through five separate lines.

Specialized 7(a):
International Trade Loans

These loans guarantee as much as $5,000,000 in combined working-capital and facilities-and-equipment loans if your business is in (or will engage in) international trade or is adversely affected by competition from imports.

Specialized 7(a):
Export Loan Programs

The Export Express Program, the Export Working Capital Program, the International Trade Loan Program, and the SBA and Ex-Im Bank Co-Guarantee Programs were designed to provide capital to exporters.

Specialized 7(a):
Community Adjustment and Investment Program

This program is aimed at aiding businesses that have been negatively affected by NAFTA.

Specialized 7(a):
Employee Trusts Program

This program provides financial assistance for employee stock ownership plans by providing up to a $1.5 million guaranty.

Specialized 7(a):
Advantage Loan Initiatives

This includes both the Small Loan Advantage and Community Advantage 7(a) Loan Initiatives. Both programs are aimed at benefiting underserved markets and communities.

Microloan Program
This program provides small loans of up to $50,000.

Certified Development Company (504 Loan) Program
This is a long-term financing tool designed to encourage economic development within a community.

The most active and expert lenders qualify for the SBA's streamlined lending programs. Under these programs, lenders are delegated partial or full authority to approve loans, which results in faster service from the SBA.

Certified lenders are those that have been heavily involved in regular SBA loan-guaranty processing and have met certain other criteria. They receive a partial delegation of authority, and the SBA gives them a three-day turnaround on their applications (they may also use regular SBA loan processing). Certified lenders account for nearly one-third of all SBA business loan guaranties.

Preferred lenders are chosen from among the SBA's best lenders and enjoy full delegation of lending authority in exchange for a reduction in the SBA guaranty. This lending authority must be renewed at least every two years, and the lender's portfolio is examined by the SBA periodically. Preferred loans account for more than 10 percent of SBA loans.

Who Are These Programs For?

An SBA loan guaranty can be used for working capital to expand an existing business or to start a new one. The capital may also be used for real estate renovation, purchase, or construction and for equipment purchases. Almost all small businesses are eligible for the SBA programs, except for those established for speculative investment, such as apartment buildings.

Eligibility

Your business generally must be operated for profit and must fall within the size standards set by the SBA. According to the SBA, in order to be eligible, a small business must be independently owned and operated and must not be dominant in its field. Depending on the industry, size-standard eligibility is based on either the average number of employees for the preceding 12 months or sales volume averaged over a three-year period. Generally, the SBA small-business standards are:

- Service industries with yearly receipts not exceeding $7 million, with some exceptions, depending on the service being provided; for example, legal and accounting services generally will not qualify for SBA loans

- Wholesale businesses employing fewer than 500 employees
- Retailers with yearly revenues not exceeding $7 million, with some exceptions depending on the type of retail operation
- General building and heavy construction contractors with yearly incomes not exceeding $33.5 million
- Special trade construction businesses with annual receipts not exceeding $14 million
- Computer programming, data processing, and systems design firms with annual receipts not exceeding $25 million
- Manufacturing businesses employing between 750 and 1,500 people, depending on the type of product manufactured

Although the SBA requirements may seem staggering to the owners of some start-ups, they should not scare away potential applicants. The SBA is one of the most popular sources of early-stage funding. For example, most commercial lenders won't approve a $50,000 loan for a start-up business. However, if the applicant secures an SBA loan guaranty, which provides the bank with a federal guaranty for repayment, the banker will be able to approve the loan.

7(a) Loan Guaranties

You can use a 7(a) loan to:

- Purchase land or buildings, including both new construction and the expansion or conversion of existing facilities
- Purchase equipment, machinery, furniture, fixtures, supplies, or materials
- Provide long-term working capital, including the payment of accounts payable and/or the purchase of inventory
- Cover short-term working capital needs, including seasonal financing, contract performance, construction financing, and export production
- Finance inventory and receivables under special conditions
- Refinance existing business indebtedness that is not already structured with reasonable terms and conditions
- Purchase an existing business

But not to:

- Refinance existing debt where the lender is in a position to sustain a loss and refinancing would mean that the SBA would take over that loss
- Effect a partial change of business ownership or a change that will not benefit the business
- Provide a reimbursement of funds owed to any owner, including any equity injection or injection of capital to permit the business's continuance until the loan supported by the SBA is disbursed
- Repay delinquent state or federal withholding taxes or other funds that should be held in trust or escrow
- Use for a nonsound business purpose

How It Works. You submit a loan application to a lender for initial review. Following your presentation, the lender checks with the SBA—before you submit a formal application—to determine the ballpark feasibility of the project. Then, if the SBA considers the project feasible and creditworthy, the lender submits a letter of intent to the SBA, if interim financing is to be supplied prior to formal consideration of the loan request.

The actual application is then forwarded to the SBA, and the lender deals directly with the SBA officers. The SBA processes can take as many as twenty working days or as few as two. If the lender has approved the loan subject to an SBA guaranty, the lender forwards a copy of the application and a credit analysis to the nearest SBA office. After SBA approval, the lender closes the loan and disburses the funds; you make monthly loan payments directly to the lender. As with any loan, you are responsible for repaying the full amount of the loan.

No balloon payments, prepayment penalties, application fees, or points are permitted with 7(a) loans. Repayment plans may be tailored to each individual business.

What You Need to Take to the Lender. Documentation requirements may vary; contact your lender for the information you must supply. Common requirements include the following:

- Purpose of the loan
- History of the business
- Business plan
- Financial statements for three years (for an existing business)

- Schedule of terms for any outstanding debts (for an existing business)
- Aging of accounts receivable and payable (for an existing business)
- Projected opening-day balance sheet (for a new business)
- Lease details
- Amount of investment in the business by the owner(s)
- Projections of income, expenses, and cash flow
- Signed personal financial statements
- Personal résumé(s)

What the SBA Looks For
- Good character
- Management expertise and commitment necessary for success
- Sufficient funds, including the SBA-guaranteed loan, to operate the business on a sound financial basis (for new businesses, this includes the resources to cover start-up expenses and the initial operating phase)
- A feasible business plan
- Adequate equity or investment in the business
- Sufficient collateral
- The ability to repay the loan on time from the projected operating cash flow

Collateral. You must pledge your readily available assets to adequately secure the loan. Personal guaranties are required from all the principal owners of the business. Liens on personal assets of the principals also may be required. However, in most cases, a loan will not be declined when insufficient collateral is the only unfavorable factor.

Specialized 7(a) SBA Express and Pilot Programs

The SBA Express program has been streamlined for success. The maximum loan amount is $350,000. The SBA response time is 36 hours or less. Both long-term and short-term credit are available, and the application has been reduced to one page. The Community Express program provides eligible loans of up to $25,000 for borrowers who are located in underserved communities. The Patriot Pilot program provides assistance for members of the military community and features the lowest interest for business loans, generally 2.25 to 4.75 percent over prime.

Specialized 7(a) CAPLines

CAPLines is the SBA's umbrella lending program that helps small businesses meet their short-term and cyclical working-capital needs. CAPLines can be used to finance:

- Seasonal working-capital needs
- The direct costs of performing construction, service, and supply contracts
- The direct cost associated with commercial and residential construction without a firm commitment for purchase
- Operating capital, by obtaining advances against existing inventory and accounts receivable, where the receivables themselves are the primary collateral, which is different from factoring

There are five distinct short-term working-capital loan programs under the CAPLines umbrella:

1. *Seasonal Line.* Finances anticipated needs during seasonal upswings in the business cycle. Repayment is made from the sale of inventory and collection on receivables created during the season.
2. *Contract Line.* Finances the direct labor and material costs associated with performing assignable contracts, such as government contracts and consulting projects. One contract line can finance more than one contract.
3. *Builders Line.* Finances the direct labor and material costs for small general contractors and builders that construct or renovate commercial or residential buildings. The building project serves as the collateral; Builders Line loans can be revolving or nonrevolving.
4. *Standard Asset-Based Line.* Provides financing for cyclical, growth, and recurring short-term needs by advancing funds against existing inventory and accounts receivable. Repayment comes from converting short-term assets into cash and remitting this cash to the lender. Businesses continually draw and repay as their cash cycle dictates. This type of credit line is generally used by businesses that provide credit to other businesses. These loans require periodic servicing and monitoring of collateral, for which the participating bank usually charges additional fees.
5. *Small Asset-Based Line.* Provides up to $200,000 under an asset-based

revolving line of credit similar to the Standard Asset-Based Line, except that some of the stricter servicing requirements are waived (provided that the business can show consistent repayment ability from cash flow for the full amount).

Loan and Guaranty Amount. CAPLines are provided only on a guaranteed basis and can be for any dollar amount, except for the Small Asset-Based Line, which is limited to $200,000. However, the maximum SBA guaranty share is limited to $3.75 million or 75 percent of the loan, whichever is less.

Loan Maturity and Disbursement. Each of the five CAPLines lines of credit has a maturity of up to five years. However, to meet the needs of the applicant, a shorter initial maturity can be established. CAPLines funds may be used as needed throughout the term of the loan to purchase short-term assets, as long as sufficient time is allowed to convert the assets into cash by maturity.

Collateral. The primary collateral will be either the current assets to be acquired with the loan proceeds or the current assets serving to secure the loan repayments. Personal guaranties will also be required from the principal owners of the business.

Credit Requirements. Applicants must:

- Demonstrate the capability to convert short-term assets into cash
- Demonstrate sufficient management ability, experience, and commitment necessary for a successful operation
- Demonstrate the capability to perform, and to collect payment for that performance
- Demonstrate the ability to repay your intended obligation from your business operation
- Provide a report detailing when income will become cash and when expenses will be paid
- Have a feasible business plan
- Have adequate equity or investment in the business
- Have the ability to provide the required updates on the status of current assets
- Pledge sufficient assets to adequately secure the loan
- Be of good character

Guaranty and Service Fees. In addition to the guaranties and fees discussed previously, the lender also may charge a servicing fee no greater than

3.5 percent of the outstanding balance on an annual basis for all CAPLines loans except the Standard Asset-Based Line, which has no fee restrictions.

Interest Rates. The rate of interest will be negotiated between the borrower and the lender, but it cannot exceed the prime rate plus 2.75 percent except for SBA Express loans, which can be prime plus 6.5 percent.

Specialized 7(a) International Trade Loans

The SBA can guarantee as much as $5,000,000 in combined working-capital and facilities-and-equipment loans if your business is in (or will engage in) international trade or is adversely affected by competition from imports. (The working-capital portion of the loan may be made according to the provisions of the Export Working Capital Program, discussed in the next section.)

Eligibility. You must establish either that the loan will significantly help your business expand, that your business will develop an export market, that your business is currently adversely affected by import competition, or that you will upgrade your equipment or facilities to improve your competitive position. Alternatively, you must be able to provide a business plan that reasonably projects export sales sufficient to cover the loan.

Specialized 7(a) Export Loan Programs

The Export Loan Programs were designed to provide working capital to exporters. In addition to the international trade loans explained previously, the SBA provides the Export Express Program, the Export Working Capital Program (EWCP), the International Trade Loan Program, and the SBA and Ex-Im Bank Co-Guarantee Program.

The Export Express Program provides streamlined financing of up to $500,000 for any business that has been in operation for at least 12 months and can demonstrate that the loan proceeds will support its export activity. The loan can be either a term loan or a revolving line of credit that is used to enhance a company's export development. The SBA response time is 36 hours or less.

The Export Working Capital Program provides lenders with up to a 90 percent guaranty on export loans as a credit enhancement. The EWCP allows financing of up to $5 million, providing short-term working-capital loans for exporters.

The International Trade Loan Program offers borrowers up to $1.75 million of SBA-guaranteed funds for business that plan to start or continue exporting, or that have been adversely affected by competition from imports. The funds may be used for the acquisition, construction, renovation, modernization, improvement, or expansion of long-term fixed assets.

The SBA and Ex-Im Bank Co-Guarantee Program is a combined effort of the SBA and the Export-Import Bank. The two agencies have joined their working-capital programs to offer a unified approach to the government's support of export financing. The guarantee coverage is for up to 90 percent of the principal and accrued interest for up to 180 days. The total working-capital line cannot exceed $2,000,000. A borrower must give the SBA a first security interest equal to 100 percent of the guaranteed amount.

Other Specialized 7(a) Loan Programs

Other 7(a) loan programs include the Community Adjustment and Investment Program, the Employee Trusts Program, the Advantage Loan Initiatives, and the Community Advantage Approved Lenders Program.

The Community Adjustment and Investment Program (CAIP) is aimed at aiding businesses that have been negatively affected by NAFTA. Under CAIP, a company that resides in an area that has been negatively affected by NAFTA may qualify for a loan that allows for the payment of fees on eligible loans, including the 7(a) loan program guaranty fee and the 504 program guaranty and lender's fees.

The Employee Trusts Program provides financial assistance for employee stock ownership plans by providing up to a $1.5 million guaranty. A qualified employee trust may relend the loan proceeds to the employer by purchasing qualified securities of the employer or may use them to purchase a controlling interest in the employer. The business must provide all the funds needed to collateralize and repay the loan.

The Advantage Loan Initiatives include both the Small Loan Advantage and Community Advantage 7(a) Initiatives. Both programs are aimed at benefiting underserved markets and communities, both offer streamlined applications for loans of up to $250,000, both will give an approval within 5 to 10 business days, and both provide guaranties of 85 percent for loans up to $150,000 and 75 percent for those over $150,000.

Microloan Program

The Microloan Program provides small loans of up to $50,000. Under this program, the SBA makes funds available to nonprofit intermediaries; these, in turn, make the loans. The average loan size is $13,000. Completed applications are usually processed by the intermediary in less than one week.

Use of Proceeds. Microloans may be used to finance the purchase of machinery, equipment, and fixtures and to make improvements to the physical location of your business. They may also be used to generate cash against a pledge of your accounts receivables and for working capital. They may not be used to pay existing debts.

Terms, Interest Rates, and Fees. Depending on the earnings of your business, you may take up to six years to repay a microloan. Rates are dependent on the intermediary lender and the costs to the intermediary from the U.S. Treasury; they rates are typically between 8 and 13 percent. There is no guaranty fee.

Collateral. Each nonprofit lending organization will have its own requirements, but it must take as collateral any assets purchased with the microloan. In most cases, your personal guaranty is also required.

Eligibility. Virtually all types of for-profit businesses that meet SBA eligibility requirements qualify.

504 Certified Development Company Program

This program, which was designed to enable small businesses to create and retain jobs, provides growing businesses with long-term, fixed-rate financing for the purchase of major fixed assets, such as land, buildings, and machinery.

According to SBA definitions, a certified development company (CDC) is a nonprofit corporation that has been set up to contribute to the economic development of its community or region. CDCs work with the SBA and private-sector lenders to provide financing to small businesses.

Usually, a 504 CDC project includes a loan from a private-sector lender, secured with a senior claim on your assets, covering as much as 50 percent of the project cost, or a loan secured with a junior position on your assets through the CDC, with SBA assistance, covering as much as 40 percent of the cost and a contribution of at least 10 percent equity from the small business that is being helped. The maximum SBA share is generally $1.5 million. Most businesses must create or retain one job for every $65,000 provided by the SBA.

Contacting the SBA

The SBA has offices located throughout the United States. For the one nearest you, call the SBA Answer Desk at 800-U-ASK-SBA (800-827-5722), or visit the SBA web site, www.sba.gov. The SBA's mailing address is U.S. Small Business Administration, 409 3rd ST, SW, Washington, DC 20416.

Chapter 9

Venture Capital

The institutional venture capital industry has its roots at the turn of the twentieth century, when wealthy families like the Rockefellers and the Du Ponts provided risk capital to small, growing companies. Following World War II, a few institutional venture capital companies were formed, the most notable being American Research and Development Corporation, founded in Boston in 1946. Owners and managers of growing companies often have mixed views concerning the institutional venture capital industry: On the one hand, they welcome the money and management support that they desperately need if they are to grow, but on the other hand, they fear the loss of control and the restrictions that the investment agreements typically place on the company. In order to achieve the delicate balance between the needs of the company and the needs of venture capitalists, business owners and managers must understand the process of obtaining venture capital financing, which is addressed in this chapter. In Chapter 10, we look at the anatomy of a venture capital transaction in detail.

Venture Capital Investing Trends

Venture capital investing trends have evolved significantly since the first and second editions of this book were published. During the heyday of venture capital in 1999 and early 2000, there were nearly three thousand investments in early-stage companies, for an aggregate investment of more than $100 billion. By 2003, the aggregate investment by venture capital firms had dropped to well under $20 billion; some of this went to a very limited handful of new portfolio companies, while the bulk of it went to follow-on investments (usually "down rounds"; see Chapter 10) to existing portfolio companies in order to keep them afloat. As market conditions slowly began to improve, the aggregate amount invested by venture capital firms began to rise. By 2004, the industry included more than a thousand venture capital investment firms with nearly $300 billion in capital under management. Because of the market conditions, however, many of these firms had not yet invested a significant portion of their capital. This dormant capital frustrated both entrepreneurs who were looking for capital and the institutional investors who had invested in the venture capital funds. This dormant capital, known as "overhang," was estimated to be as high as $68 billion by the first quarter of 2004 and was at record high levels from 2008 to 2010. By way of comparison, the private equity fund overhang was as high as $700 million in 2009, and the unallocated cash in corporate treasuries was established as being as high as $2.5 trillion in late 2011. Armed with cautious optimism, after 2004, the venture capital industry began a steady comeback, with aggregate investment amounts making slow but consistent headway. While not coming close to the levels of 1999 and 2000, by 2007, the aggregate investment amount had reached close to $30 billion.

Between 2008 and 2010, the near disappearance of debt financing in the market led to a lack of exit opportunities for venture capital firms. In 2008, the tumult in the U.S. financial markets resulted in a marked decrease in deal flow and investment compared to 2007 levels. Despite the increasing lack of leverage, however, the amount of capital invested and the number of deals done in 2008 remained relatively strong in comparison to the years 2002 through 2006.

By February 2009, the market was characterized by uncertainty and unavailability of leverage. It was the worst year for private equity fund raising since 2003—funds raised were down 68 percent from the previous year. Venture capital funds fared similarly—down 55 percent; it was their worst year since 2003.

Heading into 2011, there has been a slow but steady return of leverage and exit opportunities, which indicates a brighter future for the number of deals and the amount of capital to be invested in start-up and emerging companies in the coming years. The recession years, however, created a backlog of companies because of the lack of exit opportunities—essentially, there is an overhang somewhat similar to what we experienced in the early to mid-2000s. While firms continue to seek exits for the companies they are currently invested in (and continue to overcome the timidity the downturn has left many with), we are unlikely to see deal flow and capital invested into early-stage companies truly rally in the foreseeable future. Adding to the difficulties facing the market, there is a new regulatory framework that market players will have to successfully navigate. The financial crisis has spawned the Dodd-Frank Act, which will add new registration and record-keeping hurdles for private funds.

The dearth of debt financing and available exit opportunities (compared to historical levels) has led to changes in entrepreneurial trends and strategies. Overall, when equity capital markets become weak, there are typically fewer investments in start-ups and emerging companies, and those investments tend to gravitate toward the more extraordinary businesses. To attract financing, successful entrepreneurs will have to be more patient, resourceful, and creative, while investors are obtaining more favorable terms than have been seen in previous years. Some additional trends in the industry include:

- A smaller number of funds raising less money (for example, 37 U.S. venture funds raised $2.7 billion in the aggregate in the second quarter of 2011, the lowest level of activity since 1995)
- More syndicates, teaming, co-investing, and other risk-mitigation and knowledge-sharing techniques among investors
- The importance of the lead investor advocate (deals need a champion if they are to get to closing)
- Some shifts in negotiating leverage with the success of LinkedIn, Groupon, Zynga, Twitter, Facebook, and other such companies at being able to take money and still maintain control (balance of power)

- The evolving business models of venture capital funds and pressures on fund managers to reduce expenses and improve returns

Figure 9-1 shows some of the changes in the equity capital market and some possible trends for the future.

Primary Types of Venture Capitalists

In general, there are three primary types of traditional institutional pools of venture capital, although the lines between them have been blurring in recent years. These include public and private international venture capital firms; small-business investment companies (SBIC) and minority-enterprise SBICs (MESBICs); and corporate venture capital divisions.

Public and Private International Venture Capital Firms. These firms are typically organized as limited partnerships that themselves seek capital from venture investors, trusts, pension funds, and insurance companies, among others. They manage and invest in high-growth companies. Venture capital firms

Figure 9-1.	The Equity Capital Market—as It Was, as It Became, and as It Should Be.		
	As It Was Pre-2009	**As It Became in 2009**	**As It Should Be After 2011**
	+ Widespread leverage led to record deal flow and invested capital in 2007, followed by contraction of investment volume in 2008.	- Freezing credit markets led to historically low amount of investment, and lack of exits resulted in a glut of private equity–owned companies.	+ Thawing markets leading to increasing leverage and greater exit opportunities are creating an uptick in deals and investments.
	+ Gramm-Leach-Bliley Act allows for a minimal barrier between banks and alternative investments.	- Tumultuous markets put regulators in an uproar and in search of a way to bring stability to the economy.	- The Dodd-Frank Act has been passed and will create tighter regulations and increase costs and hurdles for private equity firms raising capital.
	* Percentage of investment dollars in deals under $50 million is lower in 2008 than in 2007.	* Percentage of investment dollars in deals under $50 million is lower in 2009 than in 2008.	* Percentage of investment dollars in deals under $50 million is lower in 2010 than in 2009.

tend to specialize in particular niches, based on either the business's *industry*, its *territory*, or its *stage of development*. Their investors expect a certain success rate and return on investment (ROI), which is critical to the firm's ability to attract future capital.

SBICs/MESBICs. Enacted in 1958, the Small Business Investment Act established a national program for licensing privately owned small-business investment companies. Minority-enterprise SBICs were added by a 1972 amendment to the act. Although the SBIC program has experienced some difficulty, it remains an integral part of the organized venture capital community. The program allows the SBA to grant licenses to certain types of venture capital firms that allow them to borrow money from the federal government at very attractive rates in exchange for certain restrictions on deal structures and on the types of businesses to which the SBIC can provide capital.

Corporate Venture Capital Divisions. Corporate venture capital (CVC) includes both formal and ad hoc venture capital divisions established by large corporations, such as Intel and Motorola, usually in hopes of funding small companies that have technology or resources that the larger companies want or need. The investment is often structured as a quasi-joint venture because corporate venture capital often brings more to the table than just money, such as access to the resources of these large companies—for example, their engineering teams, distribution channels, and key vendor relationships. Corporate venture capital efforts typically revolve around the corporation's goals to incubate future acquisitions, gain access to new technologies, engage in joint product development, share access to established distribution channels, obtain intellectual-property licenses, provide work for unused capacity, encourage and facilitate entrepreneurial thinking among current corporate staff members, find outlets for excess cash, and break into new markets. Investments usually need to both meet core financial criteria and offer a strategic fit with one or more business units within the company, either for growth opportunities or for defensive reasons. One of the key issues in being successful in raising money from these sources is to have a clear understanding of the CEO's "burning platform," key agenda, and top priorities. How does your business plan solve a problem or create an opportunity for this particular strategic investor? What's in it for the investor? What long-term sustainable competitive advantage will your technology, product, service team, or channel help the investor build and maintain?

The corporate venture capital divisions are among the fastest-growing segments of the venture capital industry as the larger technology companies try to find more creative ways to engage in deals with their more nimble counterparts and deploy the nearly $2.1 trillion that was sitting on the sidelines as of the fall of 2011. In 1996, there were only 49 companies making venture capital investments via formal "stand-alone" investment divisions; by 1999, there were nearly two hundred, accounting for more than 15 percent of all venture capital investments. However, by 2001, corporate venture capital funds had become much more cautious and focused on highly strategic deal flow and smaller investment commitments. Many suffered painful write-offs of their investments in companies that had failed or had dropped significantly in value. For example, Intel's venture capital division invested $1.3 billion in 300 start-ups in 2000, but that figure had dropped by more than half in 2004. While not approaching the levels seen in 2000, from 2004 to 2008, corporate venture capital has represented approximately 7 to 10 percent of all venture capital investments, with between $1.5 billion and $2.6 billion invested each year. In 2009, total corporate investment in venture capital fell to its lowest level since 2003 ($1.3 billion). In 2010, there was gradual improvement in corporate venture capital transactions, with approximately $1.9 billion being invested as well as the entry of new players into the market, such as ABB Technology Ventures, a division of ABB, Ltd. (a Swiss energy infrastructure company with $54 billion in market capitalization), which invested more than $75 million in nearly a dozen deals in 2010, often in partnerships or syndicates with other more traditional venture capital funds.

Preparing to Meet with Venture Capitalists

The key to obtaining an initial meeting with an institutional venture capitalist is to be sure you've done your homework and are prepared to present your business in the best light. There are three central components of the preparation process: business and strategic planning, effective networking, and narrowing the field.

A well-written business plan and financing proposal are necessary prerequisites for serious consideration by any sophisticated source of capital. These include a very compelling executive summary, a short and long review of the plan, a "killer" PowerPoint presentation, and any other supporting materials required to demonstrate and substantiate the future potential of your company. (See Chapter 3 for the elements of a business plan.)

Effective networking means using professional advisors, commercial lenders, investment bankers, and consultants who may be able to help you get your business plan into the hands of the appropriate venture capitalists. Institutional sources of capital are often flooded with unsolicited plans, which are more likely to end up in a wastebasket than before an investment committee. In a year, the average venture capital firm will see thousands of business plans, call only a few dozen candidates, and close only four to six deals. You need to find ways to increase your chances of survival as the field of choices rapidly narrows.

You can help narrow the field by remembering that most venture capitalists have preferences about the types of companies they will include in their portfolio. These preferences may be based on the nature of the company's products and services, its geographic location, its projected rates of return, its stage of development, or the amount of capital required. Rather than waste precious resources by blindly sending business plans to any and all venture capitalists in your region, take the time to research the venture capital industry to match the characteristics of the proposed investment with the investment criteria of the targeted firm.

It may turn out that your company's stage of development will determine the kind of venture capital investor you'll approach and the structure of the financing you'll receive, so it's important to identify which stage of business-development financing you need before embarking on the search for capital.

The first level is *seed financing*, in which the company receives small amounts of capital for initial product-feasibility studies, development, market research, refinement of strategies, and other preliminary analyses.

The next level of financing is *start-up* or *early-stage financing*, which is generally for the completion of product development, recruitment of a management team, refinement of the long-term business plan, and commencement of marketing efforts. Financing for companies at the starting point in their growth and development is very difficult because these companies have the highest risk of failure. Venture capitalists are now typically investing in later-stage companies, with a greater emphasis on the company's ability to generate current income and return to the investors.

First-stage financing usually funds the first phase of full-scale manufacturing, marketing, and sales. It is also at this stage that any missing components of the management team are put in place, such as the hiring of a chief financial officer or a senior vice president of sales and marketing.

Second-stage financing is typically for a company that has begun production and distribution and has established inventories, contracts, and accounts receivable, but needs working capital to fuel its expansion.

Third-stage financing is usually for a company that is already operating at a profit but needs capital for research and development of new products, expansion of physical facilities, or a significant increase in sales and marketing efforts.

Finally, in *bridge financing*, venture capitalists provide capital to a company that expects to go public within the next 12 months but requires additional working capital to bridge the gap. Firms will also consider providing capital to finance mergers and acquisitions, joint ventures, leveraged management buyouts or recapitalization, efforts to go private, or other kinds of transactions, if the return on investment meets their criteria.

If your business-plan submission survives the rigid initial review of most institutional venture-capital firms, the next step is a personal presentation of your proposal. To increase your chances of success, keep the following points in mind. Also remember how venture capitalists will interpret some of the things you say (see Figure 9-2).

Have a Dress Rehearsal

You need to rehearse your presentation many times, using a "moot court." This involves having different audiences that ask different questions, replicating the actual meeting that you'll have with the managers of the venture capital firm.

Figure 9-2.	How the Venture Capitalist Interprets Your Presentation.

What You Say:	What You Mean:
• Product's 90 percent complete	• We've got a name for it
• Leading-edge technology	• We can't make it work
• Limited downside	• Things can't get much worse
• Possibility of a shortfall	• We're 50 percent below plan
• Proven technology	• It nearly worked once before
• We're repositioning the company	• We're lost
• Upside potential	• It stopped breathing
• Customers love the product	• A cold-calling campaign starts next week

Make sure your rehearsal audiences have the background and the training (for example, lawyers, accountants, business-school professors, and entrepreneurs who have raised venture capital) to ask tough questions and critically evaluate your responses. Do your homework on the venture capital firm and learn its "hot buttons" so that you can address key issues in your presentation. As the saying goes, "You never get a second chance to make a first impression." The rehearsals will help you survive the first meeting and get to the next steps. Be prepared for the tough questions, and don't be intimidated or upset when the really hard ones start flying at you. If the venture capital firm's representatives don't ask tough questions, they are not engaged with your presentation. If they are not engaged enough to beat you up a little, there will probably be no next steps—and no deal.

Have a Mentor

It's always helpful to have a coach or mentor who either has raised venture capital or has been an advisor or negotiator in multiple venture capital transactions. The mentor or coach can help you stay focused on the issues that are important to the venture capitalists and not waste their time. He can also reassure you during the difficult and time-consuming process, teaching you to remain patient, optimistic, and level-headed about the risks and challenges you face.

Have a Detailed Game Plan

Prepare a specific presentation that isn't too long or too short (15 minutes is about right). Don't attempt to "read" every word of your business plan or put every historical fact about your company on a PowerPoint slide. Keep your presentation crisp and focused, and be prepared to answer questions and defend your key strategic assumptions and financial forecasts. Remember that every minute counts. Even the small talk at the beginning of the meeting is important because the seasoned venture capitalist is sizing you up, learning about your interests, and looking for the chemistry and the glue that is key to a successful relationship.

Have Your Team Available to Meet the Venture Capitalist

Don't overlook the "personal" component of the evaluation. In many cases, it can be the most important factor considered in the final decision. The four Cs— camaraderie, communication, commitment, and control (of your ego)—may make or break the outcome of the meeting. Any experienced venture capitalist will tell you that, at the end of the day, the decision depends on the strength of the people who will be there day to day to execute and manage the company. The venture capitalist will look for a management team that's educated, dedicated, and experienced (and, ideally, has experienced some success *as a team* before this venture). The team should also be balanced, with each member's skills and talents complementing the others' so that all the critical areas of business management are covered—from finance to marketing and sales to technical expertise.

Key Venture Capitalist Questions About Your Business Plan

- How proprietary, unique, or protectable are the company's products or services?
- How valid are the assumptions—financial or strategic—that form the basis for the projections of future success?
- Who are the early customers? How are buying decisions made? Why do these customers want what you sell?
- Are there sufficient margins throughout the various chains of distribution?
- How does the product reach the customer? What challenges exist along the way? For example, food products face a battle for shelf space, retail costs of build-out, competition for top sites, and so forth.
- Do we buy into your dream? Can the management team currently in place execute the plan?
- What are the potential upsides? Is this a small business or a growing business?

Have Passion but Not Rose-Colored Glasses

Many entrepreneurs fail to make a good impression in their initial meeting with the venture capitalist because they come on either too strong or not strong enough. An experienced venture capitalist wants to see that you have a passion for and commitment to your company and the execution of the business plan. However, she does not want to be oversold or have to deal with an entrepreneur who is so enamored of an idea or plan that he can't grasp its flaws or understand its risks.

Have a Way to Demonstrate Your Personal Commitment to the Project

All venture capitalists will seek to measure your personal sense of commitment to the business and its future. Generally, venture capitalists won't invest in entrepreneurs whose commitment to the business is only part-time or whose loyalty is divided among the business and other activities or ventures. You must have "skin in the game" to be taken seriously. The investor will look for a high energy level, a commitment to achievement and leadership, self-confidence, and a creative approach to problem solving. You will also have to demonstrate your personal financial commitment, typically by investing a significant portion of your own resources in a project before you ask others to part with their resources. Remember, any aspect of your personal life, whether it's good, bad, or seemingly irrelevant, may be of interest to the venture capitalist in the interview and due diligence process. Don't get defensive or be surprised when the questions are as broad as they are deep—venture capitalists are merely trying to predict the future by learning as much as possible about your past and current situation, as well as such things as your leadership style, how you'll handle pressures, how well you communicate with them, and whether you fit the typical archetype of a potentially successful entrepreneur. For more on this personality profiling and analysis, see *The Hypomanic Edge* by John Gartner or *Just Enough Anxiety* by Robert Rosen; both books examine the personality types and character traits that define most successful entrepreneurs and company leaders.

Have an Open and Honest Exchange of Information

One sure deal killer for venture capital firms is trying to hide something in your past or downplaying a previous business failure. During the due diligence process, a seasoned venture capitalist can and will learn about any skeletons in your closet, and she will walk away from the deal if she finds something that should have been disclosed at the outset. A candid, straightforward channel of communication is critical. A previous business failure may be viewed as a sign of experience, provided you can demonstrate that you've learned from your mistakes and figured out ways to avoid them in the future. On a related note, you must demonstrate a certain degree of flexibility and versatility in your approach to implementing your business plan. The venture capitalists may have ideas concerning the strategic direction of the company and will want to see that you are open-minded and receptive to their suggestions. If you're rigid or stubborn, they may see you as immature or assume that you're a person who can't compromise. Either one of these can be a major deal turn-off and a good excuse to walk away.

Have a Big Market and a Big Upside

Make sure that your business plan and your presentation adequately demonstrate the size of your potential market and the financial rewards and healthy margins that strong demand for your product or service will bring to the bottom line. A venture capitalist who suspects that your product or service has a narrow market, limited demand, and thin margins will probably walk away from the deal. If your target market is too mature, with already established competitors, the venture capitalist may feel that the opportunity is too limited and will not produce the expected financial returns. Venture capitalists are looking for a company that has a *sustainable competitive advantage*, demonstrated by a balanced mix of products and services that meet a new market need on both a domestic and an international basis. Remember that most venture capitalists want a 60 to 80 percent return for seed and early-stage or postlaunch deals, and at least a 25 to 35 percent return on latter-stage and mezzanine-level investments. When the Standard & Poor's 500-stock index offers 30 percent returns and when the average investor can double his money with investments in blue-chip companies, your business plan and presentation had better demonstrate that the venture capitalists' money will be better served by being invested in your company as opposed to other allocations of capital.

Have an Understanding of What Really Motivates the Venture Capitalist's Decision

David Gladstone, a seasoned venture capitalist and author of the *Venture Capital Handbook*, writes: "I'll back you if you have a good idea that will make money for both of us." That one sentence captures the essence of the venture capitalist's decision-making process. You must have a *good idea*—one that's articulated in a business plan that honestly expresses the risks and opportunities, and how your management team will influence the odds of success and survival. But then, your idea must make money for *both* of you. The venture capitalist wants deals in which both the investors *and* the entrepreneurs can enjoy the upside and the scale is not weighted in favor of either. In exchange for their capital and wisdom, venture capitalists expect to have some controls and checks and balances built into the structure of the deal and the governance of the company. Those protections ensure that their investment and their ability to participate in the growth and success of the company are secure.

Have an Exit Strategy

The saying "begin with the end in mind" clearly applies to venture capital deals. Venture capital investors aren't looking for a long-term marriage; they will be very focused on how you intend to get their original investment and return on capital back to them within four to six years (and in some markets, even faster). They are *not* necessarily interested in a long-term relationship and long strolls in the park. Your business plan and oral presentation should include an analysis and an assessment of the likelihood of the three most common exit strategies: an initial public offering (see Chapters 11 and 12), a sale of the company (see Chapter 14), or a redemption of the venture capitalists' shares of the company by the company directly. Other exit strategies include restructuring the company, licensing the company's intellectual property, converting all or a significant portion of the company to employee ownership, finding a replacement investor, or even liquidating the company. Figure 9-3 lists the key elements of a successful presentation.

Central Components of the Venture Capitalist's Investment Decision

Regardless of a company's stage of development, primary products and services, or geographic location, there are several variables that all venture capital firms will consider in analyzing any business plan presented to them for investment. The presence or absence of these variables will ultimately determine whether investors will commit capital to the project. These variables generally fall into four categories: management team, products and services, markets, and return on investment. Your team must be prepared to answer the following questions, all of which should have been addressed in your business plan:

Management Team
- What are the background, knowledge, skills, and abilities of each member of the team?
- How is this experience relevant to the proposed business plan or project?
- How are risks and problems identified, managed, and eliminated by the members of the management team?
- To what extent does each member of the management team exhibit certain entrepreneurial personality traits, such as self-confidence, leadership skills, tenacity, drive, and unbounded energy?

Figure 9-3. | **Key Elements of a Successful Presentation to a Venture Capitalist.**

Team Must:
- Be able to adapt
- Know the competition
- Be able to manage rapid growth
- Be able to manage an industry leader
- Have relevant background and industry experience
- Show a financial commitment to the company, not just sweat equity
- Be strong with a proven track record in the industry unless the company is a start-up or seed investment

Product Must:
- Be real and work
- Be unique
- Be proprietary
- Meet a well-defined need in the marketplace
- Demonstrate the potential for product expansion, to avoid being a one-product company
- Emphasize usability
- Solve a problem or improve a process significantly
- Be for mass production with potential for cost reduction

Market Must:
- Have current customers and the potential for many more
- Be growing rapidly (25 to 45% per year)
- Have a potential for market size in excess of $250 million
- Show where and how you are competing in the marketplace
- Have the potential to become a market leader
- Outline any barriers to entry

Business Plan Must:
- Tell the full story, not just one chapter
- Promote a company, not just a product
- Be compelling
- Show the potential for rapid growth and knowledge of your industry, especially your competition and your market vision
- Include milestones for measuring performance
- Show how you plan to beat or exceed those milestones
- Address all the key areas
- Detail projections and assumptions; be realistic
- Serve as a sales document
- Include a strong and well-written executive summary
- Show excitement and color
- Show a superior rate of return (a minimum of 30 to 40% per year) with a clear exit strategy

Products and Services

- At what stage of development are your products and services? What specific opportunity have you identified? How long will this "window of opportunity" remain open? What steps are necessary for you to exploit this opportunity?
- To what extent are your products and services unique, innovative, and proprietary? What steps have you taken to protect these proprietary features?
- To what extent do you control the means of production of the products and services, or are you dependent on a key supplier or licenser?
- To what extent do your products or services represent a technological breakthrough, or are they low-tech, with less risk of obsolescence?

Markets

- What stage in the life cycle is your industry in?
- What are the size and projected growth rate of your targeted market?
- What marketing, sales, and distribution methods will you use to bring your products and services to the marketplace?
- What are the strengths and weaknesses of each of your direct, indirect, and anticipated competitors?
- Will the development of your products and services create new markets? If yes, what are the barriers to entry in those markets?
- What are the characteristics of the typical consumer of the company's products and services? What has consumer reaction been thus far?

Return on Investment

- What is your current and projected valuation and performance in terms of sales, earnings, and dividends? To what extent have you substantiated these budgets and projections? Have you over- or underestimated the amount of capital you'll require?
- How much money and time have you—and your managers—already invested? How much more time and money are you willing to commit before realizing a return on your own personal investments? How well are you managing your current assets and resources?
- How much capital will you require, both currently and as projected, to bring your business plans to fruition? Could this capital be invested in

stages, tied to the performance of the company, or is the capital required all at once? What types of securities are being offered? To what extent will additional dilution be necessary to meet your growth objectives?

- What is the projected return on the proposed investment? How will this projected return be affected if you fail to meet your business plans or financial projections? What rights, remedies, and exit strategies will be available to investors if problems arise?

There are also certain *negative* factors that you should avoid at all costs because they often disqualify what might be an otherwise workable deal, such as:

- Unqualified family members filling key management positions
- Projections that provide for excessive management salaries, company cars, and other unnecessary executive benefits
- An unwillingness to provide a personal guaranty for debt financing
- An incomplete or overly slick business plan
- A business plan that projects overly optimistic or unrealistic goals and objectives

Due Diligence Is a Two-Way Street

At the same time that your business plan is under the microscope during the venture capitalist's evaluation and due diligence, you should be assessing the prospective venture capitalist's strengths and weaknesses. When the capital markets are strong, you will be able to be selective in choosing which venture capital proposal will be acceptable. Consider the following questions when determining whether the venture capital firm meets your current and projected requirements:

- How well does this firm know your industry? How often does it work with companies that are at a development stage similar to yours? To what extent has it worked with owners and managers of more-seasoned companies in a turnaround situation?
- What assistance can the venture capitalist bring in terms of management expertise, industry contacts, and support services?
- What is the reputation of this firm within the financial community? If this firm is to serve as the lead investor, how effective will it be in attracting additional investors? Has the firm asked for any special reward or compensation for serving as lead investor? What effect will this have on the willingness of other investors to participate?

- Will this firm be able to participate in later rounds of financing if the company continues to grow and needs additional capital?

To answer these questions, speak with investment bankers, attorneys, accountants, and other venture capitalists who are familiar with this particular firm. Most important, speak with the owners and managers of other companies in the investor's portfolio to determine the level of support, conflict, and communication the firm typically provides—and be sure to talk to both successful and unsuccessful portfolio companies. Find out how the venture capitalist reacted to companies that got into trouble, not just those that outstripped projections.

Balancing Your Needs and the Venture Capitalist's Wants

The negotiation and structuring of most venture capital transactions depends less on industry standards, legal boilerplate, or structural rules of thumb than on the need to strike a balance between your concerns and the venture capitalist's investment criteria. Initial negotiations and alternative proposed structures for the financing will generally depend on an analysis of the following factors.

Your Main Concerns
- Loss of management control
- Dilution of your personal stock
- Repurchase of your personal stock if you resign (voluntarily or otherwise) from the company
- Adequate financing
- Future capital requirements and dilution of the founder's ownership
- Intangible and indirect benefits of venture capitalist participation, such as access to key industry contacts and future rounds of capital

Their Main Concerns
- Your company's current and projected valuation
- The level of risk associated with this investment
- The investor's investment objectives and criteria
- Projected levels of return on investment
- Liquidity of the investment, security interests, and exit strategies in the event of business distress or failure ("downside protection")

- Protection of the firm's ability to participate in future rounds if the company meets or exceeds projections ("upside protection")
- Influence and control over management strategy and decision making
- Registration rights in the event of a public offering
- Rights of first refusal to provide future financing

Mutual Concerns

- Retention of key members of the management team (and recruitment of key missing links)
- Resolution of any conflicts among the syndicate of investors (especially where a lead investor represents several venture capital firms)
- Financial strength of the company after the investment
- Tax ramifications of the proposed investment

Understanding the Venture Capitalist's Decision Process

It is often said that a seasoned venture capitalist can recognize a bad deal within five minutes, but it can take two weeks to know if you have a good deal. So what happens during those weeks? What are the key steps and decision factors that lead to the issuance of a term sheet and an ultimate closing? Many venture capital firms receive hundreds of business plans per month, so how does yours rise to the top? Some venture capitalists refer to the "Five Pile Rule," a process whereby the business plans received each week are organized into five piles (see Figure 9-4).

You are likely to get a call requesting additional information or the scheduling of a meeting only if your business plan makes it into the target pile. This means that you need to really do your homework on the investment focus of the fund *and* ideally be introduced to the fund by someone whose business acumen and reputation the fund managers trust. Figure 9-5 shows how a venture capital firm reveals a deal's flow through each step in the decision-making process, and Figure 9-6 names some "deal killers." Other key questions that an experienced venture capitalist will be seeking to answer during the initial evaluation of the business plan include the following:

- Can we (the VC firm) add real value to this company beyond money?
- Who else says that this is a great company (such as respected angel investors that are already shareholders, the trusted resource that referred the deal to the venture capitalist, customer references, proven track record of the team, expert opinions on the market or the technology)?

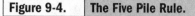

Figure 9-4.	The Five Pile Rule.

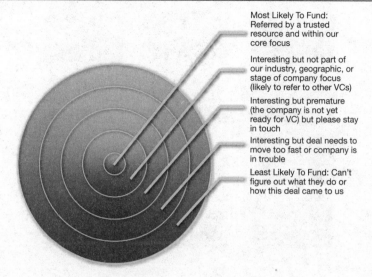

Most Likely To Fund: Referred by a trusted resource and within our core focus

Interesting but not part of our industry, geographic, or stage of company focus (likely to refer to other VCs)

Interesting but premature (the company is not yet ready for VC) but please stay in touch

Interesting but deal needs to move too fast or company is in trouble

Least Likely To Fund: Can't figure out what they do or how this deal came to us

- Should we invest in this deal alone, or should we build a syndicate in order to mitigate and share the risks as well as to tap into a pool of complementary skill sets and industry expertise?

- Do the founding entrepreneur and the team truly have the persistence, the creativity, the energy, the vision, the passion, and the focus to execute the business model? Does the team have an orientation toward measurable results and the business acumen and interpersonal/leadership skills to achieve these objectives?

- Is the market large enough to sustain the company's growth plans in light of existing and potential competitors? What is the current size, strength, and market share of these competitors? How strong (and willing to pay) are the target customers?

- What are the company's strategy, game plan, and budget for marketing, advertising, and public relations? Has it developed a clean branding strategy? Does the strategy make sense given current market conditions?

- Has the company surrounded itself with top-notch and highly respected professional service providers, board of directors members, advisory board members, and others who have a vested interest in the company's long-term success?

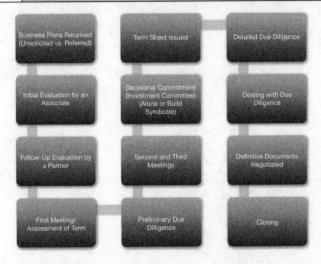

Figure 9-5.   The Venture Capitalist's Opportunity Screening Process.

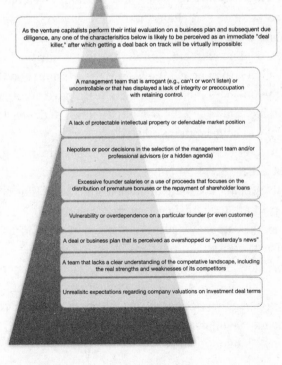

Figure 9-6.   Venture Capitalist Due Diligence "Deal Killers."

As the venture capitalists perform their intial evaluation on a business plan and subsequent due diligence, any one of the characterisitics below is likely to be perceived as an immediate "deal killer," after which getting a deal back on track will be virtually impossible:

A management team that is arrogant (e.g., can't or won't listen) or uncontrollable or that has displayed a lack of integrity or preoccupation with retaining control.

A lack of protectable intellectual property or defendable market position

Nepotism or poor decisions in the selection of the management team and/or professional advisors (or a hidden agenda)

Excessive founder salaries or a use of proceeds that focuses on the distribution of premature bonuses or the repayment of shareholder loans

Vulnerability or overdependence on a particular founder (or even customer)

A deal or business plan that is perceived as overshopped or "yesterday's news"

A team that lacks a clear understanding of the competative landscape, including the real strengths and weaknesses of its competitors

Unrealisitc expectations regarding company valuations on investment deal terms

Chapter 10

Anatomy of a Venture Capital Transaction

Once you and your potential investors have analyzed all the key relationships and the financial and structural factors and considered them from the risk, reward, and control perspectives, you can create a *term sheet*. The term sheet sets forth the key financial and legal terms of the transaction, which will then serve as a basis for preparation of the definitive legal documents. The term sheet may also contain certain rights and obligations of both parties, such as an obligation to maintain an agreed-upon valuation, to be responsible for certain costs and expenses in the event that the proposed transaction does not take place, or to secure commitments for financing from additional sources (such as the supplemental debt financing that a growing company may seek prior to closing). You'll find a sample term sheet in the appendix.

Evolution of Venture Capital Deal Terms

As discussed later in this chapter, typical deal terms for venture capital investments have evolved significantly over the past several years. In the heyday of 1998 and 1999, term sheets were drafted pretty heavily in favor of the entrepreneurs and the founding team, as venture capitalists were often competing with five or six (or more) other firms to be the source of Series A financing. By 2002, the pressures on the venture capitalists from their own investors, economic conditions, and the need to protect the downside (as companies were failing left and right) led the "deal terms pendulum" to swing all the way to the other side in favor of the source of capital. By mid-2004, market conditions were slowly improving, and venture capital deal terms began to normalize and reflect a relatively typical private equity environment. By 2008, and continuing through much of 2010, the near disappearance of debt financing in the market led to a lack of exit opportunities for venture capital firms. In 2011, there has been a slow but steady return of leverage and exit opportunities. The lack of debt financing and exit opportunities has led to changes in entrepreneurial trends and strategies. In particular, when equity capital markets are weak, there are fewer investments in start-ups and emerging companies, with investments tending to gravitate toward only the more extraordinary companies, and investment deal terms tending to lean toward the investors.

Negotiating and Structuring the Deal

Negotiations regarding the structure of the transaction will usually revolve around the types of securities involved and the principal terms of the securities. The type of securities ultimately selected and the structure of the transaction will usually fall into one of the following categories:

> *Preferred stock.* This is the most common form of security issued in connection with venture capital financing of an emerging-growth company. That's because of the many advantages that preferred stock offers—it can be converted into common stock, and it has dividend and liquidation preference over common stock. It can also have antidilution protection, a mandatory or optional redemption schedule, and special voting rights and preferences.

Convertible debenture. This is basically a debt instrument (secured or unsecured) that may be converted into equity on specified terms and conditions. Until it is converted, it offers the investor a fixed rate of return, and it offers the company tax advantages (for example, deductibility of interest payments). A venture capital company often prefers this type of security for higher-risk transactions because it wants to enjoy the position of a creditor until the risk is mitigated. Convertible debt is also used in connection with bridge financing, with the venture capitalist expecting to convert the debt to equity once additional capital has been raised. Finally, if the debentures are subordinated, commercial lenders often treat them as equity on the balance sheet, enabling the company to obtain institutional debt financing.

Debt securities with warrants. A venture capitalist generally prefers debentures or notes in connection with warrants, often for the same reasons that convertible debt is used: the ability to protect the downside by being recognized as a creditor, and the ability to protect the upside by including warrants to purchase common stock at favorable prices and on favorable terms. A warrant enables the investor to buy common stock without sacrificing the preferred position of a creditor, as it would have to do if only convertible debt were used in the financing.

Common stock. Venture capitalists rarely choose to purchase common stock from a company initially, especially at early stages of its development. Straight common stock offers the investor no special rights or preferences, no fixed return on investment, no special ability to exercise control over management, and no liquidity to protect against downside risks. One of the few times that a company that is seeking capital might issue common stock is if it wishes to preserve its Subchapter S status under the Internal Revenue Code, which would be jeopardized if it authorized a class of preferred stock. Finally, you should be aware that common-stock investments by venture capitalists could create "phantom income." That would have adverse tax consequences for employees if stock is subsequently issued to them at a cost lower than the price per share paid by the venture capital company.

Once you and the potential investors have selected the type of security you'll use, you must ensure that the authorization and issuance of the security are properly carried out in accordance with applicable state laws. For example, let's say that your corporate charter doesn't currently provide for a class of preferred stock. If this is the case, you must prepare articles of amendment, get them approved by your board of directors and shareholders, and file them with the appropriate state corporation authorities.

The nature and scope of the various rights, preferences, and privileges that will be granted to the holders of the newly authorized preferred stock will be the focus of the negotiations between you and the venture capitalist. Specifically, the terms and conditions of the voting rights, dividend rates and preferences, mandatory redemption provisions, conversion features, liquidation preferences, and antidilution provisions (sometimes referred to as "ratchet clauses") are likely to be hotly contested. In addition, if any portion of the financing from the venture capitalist includes convertible debentures, then negotiations will also focus on the term, interest rate and payment schedule, conversion rights and rates, extent of subordination, remedies for default, acceleration and prepayment rights, and underlying security for the instrument.

The kind of protection that the venture capitalist demands will depend, in part, on the specific history of your company and its corporate and capital structure. For example, let's say that several majority shareholders of the company are members of your family and that in the past you've authorized the issuance of certain shares of common stock to relatives at low prices. To protect against dilution upon conversion of the preferred stock (or the convertible debentures), the venture capitalist may require certain "ratchet" provisions to be built into the conversion terms of the preferred stock when you amend the company's corporate charter. These provisions will adjust the conversion price to allow the venture capitalist to receive a greater number of shares upon conversion than originally anticipated. A "full ratchet" adjusts the conversion price to the lowest price at which the stock that is issuable upon conversion has been sold.

There are other types of ratchet clauses, generally known as "partial ratchets," that adjust the conversion price based on a weighted-average formula in which the shares issuable upon conversion have been issued at a variety of different prices. This type of partial ratchet is generally fairer to you and your stockholders. Finally, you may wish to negotiate an exemption from the ratchet provisions for certain types of stock sales, such as those pursuant to an incentive-based employee stock option plan.

Aligning Business-Plan Analysis and Investor Concerns with Term Sheet Provisions

The strategic key to the capital-formation process is to genuinely "walk a mile in the investor's shoes" and to review your company's business plan from the perspective of the source of capital. Real or perceived holes or gaps in the business plan are likely to yield special term sheet provisions or investment agreement covenants designed to address the perceived flaw and reduce or mitigate the investor's risk prior to or after making the investment. In Figure 10-1, there are multiple examples of the connection between business-plan risks and term sheet provisions.

Figure 10-1.	Analysis of the Business Plan and the Correlation Between Investor Concerns and Term Sheet Provisions.
Business-Plan Flaws (Real or as Perceived by Investor)	**Likely Term Sheet Provision**
Weak leadership or management team	Covenant to fill gaps prior to or within a specified number of months after closing
Inexperienced outside advisory team	Covenant to hire new legal counsel and/or CPA firm prior to closing
Breadth and depth of market too narrow	Covenant to expand or deepen product or service offerings or develop a global strategy within a specified number of days after closing
Customer concentration issues	Covenant to expand the customer base and reduce dependence as a condition to closing
Absent or inadequate intellectual property protection	Closing condition to hire experienced IP counsel to develop a protection strategy (and positioning a valuation of the portfolio as well)
Capitalization table has too many "widows and orphans"	Closing condition to redeem smaller or potentially problematic shareholders prior to the next round of investment
Execution of company's strategy is dependent on third-party or regulatory approvals	Commitment by third parties or regulatory bodies to grant approval (as a condition to closing) or a legal opinion letter concerning the likelihood of approvals being granted

Business-Plan Flaws (Real or as Perceived by Investor)	Likely Term Sheet Provision
Excessive compensation or general spending by the founders or the leadership team	Ongoing covenants establishing salary and bonus limitations
Health or life risk issues among key employees	Key-person life insurance policies in place as a condition to closing
Inexperienced management team	Greater board control, required approvals, or seats or a mandatory advisory board or coach/mentor
Unproven or early-stage technology	Financing may be broken into chunks, requiring that progress milestones be met before the next tranche
The investor likes the business plans for the growth of the company but does not want to assume all of the risks	The investor may insist that the entrepreneur find co-investors or may assume responsibility for building a syndicate as a condition to closing
The investor likes the business plan but does not fully understand the company's technology	The investor may seek a more knowledgeable co-investor or analysis by an industry expert as a condition to investment
The company's balance sheet has too many "miscellaneous" obligations or shareholder loans	The investor may require an overhaul or restructuring of the balance sheet to clean up debt and possibly force conversion of shareholder loans into equity
Intellectual property of the company is "licensed" by the founders to the entity	The investor may require an assignment of the intellectual property or, at a minimum, a renegotiation of the license agreement
The company operates in a volatile and rapidly changing business environment	The investor may want a special covenant to approve any material changes in the business model, pricing, target markets, and so on
The company's management team has a track record of short-term employment commitments and opportunity-driven "ADD"	The investor may insist on "tougher than market" covenants not to compete, covenants of confidentiality, and employment agreement commitments
Unclear target market or inability to secure medium-term or long-term customer commitments	The investor may insist on periodic updates to competitive analysis and SWOT reports, customer satisfaction and loyalty surveys, improved customer feedback systems, and so on, as an ongoing post-closing covenant

Understanding the Legal Documents

The actual executed legal documents described in the term sheet must reflect the end result of the negotiation process between you and the venture capitalist. These documents contain all the legal rights and obligations of the parties, and they generally include the investment agreement, a preferred-stock resolution (to amend the corporate charter), a stockholders agreement, an employment and confidentiality agreement, a contingent proxy, and a registration rights agreement. You may also have to execute a warrant, debenture, or notes, and obtain a legal opinion of company counsel.

The Investment Agreement

This is where you'll find all the material terms of the financing. The investment agreement also serves as a form of disclosure document because the representations and warranties portion covers the relevant financial and historical information that you make available to the investor. The representations and warranties (and any exhibits) also provide a basis for evaluating the risk of the investment and the structure of the transaction. The representations and warranties section includes the following (the appendix includes some sample representations and warranties that a typical growth company is likely to be expected to make to investors):

- *Organization, qualifications, and corporate power.* This section defines the legal structure of the company and attests that it is in good standing.
- *Authorization of agreement.* The company has the legal power to enter into the agreement, and any shares issued will be valid.
- *Validity.* The agreement will be legally binding.
- *Capital stock.* This section specifies how much stock will be issued and at what price.
- *Financial statements.* This section stipulates that investors have received the latest financial statements.
- *Actions pending.* An assurance that there are no legal actions pending against the company is provided.
- *Trade secrets.* No employees have violated any third-party agreements with regard to trade secrets of the third party.
- *Governmental approvals.* There are no governmental approvals, consents, or filings necessary for the agreement to be validated.

- *Offering of the preferred stock.* No one in the company has offered or will offer any stock to anyone other than the purchasers.
- *Lack of defaults.* The company knows of no defaults or violations of any laws that would have an adverse effect on the business.
- *Veracity of statements.* Everything in the documents is true, and nothing material has been omitted.

The investment agreement will also include certain conditions that you must meet prior to the closing. These provisions require you to perform certain acts at or prior to closing as a condition to the investor's providing the financing. These *conditions to closing* are often used in negotiations to mitigate or eliminate certain risks that the investor has identified, but they usually are more of an administrative checklist of actions that must occur at closing, such as execution of the ancillary documents that are discussed on the following pages.

Perhaps the most burdensome aspects of the investment agreement, and thus the most hotly negotiated, are the various *affirmative* and *negative covenants* that will govern and restrict your future business affairs and operations. Affirmative covenants may include an obligation to maintain certain insurance policies, protect intellectual property, comply with key agreements, prepare forecasts and budgets for review and approval by the investors, and ensure that certain investors are represented on the board of directors of the company.

Negative covenants may include obligations *not* to change the nature of your business or its capital structure, declare any cash or asset dividends, issue any additional stock or convertible securities, compensate any employee or consultant in excess of agreed-upon amounts, or pledge any company assets to secure debt or related obligations.

In most cases, you can't undertake the acts covered by the various affirmative and negative covenants without the express prior approval of the investors, and such restrictions will last for as long as the venture capitalist owns the securities purchased in the financing.

Finally, the investment agreement will provide remedies for any breach of the covenants or any misrepresentations that you make. In some cases, these remedies may require a civil action, such as a demand for specific performance, a claim for damages, or a request for injunctive relief. In other cases, the remedies will be self-executing, such as an adjustment in the investor's equity position, a right of redemption of the investment securities, rights of indemnification, supermajority voting rights (special voting rights that vest with the venture capitalist in the event of a default by the company under the investment agreement), or a right to foreclose on assets securing debt securities.

Amendment to Corporate Charter

In all likelihood, you'll need to amend your corporate charter to create the Series A preferred stock. The articles of amendment will set forth the special rights and preferences that will be granted to the Series A preferred stockholders, such as special voting rights, mandatory dividend payments, liquidation preferences, and, in some cases, mandatory redemption rights. You'll find some sample provisions from a venture capital–driven amendment to a company's charter in the appendix.

Stockholders Agreement

Venture capitalists will often require your principal stockholders to become parties to a stockholders agreement as a condition to closing on the investment. Any existing stockholders agreements or buy/sell agreements will also be carefully scrutinized and may need to be amended or terminated as a condition of the investment. The stockholders agreement will typically contain certain restrictions on the transfer of your company's securities, voting provisions, rights of first refusal and cosale rights in the event of a sale of the founder's securities, antidilution rights, and optional redemption rights for the venture capital investors.

For example, the investors may want to reserve the right to purchase additional shares of your preferred stock in order to preserve their respective equity ownership in the company if you issue another round of the preferred stock. This is often accomplished with a contractual preemptive right (as opposed to such a right being contained in the corporate charter, which would make these rights available to *all* holders of the preferred stock), which might read as follows:

> Each of the investors shall have a preemptive right to purchase any share of Common Stock or any securities which the company shall issue which are convertible into or exercisable for shares of Common Stock. In determining such right, each investor holding shares of Preferred Stock shall be deemed to be holding the shares of Common Stock into which such Common Stock or Preferred Stock are convertible. Such preemptive right must be exercised by each investor within fifteen (15) days from the date that each investor receives notice from the company stating the price, terms, and conditions of the proposed issuance of the shares of Common Stock and offering to each investor an opportunity to exercise its preemptive rights.

Employment and Confidentiality Agreements

Venture capitalists will also often require key members of the management team to execute certain employment and confidentiality agreements as a condition for the investment. These agreements will define each employee's obligations, his compensation package, the grounds for termination, his obligation to preserve and protect the company's intellectual property, and posttermination covenants, such as covenants not to compete or to disclose confidential information. You'll find a commonly used sample executive employment and confidentiality agreement in the appendix.

Contingent Proxy

This document provides for a transfer to the venture capitalist of the voting rights attached to any securities held by a principal of the company upon her death. The proxy may also be used as a penalty for breach of a covenant or warranty in the investment agreement.

Registration Rights Agreement

Many venture capitalists will see an eventual public offering of your securities pursuant to a registration statement filed with the SEC as the optimal way to achieve investment liquidity and maximize their return on investment. As a result, the venture capitalist will protect his right to participate in the eventual offering with a registration rights agreement. Generally, these registration rights are limited to your common stock, and thus would require the venture capital investors to convert their preferred stock or debentures to common stock prior to the time that the SEC approves the registration statement.

The registration rights may be in the form of "demand rights," meaning that the investors have the right to *require* you to prepare, file, and maintain a registration statement. Alternatively, they may be "piggyback rights," which allow the investors to have their investment securities included in a company-initiated registration. The number of each type of demand or piggyback rights, the percentage of investors necessary to exercise those rights, allocation of the expenses of registration, the minimum size of the offering, the scope of indemnification, and the selection of underwriters and brokers will all be areas of negotiation in the registration rights agreement. You'll find a sample registration rights agreement in the appendix.

Getting Ready for the Next Round

Capital formation is an ongoing process. Upon the closing of the Series A round of venture capital financing, it is not too soon to begin thinking about positioning the company and its capital structure for the Series B round. In the heyday of 1999, the typical time between rounds could be as short as six to nine months. In 2002, the length of time between rounds slowed as long to as long as eighteen months or longer—or forever. In 2004, the length between rounds of venture capital stabilized at twelve to fifteen months. In 2010, the estimated time between rounds of financing was approximately twenty months.

Key strategic questions to ask as you prepare for the next round of financing include the following:

- What milestones and performance objectives have been put into place as a condition for our next round of investment?
- Will the next round be coming from our existing investors? If so, are those commitments firmly in place? If not, what steps have we taken to identify prospective Series B investors?
- What happens if we need money between rounds?
- What is our projected valuation and dilution of existing shareholders upon closing of the Series B round?
- How will the rights of the Series A and Series B investors be balanced? How will special approvals be determined? How will investor-based seats be allocated?
- What amendments to the charter and/or the Series A investment document will need to be made as a result of Series B financing?

Many early-stage and rapid-growth companies do not adequately prepare for the next round and either fail to analyze these key strategic questions at all or do so too late in the process. The failure to be prepared can have a detrimental effect on the capital structure of the company and the dilution of existing investors.

2002 and 2003: The "Down-Round" Dilemma

In a perfect world, each round of financing would be at a higher valuation than the previous round, and existing investors would be rewarded for having had the foresight to invest in the company at its earliest stages. But when the Nasdaq fell from 5200 to 1600 and the levels of venture capital investment dropped to $18 billion in 2003 (versus $106 billion in 2000), follow-on financings began to look far less than perfect. Valuations began dropping by as much as 95 percent from the previous rounds, and early-stage (and even Series A) investors were badly punished and highly vulnerable. The lexicon of the 2002 and 2003 venture capital investing world was dominated by "down rounds," "washouts," "cramdowns," "involuntary recapitalizations," "liquidations-preferenced bridge loans," "reverse stock splits," and my own favorite, "the death spiral convertible preferred."

Another concern during this period was litigation. Early-stage investors brought lawsuits against current-round investors because of the significant dilution that they had suffered and the restrictive terms that were placed on the company's management. Other lawsuits were filed when the early-stage investors suffered significant dilution; the fresh influx of capital had put the company on a turnaround path leading to an IPO or M&A transaction, but the early-stage investors' upside had been substantially reduced as a result of the dilution. It was not uncommon to hear of angels' 20 percent stakes being cut to 2 percent, employee stock option pools being cut from 15 percent to 1 percent, Series A venture capitalists' stakes being cut from 30 percent to 5 percent, and founding entrepreneurs' ownership being cut to almost nothing. It is amazing that founding entrepreneurs who were facing salary cuts, minimal equity ownership, a large number of disgruntled employees, and angry family, friends, and angel investors ever came back to the office. Some didn't, as their upside had been too far diluted for them to be motivated to continue building the company, while other entrepreneurs chose to fold their companies rather than face the consequences of a down round.

Some "new money" investors in 2002 and 2003 were smart enough to realize that angry investors, demoralized employees, and demotivated founders were not exactly a recipe for business success. In some cases, the liquidation preferences, control provisions, and antidilution adjustments were leading to tension and litigation, not progress and execution of the business plan. Relief and reasonableness had come back into vogue by late 2003, with upside performance adjustments if the company met its largest milestones, carve-outs for additional stock to be put into the employee option pool (or restricted stock plans replacing the options pool), warrants for angel investors who remained active in the company, a bonus pool for the leadership team, and "pay-to-play" provisions, which allowed earlier-stage investors to maintain their equity positions and certain investors' rights, but only if they put in fresh cash in the new round of investment alongside the new investors.

The Pre- and Post-2010 Market: The Big Chill and the Slow Thaw

Thanks to the accessibility of leverage before the more deleterious effects of the financial crisis took hold, 2007 saw record deal flow and investment in the private equity arena. There were more than 3,000 deals done and $595 billion invested. In 2008, the tumult in the U.S. financial markets resulted in a marked decrease in deal flow and investment compared to the historically high 2007 levels. Despite the increasing lack of leverage, however, the amount of capital invested and the number of deals done in 2008 remained quite strong in comparison to the years 2002 through 2005. Specifically, there were 2,219 deals done and $215 billion invested in 2008 compared to 2,055 deals done with $173 billion invested and 2,533 deals with $301 billion invested in 2005 and 2006, respectively.

In February 2009, the market was characterized by uncertainty and unavailability of leverage. It was the worst year for private equity fund-raising since 2003—the amount of funds raised was down 68 percent from just one year earlier. The venture capital funds had only a slightly less difficult time; they were down 55 percent from the prior year. It was their slowest year since 2003. A decrease in lending led to a fundamental shift in the private equity world: Debt became less viable as a means of investment. The fact that private equity firms hold and support their companies for longer periods of time ties up venture funds, too. The fact that venture capital firms were holding on to their companies longer had a major consequence for smaller start-ups and emerging companies: These firms started making fewer early-stage investments. Not only were there significantly fewer investments, but there was substantially less total capital invested than there had been just 24 months earlier. Specifically, in all of 2009, there was only $61 billion invested in 1,349 deals. In 2007, $595 billion had been infused into 3,002 deals.

Post-2010: The Big Thaw

One major change that is occurring in 2011 is the slow return of leverage. While this should, in theory, provide greater liquidity for start-ups and emerging companies, that trend is slow to be seen. In 2010, much of the money went primarily to larger deals—the portion of deal flow in the lower to middle market was the lowest since before 2005.

A major catalyst for the somewhat improving conditions is the greater availability of exits for private equity firms. There were more exits in the second half of 2010 than in all of 2009. While greater exits mean more liquidity for new investments, the return of capital is not proving to be a fast one. The primary reason for this sluggish return is the colossal overhang left by the crisis.

Generally, venture capital firms prefer to invest in companies that have the potential to grow quickly and generate an annual return on investment in excess of 40 percent over three to five years. Heading into 2011, private equity firms own an all-time high of 5,994 U.S. companies. This high level of company ownership wouldn't be such an impediment to firms and the companies looking for their financing if it weren't for one fact: The median hold time for companies that they exited in 2010 was more than five years. In essence, the lack of exit opportunities in 2009 has left the market with a massive backlog of investments that need to be liquidated before investment in new companies can reach precrisis levels.

The market is also seeing a new regulatory framework headed by the Dodd-Frank Act. Although the attitudes of market players toward the act have been mixed, there is no doubt that the new regulations are going to produce new hurdles for the private equity market. The exact parameters of the act have yet to be worked out by regulatory authorities, but it is clear that there will be new registration requirements for previously exempt players, greater disclosure requirements, increased scrutiny of operations, and impediments to raising funds from traditional financial intermediaries. Specifically, the Volcker Amendment to the act prohibits a banking entity from "sponsoring" any hedge fund or private equity fund, with certain exceptions and a transition period. Prior to Dodd-Frank, the more lax Gramm-Leach-Bliley Act governed the relationship between banks and alternative investments.

Until investors reach a comfort level with the new regulatory framework and the market has thawed out significantly more, deal terms are going to continue to favor investors, and it appears that this will continue for the foreseeable future.

Chapter 11

Preparing for an Initial Public Offering

An initial public offering (IPO) is a legal process through which a company registers its securities with the Securities and Exchange Commission (SEC) for sale to the general investing public. Many entrepreneurs view the process of "going public" as the epitome of their financial success and reward; however, the decision to go public requires considerable strategic planning and analysis from both a legal and a business perspective. The planning and analysis process involves weighing the costs and benefits; understanding the process and its costs; and understanding the obligations of the company, its directors, its officers, its advisors, and its shareholders once the company has successfully completed its public offering.

Recent History

By the late 1990s, IPOs (especially those in the technology sector) were created and motivated by the rapid rise in venture capital investment in the early and mid-1990s. Investments by institutional venture capital firms had soared from $4 billion in 1992 to more than $35 billion in 1999. As discussed in Chapters 9 and 10, venture capital firms are not necessarily looking for a long-term marriage, and, traditionally, their preferred exit strategy has often been the IPO, where an initial investment of a few million dollars was able to yield much more in a short time. A striking example was the $5 million investment in web-Methods, a business-to-business e-commerce software development firm, by FBR Technology Venture Partners, which reaped nearly $600 million in profits on the day webMethods went public in 2000; in 2007, webMethods was acquired by Software AG for $546 million.

By 2005, the days of numerous early-stage technology companies completing an initial public offering at maximum market valuations with minimal revenues seemed to be a thing of the past. In 2004, it appeared that market conditions had stabilized and that the IPO as a capital-formation strategy was viable for a wider variety of companies; however, they needed greater revenues and stronger management than had previously been required.

The Present and Future

In 2008, the IPO market had something of a near-death experience—the entire year saw fewer than 30 IPOs. To put this in the perspective of recent history, in 1992 and 1999, there were more than 400 IPOs, and in 2005, there were more than 160. Since 2008, the market has begun to thaw out somewhat. In 2010, there were more than 90 IPOs, and the numbers are expected to rise in the coming years. This is a far cry from the historical levels just mentioned, but it does appear that the pipeline is opening up again. The second quarter of 2011 saw 22 venture capital–backed IPOs worth more than $5.5 billion in the aggregate, the strongest three months since March 2000 in terms of value. But it is interesting to note that in 2000, it took 79 venture-backed companies to raise $5.4 billion, so while the number of *dollars* raised has rebounded, it is more concentrated in only a quarter of the total number of companies (22 vs. 79), particularly social networking giants such as LinkedIn (raising $353 million) and Pandora ($235 million) and offerings of more than a billion dollars by Groupon, Living Social, and Zynga in late 2011. The number of IPOs by month is shown in Figure 11-1.

| **Figure 11-1.** | **Chart of Recent IPO Activity.** |

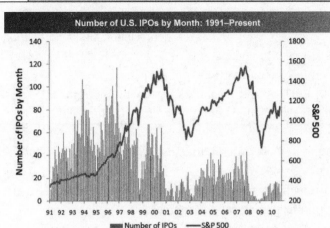

Thus, despite the shortfalls in IPO volume, proceeds from IPOs have remained relatively constant in 2010 after almost no activity in 2008 and 2009. In other words, fewer companies have been raising about the same amount of money using the public markets as it used to take significantly more IPOs to do. As in the late 1990s, technology companies have been accessing and will, for the foreseeable future, continue to access the markets through IPOs. Companies like Groupon and Pandora are looking to access the public markets to raise substantial amounts of capital, and LinkedIn's public offering was set at $45 a share, which valued the company at more than $4 billion. On LinkedIn's first day of trading in May of 2011, its shares traded at more than $100 a share, giving the company a market value of more than $10 billion—in 2010, it had $243 million in revenue. Unlike the IPO bonanza of the late 1990s, however, only a limited number of companies have been successfully accessing the public markets.

It is also important to realize that, despite the recent home runs, not every IPO is a hit. Historically, the idea has been that a small company would be able to raise a few rounds of venture capital financing, then go public in about five years, raising the capital it desired in the process. In 2010, however, the average IPO raised 14 percent less than expected, and the average age of companies was 10 years old.

With the IPO market beginning to heat up, entrepreneurs may wonder whether their company is ready to attempt to access the public markets. As a rule of thumb, a company should meet the following criteria before seriously considering an IPO in this market:

- Earnings before interest, taxes, depreciation, and amortization (EBITDA) are at least $10 million.
- Revenues are at least $100 million.
- Both EBITDA and revenue are growing more than 25 percent a year and are expected to continue to do so for the following three years.

In addition to these criteria, underwriters will be looking for these characteristics:

- A strong management team (with a vision) and governance structure (with transparency and accountability)
- Impressive gross margins and profitability growth trends
- A large, growing target market with optimistic industry forecasts for the next 12 to 36 months
- A loyal and growing customer base with demand curves on the rise and minimal customer complaints
- Genuine and demonstrable market niches protected by proprietary technology or relationships
- A strong game plan for the post-IPO allocation of proceeds via organic growth and M&A opportunities

Even where an IPO is a viable alternative, many entrepreneurs simply cannot justify the time, expense, public scrutiny, and potential risks that it takes to become and stay a publicly traded company and prefer to remain private. Even companies that had already gone public have chosen to become private as the costs of compliance began to outweigh the benefits of being a public company. In fact, for public companies with revenues of $80 million or less (or market capitalization of $40 million or less), the costs to comply with Sarbanes-Oxley, estimated at more than $1 million per annum, coupled with the significant increase in lawsuits against officers and directors of public companies, make it almost impossible to justify to shareholders that being public makes any sense.

In addition to established, successful large companies such as Cargill and Koch Industries, both of which had more than $100 billion in revenue in 2010, there has been a trend for public companies, such as CommScope, Burger King,

Gymboree, and Playboy, to go private. It is estimated that small public companies can save $2 million per year by delisting, in addition to avoiding the other burdens of being publicly listed. Facebook, a company that was recently valued at $50 billion, is an example of a company that has so far avoided the white-hot lights of public shareholder scrutiny by delaying, if not completely avoiding, an IPO.

Advantages and Disadvantages of an IPO

For a rapidly expanding privately held company, the process of going public has a number of benefits, including:

- Significantly greater access to capital
- Increased liquidity for the shares
- Market prestige
- Enhancement of public image
- Flexibility for employee ownership and participation
- Improved opportunities for mergers, acquisitions, and further rounds of financing
- An immediate increase in wealth for the founders

Advantages of Going Public

Here are more details about each of these advantages.

Cash Now and Cash Later. An IPO provides an immediate influx of capital. These additional funds are available for working capital, repayment of existing debt, marketing, research and development activities, diversification of operations, and other purposes. If your company's stock performs well in the year after it begins trading, you may be able to obtain more cash later (or provide a complete exit for shareholders) through future public offerings or through private placements.

Advantages of Equity. In contrast to money obtained through debt financing, the cash obtained from an IPO does not need to be repaid. A public offering results in an immediate increase in the company's net worth, facilitating future financing because of its improved debt-to-equity ratio.

Increased Market Value. Public companies tend to be more valuable than comparable private companies, in part because of their increased liquidity, the greater amount of available information, and a readily ascertainable value.

Mergers and Acquisitions. Going public not only raises a lot of cash that can be used for acquisitions, but also creates liquidity for your stock, which can be used as a substitute for cash to buy other companies.

Prestige, Reputation, and Enhanced Image. The visibility of your company is usually enhanced. Because a public company receives more attention from the investment community, it is likely to be accepted more easily as trustworthy and dependable. This improved visibility and reputation can help your company win customers, secure financing, or expand from the regional level to the national one. Your company's new status as a publicly owned entity may give you a competitive advantage over other companies in the same field. Publicly traded stock may be used as a vehicle for establishing stock option plans and stock purchase plans, thereby increasing your ability to attract and retain key employees. Finally, listing on a national securities exchange or Nasdaq may enhance your company's image and make it easier for you to raise additional capital in the future.

Less Dilution. Often a public offering may achieve a better share price than a private offering, resulting in less dilution of ownership for the same amount of funds received.

Personal Advantages to Shareholders. Going public gives you and your shareholders a relatively easy way to liquidate some, or ultimately all, of your investment, since you can simply sell your stock, thus achieving greater liquidity and shareholder value. Or you may use your existing stock as collateral to secure personal loans. Future sales are made easier by the existence of a public market for your company's stock. However, the SEC, the underwriter, and state securities departments place certain restrictions on sales of stock by company "insiders," which may limit your ability to dispose of large amounts of stock quickly. When a shareholder dies, his estate may have to dispose of his holdings in order to pay estate taxes. The estate will be able to do this more easily if there is a public market for the stock.

Incentives. Your customers, vendors, and employees may become shareholders. When they have a stake in your company, these individuals will have an additional incentive to work toward its success.

Disadvantages of Going Public

The many benefits of going public are not without their corresponding costs, however, and the downside of being a public company must be strongly considered in the strategic-planning process. These costs include:

- A dilution of the founders' control of the entity
- Pressure to meet market and shareholder expectations regarding growth and dividends
- Changes in management style and employee expectations
- Compliance with the complex regulations imposed by federal and state securities laws
- Stock-resale restrictions for company insiders
- Vulnerability to shifts in the stock market
- Sharing the company's financial success with hundreds or even thousands of other shareholders

Dilution and Loss of Control. You incur immediate dilution of your holdings as a result of a public offering. Future offerings could ultimately cause you to lose control of your company. In the long run, you may also risk an unfriendly takeover. Antitakeover devices may not be acceptable to the underwriters of an IPO. After a public offering, previous shareholders must share their earnings with public shareholders.

Risk. If the offering isn't successful, you will still have to bear the costs (which are incurred regardless of whether the offering is completed). If the offering is completed, these costs should be accounted for as a reduction in additional paid-in capital and thus are not expensed in the income statement (in other words, they are not tax-deductible). Additionally, the IPO market could deteriorate significantly prior to the offering.

Time and Energy. A public offering requires a great deal of management's time and energy for a period of several months. This strain and distraction could hurt your business.

Loss of Privacy. Your company immediately becomes subject to the periodic reporting and other requirements of the SEC. The stock exchanges and Nasdaq require public disclosure of all significant events that could affect an investor's decision to buy, sell, or hold your company's stock. You will need to disclose information regarding your profits, competitive position, salaries, employee benefits, and other financial information. The disclosure of this information gives your competitors an advantage that they would not otherwise have.

Additionally, significant corporate decisions will be subject to second-guessing by the investment community, shareholders, and regulators.

Reduced Flexibility. Certain decisions that previously were made unilaterally will now have to be approved by the board of directors or the shareholders. Management's decisions will have to take shareholders' interests and the public's perceptions into account.

Pressures to Pay Dividends or Improve Stock Performance. Investors' emphasis on short-term results may pressure management to sacrifice the company's long-term plan for the stockholders' short-term financial gain.

Investor Relations. You will need to establish an open channel of communication with your investors. Distributing quarterly and annual financial reports and coordinating shareholders' meetings and investment-community presentations take considerable time and money. Management, directors, and controlling shareholders owe fiduciary duties to the public shareholders. This can become a problem in situations where a parent company sells shares of a subsidiary to the public and continues to have business dealings with the subsidiary.

Volatility. Company value will be affected by the general state of the economy and overall stock market fluctuations that are not directly related to the performance of your underlying business.

Restrictions on Insider Sales. Stock sales by insiders are limited by several factors, such as "lock-up" requirements by underwriters or states. These require existing shareholders to hold their stock for a specified period following an offering (usually one year). Some states require certain shareholders' stock to be held in escrow for a significant period of time as a condition for allowing a public offering. It is also important for insider sales not to be perceived as the insiders bailing out. Insiders are also subject to civil and criminal liability if they trade in company stock on the basis of material nonpublic information.

Irreversibility. In most cases, an IPO is a one-way process. Reversing it and taking the company private again is usually difficult and costly.

Expenses. The expenses related to the IPO process are significant. They vary considerably based on the surrounding circumstances, but they typically consist of the following:

- *The underwriter's compensation.* This usually averages about 7 percent of the offering's gross proceeds. The underwriter's compensation may also include warrants, options, consulting fees, finder's fees (if the IPO leads to a merger or acquisition), preferential rights to future financing, and other "nonaccountable" expenses. The underwriter's compensation is the single largest expense incurred in going public, representing two-thirds or more of all expenses.

- *Legal fees.* These run from $100,000 to $200,000 on smaller or simpler offerings, but they can reach $600,000 or more for larger ($50 million or more) or more complex offerings. In addition, the company must pay legal and registration fees for filing with the SEC and the Financial Industry Regulatory Authority (FINRA) and for "blue sky" state security filings. These fees generally range from $20,000 to $50,000, depending on the size of the offering, the number of states in which the offering is qualified for sale, and the number of stock issues raised. You may also be required to reimburse the managing underwriter's legal fees, especially when its counsel is significantly involved in the drafting of the registration statement.

- *Accounting fees.* These range from $50,000 to $100,000 on small or simple offerings and from $150,000 to $225,000 or more on delayed, complex, or large offerings. These costs can be reduced if regular audits have been performed and if the previous year's audit has been completed. Other services that the accountants perform include reviews of the registration statement, assistance in responding to SEC comments, and preparation of the "comfort" letter to the underwriters, which assures them that there are no significant accounting problems or issues.

- *The road show.* Your top executives will need to make presentations describing your company to potential investors. This involves the expenditure of both time and money, primarily because of the extensive travel required. In an effort to reduce these costs, some companies have launched "virtual road shows," which are Web-driven opportunities for brokers and institutional investors to interact with the company's management team via the Internet.

- *Printing and engraving costs.* You can spend $50,000 to $250,000 to print the registration statement, prospectus, and underwriting documents and to engrave the stock certificates. Costs vary and can exceed this range depending on the length and number of documents, the use of color, and the number of revisions or amendments.

You'll incur all these expenses whether or not the IPO is completed, and they can easily add up to $500,000 to $800,000 for smaller offerings (about $10 million), $1 million to $1.5 million for average offerings (about $30 million), and to $2 million to $2.5 million for more complex, poorly planned, or larger offerings ($50 million or more). Expenses of completed IPOs are not tax-deductible because they are accounted for as a reduction of additional paid-in capital. On the other hand, if the IPO is not completed, such costs must be expensed. In most cases, unless there is identifiable future value, costs associated with an uncompleted IPO will be tax-deductible.

Ongoing Costs of a Public Company. Once your company goes public, you must incur some recurring expenses, such as annual administrative and investor-relations costs (quarterly reports, proxy material, annual reports, transfer agent, and public relations, for example), unexpected taxes (such as franchise, transfer, and capital stock), and indemnity insurance for errors and omissions (which is required by some underwriters).

The Hidden Legal Costs

In addition to some of the more obvious business costs, the most expensive aspect of registering securities is often the hidden costs that are imposed by federal and state securities laws. The rules and regulations imposed by the Securities and Exchange Commission make going public a time-consuming and expensive process that begins several years before the public offering and continues (by means of the SEC periodic reporting process) for as long as the company remains public. From a legal perspective, you should strongly consider the following costs and factors.

Planning and Preparing the Business for the IPO

From the day you form a company, there is a host of legal and structural pitfalls that you must avoid if an IPO is in your company's future. If they are not avoided early on, some of these pitfalls will create significant impediments to a successful IPO and will be expensive to remedy once the damage has been done. In addition, a public company requires a more formal management style from a legal perspective: You need to hold regular meetings of the board of directors, and you need to follow all the formalities imposed by state corporate laws. Therefore, it is best to operate your company as if it were public right from the start by adopting strong database-management practices and creating vehicles for communicating with your shareholders regularly.

Due Diligence and Housecleaning

Many owners (and their managers) who take their companies public complain that they feel as though their management of the company and their personal lives are conducted in a fishbowl. Federal and state securities laws dictate that a prospective investor must have access to all material information about a company that offers its securities to the public. As a result, you must go through the due diligence process well before you're ready to file a registration statement with the SEC. Before you're ready to operate in the public fishbowl, you may need to formalize, amend, or even terminate your corporate charter, bylaws, shareholder agreements, employment agreements, leases, licenses, accounting methods, and related documents and procedures.

The Registration Process

Do not underestimate the amount of time, effort, and expense required to prepare the registration statement. In fact, the 6- to 12-month time frame and the out-of-pocket expenses alone make it prohibitive for many growing businesses to go public. Although costs will vary depending on several factors, as outlined earlier, you need to be prepared to spend anywhere from $200,000 to $500,000 on legal and accounting fees, appraisal costs, printing expenses, and consulting and filing fees, in addition to the underwriter's and broker's commissions, which may run 10 percent or more of the total offering. (However, as discussed later in this chapter, the SEC has implemented new regulations for small-business owners that will reduce the cost of some of these legal and accounting fees.) Few, if any, of these costs will be contingent on the success of the offering; therefore, you must pay these fees regardless of how many shares of your company's stock you actually sell.

In addition to the registration statement, you must file exhibits and attachments that document major business transactions (such as plans to acquire, reorganize, or liquidate), customer and vendor arrangements, and your financial statements. And you must file these documents prior to the IPO. These required disclosures will result in a loss of confidentiality, and that could prove to be costly, because competitors, creditors, labor unions, suppliers, and others will have access to these documents once they become available to the public.

Periodic Reporting and Ongoing Compliance

Most public companies are subject to the ongoing periodic reporting requirements imposed by the SEC, such as quarterly financial reporting (Form 10-Q), annual financial reporting (Form 10-K), reporting of current material events (Form 8-K), and related reporting requirements, such as those for the sale of control stock and tender offers. The ongoing costs of running a public company also include an increased use of attorneys, accountants, and other advisors; the need to dedicate staff time to meet with securities analysts and the financial press; the implementation of a shareholder- and media-relations program; and the significantly greater cost of annual reports, shareholders' meetings, and solicitations of proxies when shareholder approval is needed for major corporate transactions.

Preparing for the Underwriter's Due Diligence

Before preparing the registration statement, the proposed underwriter and its financial analysts and attorneys will want to conduct extensive due diligence on your company to ensure the viability of the IPO. Due diligence entails an evaluation and scrutiny of your company's corporate records, personnel, business plans, industry trends, customer data, pricing and business models, products, key agreements, and financial data: These will be viewed as though under a microscope. The appendix provides a checklist of topics and documents that will be reviewed during due diligence.

You should begin preparing for the due diligence process well in advance of the IPO to avoid the significant expenses that will be incurred if you are unprepared and to prevent embarrassing situations if factual or strategic weaknesses or problems are unexpectedly revealed. *Remember that the underwriter's legal counsel will be looking for any problems that may impede the IPO, such as excessive compensation or expenses, a weak management team, nepotism, or problems with your company's underlying intellectual property or business model; the sooner these problems are addressed, the better.*

Conducting a Legal Audit

The best way to prepare for the due diligence process is to have your company's counsel conduct a legal audit, during which you and your key managers meet with corporate counsel to discuss strategic plans and objectives, review key documents and records, and analyze and identify current and projected problem areas that might later be identified by the underwriter's team. The goal is to solve these problems in advance of your first meeting with the underwriting team. The legal audit also lays the groundwork for a program of ongoing legal compliance and prevention to ensure that your company's goals, structure, and ongoing operations are consistent with the latest developments in business and corporate law. Finally, the legal audit helps managers identify any legal issues that can be triggered by changes in strategies, goals, or objectives and helps you plan how to handle those issues.

A comprehensive legal audit will examine a wide range of issues, from the very mundane (whether or not your company is qualified to do business in foreign jurisdictions) to the very complex (ensuring that your company's executive compensation and retirement plans are consistent with current tax and employment law regulations). The topics that must be addressed include:

- Choice and structure of the entity
- Recent acts of the board of directors and documentation (or lack thereof) relating to those decisions
- Protection of intellectual property
- Forms and methods of distribution and marketing
- Pending and threatened litigation
- Estate planning
- Insurance coverage
- Hiring and firing practices
- Employment agreements
- Securities law compliance
- Antitrust and related trade regulations
- Product liability and environmental law
- A review of sales and collection practices

Naturally, the extent and complexity of the legal audit will vary depending on the size and stage of growth of your company, the type of business (service or manufacturing, for example), the number of shareholders and employees, the extent to which your company does business in a "regulated industry," and a host of other factors.

Mechanics of the Legal Audit

The mechanics of the legal audit are described here, and a list of questions that will be covered in the audit is provided in the appendix.

The Preliminary Questionnaire. The legal audit should begin with a comprehensive questionnaire for your company's management team to review and address before the arrival of the team of attorneys that will conduct the legal audit. In the case of smaller companies, a simple checklist of issues or a formal agenda will be more than sufficient to prepare for the initial conference.

The Initial Conference. Once the documents and related materials requested in the questionnaire have been assembled and problem areas have been preliminarily identified, a meeting should be scheduled between audit counsel and the designated officers of the company who are well versed in the various aspects of its operations. Related members of the management team, such as the company's outside accountant and other professionals who play key advisory roles in the company, should be present during at least the portion of the audit that relates to their area of expertise. These initial conferences are basically an information-gathering exercise that is designed to familiarize the legal auditor with the most current information about all aspects of the company. In addition to these conferences with key personnel, the audit team should perform some on-site observations of the company's day-to-day operations. The legal audit team should also review the company's current financial statements and spend some time with the company's accounting firm.

Implementation of the Post-Audit Recommendations. Once the legal audit team has issued its post-audit evaluation to the company's management team, you can implement the recommendations of the report. What you do will vary, depending on both the growth planned by the company and the specific findings of the report. At a minimum, you should schedule meetings with key personnel to review and discuss the post-audit recommendations; prepare internal memos to educate the rank-and-file employees; conduct employee seminars to educate employees about proper procedures and compliance; and, in certain cases, develop handbooks and operations manuals to provide continued and readily available guidance for the company's staff. If significant problems are discovered during the audit, counsel should be careful as to what is included in the final written report in order to avoid potential adverse consequences under the federal or state rules of evidence. In addition, you can establish a tickler system for periodic reporting and key dates and deadlines, as well as setting a time for the next legal audit.

Additional Tips for Preparing for Due Diligence

In addition to conducting the legal audit, you should immediately implement a more formalized management structure: hold formal board meetings on a monthly or quarterly basis; maintain complete and accurate corporate minutes and resolutions; prepare periodic reports to existing shareholders; and recruit experienced, independent directors who would be acceptable to the investing public. *In short, well before your first meeting with an underwriter, begin acting as if you were already a publicly traded company in terms of management, record keeping, shareholder reporting, and financial controls. The discipline that it takes to put these practices in place while you are still privately held will expedite the IPO process and should enhance your valuation.*

Among the key concerns of any prospective underwriter or investor analyzing a company are the three Ps of due diligence: people, products, and profits.

People. Key employees should be selected carefully because their background and roles in the company will be carefully investigated during the due diligence process and subsequently disclosed in the prospectus. These employees should be subject to reasonable employment agreements, nondisclosure agreements, and incentive programs that ensure their long-term commitment to the company. A key question will be whether the management team that is currently in place has the skills and experience to lead a public company. Professional advisors should have a strong corporate and securities law background and be capable to grow with the company as its requirements for professional services become more comprehensive and complex.

Products. The products and services that your company offers should be protected to the fullest extent possible under patent, trademark, and copyright law. Any key vendor, licensee, customer, or distributor agreement that materially affects the production or distribution of these products and services should be negotiated and put in writing as formally as possible, with the eventual disclosure of these documents kept in mind. The systems used to produce the company's products or services should be fully scalable to facilitate future growth, and distribution channels should be in place to bring the company's products and services to the marketplace.

Profits. The capital structure and the company's financial performance will be under the microscope of any potential underwriter. Although the wild market of the late 1990s seemed to have little relationship to actual profits (or in the case of some high-tech companies, even revenues), the more conservative financial markets of the early 2000s are more likely to require a solid financial track record and the presence of earnings and rapid growth.

Deal Breakers to Avoid

Here are a few items that will have a negative effect on your company's valuation and an underwriter's willingness to participate in the IPO:

- An inefficient management structure or major holes in your management team
- An unprofitable business model or weak revenue base
- Overly restrictive shareholder agreements (which affect the company's control)
- Operating in a market with low barriers to entry
- Low customer loyalty to the company's brands, products, and services
- Self-dealing by members of the board of directors or key stockholders
- Weaknesses in the company's key intangible assets, such as brands or operating technology
- Inadequate corporate records
- Capital structure with excessive debt
- A series of unaudited and uncertain financial statements
- Poor earnings history

Selecting an Underwriter

At the heart of the network established for the distribution and sale of securities is the managing or lead underwriter, whose selection and negotiation is a key ingredient in the success of the IPO. A lot of time should be devoted to interviewing and selecting the lead underwriter. Consider a wide variety of underwriters, ranging from small, local firms (which may be able to devote considerable time and attention to the transaction) to larger firms with a genuine Wall Street presence and reputation (but where there is a risk that the offering will be lost among bigger transactions or delegated to junior staff members).

Many factors should be considered in selecting the lead underwriter, and you will want to interview as many prospective underwriters as possible to ensure you make the right choice. For this "beauty contest," focus on the issues set forth in the next section. The size and reputation of the underwriter your company is able to attract will depend on the strength of your company, the amount of stock being offered, and your company's business plans.

Underwriters typically offer a wide range of support services, such as management consulting services, business valuations, development of media- and shareholder-relations programs, assistance in developing an optimum capital structure or location, and analysis of merger and acquisition candidates (which may or may not be needed when you are considering a public offering). Any company (regardless of its size or industry type) should closely examine the reputation, experience, distribution capability, market-making ability, research capabilities, and specific industry expertise of the potential underwriter.

Key Factors to Consider When Selecting an Underwriter

Size requirements of the underwriter. Some major underwriters will consider only companies that have attained a particular size and level of profitability and have been in operation for some minimum period.

Size of the offering. Some underwriters will not consider offerings below a certain size (major national underwriters usually require offerings of at least $15 million).

Industry specialization. Certain underwriters possess a reputation and expertise in particular industries or fields. This knowledge affects the quality of the underwriter's due diligence, the accuracy of its pricing, and its ability to sell the company to others during and after the offering.

Research coverage. It is critical that the underwriter have strong research coverage and respect in the industry in which you will be operating. These research capabilities will be critical both in the initial valuation and road show and after the stock begins trading.

Reputation. Your company will be affected by the underwriter's image and reputation.

Quality of underwriting group. Some underwriters are able to develop stronger syndicates than others.

Distribution strength. The lead manager must control and influence the channels of distribution of the IPO. It is important that the underwriters sell out the offering and do so expeditiously.

Personal chemistry between company management and the underwriter's personnel. It is important that you begin getting to know underwriters at least six months before the offering. During the offering process, the management of the company will need to trust the underwriter's judgment, competence, commitment, credibility, and honesty. It is of paramount importance that you meet the key people in the organization and get a feeling for their philosophy. Venture capital investors may try to influence the choice of the underwriter, but the company is the one that has to live with the choice. There must be a philosophical fit.

Mix of retail and institutional customers. Some investment bankers sell primarily to institutions, and others have large retail sales organizations. The types of customers to which an underwriter directs its marketing activities may affect its ability to sell an offering in certain markets.

After-market support. Underwriters provide a variety of post-offering services, such as acting as market makers, purchasing shares for their own account, bringing the stock to the attention of analysts and investors, and facilitating the bringing of information about the company to the marketplace. A company needs a strong, deep, liquid, orderly market for its shares. This requires a number of well-capitalized market makers, starting with the managing underwriter(s) and the syndicate it (they) assemble(s). If the underwriter does not provide adequate support and ongoing reports on your company's progress, the price is likely to fall.

Quality of analysts. The underwriter's analysts should know the company's industry and must be well known in it. Additionally, they should be widely read by the investment community. The company should get a research commitment from the managing underwriter. The analysts' reputation can be checked by calling some big institutions and inquiring whether the analysts are recognized in the surveys by *Institutional Investor* or the *Greenwich Survey*.

Staffing problems. It is important to make sure that the underwriter will devote sufficient attention to the offering and that the offering will not be placed in line behind other larger, more exciting opportunities, particularly when the markets are hot.

Underwriter's references. The performance of the prospective underwriter can be checked by getting a list of the last five or ten offerings in which the underwriter participated and contacting or visiting the principals of those companies to discuss the underwriter's performance before, during, and after the offering. It is essential to determine whether the promised after-market support was there, the promised research reports were completed and published on time, the road show was well handled, the senior staff members attended the meetings, and so on. More references can be obtained from the institutions to which the underwriter sells.

The Letter of Intent

Once selected, the lead underwriter will usually execute a *letter of intent* stating the terms and conditions of the proposed distribution of the securities and setting a range for the price of the securities, hence the valuation of the company. However, the final decision on these issues will be made during the due diligence process and will be determined by the post-effective price amendment (which may adjust the price based on recent events affecting the company or changes in market conditions). Because underwriters have different methods of arriving at the preliminary valuation and pricing, be prepared to solicit competing bids if possible to ensure the best valuation for your company. The letter of intent also governs the relationship between you and the underwriter throughout the preparation and registration process because the final underwriting agreement is usually not signed until the registration statement becomes effective following SEC approval. Understanding the key terms of the letter of intent is crucial. These key terms are defined in the following sections.

Type of Underwriting. There are two basic kinds of commitments by the lead underwriter. One is the *firm commitment*, whereby the underwriter pledges to purchase all of the securities offered and then bears the responsibility for reselling the securities to the public. The other is the *best-efforts commitment*, in which the lead underwriter merely promises to use its best efforts to offer and sell the securities.

Under the best-efforts commitment, there is no assurance that the amount of capital required to meet your business objectives will be received, even though the company must still incur the extensive costs of the offering and the legal burden of being a publicly held company. One form of protection is the all-or-nothing or go–no-go amount, which provides that if a certain minimum number of shares are not sold, the entire offering will be withdrawn. An underwriter may also want to negotiate overallotment or green-shoe options, whereby the underwriter is granted the option to purchase a specific number of additional shares if the maximum number of shares to be sold is exceeded.

Compensation of the Underwriter. This usually comprises the commission schedules, ongoing consulting fees, and any warrants to purchase shares (during a certain period of time and at a fixed price). The rate of commission, the amount of advance payment, the number of warrants to be issued, and other details will depend on the company's negotiating leverage, the risk of the offering, and the underwriter's projected internal time and effort to manage the distribution network.

Offering, Size, Price, and Special Characteristics. These terms refer to the type of security to be issued, the number of shares to be sold, the price of the security per share, and any special characteristics or restrictions. The final decisions regarding these factors may not be made until just prior to the actual offering, depending on market conditions and the completion of due diligence. When this is the case, you and the underwriter should at least agree on a price range, which will be subject to the terms of the final "pricing amendment" filed with the SEC just prior to the public offering.

Responsibility for Fees and Expenses. Usually you'll be responsible for all of the company's costs and some portion of the underwriter's expenses as well. Expect that the lead underwriter will want to hold a series of parties and "dog and pony shows." To prevent excessive costs, you should establish a ceiling on these expenses.

Miscellaneous Provisions. Along with the other key terms to be negotiated, the following also apply:

- Rights of first refusal on future financing
- Responsibility for state blue sky law registration
- Selection of professional advisors
- Representations and warranties
- Restrictions on activities before and after the sale of the securities
- Accessibility of employee records for further due diligence

Selecting an Exchange

The final step in preparing to go public is to select where your stock will be listed for purchase or sale. Figures 11-2 through 11-6 explain the entry and listing requirements for a few of the major U.S. exchanges and markets:

- Nasdaq Global Select Market

- Nasdaq Global Market
- Nasdaq Capital Market
- The New York Stock Exchange (NYSE)
- The NYSE Amex Equities

As companies grow, they tend to initially seek an appropriate level of exchange and then move up to the more prestigious listing alternatives. In practical terms, the initial decision to choose one of the alternatives is going to depend on a variety of factors: the capital market accessed, market activity, initial listing requirements, and ongoing requirements, to name a few. Figures 11-2 to 11-6 lay out one of the most important factors, the initial listing requirements of the major U.S.–based exchanges.

Figure 11-2. | **Nasdaq Global Select Market Initial Listing Requirements.**

Requirements (Must Satisfy Any One of the Standards)	Standard 1	Standard 2	Standard 3	Standard 4
Pretax earnings	$11 million or higher (aggregate for prior three years) and $2.2 million (in each of prior two years)	N/A	N/A	N/A
Cash flow	N/A	Less than or equal to $27.5 million (aggregate for prior three years)	N/A	N/A

Requirements (Must Satisfy Any One of the Standards)	Standard 1	Standard 2	Standard 3	Standard 4
Market capitalization	N/A	$550 million average or more over prior 12 months	$850 million or more over prior 12 months	$160 million
Revenue	N/A	$110 million or more (prior year)	$90 million or more (prior year)	N/A
Total assets	N/A	N/A	N/A	$80 million in recent year
Stockholders' equity	N/A	N/A	N/A	$55 million
Bid price	$4	$4	$4	$4
Market makers	3 or 4	3 or 4	3 or 4	3 or 4
Corporate governance	Yes	Yes	Yes	Yes

Figure 11-3.   Nasdaq Global Market Initial Listing Requirements.

Requirements (Must Satisfy One of the Standards)	Standard 1	Standard 2	Standard 3	Standard 4
Pretax income (in prior year or two of last three prior years)	$1 million	N/A	N/A	N/A
Stockholders' equity	$15 million	$30 million	N/A	N/A
Market value of listed securities	N/A	N/A	$75 million	N/A
Total assets and total revenue (in prior year or in two of three prior years)	N/A	N/A	N/A	$75 million and $75 million

Requirements (Must Satisfy One of the Standards)	Standard 1	Standard 2	Standard 3	Standard 4
Publicly held shares	1.1 million	1.1 million	1.1 million	1.1 million
Market value of publicly held shares	$8 million	$18 million	$20 million	$20 million
Bid price	$4	$4	$4	$4
Shareholders (round-lot holders)	400	400	400	400
Market makers	3	3	4	4
Operating history	N/A	2 years	N/A	N/A
Corporate governance	Yes	Yes	Yes	Yes

Figure 11-4.   Nasdaq Capital Market Initial Listing Requirements.

Requirements (Must Satisfy One of the Standards)	Standard 1	Standard 2	Standard 3
Stockholders' equity	$5 million	$4 million	$4 million
Market value of publicly held shares	$15 million	$15 million	$5 million
Operating history	2 years	N/A	N/A
Market value of listed securities	N/A	$50 million	N/A
Net income from continuing operations (prior year or two of three prior years)	N/A	N/A	$750,000
Bid price	$4	$4	$4
Publicly held shares	1 million	1 million	1 million
Shareholders (round-lot holders)	300	300	300
Market makers	3	3	3
Corporate governance	Yes	Yes	Yes

| Figure 11-5. | NYSE Listing Requirements. | | | |

Requirements (Must Meet One of the Standards)	Standard 1 (Earnings Test)	Standard 2 (Valuation with Cash Flow)	Standard 3 (Pure Valuation with Revenues)	Standard 4 (Assets and Equity)
Round-lot holders	400 U.S.	400 U.S.	400 U.S.	400 U.S.
Public shares	1.1 million	1.1 million	1.1 million	1.1 million
Market value of public shares	$100 million	$100 million	$100 million	$100 million
Stock price	$4	$4	$4	$4
Pretax income (aggregate for last three years) and minimum in each of two prior years and third must be positive) or Pretax income (aggregate for last three years) and minimum in recent year and minimum in next recent year.	$10 million and $2 million or $12 million and $5 million and $2 million	N/A	N/A	N/A
Global market capitalization	N/A	$500 million	$750 million	$150 million
Revenues (recent 12-month period)	N/A	$100 million	$75 million (recent fiscal year)	N/A
Adjusted cash flow (aggregate for prior three years; all must be positive)	N/A	$25 million	N/A	N/A
Total assets	N/A	N/A	N/A	$75 million
Stockholders' equity	N/A	N/A	N/A	$50 million

Figure 11-6.   NYSE Amex Equities Listing Requirements.

Requirements (Must Meet One of the Standards)	Standard 1	Standard 2	Standard 3	Standard 4
Shareholders' equity	$4 million	$4 million	$4 million	N/A
Pretax income (required in last fiscal year or two of three most recent years)	$750,000	N/A	N/A	N/A
Market capitalization	N/A	N/A	$50 million	$75 million *or* at least $75 million in total assets and $75 million in revenues
Distribution	800 public shareholders and 500,000 shares publicly held *or* 400 public shareholders and 1 million shares publicly held *or* 400 public shareholders, 500,000 shares publicly held, and average daily trading volume of 2,000 shares for prior six months	800 public shareholders and 500,000 shares publicly held *or* 400 public shareholders and 1 million shares publicly held *or* 400 public shareholders, 500,000 shares publicly held, and average daily trading volume of 2,000 shares for prior six months	800 public shareholders and 500,000 shares publicly held *or* 400 public shareholders and 1 million shares publicly held *or* 400 public shareholders, 500,000 shares publicly held, and average daily trading volume of 2,000 shares for prior six months	800 public shareholders and 500,000 shares publicly held *or* 400 public shareholders and 1 million shares publicly held *or* 400 public shareholders, 500,000 shares publicly held, and average daily trading volume of 2,000 shares for prior six months
Price	$3	$3	$2	$3
Market value of public float	$3 million	$15 million	$15 million	$20 million
Operating history	N/A	2 years	N/A	N/A

Alternatives to Using a Traditional IPO

A stock offering of any type has not traditionally been the first financing strategy of small, developing companies. But a few changes in federal and state securities regulations, as well as the advent of Internet commerce, have turned the tables on the traditional methods that small businesses use to obtain equity investment. The Internet is creating new possibilities for companies that are looking to raise capital; however, it is also creating some confusion concerning what the differences are between initial public offerings and direct public offerings (DPOs).

Direct Public Offerings

A direct public offering is a primary market sale of securities (stock or debentures) from the company issuing the shares to the public buying the shares. In essence, it is a "do-it-yourself" public offering. The issuer usually performs the underwriting structuring, filing, and selling of its offer without the underwriter and selling syndicate that is used in an IPO. DPOs date back to 1976, but they have gained momentum since 1989, when the SEC simplified registrations for small companies.

The DPO made its debut on the Internet in 1995, when Spring Street Brewery displayed its offering prospectus on its web site. Potential investors could visit the site, learn about the company, download subscription documents, and, if they were interested in investing, send a check directly to Spring Street. In 1996, after experiencing the need for "Internet underwriters" firsthand, the CEO of Spring Street Brewery created Wit Capital, an online entity that integrates the functions of an investment bank, a brokerage firm, and an exchange forum.

Since the SEC ruled that "electronic delivery is good delivery," many companies have begun displaying offering literature for both direct and initial public offerings online, and DPOs on the Internet have become a popular method of raising capital for small companies. The rise of DPOs on the Internet stems from two converging trends: the rise of Internet commerce and the rise of the online investor. While a DPO is an excellent vehicle for linking small companies with investors who are willing to assume a higher degree of risk, it is not for every small business, and it is not a simple process. The stronger DPOs have been those whose companies have a loyal and wide customer base and brand affinity and where an online underwriter can be used to increase awareness of the offering.

Types of DPOs. DPOs are also referred to as exempt offerings because they are free of the intensive registration restrictions that come with an IPO. In a DPO, the company sells the deal directly to clients, members of the community, vendors, or any other constituency that has a stake in the company and its success. The steps in taking a company public through a DPO may include corporate review, due diligence, registration, and marketing and sales analysis. There are several registration options, and you should examine the requirements and limitations of each before you decide if any of them is right for your company.

Regulation A. Regulation A allows a company to raise as much as $5 million over a 12-month period. For a company to file a Regulation A offering, the company must not already be a public company and must not be an investment, oil, or gas company. There are no restrictions on the types of investors who can participate in a Regulation A offering (that is, they need not be accredited investors). Also, the issuer may engage in general marketing of the offering, such as press releases, cold calling, and television and radio commercials.

If you decide to engage in a Regulation A offering, you will be exempted from the filing provisions of the Securities Act of 1933 (the Act). That is, you will not have to file a registration statement with the SEC, although you will need to comply with the antifraud and personal-liability provisions of the Act. Despite this, you are essentially required to make the same disclosures as you would if you filed a registration statement. Regulation A offerings require that you file an offering circular with the SEC. An offering circular is basically a prospectus, but the financial statements in an offering circular need not be audited. Regulation A does not exempt your company from state securities laws, which vary greatly from state to state.

SCOR (Rule 504 under Regulation D). This type of offering allows a small company to raise up to $1 million over a 12-month period. SCOR is an acronym for Small Corporate Offering Registration (some states refer to this program as ULOR, or Uniform Limited Offering Registration). A company can either issue a SCOR offering directly to the public or use a traditional IPO model, in which an underwriter sells the stock to the public. Although it has grown in popularity since its inception in 1985, not every state has adopted the SCOR program.

For a company to launch a SCOR, it must have audited financial statements. Like a Regulation A offering, a SCOR offering must comply with the antifraud and personal-liability provisions of the Act. However, a SCOR offering does not require the issuer to file an offering circular with the SEC. A SCOR is meant to be simpler and less expensive. This is accomplished by using Form U-7. This form is in question-and-answer format and is about 30 pages long. Under Section 504 of the Act, a company engaged in an offering of up to $1 million may market the offering using television, radio, and print ads if the securities are sold in accordance with state general solicitation and advertising laws. In addition, there is no limitation on the number of purchasers allowed, and the resale of the securities is not restricted under federal law. However, make sure to check state regulations (blue sky laws) regarding further limitations in your particular state.

Trading on the Bulletin Board or Pink Sheets. One of the greatest challenges of raising capital has to do with liquidity. For many investors, the test of whether or not to invest hinges not just on the future success of the enterprise, but also on their ability to get their money out of the deal. Exempt public offerings can accommodate this need by trading on a nonlisted market such as the OTC Bulletin Board (OTCBB) or the Pink Sheets. Both the OTCBB and the Pink Sheets show quotations and facilitate trading in over-the-counter (OTC) securities. The OTCBB is operated by Nasdaq, while the Pink Sheets are owned by OTC Markets Group. Because most states have restrictions on the resale of unregistered securities, trading an exempt stock offering deal on the OTCBB or Pink Sheets is not always possible. Some states allow for the resale of shares; as a result, some companies sell a small amount to investors in those states and then commence trading on the OTCBB. Once trading begins, the company can purchase coverage in journals to gain clearance for investors in nearly 30 states to buy shares that are already trading on the market.

Advantages and Disadvantages of Internet DPOs. These are a few of the advantages of a DPO:

- The due diligence associated with exempt stock offerings is more compatible with the time constraints of running a business—a DPO takes less time than an IPO.

- The expense of hiring an investment bank to sell stocks in an IPO (4 to 7 percent of the capital raised) is saved.
- Small investors who don't generally get a share of juicy initial public offerings can have a shot at newly minted stocks, which often see immediate run-ups in price.
- DPOs help companies target long-term, small investors who are interested in the company's success.

There are also disadvantages:
- Stock sold through a direct offering can be illiquid or difficult to trade.
- In an IPO, intermediaries (primarily investment banks) screen companies that want to go public. The absence of such a screening process, along with the wide exposure provided by the Internet, may be used to defraud investors, who may then be understandably leery of other DPOs.

Initial Public Offerings on the Internet

Many companies are eager to raise more than the $5 million maximum that a Regulation A DPO offering allows, but are not in a position to attract the more prominent underwriters that generally work with large companies. For such a company, conducting an initial public offering on the Internet may be the solution.

Instead of the traditional road show, in an Internet IPO launch, the issuing company's prospectus is displayed online. Questions can be asked and replies returned via e-mail. Most companies that provide this listing service offer only a small percentage of the total amount of stock being offered. When it comes time to purchase shares, the interested party may go through the underwriter issuing the shares by placing an order online.

The Online Auction. A revolutionary idea that has become popular in recent years is the online auction. Whereas many companies have been content to set up bulletin boards that allow investors to trade without a middleman, OpenIPO, an online entity created by Bill Hambrecht, has taken that concept one step further by using the Dutch auction to take companies public. Google "went Dutch," bringing the Dutch auction style into mainstream consciousness by using this form of auction for its initial public offering in 2004.

The Dutch auction, named after the process used in Holland to bid on flowers, uses a bidding process to find an optimal market price for the stock, the lowest point at which an issuing company can sell all its shares. A similar model is used to auction U.S. Treasury bills, notes, and bonds. The highest bidders win, but the winning bidders all pay the same price—the amount of the lowest winning bid.

Investors bid on a certain number of shares at a certain price. Bids are considered indications of interest. A registration statement relating to the securities being offered will have been filed with the SEC but has not yet become effective. The securities may not be sold, nor may offers to buy be accepted, before the registration becomes effective. A bid involves no obligation or commitment prior to its acceptance after the effective date of the SEC registration statement. A bid may be withdrawn before the close of the auction. A price range is provided for each offering based on an estimate of the company's value. However, bidders are free to bid above or below this range. Once the auction closes, the calculations are done and shares are distributed to the top bidders all at the same price. All of the shares being offered are offered on the Internet. OpenIPO charges between 3 and 5 percent to underwrite the offering.

Advantages and Disadvantages of Internet IPOs. Internet IPOs have some advantages over traditional IPOs:

- They may compel major investment banks to reduce their fixed underwriting fees.
- They may be highly beneficial to companies that are seeking to raise amounts between the $5 million maximum of the DPO and the amount that would be needed to attract major investment banks.
- Electronic display of offering literature can save a company thousands of dollars.
- The underwriter may help filter out some of the fraudulent offers that are made as DPOs on the Internet. This may also add credibility to the offering.

However, Internet IPOs also have at least one disadvantage: Online offerings may not provide the appropriate bait to lure investors.

Offerings on the Internet are changing at a rapid pace. With this change comes risk. Before you undertake an offering of any kind on the Internet, you need to thoroughly investigate the listing service or the Internet underwriter if you choose to use one.

Chapter 12

The Mechanics of an Initial Public Offering

Let us assume that your company has taken all of the preparatory steps discussed in Chapter 11 and has made its selection of the lead underwriter. This chapter looks at the process of taking the company public, from the organizational meeting through to the stock offering and certain post-offering matters. It is imperative that you and your managers understand the planning and registration process before you pursue a public offering of your company's securities. You can save a lot of time and expense if you begin the planning process early, developing methods of operation and formulating strategies for your company's growth. As with any contemplated method of capital formation, going public has its costs and benefits, all of which you should carefully weigh and understand before you sell the first share of stock to the public.

The first step in an IPO is an initial meeting of all key members of the registration team: attorneys, accountants, the lead underwriter, and the company's chief executive officer and chief financial officer. This is called the "all-hands" or organizational meeting, and its purpose is to delegate responsibility for the preparation of each aspect of the registration statement and to set a timetable for the completion of each task. Figure 12-1 shows a typical agenda of topics to be covered in the organizational meeting. In connection with the preparation of the registration statement, several preliminary tasks must also be completed, including:

- Dealing with any concerns and questions that arose during the due diligence that was performed by the underwriter's counsel
- Arranging meetings of the board of directors to authorize the offering
- Preparing and completing the confidential questionnaire for the directors and officers (see the sample in the appendix)
- Conducting legal research concerning compliance with the applicable state blue sky law
- Meeting Financial Industry Regulatory Authority (FINRA) regulations (FINRA is a self-regulatory body that reviews the underwriting and distribution agreements prepared in connection with the IPO to ensure that the terms and conditions are consistent with industry practices)
- Establishing marketing and distribution strategies, including the planning and preparation for the road show

An Overview of the Registration Process

Following the organizational meeting, a series of drafting sessions will be scheduled to ensure that all of the data included in the registration statement are accurate, complete, and prepared in accordance with "plain English" drafting rules. The primary goal is a document that is truly informative to prospective investors, giving them all the information they will need to make an informed decision regarding the investment. Another goal is to anticipate SEC comments and concerns in order to reduce the number of actual comments received in the first SEC letter.

Figure 12-1.	Typical Agenda for an Organizational Meeting.

The agenda for a typical organizational meeting is as follows:

I.   REVIEW AND COMPLETE WORKING-GROUP LIST.

II. DISCUSS STRUCTURE OF OFFERING:
   A. Composition
     1. Size of offering
     2. Primary and secondary components
     3. Overallotment option (amount and source)
   B. Price range considerations/valuation
   C. Proposed Nasdaq or exchange symbol
   D. Lockup agreements with principal stockholders
     1. Stockholders covered
     2. Time period
   E. Capitalization
     1. Necessity of recapitalization or stock split
     2. Preferred stock and convertible notes/conversion at a minimum specified price
   F. Distribution objectives
     1. Institutional vs. retail
     2. Domestic vs. international
     3. Directed shares (employees, customers, others)
     4. Syndicate structure
   G. Potential existing stockholder issues
     1. Options/warrants; "cheap stock" issue
     2. Registration and piggyback rights
     3. Review market "overhang" (Rule 144)
   H. Offering expense allocation
   I. Use of proceeds

III. REVIEW TIME AND RESPONSIBILITY SCHEDULE:
   A. Review timing objectives
   B. Schedule of due diligence meetings with management, lawyers, patent counsel, litigation counsel, and auditors
   C. Drafting sessions
   D. Filing/offering timing
     1. Availability of audited financials
     2. Target filing date
     3. Target offering/closing dates
   E. SEC review period
   F. Road-show preparation
   G. Road-show schedule and sites
   H. Other lead-time matters
     1. Schedule for board of directors' meetings
     2. Communications with stockholders

IV. DISCUSS ACCOUNTING AND FINANCIAL ISSUES:
  A. Historical financial information
     1. Annual and quarterly
     2. Audited financial statements
     3. Pro forma financial statements needed because of acquisitions
  B. Availability of interim financial statements
  C. Historical and projected EPS calculations
     1. Annual and quarterly shares, options, and warrants outstanding
     2. Weighted-average shares outstanding
  D. Auditor's comfort letter
  E. Auditor's management letters and company responses
  F. Options and recent stock sales and related compensation issues
  G. Revenue recognition
  H. Accounts receivable and inventory
  I. Accounts payable
  J. Bad debt, returns, reserves
  K. Contingencies
  L. Tax issues
  M. FASB requirements
  N. Loan agreement restrictions

V. REVIEW COMPANY/CORPORATE GOVERNANCE MATTERS:
  A. Recent and upcoming senior management team additions or changes
  B. Dates of board and stockholders' meetings
  C. Composition and compensation of board
  D. Addition of outside directors, if needed or desired
  E. Audit and compensation committees
  F. Potential acquisitions
  G. Director and officer insurance—amount and scope of coverage

VI. REVIEW LEGAL MATTERS:
  A. Form of registration statement (S-1)
  B. Notice and waiver of registration rights, including indemnification
  C. Litigation—actual or threatened
  D. Waivers, restrictions, or consents needed to offer the shares
  E. Patent and technology matters; patent counsel opinion
  F. Confidential treatment of exhibits
  G. Expert opinions (patent, regulatory, etc.)
  H. Disclosure issues
     1. Certain and related-party transactions
     2. Customer/supplier/employment agreements
     3. Strategic alliances
  I. Amendment of certificate of incorporation
     1. Preferred stock
     2. Increase authorized number of shares of common stock
  J. Antitakeover provisions
  K. Selling stockholder indemnification

    L. Logistics for the board
       1. Preparation of resolutions and appropriate authorizations
       2. Formation of pricing committee
       3. Directors' and officers' questionnaires
    M. Employee stock plans
       1. Amendment of existing plans (to increase number of shares, etc.)
       2. Creation of new plans (e.g., employee stock purchase plan)
    N. Recent and proposed option grants
    O. Nasdaq issues
       1. Investment banker's compensation
       2. Venture capital restrictions
       3. Desire for immediate 1934 Act registration
    P. Possible reincorporation in Delaware (if non-Delaware) or some other state

VII. REVIEW BLUE SKY ISSUES:
    A. Listing criteria for exemption if Nasdaq national market, NYSE, or Amex. If not exempt, then go to (B), (C), (D), and (E) below
    B. Options/valuation
    C. Recent stock sales
    D. Where to file (e.g., 50 states, Canada, international)
    E. Number of states; cost

VIII. DISCUSS PUBLICITY POLICY:
    A. Prefiling, postfiling/pre-effective, posteffective
    B. Interaction with securities analysts
    C. Control of information and releases, inquiries
    D. Pending research reports/press releases/product announcements and advertising
    E. Pending newspaper/magazine articles/media interviews to be published
    F. Industry conference presentations/trade shows
    G. Other corporate announcements
    H. Offering-related press releases
    I. Communications with employees
    J. Quiet period—gun-jumping memorandum (This memorandum details how and when the company may speak to the public about its offering.)

IX. DISCUSS DUE DILIGENCE REVIEW:
    A. Status of product development
       1. New product introductions
       2. Status of product development agreements
       3. New product development and research agreements
    B. Names of principal customers or contracting parties with whom direct contacts may be made by underwriters and counsel
    C. Need for immediate contract file and technology review by underwriters and underwriters' counsel at offices of the company
    D. Timing for review of minute books, stock records, and all other contracts

    E. Discussions with patent counsel, regulatory counsel, etc.

    F. Customers, marketing and communications
1. Overview of distribution channels (sales and profitability of each)
2. Key customers
3. Marketing detail and strategy
4. Pricing strategies
5. Detailed information on competition (past, present, and future)
6. Market share vs. competition
7. Key customer wins and losses
8. Key marketing partners
9. Key distribution partners

    G. Operations
1. Overview of manufacturing operations
2. Detail of head count and function
3. Overview of suppliers

    H. Financial information
1. Overview of historical quarterly financials for two previous fiscal years
2. Top 10 customers in two previous fiscal years and in current year projected by sales volume
3. Quarterly projections for current and next fiscal years; highlights.
4. Breakout of head count by functional area
5. Sales forecasts by quarter
6. Financing history; current commercial bank lines
7. Accounts receivable aging, days' sales outstanding, and historical bad debt experience
8. Revenue recognition policy
9. Any deferred revenue or backlog
10. Policy on capitalized software
11. Discuss related-party transactions, if any

    I. Detailed stockholder table with shares, options, prices, etc. by major holder

X. **DISCUSS OTHER LOGISTICS:**
    A. Selection of transfer agent and registrar
    B. Form of stock certificates
    C. Selection of printer
    D. Use and timing of artwork and graphics in prospectus
    E. Preliminary and final prospectus quantities
    F. Location of volume printing
    G. Dress code for future meetings
    H. Preparation of exhibits for submission to the SEC's online database known as EDGAR

The dynamics of these drafting sessions can be complex and interesting, with 12 to 15 trained professionals and entrepreneurs, each with her own perspective, agenda, objectives, and turf to protect, reviewing an 80-page document word by word and line by line. This painstaking process typically results in a document that all members of the drafting team can be proud of and that can be filed with the SEC with a certain degree of confidence. A typical offering will require four or five drafting sessions over a 30- to 45-day period, including the final prefiling session, which is almost always a 24- to 36-hour session at the financial printer's facilities to edit, check, and recheck final changes.

When the initial draft of the registration statement is ready for filing with the SEC, you have two choices: You can either file the document with the transmittal letter and required fees, or you can schedule a prefiling conference with an SEC staff member to discuss any anticipated questions or problems regarding the disclosure document or the accompanying financial statements.

Once the registration statement is officially received by the SEC, it is assigned to an examining group (usually composed of attorneys, accountants, and financial analysts) within a specific industry department of the Division of Corporate Finance. The length of time required and the depth of the initial review by the examining group will depend on the history of the company and the nature of the securities offered. Be prepared, however, for an initial response roughly 30 to 60 days after the filing and a comment letter with anywhere from 50 to 200 numbered paragraphs that addresses legal and editorial changes in the text of the document and questions on the financial statements and related financial data. For example, a company that operates in a troubled or turbulent industry and is publicly offering its securities for the first time should expect a detailed review by all members of the examining group.

The comment letter will focus on the quality of the disclosure (such as the adequacy of the discussion of risk factors or the verbiage in management's discussion of the financial performance), *not* on the quality of your company or the securities being offered. In most cases, your company will be required to file a material amendment to address the staff's concerns. During this comment-and-review process, your company and the underwriter's representatives are preparing for and then participating in the road show, which is a process of presentations to institutional money managers in order to elicit initial "indications of interest," as discussed later in this chapter.

This review process continues until all concerns raised by the examining group have been addressed. The final pricing amendment is filed after the pricing meeting of the underwriters and the execution of the final underwriting agreement. The SEC has developed detailed regulations and restrictions on what information may be released to the public or the media during this period (the "quiet period"), especially those communications that appear to be designed to influence the price of the shares. These regulations are intended to prevent "gun jumping" by the issuer or its representatives. The registration statement is then declared effective, and the securities can be offered to the public. The registration statement is declared effective 20 days after the final amendment has been filed, unless the effective date is accelerated by the SEC. Most companies seek an accelerated effective date, which is usually made available if the company has complied with the examining group's suggested modifications.

In addition to SEC regulations, a company that is offering its securities to the public must meet the requirements of FINRA and state securities laws. FINRA will analyze all elements of the proposed corporate package for the underwriter in order to determine its fairness and reasonableness. The SEC will not declare a registration statement effective for public offering unless and until FINRA has approved the underwriting arrangements as fair and reasonable. Section 18 of the Securities Act states that federal securities laws do not supersede compliance with any state securities laws except in relation to the registration or qualification of a "covered security" (see subsections (a) and (b) of Section 18 of the Securities Act); therefore, the requirements of each state's blue sky laws need to be taken into account. Although various exemptions from formal registration are often available, the state securities laws for each state in which the securities will be offered must be checked very carefully with regard to the filing fees, registered-agent requirements, disclosure obligations, and underwriter or broker/dealer regulations.

The Registration Statement

The Securities Act requires the company to file a registration statement with the SEC as well as issue a prospectus to potential investors. The registration statement consists of two distinct parts: the *offering prospectus*, which is used to assist underwriters and investors in analyzing the company and the securities being offered, and the *exhibits and additional information*, which are provided directly to the SEC as part of the disclosure and registration regulations. The registration statement is part of the public record and is available for inspection.

There are a variety of formats that can be used for the registration statement; the one that you choose will depend on your company's history, industry, and size and the nature of the specific offering. The most commonly used is Form S-1. This form is complicated, with several requirements that must be fulfilled before going public, and requires a description of the company's business, its properties, material transactions between the company and its officers, pending legal proceedings, plans for distribution of the securities, and intended use of the proceeds from the IPO. Form S-3 (subject to certain requirements), which is available for companies that are already subject to the reporting requirements of the Securities Exchange Act of 1934 (the Exchange Act), is more streamlined and is useful for secondary offerings. Form S-4 is limited to filings in connection with mergers and other types of corporate combinations. All the forms are filed and processed at the SEC's headquarters office in Washington, D.C., by the Division of Corporate Finance.

The SEC's Small Business Initiatives

In 1992, the SEC implemented the Small Business Initiatives (SBIs), which significantly modified its special provisions for offerings by small businesses (formerly Regulation S-B) that were not already subject to the reporting requirements of the Exchange Act. The SBIs were designed to streamline the federal registration process for IPOs to encourage investment in "small-business issuers." Effective February 4, 2008, new rules came into effect that eliminated Regulation S-B for a larger population of smaller companies, including those small-business issuers that are now known as "smaller reporting companies." A smaller reporting company is a company that meets one of the following criteria:

- It has a common equity public float of less than $75 million.
- It has annual revenue of $50 million or less and cannot calculate its public float.

In the past, small-business issuers used to use Form SB-1 or SB-2 to register. These forms were eliminated when the new rules came into effect. Smaller reporting companies now use the same registration forms and disclosure reports as any other company but are subject to lesser disclosure requirements as generally specified in Regulation S-K.

Key Elements of the Registration Statement

Regardless of which form you ultimately use, there is a series of core procedural rules and disclosure items that must be addressed and prepared in "plain English," including but not limited to:

Cover page and forepart. The SEC has very specific requirements concerning the information that must be stated on the cover page and in the forepart of the prospectus. This includes summary information pertaining to the nature of your company's business, the terms of the offering, the determination of the offering price, dilution, the plan of distribution, risk factors, and selected financial information.

Introduction to the company. An overview of your company—its business, employees, financial performance, and principal offices.

Risk factors. A description of the operating and financial risk factors affecting your company's business, with particular regard to the offering of the securities (such as whether your business depends on a single customer or supplier, or on key personnel; the absence of an operating history in the new areas of business that the company wants to pursue; an unproven market for the products and services offered; or a lack of earnings history).

Use of proceeds. A discussion of the anticipated use of the proceeds that will be raised by the offering.

Capitalization. A description of the company's capital structure, including debt obligations; your company's anticipated dividend policy; and dilution of the investors' equity.

Description of business and property. A description of the key assets, principal lines of business, human resources, properties, marketing strategies, and competitive advantages of your company and any of its subsidiaries for the last five years.

Management and principal shareholders. A discussion of the key management team and a description of each member's background, education, compensation, and role in the company, as well as a table of all shareholders who hold a beneficial interest of 5 percent or more.

Litigation. A statement of any material litigation (past, pending, or anticipated) affecting your company, or any other adverse legal proceedings that would affect an investor's analysis of the securities being offered.

Management's discussion and analysis (MDA). This section is a summary of your company's business plan, including a "state of the union" presentation of its goals and successes to date. Note that preparing the MDA section may cause your company's management team to take its first hard, objective look at its business model, management practices, and financial statements and how the company got to where it is; there may be some interesting revelations uncovered during the process.

Financial information. A summary of financial information, such as the company's sales history, net income or losses from operations, long-term debt obligations, dividend patterns, capital structure, founder's equity, and shareholder loans.

Securities offered and underwriting arrangements. A description of the underwriting arrangements, the distribution plan, and key characteristics of the securities being offered.

Experts and other matters. A brief statement regarding the identity of the attorneys, accountants, and other experts retained, as well as the availability of additional information from the registration statement filed with the SEC (such as indemnification policies for the directors and officers, recent sales of unregistered securities, a breakdown of the expenses of the offering, and a wide variety of corporate documents and key agreements).

A typical schedule for an initial public offering is given in Figure 12-2.

Figure 12-2.	Detailed Schedule for an IPO.

The following is a typical schedule for an initial public offering. Printed in bold type at the end of each action is an indication of who is responsible for the execution of that action.

1. Conduct the organizational meeting with company officers, underwriters, counsel, and accountants to discuss the tentative schedule and review the structure of the offering, including the following **(all)**:
   (a) Discuss the amount of common stock to be offered, the identity of selling stockholders, if any, and other parameters of the offering;
   (b) Determine type of 1933 Act registration statement;
   (c) Discuss the tentative time and responsibility schedule;
   (d) Discuss financial/accounting matters, and decide on financials to be included in registration statement;
   (e) Discuss registration rights and preemptive rights, and waiver if necessary;
   (f) Discuss the need for reincorporation, reorganization, or recapitalization, or certificate of incorporation and bylaws amendments, including revisions to be made for publicly held corporation and possible increase in authorized capital and antitakeover provisions;

(g) Discuss the composition of the board of directors; addition of outside directors; audit committee and other committees;

(h) Discuss desired trading symbol and listing of stock with Nasdaq, American Stock Exchange (Amex), or New York Stock Exchange (NYSE) and listing criteria;

(i) Discuss blue sky procedures, potential problem areas and states, and any distribution outside of the United States; and discuss any other necessary action with respect to the offering.

2. Begin preparing the following:
   (a) Registration statement:
       (i) cover page, back cover, underwriting section of prospectus **(underwriter counsel)**;
       (ii) capitalization table and audited financial statements and schedules **(accountant)**;
       (iii) remainder, including exhibits **(company; company counsel)**;
   (b) Directors' and officers' questionnaires **(company counsel)**;
   (c) Powers of attorney for registration statement and amendments **(company counsel)**;
   (d) Any necessary amendments to certificate of incorporation and bylaws **(company counsel)**;
   (e) Resolutions for directors' meetings **(company counsel)**;
   (f) Underwriting documents **(underwriter counsel)**;
   (g) Gather company documents to be reviewed and reproduced as exhibits to registration statement, determine which documents or parts of documents require confidential treatment, arrange for disks of exhibits and input of documents not available on disks for EDGAR filing **(company counsel)**; and
   (h) Selling stockholders' documents **(company counsel)**.

3. Send notice of registration to persons holding registration rights and initial letter of inquiry to potential selling stockholders **(company counsel)**.

4. Begin taking steps necessary to accomplish the following:
   (a) Review corporate records to ensure completeness **(company counsel)**;
   (b) Reserve stock-trading symbol **(company)**;
   (c) Select banknote company and form of stock certificate **(company counsel)**;
   (d) Select transfer agent and registrar **(company)**;
   (e) Select financial printer **(company)**.

5. Distribute first draft of 1993 Act registration statement (without financial statements) to working group **(company counsel)**.

6. Meet for the following **(all)**:
   (a) Overview of company's operations;
   (b) Due diligence sessions with officers.

7. Meet to review draft of registration statement **(all)**.

8. Discuss graphics and photos for prospectus, if desired **(company)**.

9. Make initial determination of selling stockholders **(company)**.

10. Send EDGAR Form ID to SEC to obtain EDGAR access codes **(company)**.

11. Obtain CUSIP number from Standard & Poor's **(company counsel)**.

12. Distribute second draft of registration statement **(company counsel)**.

13. Distribute draft underwriting agreement and other underwriting documents **(underwriter counsel)**.

14. Distribute directors' and officers' questionnaires **(company counsel)**.

15. Meet to review registration statement and conduct additional due diligence sessions with officers **(all)**.

16. Make draft financial statements available **(accountant)**.

17. Discuss underwriting agreement **(all)**.

18. Prepare stock-exchange listing application **(company counsel)**.

19. Distribute third draft of registration statement (including draft financial statements and MD&A) **(company counsel)**.

20. Meet to review registration statement **(all)**.

21. Send registration statement to financial printer **(all)**.

22. Hold meeting of board of directors to adopt resolutions relating to **(all)**:
    (a) Issuance and sale of common stock to be sold by company;
    (b) Authorizing execution and filing of 1933 Act registration statement and amendments, including decision as to number of shares to be sold and overallotment option ("green shoe");
    (c) Appointing attorneys-in-fact to sign amendments to registration statement;
    (d) Execution and delivery of underwriting agreement and creation of pricing committee (if appropriate);
    (e) Authorizing registration of the common stock with state and foreign jurisdictions and other blue sky matters;
    (f) Authorizing listing of stock on Nasdaq, Amex, or NYSE, and 1934 Act registration;
    (g) Form of certificate for common stock;
    (h) Other corporation cleanup matters (e.g., amendment of bylaws, stock splits, recapitalizations, etc.)

23. Commence assembly of exhibits for registration statement and conversion to EDGAR format **(all)**.

24. Deliver working proof of registration statement to working group **(printer; company counsel)**.

25. Discuss proposed contents of comfort letter with accountants **(underwriter counsel; accountant)**.

26. Prepare 1934 Act registration statement (Form 8-A) **(company counsel)**.

27. Meet to review registration statement **(all)**.

28. Prepare draft of filing press release and clear with parties concerned **(company counsel)**.

29. Obtain signature pages and powers of attorney for registration statement and amendments from directors and officers **(company counsel)**.

30. Receive executed directors' and officers' questionnaires; furnish copy to underwriter counsel **(company counsel)**.

31. Complete selling stockholder documents **(all)**.

32. Complete preliminary blue sky memorandum **(underwriter counsel)**.

33. Obtain checks for FINRA, blue sky filings, and listing application **(company)**.

34. Distribute draft comfort letter and internal control letter **(accountant)**.

35. Finalize underwriting agreement and FINRA filing letter **(underwriter counsel)**.

36. Prepare request for confidential treatment, if necessary **(company counsel)**.

37. Update due diligence findings **(all)**.

38. Send wire-transfer filing fees to SEC's lockbox **(company)**.

39. File 1933 and 1934 Act registration statements with SEC via EDGAR (If this is the first EDGAR filing, also submit paper copy of filing.) **(company counsel)**.

40. Release press release **(company)**.

41. File listing application for inclusion on Nasdaq, Amex, or NYSE **(company counsel)**.

42. Complete FINRA and blue sky filings **(underwriter counsel)**.

43. Contact SEC to determine review period **(company counsel)**.

44. Begin preparation of road-show presentation, road-show schedule, and travel arrangements **(underwriter; company)**.

45. Receive and respond to SEC comments **(company counsel; underwriter counsel)**.

46. Furnish corrections and changes to printer; file Amendment No. 1 and any letter furnishing supplemental information via EDGAR **(all)**.

47. File Amendment No. 1 with FINRA and Nasdaq, Amex, or NYSE, as applicable **(company counsel; underwriter counsel)**.

48. Prepare underwriters' power of attorney and transmittal letters to underwriters and dealers to accompany preliminary material; give mailing instructions and labels to printer **(underwriter)**.

49. Prepare letters and obtain labels for mailing to **(underwriter)**:
    (a) Underwriters;
    (b) Institutions;
    (c) Dealers; and
    (d) Financial publications.

50. Obtain quantities of preliminary prospectus, create labels for mailing of preliminary prospectus to offices of underwriters' representatives **(underwriter)**.

51. Release printer to print preliminary prospectuses **(company counsel; underwriter counsel)**.

52. Mail to prospective underwriters preliminary prospectus, preliminary blue sky

memorandum, underwriting agreement, other underwriting documents, and power of attorney with managing underwriters' letter of transmittal **(underwriter)**.

53. Order stock certificates from banknote company to be available at closing **(company)**.

54. Informational meetings (begin road show) **(company; underwriter)**.

55. Procure requests for acceleration from underwriters and company; letter regarding distribution of prospectus **(company counsel; underwriter counsel)**.

56. If demand indicates, prepare abbreviated registration statement pursuant to Rule 462(b) to increase offering by up to 20 percent **(company counsel)**.

57. Receive and respond to second set of SEC comments **(all)**.

58. Furnish all corrections and changes to printer; file Amendment No. 2 via EDGAR, together with letters from underwriters as to distribution of preliminary prospectus, requests for acceleration, etc. **(company counsel; underwriter counsel)**.

59. File Amendment No. 2 with FINRA and Nasdaq, Amex, or NYSE, as applicable **(company counsel; underwriter counsel)**.

60. Complete supplemental blue sky memorandum **(underwriter counsel)**.

61. Approve tombstone advertisement (the format of the advertisement that will appear to announce the offering and the syndicate of underwriters) **(underwriter)**.

62. Prepare updated press release announcing the offering, and clear with concerned parties **(all)**.

63. Receive executed selling stockholders' powers of attorney (including questionnaires), custody agreements, and stock certificates **(company counsel)**.

64. Arrange for delivery of good-standing certificates at closing **(company counsel)**.

65. Notify Nasdaq, Amex, or NYSE of expected offering date **(company counsel)**.

66. If necessary, file Rule 462(b) registration statement with SEC **(company counsel)**.

67. If you meet Rule 430A requirements, declare registration statements effective **(company; company counsel)**.

68. Meeting of board of directors or pricing committee **(company)**.

69. Determine public-offering price of common stock and commissions **(company; accountant; underwriter)**:
    (a) Approve final prospectus and pricing terms;
    (b) Approve final underwriting agreement and authorize execution; and
    (c) Ratify acts of officers in connection with offering.

70. Deliver comfort letter and letter regarding internal controls **(accountant)**.

71. Execute and deliver underwriting agreement **(underwriter counsel; company counsel)**.

72. Prepare form of final prospectus **(all)**.
73. Complete blue sky registrations **(underwriter counsel)**.
74. Release wire transfer of funds to underwriters and dealers **(underwriter)**.
75. Release press release with final terms of offering **(underwriter)**.
76. Public offering **(company)**.
77. Give printer labels and printing information for final prospectus; OK printing **(underwriter)**.
78. Begin preparation of the accountant's comfort letter **(accountant)**.
79. Commence preparation of legal opinions, certificates, and other closing documents **(company counsel; underwriter counsel)**.
80. Tombstone advertisement appears **(underwriter)**.
81. Supply transfer agent with legal opinions and other required documents **(company counsel)**.
82. Transmit final prospectus via EDGAR, pursuant to rule 424(b) **(company counsel)**.
83. Mail final prospectus to FINRA and state blue sky authorities **(underwriter counsel)**.
84. Distribute draft closing memorandum **(all)**.
85. Furnish company with names and denominations for stock certificates **(underwriter counsel)**.
86. Preclosing **(all)**.
87. Closing (if priced after market closing, then closing is usually within four days) **(all)**.

The Road Show

Once an agreement has been signed, the lead underwriter will organize a group of co-underwriters to share in the risk of the offering and to establish the network of participating registered broker/dealer firms. The role of the broker/dealer firms is to sell the company's securities to their clientele. During this period of negotiations, your company's management team and operations will be closely reviewed and scrutinized by the members of the distribution network. This review process is commonly referred to as the "road show," and it allows the members of the syndicate to learn more about your company and the proposed offering; it also builds excitement about the impending offering.

The road show is designed to whet investors' appetites for an IPO, and it is often a crucial element in determining the value of an offering and building initial demand for the company's shares. If your road show goes poorly before key pundits and money managers on Wall Street, you'll see the demand for your stock issue wilt. If the road show goes well, you'll ensure robust demand and a strong aftermarket in the stock.

A road show is a whirlwind, two-week campaign through a dozen or more financial markets across the country and sometimes beyond. Presentations typically run half an hour and should be in the format and the style that fund managers have become accustomed to. Top management may make several presentations in one day, appearing at a "one-on-one" breakfast meeting with a single investor group, then heading off to a stand-up presentation in a room crowded with mutual fund managers and other institutional investors and analysts representing pension funds and other investment sources. Most of those attending these presentations are old hands at picking winners and know all the right questions to ask the company.

Remember that astute institutional buyers have seen a whole slew of presentations come and go. They've been burned, and they've been successful. So they've developed a pretty good nose for how much of your presentation is fluff and how much is solid, including an analysis of all your financial data and whether your management team seems capable and authentic.

By the time your team hits the road, it should have been thoroughly coached by your underwriters. In fact, some institutional money managers will not let anyone except the company's representatives be in the room for the presentations, so your team had better be ready to answer questions without relying on the underwriters. Managers also have the good name of the underwriters behind them, and that counts for a lot. Good underwriters gain their reputation by backing companies that they feel will succeed in the market, and also by ensuring a strong aftermarket in the stock for the investors. The goal of this intense two-week schedule of limos, five-star restaurants, and fancy hotels is to have preliminary indications of interest for at least four times the number of shares to be offered.

The Waiting Period

Following the regulatory filings, the managing underwriter will circulate invitations to proposed members of the underwriting groups. As the underwriting syndicate takes shape during the waiting period, the underwriters may be circulating the preliminary prospectus (called a "red herring") to ascertain indications of interest among their retail and institutional clients. Other than the road shows and the use of the red herring, marketing activities are severely restricted during the waiting period under Section 5 of the Securities Act. This is the quiet period, so the distribution of catalogs, brochures, television ads, and articles about the issuer is prohibited. Videotapes are acceptable at the road show if they show nothing more than a person talking, and if someone from the issuer is also present. Slide presentations are also acceptable if the slides are not distributed, and all materials must be 100 percent consistent with the information contained in the prospectus.

Valuation and Pricing

There is no standard formula for the valuation process, although certain factors are always included. The most important determinant is the company's past and projected operating results and financial condition. Other factors such as its competitive position, management team, industry, and growth potential; current economic conditions; and the state of the stock market also play roles in the valuation of a company's stock. *Ultimately, however, investor demand (generated as a result of the road show) determines the final IPO valuation.*

An analysis of the stock market's current valuation of comparable companies is the most basic and most effective valuation tool for investment bankers, who will use such analyses to determine and substantiate the IPO price. Prices of other successful and similar offerings will also come into play, as will the company's projected earnings and cash flow at the time of the offering. The price/earnings ratios and return on sales of other companies in the industry may be used to extrapolate the price of the stock.

Taking all this into account, the underwriter will most likely choose a slightly lower price than the estimate. This is to guard against a weak aftermarket and to give buyers an incentive. An aggressive valuation may increase investors' expectations and put more pressure on the company's performance in the aftermarket. A higher valuation is also likely to reduce the stock's rate of appreciation. Strong aftermarket performance is desirable because it generates credibility with investors, creates positive visibility for your company, and increases the company's ability to pursue follow-on financings. Consequently, companies should seek the highest *sustainable* valuation rather than the highest *attainable* valuation. Major-bracket underwriters generally prefer a price range of $10 to $20 a share. Underpricing or overpricing occurs when the first trades of the newly issued stock are made at prices above or below the offer price. Underpricing is more common than overpricing. This underpricing, if reasonable, has some merits, for the reasons explained previously.

Keep in mind that the underwriters must balance the price in such a way that neither the company nor the investor comes away totally satisfied. There is tension between the company, which wants to maximize the proceeds of the offering, and the institutional and retail bankers, who want to deliver the best price and value to their clients. Underwriters will attempt to maximize the offering price to the company and provide a reasonable return to investors.

In any case, it is likely that the company won't know the actual pricing of the offering until the day before it becomes effective and the underwriter's agreement is signed. Until that point, the underwriter is not obligated to conduct the offering at any previously mentioned price or price range. After the initial offering, naturally, the market will control the price; some Internet and technology offerings have seen their prices double, triple, and even quadruple on the first day of trading.

The Closing and Beyond

Once the final underwriting agreement is signed and the final pricing amendment is filed with the SEC, the registration statement is declared effective and the selling process begins. Throughout the selling period, *wait patiently* and hope that any minimum sales quotas (as in "all-or-nothing" offerings) are met and that the offering is well received by the investing public.

To facilitate the mechanics of the offering process, consider retaining the services of a registrar and transfer agent, who will be responsible for issuing stock certificates, maintaining stockholder ownership records, and processing the transfer of shares from one investor to another. These services are usually offered by commercial banks and trust companies (which also offer ongoing support services, such as annual report and proxy mailing, disbursement of dividends, and custody of the authorized but unissued stock certificates). Once the offer and sale of the shares to the public has been completed, a closing must be scheduled to exchange documents, issue stock certificates, and disburse the net proceeds.

Ongoing Reporting and Disclosure Requirements

The Exchange Act generally governs the ongoing disclosure and periodic reporting requirements of publicly traded companies. Section 13 grants the SEC broad powers to develop documents and reports that must be filed. There are three primary reports required by Section 15(d):

Form 10-K. This is the *annual* report that must be filed after the close of the fiscal year covered by the report. The timing of the filing depends on whether the issuer is a large accelerated filer (60 days after the end of the fiscal year), an accelerated filer (75 days after the end of the fiscal year), or not an accelerated filer at all (90 days after the end of the fiscal year). It must include a report of all significant activities of the company during its fourth quarter, an analysis and discussion of the company's financial condition, a description of the current officers and directors, and a schedule of certain exhibits. The 10-K generally requires the issuer's income statements for the prior three years and the balance sheets for the prior two years; however, the lesser disclosure requirements that are available for smaller reporting companies allow such issuers to choose to provide the information specified in Article 8 of Regulation S-X instead of the required financial statements.

Form 10-Q. This is a *quarterly* report that must be filed no later than 40 days after the end of each of the first three quarters of each fiscal year for a large accelerated filer or 45 days after the end of the quarter for a company that is not a large accelerated filer. This filing includes copies of quarterly financial statements (accompanied by a discussion and analysis of the company's financial condition by its management) and a report concerning any litigation, as well as any steps taken by the company that affect shareholder rights or require shareholder approval.

Form 8-K. This is a *periodic* report designed to ensure that *all material information* pertaining to significant events that affect the company is disclosed to the investing public as soon as it is available, but in general not later than four business days (periods may vary) after the occurrence of the particular event that triggers the need to file the Form 8-K. The duty to disclose "material information" (whether as part of an 8-K filing or otherwise) to the general public is an ongoing obligation that continues for as long as the company's securities are publicly traded.

You'll need to establish an ongoing compliance program to ensure that all *material* corporate information is disclosed as fully and promptly as possible. A fact is generally considered to be material if there is a substantial likelihood that a reasonable shareholder would consider it important in his investment decision (whether to buy, sell, or hold, or how to vote on a particular proposed corporate action). The following kinds of information are examples of what is typically considered material for disclosure purposes:

- Acquisitions and dispositions of other companies or properties
- Public or private sales of debt or equity securities
- Bankruptcy or receivership proceedings affecting the issuer
- Significant contract awards or terminations
- Changes in the key management team

Additional Reporting and Disclosure Requirements

Pursuant to Section 12(g) of the Exchange Act, certain publicly traded companies are subject to additional registration, reporting, and disclosure requirements for a class of equity security that is held by more than 500 shareholders, even though such companies did not have the intention of registering such securities publicly. Once registration pursuant to Section 12(g) takes place, a company will also be subject to the rules developed by the SEC for proxy solicitation, reporting of beneficial ownership, liability for short-swing transactions, and tender-offer rules and regulations.

Proxy Solicitation. Because of the difficulty of assembling all the shareholders of a corporation for matters that require a shareholder vote, voting by proxy is a fact of life for most publicly held corporations. When soliciting the proxies of shareholders for voting at annual or special meetings, special statutory rules must be followed carefully. The request for the proxy must be accompanied by a detailed proxy statement that specifies the exact matters to be acted on and any information that the shareholder would require in order to reach a decision.

Reporting of Beneficial Ownership. Section 16(a) requires that all officers and directors, and any shareholders who own at least 10 percent of the voting stock, file a statement of beneficial ownership of securities. Filed on Form 3, the statement must reflect all holdings, direct and indirect. Section 16(a) also requires that whenever the officers and directors increase or decrease their holdings by purchase, sale, gift, or otherwise, the transaction must be reported on Form 4 no later than two business days after the transaction occurred.

Liability for Short-Swing Transactions. Section 16(b) requires that officers, directors, employees, or other insiders return to the company any profit they may have realized from any combination of sales and purchases (or purchases and then sales) of securities made by them within any six-month period. Any acquisition of securities (regardless of the form of payment) is considered a purchase. The purpose of Section 16(b) is to discourage even the possibility of directors and officers taking advantage of inside information by speculating in a company's stock. Liability occurs automatically if there is a sale and a purchase within six months, even if the individual involved in the transaction did not actually take advantage of inside information.

Tender-Offer Rules and Regulations. Sections 13 and 14 generally govern the rules for parties who wish to make a tender offer to purchase the securities of a publicly traded corporation. Any person acquiring (directly or indirectly) beneficial ownership of more than 5 percent of an equity security registered under Section 12 must report the transaction by filing a Schedule 13D within 10 days from the date of acquisition. Schedule 13D requires the disclosure of certain material information, such as the identity and background of the purchaser, the purpose of the acquisition, the source and amount of funds used to purchase the securities, and disclosure of the company.

If the purchase is in connection with a tender offer, the provisions of Section 14(d) also apply, pursuant to which the terms of the tender offer must be disclosed (as well as the plans of the offeror if it is successful, and the terms of any special agreements between the offeror and the target company). Section 14(e) imposes a broad prohibition of the use of false, misleading, or incomplete statements in connection with a tender offer.

Insider Trading and Rule 10b-5. The business and financial press has devoted a great deal of attention to the SEC's Rule 10b-5 and its application in the prosecution of insider-trading cases. Here's the text of Rule 10b-5:

It shall be unlawful for any person, directly or indirectly, by the use of any means or instrumentality of interstate commerce, or of the mails or of any facility of any national securities exchange:

(a) to employ any device, scheme or artifice to defraud;

(b) to make any untrue statement of a material fact or to omit to state a material fact necessary in order to make the statements made, in light of the circumstances under which they were made, not misleading; or

(c) to engage in any act, practice, or course of business which operates or would operate as a fraud or deceit upon any person, in connection with the purchase or sale of any security.

Rule 10b-5 has been enforced in insider-trading cases, typically those in which an officer, director, or some other person who has a fiduciary relationship with a corporation buys or sells the company's securities while in the possession of material, nonpublic information. However, Rule 10b-5 is also used in a variety of other situations such as:

- When a corporation issues misleading information to the public or keeps silent when it has a duty to disclose information
- When an insider selectively discloses material, nonpublic information to another party, who then trades securities based on the information (generally called tipping)
- When a person mismanages a corporation in ways that are connected with the purchase or sale of securities
- When a securities firm or another person manipulates the market for a security traded in the over-the-counter market
- When a securities firm or securities professional engages in certain other forms of conduct connected with the purchase or sale of securities

It is imperative that all officers, directors, employees, and shareholders of publicly traded companies (or companies that are considering being publicly traded) be keenly aware of the broad scope of this antifraud rule in transactions that involve the company.

Disposing of Restricted Securities

All shares of a public company that are held by its controlling persons (which typically includes its officers, directors, and any 10 percent shareholders) are deemed "restricted securities" under the Securities Act. The sale of restricted securities is generally governed by Rule 144, which requires as a condition of sale that:

- The company is current in its periodic reports to the SEC.
- The restricted securities have been beneficially owned for at least six months preceding the sale.
- The amount of securities that may be sold in any three-month period is limited to either 1 percent of the outstanding class of securities or the average weekly reported volume of trading in the securities on a registered national exchange (if the securities are listed), whichever is greater.

- The securities may be sold only in brokers' transactions, and the notice of the sale must be filed with the SEC concurrently with the placing of the sale order.
- If the sale involves 500 shares or more than $50,000 in any three-month period, a report of the transaction on Form 144 must be filed.

Private Investment in Public Entities (PIPEs)

A PIPE is a private sale of unregistered securities by a public company to a select group of individuals or institutions. PIPE offerings became a very popular strategy in the early 2000s, when companies that were already public had difficulty raising capital in the public markets because of the very tough market and economic conditions, often resulting in disappointing operating performance and a depressed stock price. In a traditional or "pure" PIPE transaction, the investors enter into a purchase agreement for a fixed amount of the public company's securities at a predetermined price in a private placement offering (see Chapter 6), and the closing is conditioned on the filings and effectiveness of a resale registration statement for these securities. In this type of PIPE, the investors do not actually provide the funds until closing. In a standard PIPE, the investors purchase and pay for restrictive securities in a private placement, however, the company agrees to file and make effective a resale registration statement *following* the closing. In a traditional PIPE, the investors bear the pricing risk prior to closing, whereas in a standard PIPE, the investors bear the risk of the company's ability to get the offering filed and effective *after* the closing.

PIPE transactions provide a strategy for raising private capital in a turbulent public market; the timetable is often much faster than that of a traditional secondary offering, the transaction costs are much lower, and typically there is no need for an expensive and time-consuming road show. From the investor's perspective, she is issued a nearly liquid security at a discount from market, essentially on the assumption and the hope that market conditions will improve and the price of the stock will rise in the future. The securities offered in all types of PIPEs can be common stock, convertible preferred stock, or even convertible debt. The PIPE investors must be accredited and typically include hedge funds, pension funds, specialized PIPE-focused funds, mutual funds, and strategic investors. The company files with the SEC to register the shares (either prior to closing or thereafter, depending on the type of PIPE) on a Form

S-3, provided that the issuer has its SEC filings current for the past year and is not in material default on any major obligations, such as office leases or commercial loans.

PIPEs Market Data

- In 2003, there were 1,075 common stock and 309 convertible securities PIPEs transactions, raising $13.7 billion and $4.8 billion, respectively. By May 31, 2004, nearly $7 billion in capital had been raised in PIPEs transactions in 2004. During 2010, there were approximately 1,203 PIPEs transactions, raising $40.2 billion.
- Conversion or purchase discounts range from as little as 10 percent to as high as 40 percent, depending in part on the current performance and industry type of the issuer.
- The market capitalization of the average PIPEs transaction issuer ranges from $10 million to $300 million and higher (in general, the smaller deals have higher incidences of warrant coverage and deeper purchase/exercise discounts).
- Over one-half of all PIPEs transactions include the issuance of warrants to buy additional shares of the issuer based on a variety of discounted or market pricing formulas, especially in smaller transactions, where the percentage is closer to 75 percent.

Resources on IPOs and the Public Securities Markets

- *U.S. Securities and Exchange Commission:* www.sec.gov
- *Nasdaq Stock Market:* www.nasdaqomx.com
- *Securities Industry Association:* www.siaonline.com
- *American Association of Individual Investors:* www.aaii.com
- *National Association of Corporate Directors:* www.nacdonline.org
- *Bloomberg IPO Center:* www.bloomberg.com
- *123Jump Financial Center:* www.123jump.com
- *WSJ Market Watch:* www.marketwatch.com

Chapter 13

Franchising, Joint Ventures, Co-Branding, and Licensing

Until this point, the focus of this book has been on the many ways in which you can raise equity or debt capital to facilitate the growth of your business. As we have seen, equity has its costs in terms of dilution of ownership and control, and debt can weigh heavily on an entrepreneur, both because of the burden of repayment and because of the accompanying covenants that will govern and restrict the company's day-to-day operations. Therefore, some entrepreneurs choose an alternative strategy when it comes to developing ways to grow their businesses—one that uses the resources of *others* to meet *their* growth objectives. These strategies can also be used to enhance the company's business model to generate new revenue streams and profit centers, which may be a condition for an existing or prospective investor making a commitment to the next round of financing.

You may be thinking, "Wait a minute; using the resources of others to implement my business plan sounds a little like grand larceny!" Of course, it's not. We're talking here about *leveraging your intangible assets* and *developing strategic relationships* through such means as franchising, joint ventures, co-branding, and licensing to meet your business-planning and growth objectives. These strategies not only are an efficient way to build your brand awareness, customer base, and market share, but also are a cost-effective way to achieve growth compared with traditional capital-formation strategies. For more information on these topics, see two of my other books: *Harvesting Intangible Assets* (AMACOM, 2011) and *Franchising and Licensing*, fourth edition (AMACOM, 2011).

For example, a successful chain of five retail stores could go into the capital markets seeking to raise debt or equity to build five more stores. *Or* it could invest an amount equal to the cost of one store into building the systems and infrastructure for franchising 50 stores. Similarly, a young technology company could try to raise the money to build distribution channels and brand awareness from scratch. *Or* it could achieve virtually overnight recognition by seeking joint ventures, strategic alliances, and co-branding relationships with already established companies operating in the same marketplace. Finally, an early-stage medical-products company could spend the next 12 to 18 months searching for capital to complete its research and development and deal with the many hurdles in bringing its proprietary product to the market. *Or* it could streamline its costs and overhead by finding an already established medical-products conglomerate that would license the proprietary technology and pay license fees and royalties for the rights to use that technology. Figure 13-1 shows a number of strategies for harvesting intangible assets.

As you can see, these strategies may be viable alternatives to traditional capital formation, and in some cases they should be carefully considered as a lead strategy, with capital formation for internal growth as the backup plan. In other cases, such as business-format franchising, it will still be necessary for you to raise some money so that you have the resources to recruit and support your franchisees properly, but it is likely to be far less than you would need if you were to develop all of these markets yourself, and the capital is likely to cost less, too.

Let's take a look at these strategies in greater detail, starting with franchising.

Figure 13-1.   Harvesting Intangible Assets.

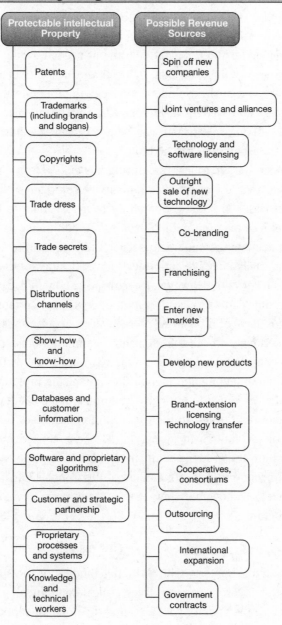

Protectable intellectual Property	Possible Revenue Sources
Patents	Spin off new companies
Trademarks (including brands and slogans)	Joint ventures and alliances
Copyrights	Technology and software licensing
Trade dress	Outright sale of new technology
Trade secrets	Co-branding
Distributions channels	Franchising
Show-how and know-how	Enter new markets
Databases and customer information	Develop new products
Software and proprietary algorithms	Brand-extension licensing Technology transfer
Customer and strategic partnership	Cooperatives, consortiums
Proprietary processes and systems	Outsourcing
Knowledge and technical workers	International expansion
	Government contracts

Business-Format Franchising

Franchising can be viewed as an alternative growth strategy because the original founders of a company avoid dilution of their ownership and are no longer directly responsible for the financial investment needed to fuel the company's growth and expansion. Instead, this financial responsibility is shifted to third-party franchisees and area developers, who pay the franchisor for the right to use its trademarks and systems in exchange for initial franchise fees and royalties. Over time, this income stream can be a very valuable and lucrative asset around which an estate plan can be built.

Over the past three decades, franchising has emerged as a popular expansion strategy for a variety of product and service companies. Retail sales from franchised businesses in 2010 accounted for over $2 trillion in total sales, and franchises employed over ten million people. You don't have to have the ambition to become a national or multinational corporation to consider franchising, as it can be an especially effective option for smaller businesses that cannot afford to finance internal growth. However, franchising as a method of marketing and distributing products and services is appropriate only for certain kinds of companies. A host of legal and business prerequisites must be satisfied before any company can seriously consider franchising as a method for rapid expansion.

Many companies prematurely choose franchising as a growth alternative or exit strategy, then assemble and launch the franchising program haphazardly. Other companies are urged to franchise by unqualified consultants or advisors who may be more interested in their own professional fees than in the long-term success of the franchising program. This has caused financial distress and failure for both the growing company and the franchisee, usually resulting in litigation. Current and future members of the franchising community must be urged to take a responsible view of the creation and development of their franchising programs.

The Essentials of Franchising

Responsible franchising starts with an understanding of the strategic essence of the business structure. There are three critical components of the franchise system: the brand, the operating system, and the ongoing support provided by the franchisor to the franchisee.

First, the brand creates the demand, allowing the franchisee to initially *attract* customers. The brand includes the franchisor's trademarks and service marks, its trade dress and decor, and all the intangible factors that create customer loyalty and build brand equity. Next, the operating system essentially delivers the promise, allowing the franchisee to *maintain* customer relationships and build loyalty. Finally, the ongoing support and training provide the impetus for growth, providing the franchisee with the tools and tips that it needs if it is to *expand* its customer base and build its market share.

A responsibly built franchise system is one that provides value to its franchisees by teaching them how to get and keep as many customers as possible, customers who consume as many products and services as possible—and as often as possible. In fact, most litigation in franchising revolves around the gap between the *actual* needs of the franchisees if they are to remain competitive in the marketplace and the *reality* of the support that the franchisor is able to provide. The genesis of the disappointment often begins during the recruitment phase and continues beyond the start-up as the franchisee struggles to remain competitive, *unless* the franchisor delivers on its promises and is committed to providing excellent initial and ongoing training and support.

Reasons for Franchising

There are many reasons why successful growing companies have selected franchising as a method of growth and distribution. By franchising their product or service, these companies can:

- Obtain operating efficiencies and economies of scale.
- Achieve more rapid market penetration at a lower capital cost.
- Reach targeted consumers more effectively through cooperative advertising and promotion.
- Sell products and services to a dedicated distributor network.
- Replace the need for internal personnel with motivated owner-operators.
- Shift the primary responsibility for site selection, employee training, personnel management, local advertising, and other administrative concerns to the franchisee.

In a typical franchising relationship, the franchisee shares the risk of expanding the market share of the growing company by committing its capital and resources to the development of satellite locations that are modeled after the proprietary business format of the growing company. The risk of business failure of the growing company is further reduced by the improvement in its competitive position, reduced vulnerability to cyclical fluctuations, the existence of a captive market for the growing company's proprietary products and services (because of the network of franchisees), and the reduced administrative and overhead costs enjoyed by a growing company.

The Foundation for Responsible Franchising

Responsible franchising is the *only* way in which growing companies and franchisees will be able to coexist harmoniously in the twenty-first century. Responsible franchising means that there must be a secure foundation from which the franchising program is launched. Any company that is considering franchising as a method of growth and distribution or any individual who is considering franchising as a method of getting into business must understand the components of this foundation. The key components are:

A proven prototype location (or chain of stores) that will serve as a basis for the franchising program. The store or stores must have been tested, refined, and operated successfully, and must be consistently profitable. The success of the prototype should not depend too much on the physical presence or specific expertise of the founders of the company.

A strong management team made up of internal officers and directors (as well as qualified consultants) who understand both the particular industry in which the company operates and the legal and business aspects of franchising as a method of expansion.

Sufficient capitalization to launch and sustain the franchising program. Enough capital should be available so that the growing company can provide both initial and ongoing support and assistance to franchisees. A poorly prepared business plan and an inadequate capital structure are often the principal causes of failure of early-stage franchisors.

A distinctive and protected trade identity that includes federal- and state-registered trademarks as well as a uniform trade appearance, signage, slogans, trade dress, and overall image.

Proprietary and proven methods of operation and management that can be provided in a comprehensive operations manual, resist duplication by competitors, maintain their value to the franchisees over an extended period of time, and be enforced through clearly drafted and objective quality-control standards.

A comprehensive training program for franchisees that integrates all the latest education and training technologies and can be conducted both at the company's headquarters and on-site at the franchisee's proposed location, both at the outset of the relationship and on an ongoing basis.

Field support staff who are skilled trainers and communicators and who are available to visit, inspect, and periodically assist franchisees, and also monitor quality control.

A set of comprehensive legal documents that reflects the company's business strategies and operating policies. The offering documents must be prepared in accordance with applicable federal and state disclosure laws, and franchise agreements should strike a delicate balance between the rights and obligations of the growing company and the franchisee.

A demonstrated market demand for the products and services developed by the growing company that will be distributed through the franchisees. The growing company's products and services should meet certain minimum quality standards, should not be subject to rapid shifts in consumer preferences (fads), and should be proprietary in nature. Market research and analysis should be sensitive to trends in the economy and the specific industry, the plans of direct and indirect competitors, and shifts in consumer preferences.

A carefully developed set of uniform site-selection criteria and architectural standards that can be readily and affordably secured in today's competitive real estate market.

A genuine understanding of the competition (both direct and indirect) that the growing company will face as it markets and sells franchises to prospective franchisees, as well as the competition that the franchisees will face when marketing the growing company's products and services.

Relationships with suppliers, lenders, real estate developers, and related key resources as part of the operations manual and system.

A franchisee profile and screening system to identify the minimum financial qualifications, business acumen, and understanding of the industry that will be required for success.

An effective system of reporting and record keeping to maintain the performance of the franchisees and ensure that royalties are reported accurately and paid promptly.

Research and development capabilities for the introduction of new products and services for consumers through the franchised network on an ongoing basis.

A communication system that facilitates a continuing and open dialogue with the franchisees, and as a result reduces the chances for conflict and litigation with the franchise network.

National, regional, and local advertising, marketing, and public relations programs designed to both recruit prospective franchisees and attract consumers to the sites operated by franchisees.

The Regulation of Franchising

The offer and sale of franchises is regulated under federal and state law. Federal franchise law is embodied principally in a regulation promulgated by the Federal Trade Commission (FTC) and commonly referred to by those involved in franchising as the "FTC Rule" (codified at 16 CFR §437). The FTC Rule, which became law in 1979 and was formally titled "Disclosure Requirements and Prohibitions Concerning Franchising and Business Opportunity Ventures," requires franchisors to make certain disclosures to prospective franchisees in the United States and its territories. The FTC Rule applies to product and business-format franchises that have three elements: (1) the franchisee sells goods or services or operates a business identified by or associated with the franchisor's trademark, service mark, trade name, advertising, or other commercial symbol designating the franchisor (the Mark); (2) the franchisor exercises significant control or provides significant assistance in the franchisee's method of operation; and (3) the franchisee is required to make payment of $500 or more to the franchisor or a person affiliated with the franchisor at any time before or within six months after the business opens.

In addition to the FTC Rule, more than a dozen states (known as the "registration states") have enacted their own rules and regulations governing the offering and sale of franchises. The franchise laws of a particular registration state typically apply to the offer or sale of a franchise when the franchisee is a resident of that state or when the franchise will be operated within that state's borders. The registration states include most of the nation's largest commercial marketplaces, such as California, New York, and Illinois. State franchise laws typically use a three-element (or "three-legged stool") definition similar to the FTC Rule, although there are some differences in each of the "legs"; these are discussed later in this chapter.

In 2007, the FTC adopted amendments to the FTC Rule, now entitled "Disclosure Requirements and Prohibitions Concerning Franchising" (referred to as the "Amended FTC Rule"). These were the first changes to the FTC Rule since its adoption almost 30 years earlier. Among other things, the Amended FTC Rule dictated the use of a single disclosure document to provide the potential franchisee with the information he needed to facilitate an informed purchase. This new format is called (not surprisingly) the "Franchise Disclosure Document" (FDD), and it may be used anywhere in the United States. This change is significant because prior to the adoption of the Amended FTC Rule, a franchisor could choose to follow one of two different formats, the FTC format or the Uniform Franchise Offering Circular (or UFOC) format. The FTC format was prescribed by the original FTC Rule, while the UFOC format was developed by the Midwest Securities Commissioners Association in 1975 and later monitored and revised by the successor organization, the North American Securities Administrators Association. Most franchisors used the UFOC format, however, because it was the format required in the registration states. The Amended FTC Rule simplified the disclosure process by eliminating the dual-format system and prescribing one standard for the specific information that must be included in the FDD and the format in which that information must be disclosed. The Amended FTC Rule also prescribes the timing for the delivery of the FDD, which must occur at least 14 days before any binding agreement is signed or any payment to the franchisor is made.

Other key improvements in the Amended FTC Rule have made it easier for both U.S. and overseas franchisors to explore opportunities in the U.S. market. These improvements may help reduce the amount of preliminary effort and expense required of franchisors who want to "test the waters" of franchise expansion in the United States. Some of these are summarized in the next section.

Key Improvements in the Amended FTC Rule

1. *New exemptions for larger, sophisticated, or experienced franchisees.* Under the Amended FTC Rule, three new exemptions are available for transactions involving larger, sophisticated, or experienced franchisees. If a franchisor can take advantage of one or more of these exemptions, then the franchise disclosure and related compliance requirements will not apply. These new exemptions are available if:

    a.   The franchisee is a high-net-worth company or individual (at least USD 5 million) and has been in business for at least five years.

b. The franchisee must make a large initial investment (more than USD 1 million).

c. The franchisees are "insiders," such as officers, directors, general partners, managers, or owners of a franchisor.

In addition to these new exemptions, the exemptions that were included in the original FTC Rule are still available. These include exemptions for (1) fractional franchises, (2) leased department arrangements, (3) purely verbal agreements, and (4) minimum required payments within the first six months of operations that are below the $500 threshold (which really is simply a method of avoiding the required-payment element of the franchise definition under the Amended FTC Rule). Another important exemption that is related to the required-payment element is the "inventory exemption." Under the Amended FTC Rule (and in the original FTC Rule), the definition of a required payment specifically excludes payments for the purchase of "reasonable amounts of inventory at bona fide wholesale prices for resale or lease." A "reasonable amount" is an amount that is not more than what a "reasonable businessperson" would normally purchase for a starting inventory or supply, or to maintain an ongoing inventory or supply. This inventory exemption also includes goods intended to be furnished to the public through lease. This means that franchisees who are in the auto or furniture rental business, for example, can take advantage of this exemption. The inventory exemption does not include goods that a franchisee must purchase for its own use in the operation of the business, such as equipment or ordinary business supplies, however.

Finally, the Amended FTC Rule also excludes (1) relationships between employer and employees and among general partners (but not limited partners) in a business, (2) membership in retailer-owned cooperatives, (3) certification and testing services, and (4) single trademark licenses. This last exclusion includes one-on-one licensing arrangements, where a trademark is licensed to a single licensee who manufactures the trademarked goods according to the licensor's specifications. This is common, for example, in the clothing industry, where trademark owners license the manufacture of textiles. The single trademark license exclusion also includes "collateral product" licensing, where a trademark that is well known in one context (for example, a soft drink logo) is licensed for use in another (for example, on clothing or decorative items embossed with the soft drink logo).

2. *No more "first personal meeting" disclosure requirement.* In the past, many domestic and foreign franchisors have avoided the United States because they were required to commit considerable resources to the preparation of a disclosure document before they could even meet with a prospective franchisee. Under the Amended FTC Rule's new process, however, a franchisor may now "test the waters" for its concept before incurring the expense of disclosure compliance. Specifically, a franchisor now may exhibit at U.S. trade shows and engage in discussions with prospective franchisees without having to deliver an FDD. Prior to the Amended FTC Rule, a franchisor had to deliver disclosure documents to a prospective franchisee at the time of the "first personal meeting" to discuss a possible franchise relationship. However, the Amended FTC Rule now simply requires that the disclosures be provided at least 14 calendar days before a prospective franchisee makes any payment to the franchisor or its affiliate and before signing any binding agreement in connection with the franchise sale.

The benefit to would-be franchisors is that they no longer have to incur the legal, accounting, and market research expenses necessary to prepare an FDD in order to attend trade shows and evaluate franchise opportunities in the United States. Under the Amended FTC Rule, the time, effort, and expense of preparing the FDD (including audited financial statements and franchise agreements) can be deferred until one or more legitimate franchisee candidates are identified. These expenses can be significant, especially with respect to the preparation and audit of financial statements.

3. *Electronic disclosure is specifically permitted.* The Amended FTC Rule expressly permits franchisors to deliver disclosure documents by electronic means, such as on a compact disc, through e-mail, through Internet downloads, or posted on Web pages. While the disclosure documents must still be in writing, it is no longer necessary to incur the expense of preparing and delivering paper copies of the often lengthy FDD.

4. *No more waiting period after mutually negotiating changes to the franchise agreement.* Before the Amended FTC Rule, a prospective franchisee had to have been furnished fully completed, final form franchise and related agreements at least five business days before executing them. This meant that even nonmaterial "fill-in-the-blank" terms inserted into the standard form would trigger a

new five-business-day waiting period. And if any negotiated terms of the standard agreements benefited the franchisor, the waiting period restarted. Under the Amended FTC Rule, however, there is no need to restart the waiting period after negotiating changes initiated by the prospective franchisee and revising the agreements accordingly. If a franchisor *unilaterally* and *materially* alters the terms of basic agreements attached to the FDD, however, a new waiting period will start.

5. *More flexibility in accounting and audit requirements for financial statements.* For foreign franchisors, meeting the requirement that audited financial statements be included in the FDD often involves significant amounts of time and expense. Before the Amended FTC Rule, a franchisor's financial statements were required to be prepared in accordance with U.S. generally accepted accounting principles (GAAP). However, foreign franchisors will typically prepare their financial statements in accordance with their own country's GAAP. Furthermore, the audit of the franchisor's financial statements was required to be done in accordance with U.S. generally accepted auditing standards (GAAS). This typically limited the choice of auditor to a U.S. accounting firm, one that would probably not be familiar with the franchisor or its financial history.

Under the Amended FTC Rule, foreign franchisors may prepare their financial statements using a comprehensive set of accounting standards other than U.S. GAAP, as long as there is an audited reconciliation to U.S. GAAP. Also, foreign franchisors now may now use a non–U.S. accounting firm as long as that firm (1) is registered with the Public Company Accounting Oversight Board (PCAOB), the U.S. entity charged with monitoring auditing standards for public companies, and (2) has recently audited one or more financial statements included in a filing with the U.S. Securities and Exchange Commission (SEC). Foreign accountants who are registered with the PCAOB are subject to the same auditing standards as their U.S. counterparts.

One additional change involves the regulation of business opportunity ventures: The original FTC Rule regulated both franchises and business opportunity ventures (as indicated by the formal title of the original FTC Rule). Business opportunity ventures are similar to franchises in some way, but are defined by a different set of three characteristics (where the company is similar to the franchisor and the buyer is similar to the franchisee): (1) the company sells goods or services that are supplied by the company or a person affiliated with the company; (2) the company assists the buyer in any way with respect to securing accounts for the buyer, or securing locations or sites for vending machines or rack displays, or providing the services of a person able to do either; and (3) the buyer is required to make a payment of $500 or more to the company or a person affiliated with the company at any time either before or within six months after the business opens. With the adoption of the Amended FTC Rule, however, the FTC created a separate regulation covering business opportunity ventures (16 CFR §437). The Amended FTC Rule no longer regulates business opportunity ventures.

The Registration States. Almost 10 years before the FTC adopted the FTC Rule, California had already begun to regulate the offer and sale of franchises when, in 1970, the California legislature enacted the California Franchise Investment Law. Many states followed California's lead, and today there are 15 states that regulate franchise offers and sales. The states that require full registration and merit review of a proposed franchise prior to the "offering" or selling of a franchise are California, Maryland, Minnesota, New York, North Dakota, Rhode Island, Virginia, and Washington.

Other states that regulate franchise offers include Hawaii, which requires the filing of a Franchise Disclosure Document (FDD) and will engage in a limited review of the franchisor's FDD; Indiana and Wisconsin, which require filing the FDD with the state authorities; Michigan, which requires the filing of a "Notice of Intent to Offer and Sell Franchises," and Oregon, which requires only that presale disclosure be delivered to prospective investors, consistent with the Amended FTC Rule. Some states that regulate the sale of "business opportunities" or seller-assisted marketing plans, such as Connecticut, Kentucky, Florida, Texas, Utah, and Nebraska, have exemptions available for franchisors that comply with the Amended FTC Rule or that offer a franchise that includes the licensing of a federally registered trademark. These states require the filing of a notice of exemption with the appropriate state agency.

Guidelines for Determining What *Is* and What Is *Not* a Franchise

Companies frequently seek advice on how to structure a relationship that avoids the definition of a franchise under federal or state laws. The first question I ask is, "Why?" to ensure that they are seeking to avoid having to comply with these registration and disclosure laws for appropriate legal or strategic reasons. Most answers fall into one of the following categories:

1. An overseas franchisor who is uncomfortable with having to make disclosures that would not be required in its country of origin
2. A midsize or large company that feels that (as a pioneer) its industry is not ready for or will react adversely to the kinds of controls that a franchise relationship typically implies
3. A company or individual officer who has an aspect of her past that she would prefer not to be disclosed (raising other legal problems)
4. A small company that is concerned with the perceived costs of preparing and maintaining the legal documents
5. The real or perceived belief that by becoming a franchisor, the company somehow increases its chances of being sued (a myth that I usually try to debunk)
6. Some other specific circumstances or myth or fear that the company's management team has concerning franchising

Before dealing with the parameters that have been developed by the courts and regulatory authorities over the years, which provide some (but not complete) insight into which relationships will be considered franchises and which will not, we usually try to use creative thinking and structural alternatives to solve the company's problem. For example, in the first case given previously, a foreign franchisor may be able to set up a new subsidiary rather than disclosing the financial statements of the parent company (this usually arises in the case of a privately held company). If the subsidiary is properly capitalized and certain other specific conditions are met, the confidentiality of the parent company's data may be preserved. In the second case, we have often created the "nonfranchise franchisor," which is a company that has essentially agreed to prepare and provide an FDD even though the details of its relationships are in a regulatory gray area. This way, the franchisor appeases the regulators but also placates industry participants who may be more comfortable with a "strategic partner" or "licensee" designation than with a franchisor-franchisee relationship.

If the company is insistent on avoiding the need to comply with federal and state franchise laws, we then go through an exercise of determining from a cost-benefit analysis which leg of the "three-legged stool" (representing the three elements required to be a franchise) may be sacrificed. In today's brand-driven environment, the willingness to license the system without the brand to avoid the trademark license leg has not been very popular. Similarly, in an economy in which "cash flow is king," most of these clients have not been willing to waive the initial franchise fee or wait more than six months for their financial rewards. And the age-old trick of "hiding" the franchise fee in a training program or initial inventory package was figured out by the regulators a long time ago.

So it is often the third leg of the stool, the one that is most difficult to interpret, where the creative structuring must take place. The courts and the federal and state regulators have not provided much clear guidance concerning the *degrees* of support or the *degrees* of assistance that will meet the definition and those that will not. The mandatory use of an operating system or marketing plan will meet the third element of the test, but what if the use of the system is optional? What if the plan or system is not very detailed and provides lots of room for discretion on the part of the franchisee, without penalty for adapting the plan or system to meet local market conditions? And if you choose this path, does allowing this degree of discretion and flexibility sacrifice your ability to maintain quality control? In addition, in a competitive environment in which most growing companies are trying to provide *more* support and assistance to their partners in the distribution channel (and also exercise more control over them), would providing less than the norm just to avoid the definition of a franchise really make sense? These legal and strategic decisions should not be made hastily without the long-term implications being properly analyzed.

Joint Ventures

Joint ventures are legal structures that offer another alternative to capital formation for small and growing companies. A joint venture is typically structured as a partnership or as a newly formed co-owned corporation or limited-liability company, in which two or more parties are brought together to achieve a series of strategic and financial objectives on a short-term or long-term basis. A less formal method of meeting some of the same objectives without the legal structure can be achieved by creating strategic alliances or co-branding (discussed in detail later in this chapter). Entrepreneurs who wish to explore creating a joint venture should give careful thought to the type of partner they are looking for and what resources each will contribute to the newly formed entity.

Each party to the transaction will be making his respective contribution of skills, abilities, and resources. From the entrepreneur's perspective, a larger joint-venture partner often already has in place capital, human resources, and strategic market relationships that would take years to develop on a stand-alone basis. In addition to access to resources, the entrepreneur may enjoy other benefits from the relationship, such as a boost in credibility from "piggy-backing" on the goodwill and reputation of the larger corporate partner (which will, in turn, open up capital markets and potential customer relationships) and, in some cases, the opportunity to work with, instead of against, an otherwise direct or potential competitor. The key to these relationships is to define the expectations and goals clearly in advance, so that each party knows what assets it is contributing to this newly formed entity and how the rewards will be divided.

Here are eight reasons you might consider a joint venture or strategic alliance:

1. To develop a new market (domestic or international)
2. To develop a new product
3. To develop and share technology
4. To combine complementary technology
5. To pool resources to develop a production and distribution facility
6. To acquire capital
7. To execute a government contract
8. To access a distribution network or sales and marketing capability

For example, suppose that a small business named ProductCorp has patents that will protect the technology necessary for a wide range of new consumer products. The company can commence a search for a capital-rich partner that will invest in the construction of a manufacturing facility, to be owned and operated by the newly established entity. As an alternative, ProductCorp could enter into a joint venture with a larger competitor that already has the manufacturing capability to produce the products.

Each strategy has its advantages and disadvantages. The capital-rich joint-venture partner brings the necessary financial resources to achieve ProductCorp's objectives, but it cannot contribute experience in the industry. The larger competitor may offer certain operational and distribution synergies and economies of scale, but it may seek greater control over ProductCorp's management decisions.

All successful joint-venture and strategic-alliance relationships share some essential factors. These critical success factors apply to virtually all industries and all types of strategic relationships and include:

- A complementary unified force or purpose that binds the two or more companies together
- A management team that is committed to the success of the venture, free from politics or personal agendas
- A genuine synergy in which the whole truly exceeds its collective individual parts
- A cooperative culture and spirit among the strategic partners that leads to trust, resource sharing, and a friendly chemistry among the parties
- A degree of flexibility in the objectives of the joint venture to allow for changes in the marketplace and an evolution of technology
- An actual alignment of management styles and operational methods, at least to the extent that it affects the underlying project (as in the case of a strategic alliance) or the management of the new company that has been created (as in the case of a formal joint venture)
- The general levels of focus and leadership from all key parties that are necessary to the success of any new venture or business enterprise

The Mating Dance: Searching for the Right Joint-Venture Partner

Embarking on a search for a joint-venture partner is a bit like searching for an appropriate spouse. You should review prospective candidates carefully and thoroughly and conduct extensive due diligence on the final few whom you are considering. Develop a list of key objectives and goals to be achieved by the joint venture or licensing relationship, and compare this list with those of your final candidates. Take the time to understand the corporate culture and decision-making process within each company. Consider some of the following issues: How does each prospective partner's operation fit with your own processes? What about each prospective partner's previous experience and track record with other joint-venture relationships? Why did these previous relationships succeed or fail?

In many cases, smaller companies looking for joint-venture partners wind up selecting a much larger Goliath that offers a wide range of financial and non-financial resources that will allow the smaller company to achieve its growth plans. Under these circumstances, the motivating factor for the larger company is to get access and distribution rights to new technologies, products, and services. In turn, the larger company offers access to pools of capital, research and development, personnel, distribution channels, and general contacts that the small company desperately needs.

But proceed carefully. Be sensitive to the politics, red tape, and different management practices that may be in place at a larger company but will be foreign to your company. Try to distinguish between what is being promised and what will actually be delivered. If your primary motivating force is really only capital, consider exploring alternative (and perhaps less costly) sources of money. Ideally, the larger joint-venture partner will offer a lot more than just money. If your primary motivating force is access to technical personnel, consider purchasing these resources separately rather than entering into a partnership in which you give up a certain measure of control. Also, consider whether strategic relationships or extended-payment terms with vendors and consultants can be arranged in lieu of the legal structure of a joint venture. Figure 13-2 highlights the differences between joint ventures and strategic alliances.

Figure 13-2.	Comparing Joint Ventures and Strategic Alliances.	
	Joint Ventures	**Strategic Alliances**
Term	Usually medium- to long-term	Short-term
Strategic objective	Often serves as the precursor to a merger	Flexible and noncommittal
Legal agreements and structure	Actual legal entity formed	Contract-driven
Extent of commitment	Shared equity	Shared objectives
Capital and resources	Each party makes a capital contribution of cash or intangible assets	No specific capital contributions (may be shared budgeting on even cross-investment)
Tax ramifications	Be on the lookout for double taxation unless pass-through entities utilized	No direct tax ramifications

Also consider the following key strategic issues before and during joint-venture or strategic-alliance negotiations:

- *Exactly what types of tangible and intangible assets will each party contribute to the joint venture?* Who will have ownership rights to the property contributed during the term of the joint venture and thereafter? Who will own property developed as a result of joint development efforts?
- *What covenants of nondisclosure or noncompetition will be expected of each joint venturer during the term of the agreement and thereafter?*
- *What timetables or performance quotas for completion of the projects contemplated by the joint venture will be included in the agreement?* What are the rights and remedies of each party if these performance standards are not met?
- *How will issues of management and control be addressed in the agreement?* What will be the respective voting rights of each party? What are the procedures in the event of a major disagreement or deadlock? What is the fallback plan?

Once you and your prospective partner have discussed all of these preliminary issues, you should prepare, with the assistance of counsel, a formal joint-venture agreement or corporate shareholders' agreement. The precise terms of the agreement between your company and your joint-venture partner will naturally depend on both of your specific objectives.

Co-Branding

Co-branding is a form of informal partnership in which two or more established brand names combine to bring added value, economies of scale, and customer recognition to each product. Co-branding can be arranged between two franchise companies, two nonfranchise companies, or a franchise company and a nonfranchise company. It has many forms, including the following:

Financial services co-branding. In the early 1990s, credit card companies pioneered co-branding, pairing up with airlines or telecommunications companies for mutual branding and shared rewards.

Consumer-product ingredient co-branding. One brand appears as an ingredient in another as an enhancement to drive sales and cross-consumer loyalty. Examples include Post Raisin Bran's use of Sun-Maid raisins in its cereal; Archway's use of Kellogg's All-Bran in its cookies; Ben & Jerry's Heath Bar Crunch ice cream; and PopTarts with Smuckers fruit fillings.

Implied endorsement co-branding. The co-branded name or logo is used to build consumer recognition, even if no *actual* ingredient from that brand is used in the product—for example, the John Deere logo stamped on the back of a Florsheim boot; the Doritos Pizza Craver tortilla chips, whose packaging features Pizza Hut's logo; or Doritos Taco Supreme chips, where the packaging features Taco Bell's logo.

Actual composite co-branding. The co-branded product actually uses a branded pairing of popular manufacturing techniques or processes— Timberland boots with Gore-Tex fabric, furniture with Scotchgard protectants, Dell or Gateway computers with Intel inside, and so on.

Designer-driven co-branded products. Certain manufacturers have co-branded with well-known designers to increase consumer loyalty and brand awareness. For example, the Eddie Bauer edition of the Ford Explorer has been a very strong seller with product differentiation.

Retail business format co-branding. This type of co-branding is growing rapidly within the retailing, hospitality, and franchising communities to attract additional customers. This type of co-branding includes creating complementary product lines to offset different consumer tastes (such as Baskin-Robbins and Dunkin' Donuts, whose products are now offered at the same co-branded locations) or consuming patterns (combining a traditional breakfast-only consumer traffic with a lunch-only traffic pattern); or selling additional products or services to a "captured customer" (such as selling Starbucks coffee at an auto-service mini-mall while customers wait for their cars to be repaired).

Why Should a Company Think About Co-Branding as a Growth Strategy?

Co-branding is one of four leveraging options; the other three are line extensions, stretching the brand vertically in the existing product class, and creating brand extensions into different product classes. Co-branding should be considered for the following reasons:

- It is a way to leverage the company's intangible assets (including brand awareness and customer loyalty) by entering another product class.
- It can provide added value in the form of customer convenience,

thereby creating a point of differentiation from competitive products and services.

- It is easier and less risky than trying to build a strong brand because there are many internal and external impediments to the latter, such as a corporate bias against innovation, short-term orientation, price pressures, and competitive threats.

- It can gain marketplace visibility and create new customer interest, which helps a company maintain brand equity in the face of competitors' new-product introductions and declining brand awareness.

- It can change the perception of a brand. The company can create a new brand personality (for example, the use of Bart Simpson with Butterfingers), or at least update it.

- It can help a company gain access to new product categories that otherwise would have involved a significant investment of time, money, and resources to enter.

- It can provide greater assurance about product quality. A brand name assists consumers in understanding a product's characteristics, and the presence of a second brand may signal to potential customers that another firm is willing to stake its reputation on the product.

- It can reach a new customer base far more quickly than the launch of a new brand, which usually takes several years (three to five years in the credit card industry, for example).

- It offers a shortcut to an image upgrade, such as Ford's Special Eddie Bauer Editions.

- It offers a way to target a key demographic audience, such as Master-Card's creating a co-branded card with universities to reach college students and alumni.

Things to Consider Before Entering a Co-Branding Arrangement

- Be aware of the fit of the brands. For example, a hypothetical Godiva/Slim-Fast line of chocolate snack bars would benefit the Slim-Fast brand by its association with superior chocolates produced by Godiva. However, this would detract from Godiva's upscale brand image. In this scenario, there is not a fit between the brands.

- Understand consumer perceptions of your product and its attributes to better determine whether the two brands have a common set of attributes.

- Examine the degree to which the two brands complement each other.
- Rate how each brand is regarded in the marketplace separately, then rate the co-branded product.
- Explore the relative contribution that each brand will make to the effectiveness of the co-branded product.
- What types of partners would enhance your identity?
- What types of partners would help reduce the limitations of your identity?

Figure 13-3 provides some examples of co-branding.

Advantages and Disadvantages of Co-Branding

Co-branding offers many advantages for your business:

- Shares costs, including marketing and packaging, but also rent and utilities if the two companies are in same location.
- Permits complementary services to achieve marketing and expense benefits. For example, many gas stations and restaurants co-brand, and quick-service restaurants have teamed up with each other to serve different but complementary meals. One brand finds another brand that will not compete directly against it but will bring business in the door at a time of the day when it does not get high traffic.

Figure 13-3.	Examples of Co-Branding.

- Adidas and Polar Electro created Project Fusion, which takes sports apparel equipment and integrates speed-monitoring equipment.
- Apple and Nike created Sports Kit, which allows shoes to talk to an iPod.
- The Art of Shaving designed a power razor that is compatible only with Gillette blades.
- The Nokia 8800 was a collaboration by Nokia and Aston Martin.
- Sperry designed shoes for J. Crew.
- Michael Jordan and Nike came together to create the Air Jordan shoes.
- T.G.I. Friday's has created specialty items with Jack Daniels–flavored sauces.
- Eddie Bauer joined with Ford to create a special-edition SUV.
- Philips joined with Douwe Egberts to create the Senseo coffeemaker.

- Facilitates expansion into international markets.
- Makes it easier to get brand recognition for your brand in foreign markets if it's tied to a well-known domestic brand. Many foreign markets enjoy American products, so the co-branding works to their advantage.
- Creates convenience for customers, which can increase business for both companies.
- Taps into the national image and awareness of the brand of the issuing company.
- Increases the distribution network.
- Enhances market clout in terms of the value and quality communicated to customers.
- Doubles brand recognition, doubles the endorsement power, and doubles consumer confidence in the co-branded products.

There are also some disadvantages of co-branding:
- Agreements between co-branding partners can be hard to construct and agree upon.
- Marketing must be agreed upon by both parties, which can delay time to market and reduce the flexibility of your marketing plans.
- Bad publicity for one company can affect the other company.
- If one brand fails to live up to the promises it made to the other, the co-branding relationship can dissolve.
- If co-branding fails, both companies suffer, and consumers may become confused about new products, diminishing the value of both of the companies involved in the co-branding relationship.

Preparing a Co-Branding Agreement

Once your company has determined the type of partner you want to pursue, ask yourself the following questions:
- How will the co-branded opportunity be marketed?
- Which company will provide the services and assistance?
- Which partner's team will operate the co-branded stores or sell the co-branded products? Will it vary?

When you and another company have determined that you want to develop a co-branding arrangement, you'll need to formalize the deal by executing a co-branding agreement that addresses the following issues:

- Designated territory
- Initial term and renewal (if any) of the co-branding agreement
- Duties of each party
- Licensing of the intellectual property
- Licensing fees
- Financial reporting
- Quality control
- Noncompete clauses
- Termination (including operation of the co-branded units upon termination)
- Dispute resolution

Before you launch the deal, implement a pilot program to work out any kinks in the arrangement. The pilot program should determine whether the co-branded and combined operations will produce the projected synergies and increased sales for both companies and the projected reductions in operating costs as a percentage of revenue. The test should also reveal whether equipment, labor, and other needs are compatible. Testing should enable your company to develop and refine its operating procedures for the preparation and delivery of the products or services of both businesses in and from the same facility, and to develop an operations manual and training programs for the co-branded unit. Finally, the test period should offer both companies the time to develop a productive working relationship.

The following parameters and goals of the test must be established before the test is begun:

- Duration of the test period
- Number and types of products to be tested
- Goals that the co-branded products are expected to achieve
- Whether the co-branded products will be in or at company-owned or franchisee-operated units

Licensing

Licensing is a contractual method of developing and exploiting intellectual property by transferring the rights of use to third parties without the transfer of ownership. Virtually any proprietary product or service can be the subject of a licensing agreement. Examples range from the licensing of the Mickey Mouse character by Walt Disney Studios in the 1930s to modern-day licensing of computer software and high technology. From a legal perspective, licensing involves complex issues of contract, tax, antitrust, international, tort, and intellectual-property law. From a business perspective, licensing involves weighing the economic and strategic advantages of licensing against those of other methods of bringing a product or service to the marketplace—methods such as direct sales, distributorships, and franchises.

Licensing can be viewed as an alternative growth strategy because the founders of the company are no longer directly responsible for the financial investment needed to fuel its growth and expansion. Instead, the capital-formation and investment burden is shifted to another, who pays the licensor for the right to use its technology or its brand name in exchange for initial license fees and royalties.

The decision to shift to being a licensor of technology instead of bringing products and services directly to the market significantly reduces the amount of capital your company will need; it may also lead to your company's becoming a virtual corporation that has only limited day-to-day operations and is really just a holding company that receives and distributes licensing fees.

Many of the benefits of licensing that can be enjoyed by a growing company closely parallel the advantages of franchising, namely:

- Spreading the risk and cost of development and distribution
- Achieving more rapid market penetration
- Earning initial license fees and ongoing royalty income
- Enhancing consumer loyalty and goodwill
- Preserving the capital that would otherwise be required for internal growth and expansion
- Testing new applications for existing and proven technology
- Avoiding or settling litigation regarding a dispute over ownership of the technology

The disadvantages of licensing are also similar to the risks inherent in franchising, such as:

- A diminished ability to enforce quality-control standards and specifications

- A greater risk of another party's infringing on the licensor's intellectual property
- A dependence on the skills, abilities, and resources of the licensee as a source of revenue
- Difficulty in recruiting, motivating, and retaining qualified and competent licensees
- The risk that the licensor's entire reputation and goodwill may be damaged or destroyed by the act or omission of a single licensee
- The administrative burden of monitoring and supporting the operations of the network of licensees

Failure to consider all of the costs and benefits of licensing could easily result in a regrettable strategic decision or being stuck with the terms of an unprofitable license agreement. This could occur if you underestimate the licensee's need for technical assistance and support, or if you overestimate the market demand for your products and services. To avoid such problems, you should conduct a certain amount of due diligence before engaging in any serious negotiations with a prospective licensee. This preliminary investigation should cover the following areas:

- Market research
- Legal steps to fully protect intellectual property
- An internal financial analysis of the technology with respect to pricing, profit margins, and costs of production and distribution
- A more specific analysis of the prospective licensee with respect to its financial strength, research and manufacturing capabilities, and reputation in the industry

Once you've decided to enter into more formal negotiations, you should discuss the terms and conditions of the license agreement with the licensee. These provisions will vary, depending on whether the license is for merchandising an entertainment property, exploiting a given technology, or distributing a particular product to an original-equipment manufacturer or value-added reseller.

There are two main types of licensing: *technology licensing*, where the strategy is to find a licensee who can exploit industrial and technological developments; and *merchandise and character licensing*, where the strategy is to license a recognized trademark or copyright to a manufacturer of consumer goods in markets that the licensor does not currently serve.

Technology Licensing

The principal reason for technology transfer and licensing agreements is to make a marriage between the technology proprietor (you, as licensor) and an organization that has the resources to develop and market the technology properly (as licensee). This marriage is made between companies and inventors of all sizes, but it often occurs between an entrepreneur who has the technology but lacks the resources to penetrate the marketplace adequately, and therefore becomes a licensor, and a larger company that has the research and development, production, human resources, and marketing capability to make the best use of the technology. Many successful entrepreneurs have relied on the resources of larger organizations to bring their products to market, including Chester Carlson (the inventor of xerography), Edwin Land (Polaroid cameras), and Willis Carrier (air-conditioning). As the base for technological development becomes broader, large companies are looking not only to entrepreneurs and small businesses for new ideas and technologies, but also to foreign countries, universities, federal and state governments, and one another to serve as licensors of technology.

In the typical licensing arrangement, the owner of intellectual-property rights (patents, trade secrets, trademarks, and so on) permits another party to use these rights under a set of specified conditions and circumstances set forth in a license agreement. Licensing agreements can be limited to a very narrow component of the proprietor's intellectual-property rights, such as one specific application of a single patent, or they can be much broader, such as in a "technology-transfer" agreement, where an entire bundle of intellectual-property rights is transferred to the licensee in exchange for initial fees and royalties. Figure 13-4 provides examples of the different types of licensing strategies. The technology-transfer arrangement is actually closer to a sale of the intellectual-property rights, an important difference being that the licensor retains the right to get the intellectual property back if the licensee fails to meet its obligations under the agreement. An example of this type of transaction might be bundling a proprietary environmental cleanup system and technical support and training services to a master overseas licensee, with reversionary rights in the event of a breach of the agreement or the failure to meet a set of performance standards.

As a rule, any well-drafted technology license agreement should address the following topics.

Scope of the Grant. Define the exact scope and subject matter of the license

Figure 13-4.	One Patent, Multiple Revenue Streams.

Patent X					
↓	↓	↓	↓	↓	↓
Direct Use and Application in Company's Core Business	Licensed to Third Party for a Parallel, Noncompetitive Use (Limited Use)	Licensed to a Competitor Abroad (Limited Geographic Area)	Consortium (Nonexclusive)	Research and Development (to User Who Hopes to Find Other Applications Within Noncompeting Industries/ Option to License)	Licensed to Aftermarket Service Provider (Service, Maintenance, Training, Parts, etc.)

carefully. Clearly set forth any restrictions on the geographic scope, rights of use, permissible channels of trade, restrictions on sublicensing, limitations on assignability, or exclusion of improvements to the technology covered by the agreement.

Term and Renewal. This section specifies the commencement date, duration, renewals and extensions, conditions for renewal, procedures for providing notice of intent to renew, grounds for termination, obligations upon termination, and your reversionary rights to the technology.

Performance Standards and Quotas. To the extent that your primary revenues as the licensor will depend on royalty income that will be calculated based on the licensee's gross or net revenues, you may want to impose certain minimum levels of performance in terms of sales, advertising and promotional expenditures, and human resources to be devoted to the exploitation of the technology. The licensee will probably argue for a "best efforts" provision that is free from performance standards and quotas. In this event, you may want to insist on a minimum royalty level that will be paid regardless of the licensee's actual performance.

Payments to the Licensor. Virtually every type of license agreement will include some form of initial payment and ongoing royalty to the licensor. Royalties vary widely, however, and may be based on gross sales, net sales, net profits, fixed sum per product sold, or a minimum payment to be made to the licensor over a given period of time; they may also include a sliding scale to provide some incentive to the licensee as a reward for performance.

Quality Assurance and Protection. Here, you should set forth quality-control standards and specifications for the production, marketing, and distribution of the products and services covered by the license. In addition, the agreement should include procedures that give you the opportunity to *enforce* these standards and specifications, such as a right to inspect the licensee's premises; a right to review, approve, or reject samples produced by the licensee; and a right to review and approve any packaging, labeling, or advertising materials to be used in connection with the exploitation of the products and services that are within the scope of the license.

Insurance and Indemnification. You should take all necessary and reasonable steps to ensure that the licensee has an obligation to protect and indemnify you against any claims or liabilities resulting from the licensee's exploitation of the products and services covered by the license.

Accounting, Reports, and Audits. You must impose certain reporting and record-keeping procedures on the licensee to ensure that you receive an accurate accounting for periodic royalty payments. In addition, you should reserve the right to audit the licensee's records in the event of a dispute or discrepancy, along with provisions as to who will be responsible for the cost of the audit in the event of an understatement.

Duties to Preserve and Protect Intellectual Property. Carefully define the obligations that the licensee and its agents and employees have to preserve and protect the confidential nature and acknowledge the ownership of the intellectual property that is being disclosed in connection with the license agreement. Also describe in this section any required notices or legends that must be included on products or materials distributed in connection with the license agreement (such as the status of the relationship or the actual owner of the intellectual property).

Technical Assistance, Training, and Support. This section of the agreement delineates any obligation you have as licensor to assist the licensee in developing or exploiting the subject matter that is being licensed. This assistance may take the form of personal services or of documents and records. Either way, this section should also specify any fees over and above the initial license and ongoing royalty fee that are due you for such support services.

Warranties of the Licensor. A prospective licensee may demand that you provide certain representations and warranties in the license agreement. These may include warranties that you own the technology, with no known infringements or restrictions on the ability to license the technology, or that the technology has the features, capabilities, and characteristics that were previously represented in the negotiations.

Infringements. The license agreement should contain the procedures by which the licensee must notify you of any known or suspected direct or indirect infringements of the subject matter being licensed. The responsibilities for the cost of protecting and defending the technology should also be specified in this section.

Merchandise- and Character-Licensing Agreements

The use of commonly recognized trademarks, brand names, sports teams, athletes, universities, television and film characters, musicians, and designers to foster the sales of specific products and services is at the heart of today's merchandise- and character-licensing environment. Manufacturers and distributors of a wide range of products and services license words, images, and symbols. Certain brand names and characters have withstood the test of time, while others are fads that fall prey to consumer shifts and stiff competition.

The trademark and copyright owners of these properties and character images are motivated to license them for a variety of reasons. Aside from the obvious desire to earn royalty fees and profits, many manufacturers view licensing as a form of merchandising that promotes the underlying product or service. The licensing of a trademark for application on a line of clothing helps to establish and reinforce brand awareness at the consumer level. For example, when consumer products companies license their brands for apparel merchandising, the goal is not only to enjoy the royalty income from the sale of the clothing line, but also to sell more of its underlying products, appeal to the lifestyle of targeted consumers, and maintain consumer awareness. Manufacturers have adopted similar strategies to revive a mature brand or failing product. In certain instances, the product that has been licensed has been almost as financially successful as the underlying product it was intended to promote.

Owners of brand names, celebrities, and academic institutions must be very careful not to grant too many licenses too quickly. The financial rewards from a flow of royalty income from hundreds of different manufacturers can be quite seductive, but it must be weighed against the possible loss of quality control and dilution of the brand name, logo, or character. The loyalty of the licensee network is also threatened when too many licenses are granted for closely competing products.

Retailers will also become cautious when purchasing licensed goods from a licensee if there is a fear that quality control has suffered or that the popularity of the licensed character, celebrity, or image will be short-lived. This may result in smaller orders and an overall unwillingness to carry inventory. This is especially true in the toy industry, where purchasing decisions are being made (or at least influenced) by the whims of a five-year-old child who may strongly identify with a character one week and then turn her attention to a different character the next week. It is incumbent upon the manufacturers and licensees to develop advertising and media campaigns that will hold the consumer's attention for an extended period of time. Only then will the retailer be convinced of the potential longevity of the product line. This will require a balancing of the risks and rewards between licensor and licensee in the character-licensing agreement in the areas of compensation to the licensor, advertising expenditures by the licensee, scope of the exclusivity, and quality-control standards and specifications.

In the merchandise-licensing community, the name, logo, symbol, or character is typically referred to as the "property," and the specific product or product line produced (the T-shirts, mugs, posters, and so on) is referred to as the "licensed product." This type of licensing offers opportunities and benefits to both the owner of the property and the manufacturer of the licensed product. For the owner of the property, licensing strengthens and expands brand recognition, goodwill, and royalty income. For the manufacturer of the licensed products, there is an opportunity to leverage the goodwill of the property to improve sales of the licensed products. The manufacturer has an opportunity to hit the ground running in the sale of merchandise by gaining access to and use of an already established brand name or character image.

The licensor and the licensee should conduct due diligence on each other. From your perspective as the owner of the property, you should ensure that the manufacturer of the licensed product demonstrates an ability to meet and maintain quality-control standards, possesses financial stability, and offers an aggressive and well-planned marketing and promotional strategy. From the perspective of the manufacturer of the licensed product, you as the owner of the property should display integrity and a commitment to quality, disclose your future plans for the promotion of the property, and be willing to participate and assist in the overall marketing of the licensed products. For example, if a star basketball player were unwilling to appear at promotional events designed to sell his own specially licensed line of shoes, this would present a major problem and could lead to a premature termination of the licensing relationship.

When preparing and negotiating a merchandise-licensing agreement, there are several key areas that must be addressed:

- Scope of the territorial and product exclusivity
- Assignability and sublicensing rights
- Definition of the property and the licensed products
- Quality control and approval
- Ownership of artwork and designs
- Term renewal rights and termination of the relationship
- Initial license fee and ongoing royalty fees
- Performance criteria for the licensee
- Liability insurance
- Indemnification
- Duty to pursue trademark and copyright infringement
- Minimum advertising and promotional requirements
- Accounting and record keeping by the licensee
- Inspection and audit rights of the licensor
- Rights of first refusal for expanded or revised characters and images
- Limitations on the licensee's distribution to related or affiliated entities
- Representations and warranties of the licensor with respect to its rights to the property
- Availability of the licensor for technical and promotional assistance
- Miscellaneous legal provisions, such as law to govern, inurement of goodwill, nature of the relationship, notice, and force majeure

Turning Lemons into Lemonade: A Case Study

The licensing of intellectual capital and technology to industries that are beyond your competencies can be not only a way to harvest new opportunities, but also a strategy for salvaging a product line or application that has been an actual or near disaster. One of the highest-profile examples of this was Procter & Gamble's development of its proprietary Olestra molecule. When Olestra was introduced, it was touted as a revolutionary new low-fat ingredient, but unpleasant side effects (including stomach pains and gas) surfaced, and millions of dollars in plant and equipment ran the risk of sitting dormant unless an alternative application of the molecular formation could be uncovered. After working with a team of internal technologists and outside strategic advisors, a number of potential applications had been identified, but, surprisingly, the most successful application was in the field of environmental remediation—a far cry from potato chips. Apparently, when poured on contaminated soil or sludge, the Olestra molecule binds itself to pollutants, making them easier to remove.

Chapter 14

Mergers and Acquisitions

The merger-and-acquisition frenzy that took place in 1999 and 2000 affected owners and managers of businesses of all types and sizes, and brought us megadeals such as AOL Time Warner, ExxonMobil, and Daimler-Chrysler. The market went on a short hiatus in 2002 and 2003, but then made a resurgence, bringing in deals between Bank One and JPMorgan Chase, AT&T Wireless and Cingular, and Oxford Health and United Health, all valued at billions of dollars. The financial crisis, however, took its toll on the M&A market. It is estimated that in 2007, there were approximately 15,700 deals done in the global market; by 2009, that number had fallen to 9,400.

There has been a thawing of deal flow in the past two years, and there is good reason to believe that M&A activity will continue to recover in the coming years. The recent uptick in M&A activity from the recessionary lows has trickled down to the middle markets and smaller companies. In 2010, there were $129.4 billion in deals done that were valued at up to $50 million—a 14.7 percent increase over 2009. Like initial public offerings, discussed in Chapter 11 and 12, mergers and acquisitions can also be an exit strategy and liquidity event for entrepreneurs, angels, strategic investors, and venture capital firms. The number of "venture-backed" companies that are bought varies from year to year depending on economic cycles and capital market conditions. After the challenging years of 2008 and 2009, marked by a slow economy and low multiples/valuations for sellers, activity picked up significantly in 2010, when there were 400 completed acquisitions of venture-backed companies, the biggest number since the National Venture Capital Association (NVCA) started keeping track of these data in 1985. The average disclosed deal size was approximately $157 million, with the largest venture-backed acquisition in 2010 being the purchase of Bravo Health, a Baltimore-based provider of health-care services, by Health Spring for $545 million. The information technology sector saw the highest number of venture-backed M&A deals in 2010, with a total of 72 deals with a disclosed total dollar value of $2.8 billion in the aggregate. In most cases, the return to the venture investor was 2 to 10 times its original investment (67 percent of the time), with the valuation being *below* the original investment only 24 percent of the time, and at the other extreme, 10 percent of the total deals yielding more than 10 times the original investment.

Although the capital to finance an acquisition is usually not a challenge for corporate titans, as the owner or manager of a small to medium-size company, you may be considering a merger or acquisition for strategic or financial reasons but lack the capital to move forward. This chapter is written primarily from the perspective of an emerging-growth company that is considering the purchase of another business of similar size as a method of strategic growth or diversification. (If you're considering selling your business rather than purchasing someone else's, the information in this chapter will also be useful because it will provide insight into the buyer's strategies and areas of concern.) The chapter discusses due diligence, valuation, pricing, and structuring the proposed transaction. For more information, see my book *Mergers and Acquisitions from A to Z*, third edition (AMACOM, 2010).

Current Trends Affecting Mergers and Acquisitions in a Turbulent Environment

At what rate does an iceberg melt? One drop at a time. For many merger-and-acquisition professionals, that's how the market has appeared since the financial crisis ... things have been improving, and the speed at which the M&A iceberg has been thawing is picking up. Whether you are the principal or an officer of a company, a lawyer or accountant whose practice is M&A-driven, an investment banker, or a consultant, the consensus is that mergers and acquisitions are actively picking up and conditions are improving in the broader market, but things are just starting to really move along, and there is a certain fragility that has made it somewhat of a defensive market. Because (overall) the market is still wary, there are many deals, even good deals, that are not getting done; this is beginning to change, however, and the M&A iceberg is poised to start thawing out at a much quicker pace than it has been. This is especially true in the "middle market" (deals in the $20 million to $300 million range), where deals have been heating up at a faster pace than in the rest of the M&A market.

Deals today need to be fairly structured, be reasonably priced, and genuinely make sense, or they will not get done. And while valuations have not reached the prerecession levels, the gap between buyers and sellers in valuing businesses has begun to close. There is now optimism that a good deal *can* get done in this market—especially for middle-market deals. In fact, 2010 experienced the highest transactional total in the middle market since the Internet bubble of 2000. Further, with corporate balance sheets heavy with cash, increasing valuations, modest economic growth projections, and increasing (but cautious) optimism among executives, larger corporations are likely to continue making middle-market strategic bets instead of "bet the farm" large transactions—*making M&A the emerging-growth company's exit vehicle of choice for the foreseeable future.*

What conditions have fueled the thawing of the iceberg? A recovering and more stable stock market; improvements in the economy; interest rates remaining low; improvements in financial controls, systems, and corporate governance; cross-border deals on the rise; a willingness of sellers to be more realistic from a valuation perspective; and a genuine focus on the quality of transactions. Yes, we will still have uncertainty about future financial regulations, uncomfortably high levels of unemployment, and weakness in certain sectors, but the market's willingness to shrug off these troubling conditions has led to a measurable uptick in M&A activity.

Business strategists often say that it is "cheaper to buy than to build" a business. With recovering, modest global economic growth projections, the prospect of a double-dip recession being unlikely, gradual additions to payroll, and increasing leverage levels, the weight is leaning on the buy side of the "buy versus build" scale. Also, a recent IPO market that has been less hospitable to most emerging-growth companies is likely to provide incentives for matchmaking between well-run, valuable businesses and strategic acquirers. All these factors also permit the emerging company to develop by acquiring other businesses at a strategic value.

Notwithstanding the continuing development of the perfect middle-market M&A storm, the purchase and/or selling of a business is a complex and challenging task. There are many different ways to buy and sell a business. This chapter will lead the buyer and seller through the process, and give both the buyer and the seller an understanding of the other's perspective (see Figures 14-1 and 14-2).

Buy-Vs.-Build Analysis

At what point is it better to buy capabilities than it is to develop them organically? Factors to consider include the following:

- Costs (tangible and intangible)
- Speed to market
- Quality/expertise
- Degree of competition in the market
- Speed and difficulty in building or access to a distribution channel
- Market fragmentation
- Regulation
- Access to financing
- Governance issues
- Customer acquisition costs/time frame/loyalty
- Supplier acquisition costs/time frame/loyalty
- Research and development capabilities
- Human capital

Figure 14-1.	Contrasting and Understanding Buyers' and Sellers' Motivations.

Sellers' Motivations	Buyers' Motivations
• Founder's health or retirement	• Growth
• Serial entrepreneur burnout	• Use of shares as currency
• Shareholder liquidity	• Typically harder to build
• Competitive necessity	than to buy
• Scale	• Competitive response
• Distribution	• Lack of internal innovation
• Capitalize on innovation	• Industry consolidation
• Industry consolidation	• Economic considerations
• Economic conditions	• Diversification

Figure 14-2.	Contrasting and Understanding Buyers' and Sellers' Motivations.

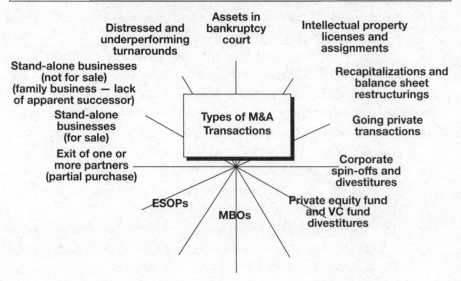

Develop an Acquisition Plan

Entrepreneurs and middle-market companies use acquisitions when it is more efficient to acquire assets and resources from outside rather than expand internally. The process begins with an acquisition plan, which identifies the specific objectives of the transaction and the criteria to be applied in analyzing a potential target company. The acquisition plan will be presented to sources of acquisition financing to provide the capital needed. Although the reasons for considering growth by acquisition will vary from industry to industry and from company to company, the most common strategic advantages from your perspective as a buyer include:

- You can achieve operating and financial synergies and economics of scale in areas such as production and manufacturing, research and development, management, marketing, and distribution.
- Your company may be able to develop the full potential of the target company's proprietary products or services if they are suffering from lack of capital to move projects forward.
- The target company may stand to lose its management team because of the lack of career growth potential unless it is acquired by a business that offers higher salaries, increased employee benefits, and greater opportunity for advancement. Conversely, you may have a surplus of strong managers who are likely to leave unless your company acquires other businesses that they can operate and develop.
- You may want to stabilize your company's earnings stream and mitigate its risk of business failure by diversifying your products and services through acquisition rather than internal development.
- Your company may need to deploy excess cash in a tax-efficient project (because both the distribution of dividends and stock redemptions are generally taxable events to your shareholders).
- Your company may want to achieve certain production and distribution economies of scale through vertical integration, which would involve the acquisition of a key supplier or customer.
- The target company's management team may be ready for retirement or a key manager may have recently died (leaving the business with residual assets that your company can utilize).
- You may wish to increase your market power by acquiring competitors, which may be a less costly method of achieving growth than internal expansion.
- You may be weak in certain key business areas, such as research and development or marketing, and it may be more efficient to fill these gaps through an acquisition than to build these departments internally.
- Your company may have superior products and services but lack the consumer loyalty or protected trademarks needed to gain recognition

in the marketplace. The acquisition of an older, more established firm can be a more efficient method of developing goodwill.

- Your company may want to penetrate new geographic markets and conclude that it is cheaper to acquire firms that are already doing business in those areas than to establish market diversification from scratch.

- Your company may be able to provide the technical expertise or capital that the target company needs to grow to the next stage in its development.

Steps Involved in an Acquisition

- Develop acquisition objectives.
- Analyze the projected economic and financial gains to be achieved by the acquisition.
- Assemble an acquisition team (typically managers, attorneys, accountants, a business appraiser, and investment bankers).
- Conduct a search for acquisition candidates.
- Perform due diligence analysis of prime candidates
- Conduct initial negotiations and valuation of the selected target.
- Select the structure of the transaction.
- Identify sources of financing for the transaction.
- Conduct detailed bidding and negotiations.
- Obtain all shareholder and third-party consents and approvals.
- Structure the legal documents.
- Prepare for the closing.
- Close the deal.
- Perform postclosing tasks and responsibilities.
- Implement the strategic integration of your company and the acquired company.

Pitfalls to Avoid

In developing a defined set of acquisition objectives, it is crucial that you avoid certain pitfalls. For example, when you are determining the valuation of a target, do not rely too heavily on the previous year's earnings or a "multiple of sales" formula. Instead, look closely at the fundamentals of the target's business, such as economic and technological trends affecting its outlook, the quality of its assets and management team, its dependence on a particular key supplier or customer, and the extent to which its intellectual property has been protected.

Also examine other financial data about the target (in addition to its sales figures), such as cash flow, accounts receivable management, credit ratings, and cost of goods sold. Probe beyond the data contained in the financial statements provided by the prospective target; they can be incomplete or misleading. Many target companies have spent years trying to understate their performance in order to avoid excessive tax liability or the percentage paid to lessors and licensors. Now they may seek to overstate their financial performance by capitalizing items that are normally taken as direct expenses, overstating the value of assets, and understating the extent of liabilities to make the financial statements more attractive in anticipation of a sale.

Another common acquisition misperception is that diversification significantly reduces the risk of business failure. Although having a diversified line of products and services does tend to stabilize a company's earnings stream, developing such a line can be a very dangerous and expensive acquisition strategy. For example, the negotiation and structure of the transaction will often be driven by an awareness of the special issues affecting the industry in which the target operates. You will be at an extreme disadvantage, *both during the negotiations and beyond the closing,* if you misunderstand or lack knowledge about the particular industry. It is therefore imperative that your acquisition team conduct meaningful due diligence, which it can do if it has a background and experience with a business that is similar or related to the target. An alternative is to structure part of the purchase price in the form of a postclosing long-term consulting contract so that the benefits of the target company's management expertise are preserved. That way the target company's knowledge is transferred to the employees who will be responsible for managing the company once the target company's personnel depart.

A final pitfall to avoid when developing acquisition objectives is the assumption that the best opportunities can be found in turnaround situations. Although a financially distressed target may be available at a lower price than a healthy firm, the difference in price may not be worth the drain on resources that will be needed to rehabilitate the target. For example, a target company that has been grossly mismanaged may be able to be put back on its feet with an infusion of fresh management talent. But some companies that are available to be acquired may have been divisions that were spun off by larger companies because they had been a resource drain for the parent since their inception or should have never been started. In such cases, it will be especially difficult (if not impossible) for you to commit enough talent, expertise, and capital to achieve a successful turnaround. The most effective way to distinguish between a target that truly has kinetic energy and salvageable assets and one that will always be the "walking dead" is through effective due diligence and analysis.

Analyzing Target Companies

The analysis begins with the assembly of your acquisition team, which is made up of the key officers of your company, your lawyer, your accountant, and other strategic or financial advisors, such as investment bankers. The acquisition team will help you to identify the key strategic and financial objectives of the transaction, and these will then be used as the criteria for screening candidates.

After the team has identified the acquisition objectives and developed the criteria for analyzing a target company, the next logical step for the team is to identify appropriate candidates and then narrow the field. The transaction should achieve one or more of your developed objectives, and the target company should meet many (if not all) of the criteria identified. A candidate that is under serious consideration should possess most or all of the following criteria:

- Be operating in an industry that demonstrates growth potential.
- Be protective of the proprietary aspects of its products and services.
- Demonstrate a well-defined and established market position.
- Be involved in a minimal amount of litigation (especially if the litigation is with a key customer or supplier).
- Be in a position to readily obtain key third-party consents from lessors, bankers, creditors, suppliers, and customers. *Failure to obtain the necessary consents to the assignment of key contracts will serve as a substantial impediment to the completion of the transaction.*
- Be positioned for a sale (except in hostile takeover situations) so that negotiations focus on the terms of the sale and *not* on whether to sell in the first place.
- Have its principal place of business located within an hour (via air) of your company's headquarters or satellite offices (*unless*, of course, your primary objective is to enter new geographic markets).

Selecting the Target Company

Once you have narrowed the field of candidates, it's time to select the company that you want to acquire. Effective rating and analysis of the finalists will involve two phases: the *acquisition review* and, once you think you've identified the specific company you want to acquire, the detailed legal and business *due diligence*.

Acquisition Analysis

The acquisition review is the preliminary analysis of the two or three finalists that most closely meet your objectives. In all likelihood, the prospective targets will have different strengths and weaknesses, which makes the selection of the winner that much more difficult. As a result, the primary goal of the acquisition review is to collect data that will help you determine the value of the finalists for negotiation and bidding purposes.

The key areas of inquiry at this stage in the transaction include:

- The targets' management teams
- Financial performances (current and projected)
- Areas of potential liability to a successor company
- Legal or business impediments to the transaction
- Confirmation of any facts underlying the terms of the proposed valuation and bid
- The extent to which the intellectual property of the target companies has been protected

This information can be obtained from meetings with and requests for information from the targets' management teams or from external sources such as trade associations, the targets' customers and suppliers, industry publications, chambers of commerce, securities law filings, or private data sources such as Dun & Bradstreet, Standard & Poor's, and Moody's Investors Service.

When you have the data for the finalists, assemble your acquisition team to analyze the information, select the target company, and structure the terms of the offering. The result should be a letter of intent or preliminary agreement with the target company selected. Often, the buyer and seller execute a letter of intent as an agreement in principle to consummate the transaction. The parties should be very clear as to whether the letter of intent is a binding preliminary contract or merely a memorandum from which the formal legal documents can be drafted once due diligence is completed. The letter of intent has many advantages to both parties, which include:

- A psychological commitment to the transaction
- A way to expedite the formal negotiations process
- An overview of the matters that require further discussion

One difficult issue in drafting the letter of intent is whether to include a price. From your perspective as buyer, you don't want to set the purchase price until you have completed due diligence. However, the seller may hesitate to proceed without a price commitment. Therefore, you should establish a price range with a clause that states the factors that will influence the final price. As the buyer, always reserve the right to change the price and the terms in the event that you discover information during due diligence that will reduce the target's value (or to draft "holdback" clauses to allow for any unforeseen liabilities or events). Finally, it is not unusual for a seller to request that you execute a confidentiality agreement before you conduct extensive due diligence. Negotiate the narrowest possible scope in connection with such agreements, especially if you are in the same or a similar industry as the target.

Following the execution of a letter of intent, one of the first responsibilities of your attorney is to complete a comprehensive schedule of activities well before you begin the due diligence process. The primary purpose of the schedule is to outline all the events that must occur and list all the documents that must be prepared both before the closing date and beyond. In this regard, your attorney acts as an orchestra leader, assigning primary areas of responsibility to various members of the acquisition team and to the target company and its counsel as well. Once all tasks have been identified and assigned (and a realistic timetable established for their completion), then you can determine a firm closing time and date.

The exact list of legal documents that must be prepared and the specific tasks to be outlined in the schedule will vary from transaction to transaction. These usually depend on the specific facts and circumstances of the particular deal, such as whether the transaction is a stock or an asset purchase, the form and terms of the purchase price, the nature of the target's business, the nature and extent of the assets being purchased or liabilities being assumed, and the sophistication of the parties and their respective attorneys.

A comprehensive discussion of the preparation and negotiation of all of the documents that must be developed in connection with the transaction is beyond the scope of this chapter. It is important, however, for the acquisition team to understand the key points to be negotiated in the primary documents.

Conducting Due Diligence

After you have reached a preliminary agreement with your target acquisition, you and your acquisition team should immediately embark on the extensive legal and business due diligence that must occur prior to closing the transaction. The legal due diligence focuses on the potential legal issues and problems that may impede the transaction, shedding light on how the documents should be structured. The business due diligence focuses on the strategic issues surrounding the transaction, such as integration of the human and financial resources of the two companies; confirmation of the operating, production, and distribution synergies and economies of scale to be achieved by the acquisition; and the gathering of the information necessary for financing the transaction.

The due diligence process can be tedious, frustrating, time-consuming, and expensive. Yet it is necessary for a well-planned acquisition, and it can be quite revealing in terms of analyzing the target company and measuring the costs and risks of the transaction. You can expect sellers to become defensive, evasive, and impatient during this phase of the transaction. Most entrepreneurs do not enjoy having their business policies and decisions examined under a microscope (especially for an extended period of time and by a party that is searching for skeletons in the closet), and they can become especially frustrated when you and your advisors probe and second-guess key decisions from the past. Eventually, the target may give the prospective buyer an ultimatum: "Finish the due diligence soon or the deal is off." When negotiations have reached this point, it's probably best to end the examination process.

Keep in mind that due diligence is *not* a perfect process. Information will slip through the cracks, which is precisely why broad representations, warranties, and indemnification provisions should be structured into the final purchase agreement to protect you, as the buyer. The nature and scope of these provisions are likely to be hotly contested during the negotiations.

One way to expedite the due diligence process and ensure that virtually no stone remains unturned is through effective due diligence preparation and planning. In analyzing the target company, work closely with your attorney to gather and review the legal documents (which may be relevant to the structure and pricing of the transaction, your potential legal risks, and liabilities following the closing) and to identify all of the concerns and approvals that must be obtained from third parties and government agencies. With the assistance of your legal and financial advisors, develop a comprehensive checklist that enables you to evaluate the history of the company and potential risks so that they can be properly analyzed prior to closing.

Assessing the Legal Issues of Due Diligence

In reviewing the legal documents and business records, your acquisition team should gather the data necessary to answer the following types of preliminary legal questions:

- What legal steps will need to be taken to complete the transaction (for example, does it require director and stockholder approval, or are there share-transfer restrictions or restrictive covenants in loan documentation)?
- What antitrust problems (if any) are raised by the transaction? Will filing under the premerger notification provisions of the Hart-Scott-Rodino Act be necessary?
- Will the transaction be exempt from registration under applicable federal and state securities laws under the "sale of business" doctrine?
- What potential adverse tax consequences to you, the seller, and your respective stockholders may be triggered by the transaction?
- What are your potential postclosing risks and obligations? To what extent should the seller be responsible for such potential liability? What steps (if any) can be taken to reduce these potential risks or liabilities? What will it cost to implement these steps?
- What are the impediments to your ability to sell key tangible and intangible assets of the target company (such as real estate, intellectual property, favorable contracts or leases, human resources, or plant and equipment)?
- What are your and the seller's obligations and responsibilities under applicable environmental and hazardous waste laws?
- What are your and the seller's obligations and responsibilities to the creditors of the target?
- What are your and the seller's obligations and responsibilities under applicable federal and state labor and employment laws? (For example,

will you be subject to successor liability under federal labor laws and, as a result, be bound by existing collective-bargaining agreements?)

- To what extent will employment, consulting, confidentiality, or non-competition agreements need to be created or modified in connection with the proposed transaction?

Finally, the acquisition team and legal counsel should carefully review the documents and records received from the target to determine how the information gathered will affect the structure or the proposed financing of the transaction.

Analyzing the Business Issues of Due Diligence

In conducting due diligence from a business perspective, you are likely to encounter a variety of financial problems and risk areas when you analyze the target company. These typically include:

- Undervaluation of inventories
- Overdue tax liabilities
- Inadequate management information systems
- Incomplete financial documentation or customer information
- Related-party transactions (especially in small, closely held companies)
- An unhealthy reliance on a few key customers or suppliers
- Aging accounts receivable
- Unrecorded liabilities (for example, warranty claims, vacation pay, claims, or sales returns and allowances)
- An immediate need for significant expenditures as a result of obsolete equipment, inventory, or computer systems

Each of these problems poses different risks and costs, and you should weigh these against the benefits to be gained from the transaction. An experienced buyer must be prepared to walk away from any deal at any time (in other words, do not fall in love with any deal), and the due diligence process is designed to help ensure that you are actually getting what you bargained for at the outset of the negotiations. Don't feel trapped into proceeding if the process uncovers unpleasant or unacceptable surprises, even if you have a lot of time and money invested in the deal.

Keeping the Transaction on Track

One of the challenges for the management and advisory team of an emerging-growth buyer is to keep a transaction on track once it has commenced. Communication, coordination, and momentum are critical, and each party or team involved in the transaction should have a designated quarterback and point of contact. This quarterback must have the business acumen and transactional experience to diagnose "deal killers" and have the tools to destroy them.

Valuation, Pricing, and Sources of Acquisition Financing

When you have completed your due diligence, but before you structure and draft the formal legal documentation, the acquisition team should reach certain conclusions regarding the valuation, pricing, and financing for the proposed transaction.

One of the key members of the acquisition team should always be a qualified business appraiser who understands the special issues involved in assessing the value of a closely held company. By determining the valuation parameters of the target, the appraiser plays an important role in determining the proposed structure, pricing, and source of financing for the acquisition. Most of the information that an appraiser will need in order to analyze the value of the target can be gathered as part of the ordinary due diligence process. The appraiser's job is to answer the following questions:

- How will the value of the target be affected by the loss of its current management (if applicable)?
- How should the goodwill of the target be valued? What are the various components that make up the target's goodwill?
- How and to what extent should the target's intangible assets be assigned some relative tangible value? (Intangible assets may include customer lists, intellectual property, licenses and distributorship agreements, regulatory approvals, leasehold interests, and employment contracts.)
- If less than complete ownership of the target is being acquired, what effect do the remaining minority shareholders have on the target's overall value?
- If the transaction is being structured as a stock rather than an asset acquisition, what effect do the unknown contingent liabilities have on overall value? This assumes that there is no comprehensive indemnification provision.

- What effect should the target's accounting methods, credit ratings, business plans or projections, or income tax returns have on the overall value of its business?

Although a comprehensive discussion of the various methods of valuation is beyond the scope of this chapter, it is crucial for the acquisition team to take the time to learn how the appraiser will arrive at the range of values for the target company. Most methods of valuation fall into one of three general categories: comparable worth, asset valuation, or financial performance. The determination of which method or methods the appraiser should use will depend on the individual facts and circumstances surrounding each target company.

Financing the Acquisition

Many smaller-scale acquisitions are financed primarily by the buyer's excess cash or retained earnings. Under such circumstances, little or no external debt or equity financing is required, and the only key issues become pricing the stock or assets to be purchased and the terms of payment. However, if you lack the cash required to finance the transaction, you have two choices: You can offer the shareholders of the target company some form of consideration other than cash, such as equity securities, promissory notes, or a share of the post-closing earnings (earn-outs), or you can identify an external source of capital to finance the purchase.

In identifying external sources of financing, coordinating the timing of the closing of both transactions is critical. Many companies have successfully used private placements, commercial lenders, venture capitalists, and even public offerings of their securities to finance the growth of their business. Depending on the size and complexity of the transaction, your acquisition team may want to retain the services of an investment banker. Most investment banking firms have merger and acquisition specialists who can assist you in arranging and negotiating the necessary financing for the transaction, usually in exchange for a consulting fee and a percentage of the capital raised. The investment bankers may also be available to help you prepare the proposal that you will present to potential sources of capital, structure the transaction, and perform the valuation of the target. These services may also be available from accountants, attorneys, business brokers, and merchant bankers for smaller-scale transactions. Once the decision to acquire the target company has been made, strategies must be developed to determine the structural alternatives for the transaction.

The options available to finance an acquisition depend on the size and complexity of the transaction, the amount of cash you have available, the market for your securities, the terms of the purchase price, and the financial-market conditions at the time of the purchase.

In many cases, sellers are willing to provide some of the purchase price in *takeback financing*, particularly if they don't have an immediate need for the cash or if they believe that the company is worth more than you are able (or willing) to pay. Similarly, you may use seller financing either to keep the seller motivated to support the company's future success or to force the seller to prove that the business truly has the upside potential that has been represented. In other words, the seller would absorb or continue to assume some of the risk of the transaction by deferring its compensation until after closing. Seller financing may also be a necessary option if you are having difficulty obtaining a commitment from lenders or investors.

There are two forms of seller financing: fixed and contingent. An example of fixed financing is a simple installment sale or an unsecured promissory note or equity, such as the seller's taking some of the buyer's common or preferred stock (or convertible debt) as payment. An example of contingent financing is a warrant (option to purchase the shares at a fixed price at a later time) or some other type of conditional payments, such as earn-outs. With an earn-out, the seller might receive additional payments in the event of certain contingencies such as:

- If the acquired business performs above a specified level in the future
- If a specific postclosing condition is met
- If a given event occurs, such as FDA approval or the issuance of a patent

Sellers who agree to accept a portion of their payment in this manner must recognize the economic risks, such as the possibility that the buyer will default on its obligations or that the postclosing condition will not be met.

Structuring the Deal

There are a multitude of ways in which a corporate acquisition may be structured, and the structure selected may affect the range of financing alternatives available. There are also a wide variety of corporate-, tax-, and securities-law issues that affect the final decision concerning the structure of any transaction.

Each issue must be carefully considered from a legal and accounting perspective. However, at the heart of each alternative are the following basic issues:

- Will you be acquiring the stock or the assets?
- What form of payment will be made (cash, notes, securities, etc.)?
- Will the purchase price be fixed, contingent, or payable over time on an installment basis?
- What are the tax consequences of the proposed structure for the acquisition?

Perhaps the most fundamental issue in structuring the acquisition of a target company is whether the transaction will take the form of an *asset* or a *stock* purchase. Each form has its advantages and disadvantages, depending on the facts and circumstances surrounding the transaction. The acquisition team should consider the following factors in determining the ultimate form of the transaction:

Advantages of a Stock Purchase

- The business's identity, licenses, and permits can usually be preserved.
- Continuity of the corporate identity, contracts, and structure are maintained.

Disadvantages of a Stock Purchase

- There is less flexibility to cherry-pick key assets of the seller.
- The buyer may be liable for unknown, undisclosed, or contingent liabilities (unless the purchase agreement provides adequate protection against this).
- The buyer will be forced to contend with the seller's minority shareholders unless all the shares of the company are purchased.
- The offer and sale of the securities may need to be registered under federal or state securities laws.

Advantages of an Asset Acquisition

- The buyer can be selective concerning which assets of the target company will be purchased.
- The buyer is generally not liable for the seller's liabilities unless they are specifically assumed under the contract.

Disadvantages of an Asset Acquisition

- The bill of sale must be comprehensive enough to ensure that no key assets are overlooked and as a result are not transferred to the buyer.
- A variety of third-party consents to transfer key tangible and intangible assets to the purchaser will typically be required.
- The seller will be responsible for liquidating the remaining corporate "shell" and distributing the proceeds of the asset sale to its shareholders, which may result in double taxation unless a special tax election is made.
- Compliance with applicable state bulk-sales statutes is required.
- State and local sales and transfer taxes must be paid.

Preparing the Definitive Legal Documents

Once you have completed the due diligence, conducted all valuations and appraisals, negotiated the terms and price, and arranged the financing, your acquisition team must work carefully with your attorneys to structure and begin preparing the definitive legal documentation that will formalize the transaction. Drafting and negotiating these documents usually focuses on the following issues:

- The nature and scope of the seller's representations and warranties
- The terms of the seller's indemnification to the buyer
- Conditions for closing the transaction
- Responsibilities of the parties between the execution of the purchase agreement and actual closing
- The terms of payment of the purchase price
- The scope of postclosing covenants of competition
- Predetermined remedies (if any) for breach of the covenants, representations, or warranties

Other Key Issues in Preparing and Negotiating the Purchase Agreement in 2012 and Beyond

Allocation of Risk. As discussed earlier, the heart and soul of the acquisition agreement is, in many ways, merely a tool for *allocating risk*. The buyer will want to hold the seller accountable for any postclosing claims or liabilities that arose as a result of a set of facts that occurred while the seller owned the company or that have occurred as a result of a misrepresentation or material omission by the seller. The seller, on the other hand, wants to bring as much finality to the transaction as possible to allow some degree of sleep at night. When both parties are represented by skilled negotiators, a middle ground is reached, both in general and on specific issues of actual or potential liability. The buyer's counsel will want to draft changes, covenants, representations, and warranties that are strong and absolute. The seller's counsel, on the other hand, will seek to insert phrases like "except insignificant defaults or losses that have not, or are not likely to, at any time before or after the closing, result in material loss or liability to or against the buyer," leaving some wiggle room for insignificant and nonmaterial claims. The battleground will be the indemnification provisions and any exceptions, carve-outs, or baskets that are created to dilute these provisions.

Scope of the Assets. The typical buyer will want to specify a virtual laundry list of categories of assets to be purchased, but the classic seller will want to modify the list by using words like "exclusively" or "primarily." The seller may want to exclude all or most of the cash on hand from the schedule of assets to be transferred. In some cases, the seller may want to license some of the technology rights in lieu of an outright sale or, at the very least, obtain a license back of what has been sold.

Security for the Seller's Takeback Note. When the seller is taking back a note from the buyer as all or part of the consideration, the issue of security for the note is always a problem. Naturally, the seller will want noncontingent personal and corporate guaranties from the buyer and anyone else that it can manage to get them from. The buyer will be reluctant to offer such broad security. Several "creative" compromises between the parties have been reached, including partial or limited guaranties, the acceleration of the note based on postclosing performance, the right to repurchase the assets in the event of a default, commercial lender–like covenants to prevent the buyer from getting into a position where it is unable to pay the note (such as dividends restrictions, limitations on excessive salaries, and so on), or contingent consulting agreements in the event of a default.

Who's on the Line for the Financial Statements? The financial statements provided by the seller to the buyer in connection with the due diligence and prior to closing are often a hotly contested item. The timing and scope of the financial statements and the standard to which they will be held is at issue. The buyer and its team may prefer a "hot-off-the-press" and recently completed set of financials audited by a Big 4 accounting firm, and the seller will want to serve up a "best-efforts" unaudited and uncertified guesstimate. Somewhere in between is where most deals wind up, with verbiage such as "of a nature customarily reflected" and "prepared in substantial accordance with GAAP" and "fairly present the financial condition" being bantered around. The scope of the liabilities included on the financial statement and who will bear responsibility for unknown or undisclosed liabilities will also be negotiated in the context of the overall financial statement discussion.

The Existence and Scope of the Noncompete. It is only natural for the buyer to expect that the seller will agree to stay out of the business being sold for some reasonable amount of time. Depending on the seller's stage of life and postclosing plans, which may include actual retirement, the parties are likely to argue over the scope, duration, and geographic focus of the covenant of noncompetition. The more difficult issues often arise when a conglomerate is spinning off a particular division or line of business and the remaining divisions will continue to operate in an industry that is similar or parallel to the business being sold to the buyer. The allocation of the purchase price to a noncompete covenant raises certain tax issues that must be analyzed, and these covenants may have only limited enforceability under applicable state laws if their scope or duration is deemed unreasonable or excessive.

Tips for Buyers Acquiring Other Companies

Before you embark on the acquisition trail, here are a few tips to keep in mind:

- Accept nothing less than a "known and should have known" standard in the representations and warranties.
- Don't skimp on due diligence.
- Negotiate an adequate holdback for unforeseen liabilities.
- Assemble a dynamic acquisition team that understands all the legal, strategic, and financial issues involved.
- Try to convince the target to take a portion of the purchase price on an earn-out or installment basis.
- Be certain that all postclosing synergies and challenges have been identified.
- Before closing, be certain that all the necessary acquisition capital is available and in your possession. *Timing is everything.*

Postclosing Matters

After the closing, a variety of legal and administrative tasks must be carried out to complete the transaction. The nature and extent of these tasks will vary depending on the size of your transaction and the source of capital that you select. The parties to any acquisition must be careful to ensure that the pure jubilation of closing does not cause any postclosing matters to be overlooked.

In an asset acquisition, these postclosing tasks might include a final verification that all the assets acquired are free of liens and encumbrances; the recording of financing statements and transfer-tax returns; the recording of any assignments of intellectual property with the Library of Congress or the U.S. Patent and Trademark Office; notification of employees, customers, distributors, and suppliers concerning the sale; and adjustments to bank accounts and insurance policies.

In a stock acquisition (or merger), postclosing matters may entail all of the above, plus the filing of articles of amendment to the corporate charter or articles of merger; completion of the transfer of all stock certificates; amendments to the corporate bylaws; and the preparation of all appropriate postclosing minutes and resolutions.

M&A Resources

There are four key organizations devoted to the educational and training needs of M&A professionals. They are:

- **Middle Market Investment Bankers Association (MMIBA)** (www.mmbia.com)
  Founded in 2008 and managed by the National Association of Certified Valuers and Analysts (NACVA), this organization focuses on networking, education, and contribution of middle-market investment banking professionals
- **International Network of M&A Professionals (IMAP)** (www.imap.com)
  Founded in 1973, IMAP is an exclusive global partnership of leading M&A advisory firms
- **Alliance of Merger and Acquisition Advisors (AMAA)** (www.amaaonline.com)
  Founded in 1998, AMAA has over 750 professional service firm members in North America
- **Association for Corporate Growth (ACG)** (www.acg.org)
  Founded in 1954, ACG has 14,000 members in 56 chapters worldwide

There are dozens of web sites that provide resources and data on mergers and acquisitions. Some of my favorites include:

- M&A Advisor (www.maadvisor.com)
- Acquisitions Monthly (www.aqm-e.com)
- Mergers & Acquisitions Report (www.themiddlemarket.com)
- Tech Dealmaker (www.the451group.com)

Chapter 15

Capital-Formation and Business Growth Resources Directory

There are literally thousands of trade associations, networking groups, venture clubs, and other organizations that focus directly or indirectly on the needs of small-business owners, entrepreneurs, growing companies, women-owned businesses, minority-owned businesses, importers and exporters, and virtually every other group that shares common interests. Some of the more established groups with a genuine nationwide presence and solid track record include:

U.S. Chamber of Commerce
1615 H Street, NW
Washington, DC 20062
(202) 659-6000

http://www.uschamber.com

The U.S. Chamber of Commerce represents 3,000,000 businesses, 3,000 state and local chambers of commerce, 830 business associations, and 87 American Chambers of Commerce abroad. It works with these groups to support national business interests and includes a Small Business Center.

Association for Corporate Growth Headquarters
71 S. Wacker Drive
Suite 2760
Chicago, IL 60606
(312) 957-4260
http://acg.org

The Association for Corporate Growth provides programs, education, and networking in the areas of middle-market corporate growth, corporate development, and mergers and acquisitions. The association has about 5,500 members representing 2,500 companies in 36 chapters throughout North America and the United Kingdom.

National Association of Seed and Venture Funds
http://www.nasvf.org

The National Association of Seed and Venture Funds is an organization of innovation capital leaders: private, public, and nonprofit organizations that are committed to building their local economies by investing in local entrepreneurs.

Y Combinator
320 Pioneer Way
Mountain View, CA 94041
http://ycombinator.com

Y Combinator is a seed-stage start-up-funding firm. It provides seed money, advice, and connections as part of a three-month cycle. After an application process and acceptance by Y Combinator, founders of start-ups move to Silicon Valley for three months, where the firm works with the founders to refine the start-ups and prepare the founders to pitch to investors. At the end of the cycle, founders participate in "Demo Day," where they present their start-up to a room full of investors. On average, Y Combinator invests $18,000 in each chosen start-up in exchange for 7 percent equity.

Ewing Marion Kauffman Foundation
4801 Rockhill Road
Kansas City, MO 64110
(816) 932-1000
http://www.kauffman.org

The Kauffman Foundation sponsors the entrepreneurship.org web site, which serves as a critical resource for entrepreneurs who are starting and growing businesses, and provides links to other resources on the Web.

International Franchise Association (IFA)
1501 K Street, NW
Suite 350
Washington, D.C. 20005
(202) 628-8000
http://franchise.org

The IFA serves as a resource center for current and prospective franchisees and franchisors, the media, and the government. It has promoted programs to expand opportunities for women and minorities in franchising.

SCORE
http://www.score.org
(800) 634-0245

SCORE is a nonprofit organization, partnered with the Small Business Administration, that provides free online and in-person business counseling. SCORE also offers business counseling and low-cost workshops through almost 400 chapters nationwide.

National Association of Development Companies (NADCO)
6764 Old McLean Village Drive
McLean, VA 22101
http://www.nadco.org

NADCO is the trade group of community-based nonprofit organizations, known as Certified Development Companies (CDC), that promote small-business expansion and job creation through the Small Business Administration 504 loan program.

National Association of Manufacturers (NAM)
1331 Pennsylvania Avenue, NW
Suite 600
Washington, DC 20004
(202) 637-3000
http://www.nam.org

NAM serves as the voice of the manufacturing community and is active on all issues concerning manufacturing, including legal system reform, regulatory restraint, and tax reform.

National Association for the Self-Employed (NASE)
P. O. Box 241
Annapolis Junction, MD 20701
(800) 649-6273
http://www.nase.org

NASE helps members become more competitive by providing more than 100 benefits that save money on services and equipment. NASE's members consist primarily of small-business owners with few or no employees.

National Association of Small Business Investment Companies (NASBIC)
1100 H Street, NW
Suite 610
Washington, DC 20001
(202) 628-5055
http://www.nasbic.org

The National Association of Small Business Investment Companies is dedicated to promoting a strong small-business investment company industry. NASBIC provides professional programs and representation in Washington to promote the growth and vitality of this sector of the business community.

National Federation of Independent Business (NFIB)
53 Century Boulevard
Suite 250
Nashville, TN 37214
(800) NIFB-NOW (634-2669)
(615) 872-5800
http://nfib.com

NFIB disseminates educational information about free enterprise, entrepreneurship, and small business. It represents more than 60,000 small and independent businesses before legislatures and government agencies at the federal and state level.

National Small Business United (NSBU)
1156 15th Street, NW
Suite 1100
Washington, DC 20005
(202) 293-8830

The NSBU is a membership-based association of business owners that presents small business's point of view to all levels of government.

Let's Talk Business Network
58 Harwood Drive East
Glen Cove, NY 11542
(917) 408-6173
http://www.ltbn.com

Let's Talk Business Network acts as an entrepreneurial support community, providing products, a radio network, and a support network of over 5,000 contacts for entrepreneurs who wish to discuss common business experiences and challenges.

National Venture Capital Association
1655 North Fort Meyer Drive
Suite 850

Arlington, VA 22209
(703) 524-2549
http://www.nvca.org

The National Venture Capital Association's mission is to define, serve, and promote the interests of the venture capital industry, to increase the understanding of the importance of venture capital to the U.S. economy, and to stimulate the flow of equity capital to emerging-growth and developing companies.

National Association of Investment Companies (NAIC)
1300 Pennsylvania Avenue, NW
Suite 700
Washington, DC 20005
(202) 204-3001
http://www.naicvc.com

NAIC is the industry association for venture capital firms that dedicate their financial resources to investment in minority businesses.

National Association of Women Business Owners (NAWBO)
601 Pennsylvania Avenue, NW
South Building
Suite 900
Washington, DC, 20004
(800) 55-NAWBO (556-2926)
http://nawbo.org

NAWBO uses its collective influence to broaden opportunities for women in business, and is the only dues-based national organization representing the interests of all women entrepreneurs in all types of business.

National Association for Female Executives (NAFE)
P. O. Box 3052
Langhorne, PA 19047
(800) 927-6233
http://www.nafe.com

Through education and networking programs, NAFE helps women share the resources and techniques needed to succeed in the competitive business world.

National Business League (NBL)
4308 Georgia Avenue, NW
Washington, DC 20011
(202) 726-9100
http://www.eaglenews.com/NBL/NBLHome.html

NBL is primarily involved in business development among African Americans and serves as a voice for black businesses on Capitol Hill and in the federal government.

U.S. Hispanic Chamber of Commerce (USHCC)
1424 K Street NW
Suite 401
Washington, DC 20005
(800) USHCC86 (874-2286)
(202) 842-1212
http://www.ushcc.com

USHCC advocates the business interests of Hispanics and develops minority business opportunities with major corporations and at all levels of government.

National Black Chamber of Commerce (NBCC)
1350 Connecticut Avenue, NW
Suite 405
Washington, DC 20036
(202) 466-6888
http://www.NationalBCC.org

NBCC focuses on economically empowering African American communities through entrepreneurship.

U.S. Pan Asian American Chamber of Commerce (USPAACC)
1329 18th Street, NW
Washington, DC 20036
(800) 696-7818 or (202) 296-5221
http://www.uspaacc.com

USPAACC is the largest national, nonprofit, nonpartisan organization representing all Asian American and Asian American–related groups in business, sciences, the arts, sports, education, and public and community service. USPAACC serves as a gateway to corporate and government contracts, Asian American suppliers, information, and the Asia market.

National Foundation for Teaching Entrepreneurship (NFTE)
120 Wall Street, 18th Floor
New York, NY 10005
(800) 367-6383
http://www.nfte.com

NFTE is an international nonprofit organization that introduces poor and at-risk young people to the world of entrepreneurship by showing them how to operate their own small-business enterprises.

Opportunity International
2122 York Road
Suite 150
Oak Brook, IL 60523

(800) 7WE-WILL (793-9455)
http://www.opportunityinternational.org

With partner organizations, Opportunity International provides loans and basic training in business practices to the poor, thereby breaking the cycle of poverty.

American Farm Bureau Federation
600 Maryland Avenue, SW
Suite 1000W
(202) 406-3600
http://www.fb.org

As the nation's largest farm organization, the American Farm Bureau Federation promotes policies and provides programs that improve the financial well-being and quality of life for farmers and ranchers.

TechAmerica
Commercial Development Office
5201 Great America Parkway, #400
Santa Clara, CA 95054
(408) 987-4200
http://www.itaa.org/offices or http://www.techamerica.org/offices

TechAmerica is the technology industry's leading trade association, giving the tech sector a voice and offering companies a broad array of programs and services. TechAmerica represents nearly 1,200 companies and maintains 20 offices.

American Financial Services Association (AFSA)
919 18th Street, NW
Suite 300
Washington, DC 20006
(202) 296-5544
http://www.americanfinsvcs.com

AFSA acts as the national trade association for market-funded providers of financial services to consumers and small businesses.

National Small Business Association (NSBA)
1156 15th Street, NW
Suite 1100
Washington, DC 20005
(202) 293-8830
http://www.nsba.biz

NSBA is a volunteer-driven organization that advocates state and federal policies beneficial to small businesses.

American Society of Association Executives (ASAE)
1575 I Street, NW
Washington, DC 20005
(888) 950-2723 or (202) 371-0940
http://asaecenter.org

ASAE serves as an advocate for the nonprofit sector of the economy, and represents more than 11,000 organizations.

Association of American Publishers (AAP)
455 Massachusetts Avenue, NW
Suite 700
Washington, DC 20001
(202) 347-3375
http://www.publishers.org

AAP assists publishers by expanding the market for American books both nationally and abroad, promotes intellectual freedom and opposes censorship, and offers practical advice and information to assist members in the management and administration of their companies.

National Association of Convenience Stores (NACS)
1600 Duke Street
Alexandria, VA 22314
(703) 684-3600
http://www.nacsonline.com

NACS is an international trade association representing more than 2,100 retail and 1,500 supplier company members, assisting these entities to increase their current effectiveness and profitability.

National Association of Wholesaler-Distributors (NAW)
1325 G Street, NW
Suite 1000
Washington, DC 20005
http://www.naw.org

NAW is a trade association that represents the wholesale distribution industry; it is active in the areas of government relations and political action, research and education, and group purchasing.

National Restaurant Association (NRA)
1200 17th Street, NW
Washington, DC 20036
(202) 331-5900
http://www.restaurant.org

NRA represents, promotes, and educates the restaurant industry. It represents more than 380,000 businesses and provides them with educational and other resources.

National Retail Federation (NRF)
325 7th Street, NW
Suite 1100
Washington, DC 20004
(800) NRF-HOW2 (637-4692) or (202) 783-7971
http://www.nrf.com

NRF is the world's largest retail trade association, providing programs and services in education, trading, information technology, and government affairs to advance its members' interests.

Business Software Alliance (BSA)
1150 18th Street, NW
Suite 700
Washington, DC 20036
(202) 872-5500
http://www.bsa.org

BSA is the largest and most international IT industry group, with policy, legal, and/or educational programs in 80 countries. While several of BSA's initiatives are global in scope, most of its policy, legal, and educational efforts are led and conducted at the national level, with a growing emphasis on emerging economies.

American Intellectual Property Law Association (AIPLA)
241 18th Street South
Suite 700
Arlington, VA 22202
(703) 415-0780
http://www.aipla.org

AIPLA is a national bar association composed mainly of lawyers that strives to improve the nation's intellectual property laws and their interpretation by the courts, and provides legal education to the public and to organization members on matters involving intellectual property.

International Trademark Association (INTA)
1133 Avenue of the Americas
New York, NY 10036
(212) 768-9887
http://www.inta.org

INTA is a worldwide membership organization of trademark owners and advisors; it seeks to shape public policy, advance practitioners' knowledge, and educate the public and the media about the significance of trademarks in today's commercial environment.

National Association of Professional Employer Organizations (NAPEO)
707 North Saint Asaph Street

Alexandria, VA 22314
(703) 836-0466
http://www.napeo.org

NAPEO is the recognized voice of the PEO industry and is dedicated to working toward the goals of PEOs, their clients, and the regulatory and legislative bodies that monitor the industry.

Turnaround Management Association (TMA)
150 South Wacker Drive
Suite 900
Chicago, IL 60606
http://www.turnaround.org

TMA is the only international nonprofit association dedicated to corporate renewal and turnaround management. TMA has more than 9,000 members in 47 chapters.

United States Association for Small Business and Entrepreneurship (USASBE)
Belmont University
1900 Belmont Boulevard
Nashville, TN 37212
http://www.usasbe.org

USASBE is the largest independent, professional, academic organization in the world dedicated to advancing the discipline of entrepreneurship. With more than 1,000 members, USASBE provides educational and other resources for educators and practitioners.

The American Small Business Coalition (The ASBC)
P. O. Box 2786
Columbia, MD 21045
(410) 381-7378
http://www.theasbc.org

The ASBC is a member-driven community of individuals and organizations that aids in developing, refining, and implementing strategies for doing business in the government sector.

Angel Capital Association (ACA)
10977 Granada Lane
Suite 103
Overland Park, KS 66211
(913) 894-4700
http://www.angelcapitalassociation.org

ACA is a trade association of angel investment groups, providing professional development, best practices, networking, and collaboration for member angel groups. For entrepreneurs, ACA provides educational resources and contact information for angel groups.

Center for Innovative Technology (CIT)
2214 Rock Hill
Suite 600
Herndon, VA 20170
(703) 689-3000
http://www.cit.org

CIT Entrepreneur invests and leverages available funds for early-stage technology companies with a high potential for technology commercialization, rapid growth, and downstream private equity financing. CIT Entrepreneur offers four distinct programs: Gap Fund, Federal Funding Assistance Program, Entrepreneurial Education Program, and the Virginia South Technology Acceleration Pilot Program.

Edward Lowe Foundation
58220 Decatur Road
P. O. Box 8
Cassopolis, MI 49031
(800) 232-LOWE (5693)
http://www.edwardlowe.org

The Edward Lowe Foundation provides information, research, and educational experiences that support entrepreneurship. The foundation focuses primarily on second-stage entrepreneurs.

Entrepreneurs' Organization
Global Headquarters
500 Montgomery Street
Suite 500
Alexandria, VA
(703) 519-6700
http://www.eonetwork.org

The Entrepreneurs' Organization is a dynamic, global network of more than 8,000 business owners in 45 countries. EO is a catalyst that enables entrepreneurs to learn and grow from one another, and publishes *Octane*, a quarterly magazine giving business lessons, experiential advice, and tips and entrepreneurship best practices.

Collegiate Entrepreneurs' Organization
3105 N. Ashland Avenue
Chicago, IL 60657
(773) 360-8426
http://www.c-e-o.org

CEO has chapters on university campuses across North America. It informs, supports, and inspires college students seeking to be entrepreneurial and looking for opportunity through enterprise creation.

The Consortium for Entrepreneurship Education
1601 West Fifth Avenue, #199
Columbus, OH 43212
http://www.entre-ed.org

The consortium provides advocacy, leadership, networking, technical assistance, and resources nationally across all levels and disciplines of education.

Federal Agencies

U.S. Small Business Administration (SBA)
409 Third Street, SW
Washington, DC 20416
(800) 827-5722
http://sba.gov

The SBA offers a wide variety of financing programs, workshops and seminars, and management and technical assistance through its many district offices.

Export-Import Bank (Eximbank)
811 Vermont Avenue, NW
Washington, DC 20571
(800) 565-3946
www.exim.gov

Eximbank offers financing assistance for potential exporters and companies of all sizes interested in doing business abroad.

U.S. Department of Commerce (DOC)
Herbert C. Hoover Building
1401 Constitution Avenue
Washington, DC 20230
(202) 482-2000
http://www.commerce.gov

The DOC offers a wide variety of programs and services relating to economic development, international trade, and minority business. The U.S. Patent and Trademark Office [(800) 786-9199] is a division of the DOC that processes federal patent and trademark applications and publishes various resources on the protection of intellectual property.

Federal Trade Commission (FTC)
600 Pennsylvania Avenue, NW
Washington, DC 20852
(202) 362-2222
http://ftc.gov

The FTC provides guidance to businesses that may need to comply with a variety of federal rules and regulations.

Trade Information Center
International Trade Administration
U.S. Department of Commerce
1401 Constitution Avenue
Washington, DC 20230
(800) USA-TRAD(E) (872-8723) or (202) 482-0543
http://www.trade.gov

The center provides comprehensive resources for information on all U.S. federal government export assistance programs.

Export Assistance Center
1401 Constitution Avenue
Washington, DC 20230
(800) USA-TRAD(E) (872-8723)
http://www.export.gov

Export.gov brings together resources from across the U.S. government to assist American businesses in planning their international sales strategies and succeeding in today's global marketplace.

Bureau of Industry and Security
Office of Exporter Services
14th Street and Constitution Avenue, NW
U.S. Department of Commerce
Washington, DC 20230
(202) 582-4811
http://bis.doc.gov

The BIS is responsible for counseling exporters, conducting export control seminars, and drafting and publishing changes to the Export Administration Regulations.

In addition to the agencies above, all major federal departments and agencies have an Office of Small and Disadvantaged Business Utilization (OSDBU), which is responsible for ensuring that an equitable share of government contracts is awarded to small and minority businesses. Sample OSDBU office phone numbers within selected agencies include:

Department of Agriculture
(202) 720-7117
http://www.usda.gov

Department of Defense
(703) 614-1151
http://www.defense.gov

Department of Justice
(202) 616-1151
http://www.usdoj.gov

Agency for International Development
(703) 875-1551
http://www.usaid.gov

Office of Personnel Management
(202) 606-2180
http://www.opm.gov

Business Growth Resources on the Web

Over the past few years, hundreds of web sites have been developed to provide support to entrepreneurs and growing companies. Web sites come and go quickly and change often, so it's probably best to use one of the popular search engines and enter keywords that will narrow the scope of your search or particular resource need. Next time you are surfing the Net, here are some web sites that are worth visiting:

Name	Internet Address	Main Features
National Survey of Small Business Finances	http://www.bog.frb.fed.us/pubs/oss/oss3/nssbftoc.htm	Provides a wealth of information on American small businesses, including information such as financial characteristics, firm size, and income and balance sheets
IdeaCafe	http://www.businessownersideacafe.com	Small-business meeting place
International Franchise Association	http://www.franchise.org	Provides information on franchising opportunities, trends, and developments
IFX International	http://www.centercourt.com	Articles and information on franchising
IFA Online	http://www.franchise.org	Offers IFA's *Franchise Opportunities Guide*, *Franchising World*, bulletin boards, calendar of events, and more for franchisors and franchisees
Legaldocs	http://legaldocs.com	Low-cost legal forms

Name	Internet Address	Main Features
Venture Capital Institute	http://vcinstitute.org	Wide range of venture capital resources
Dun & Bradstreet Information	http://dnb.com	A comprehensive source of financial and demographic information
EDGAR	http://www.sec.gov/edgarhp.htm	A database that contains all corporate annual and quarterly reports (and exhibits) filed with the Securities and Exchange Commission
The Wall Street Journal's Interactive Edition	http://www.wsj.com	Allows users to access news and financial information about specified companies
Inc. Online	http://www.inc.com	Allows users to (1) build their own web sites, (2) read the current issue or browse through *Inc.* magazine's extensive archives, and (3) interact with other entrepreneurs, experts, and *Inc.* editors
"Ask the Lawyer"	http://www.fairmeasures.com	A web site that offers practical advice for complying with employee law and preventing lawsuits
Business Journal	http://www.bizjournals.com	Features expert advice for small businesses on topics such as sales and marketing, technology, business financing, and tips on shopping for business products and services
Monster Board	http://www.monster.com	Covers a variety of issues, from hiring to staffing to other related topics for human resource executives
Interbiznet's	http://www.interbiznet.com	Lists recruiting sites
CareerPath	http://www.careerpath.com	Launched by the *Boston Globe, Chicago Tribune, Los Angeles Times, New York Times, San Jose Mercury News,* and *Washington Post,* divides hundreds of listings by journal and by field of interest
SHRM (Society for Human Resource Management)	http://www.shrm.org	Lists a variety of services and products for human resource professionals

Name	Internet Address	Main Features
SBA Women in Business	http://www.sba.gov/womeninbusiness	Provides training, advice, and guidance to women who may be starting businesses
The Center for Association Leadership	http://www.asaenet.org	Provides a newsroom, a bookstore, and links to various upcoming events and meetings
Income Opportunities Magazine	http://www.incomeops.com	Provides advice and tips on starting and succeeding in your own e-commerce venture
Span Link Communications	http://www.spanlink.com	Provides a broad range of communications products and services to businesses and enterprises
Switchboard	http://www.switchboard.com	Contains a searchable database to locate businesses nationwide
Red Herring Magazine	http://www.redherring.com	Contains news, research, event listings, and other information for investors and entrepreneurs
The Small Business Advocate	http://www.smallbusinessadvocate.com	Provides access to a live radio talk show, audio archives of past shows, links to small-business–related articles, and links to related small-business web sites
CFO Mergers & Acquisitions Center	http://www.cfonet.com	A collection of articles, resources, and an M&A discussion group from *CFO* magazine
The Online Investor M&A	http://www.theonlineinvestor.com/mergers.shtml	Weekly information on new M&A announcements
TradePort	www.tradeport.org/	Repository of free information and resources for businesses involved in all aspects of global trade.
Global Edge	http://globaledge.msu.edu	A knowledge Web portal that connects professionals worldwide to a wealth of information, insights, and learning resources on global business activities.
Trade Resources	www.usitc.gov	Provides tariff and trade information services, industry economic analysis, and trade policy support.

Internet Resources to Learn More About Private Placements, Angel Investors, Venture Capital Networks, Accelerator Programs, and Other Alternative Sources of Funding

Name	Internet Address	Main Features
FundingPost	www.fundingpost.com	Connects angel and venture capital investors with entrepreneurs
PrivateRaise	www.privateraise.com	Private Raise offers a comprehensive database of alternative public offering transactions and a proprietary directory of market participants
North American Securities Administrators Association	www.nasaa.org	Is the voice of state securities agencies responsible for efficient capital formation and grassroots investor protection
Regulation D Resources	www.regdresources.com	Provides services for the preparation of private placement memorandum documentation, subscription documents, SEC Form D filing preparation, and consulting related to the structuring and execution of private placement offerings
Venture Capital Access Online	www.vcaonline.com	Provides online services and tools to entrepreneurs and investors
Private Equity International	www.privateequityinternational.com	Provides private equity news
Private Placement Letter	www.privateplacementletter.com	Provides market data
Xpert Financial	www.xpertfinancial.com	Enables private companies to raise capital, investors to access high-quality private company investments, and shareholders to trade private company securities
Second Market	www.secondmarket.com	An SEC-regulated alternative trading system
Active Angel Investors	www.activeangelinvestors.com/index.htm	A membership network of accredited investors who desire to invest in seed-stage opportunities in the Mid-Atlantic region

Name	Internet Address	Main Features
Mid-Atlantic Angel Group	www.magfund.com	Created to bridge the gap between angel funding and institutional venture capital funding serving the Greater Philadelphia region
ARC Angel Fund	www.arcangelfund.com	ARC Angel Fund invests in seed and early-stage companies with high growth potential
Angel Investment Network	www.midwestinvestmentnetwork. com	Includes a wide range of U.S. and international investors looking for investment opportunities
Investor's Circle	www.investorscircle.net	A network of more than 150 angel investors, professional venture capitalists, foundations, and family offices that are using private capital to promote the transition to a sustainable economy
Minority Angel Investor Network	www. minorityangelinvestornetwork. com	A network of accredited investors with an interest and commitment to invest in high–growth, minority-owned or minority-led companies
Rain Source Capital	www.rainsourcecapital.com	One of the nation's largest multi-state angel fund networks
Venture Funding Network	www.venturefundingnetwork.com	An online network that brings entrepreneurs, investors, financiers, and service providers together
Mid-Atlantic Venture Association	www.mava.org	Provides a wide range of programs, information, and forums designed to stimulate revenue and company growth, facilitate quality deal flow, encourage collaboration, and foster relationships among entrepreneurs, investors, strategic partners, and customers
The Angels' Forum	www.angelsforum.com	Investing in, mentoring, and advising Silicon Valley start-ups from the seed stage all the way through a meaningful exit
SBIC Program	www.sba.gov/INV	Created to fill the gap between the availability of venture capital and the needs of small businesses in start-up and growth situations

Name	Internet Address	Main Features
Technology Capital Network at MIT	www.thecapitalnetwork.org	Boston's leading nonprofit organization providing extensive educational programs and a community to help early-stage entrepreneurs master the entire funding process and successfully raise seed capital for financing their high-growth start-ups
Go Big Network	http://www.gobignetwork.com	A national network of investors
Funding Universe	www.fundinguniverse.com	Matches qualified small-business owners with active banks, credit unions, and other lending sources
The Funded	www.thefunded.com	An online community of more than 16,500 CEOs, founders, and entrepreneurs to discuss fundraising, rate and review investors, and discuss strategies to grow a start-up business
Angel Capital Association	www.angelcapitalassociation.org	Trade association of leading angel investment groups in North America
Y Combinator	www.ycombinator.com	Y Combinator does seed funding for start-ups.
Launch Pad Ignition	www.launchpadignition.com	A new start-up accelerator
Spark Business Accelerator	www.annarborusa.org/start-ups/spark-business-accelerator	Accelerator program in Ann Arbor, Michigan
Lending Club	www.lendingclub.com	An online financial community that brings together creditworthy borrowers and savvy investors so that both can benefit financially
Prosper	www.prosper.com	Prosper is the world's largest peer-to-peer lending marketplace
ACCION USA	www.accionusa.org	A leader in U.S. microfinance loans
Kickstarter	www.kickstarter.com	The largest funding platform for creative projects in the world

International Finance Institutions on the Web

All of the international finance institutions maintain web sites with extensive information and data on the countries in which they work. These sites also provide a detailed listing of projects under consideration and contact information for businesses interested in working with these institutions.

Export-Import Bank of the United States
www.exim.gov

The Export-Import Bank web site posts information about the bank's program, including detailed information for companies interested in the Working Capital Guarantee Program.

Inter-American Development Bank
www.iadb.org

This site lists upcoming procurement and business opportunities generated by the bank's lending programs. The lists are arranged by country and by sector. The IDB's basic procurement policies, contract award information, and contact information are included on the web site. The site also posts research and statistics, and notices about business seminars hosted by IDB in Washington, D.C., and in cities across the United States and abroad.

International Monetary Fund
www.imf.org

The IMF's web site is loaded with statistical information on the economies of most countries, including detailed forecasts for growth and reports on business conditions. It also includes links to many important regional institutions and other sources of data.

Overseas Private Investment Corp.
www.opic.gov

OPIC is an independent U.S. government agency that sells investment services to U.S. companies investing in 140 emerging economies. Its web site includes detailed investment information, including special information on opportunities for small businesses, plus descriptions of OPIC's political risk insurance and project finance and investment funds.

U.S. Agency for International Development
www.info.usaid.gov

USAID is the federal agency for foreign assistance programs, which include agency-financed procurement opportunities. Its web site posts notices for procurement projects and recent awards, plus contact information.

U.S. Department of Commerce
www.commerce.gov

The Commerce Department and its International Trade Administration (www. ita.doc.gov) post extensive information on the levels of direct investment and trade with other countries and provide contacts for assistance.

U.S. Trade and Development Agency
www.ustda.gov

The TDA web site offers trade and export news, reports on agency programs by region and sector, dates for business briefings, and announcements of export opportunities.

The William Davidson Institute
www.wdi.umich.edu

The William Davidson Institute is a nonprofit, independent institute that works with international finance institutions and private companies that are interested in investing in emerging economies. The institute offers management training, executive education, consulting expertise, and project-based assistance to corporations operating abroad.

World Bank
www.worldbank.org

The World Bank site is a huge source of information on economic and business conditions in developing nations plus the bank's programs for procurement, investment, and risk management. The bank's Business Partnership Center posts detailed information about working with the bank to finance projects, obtain insurance, and identify private partners. The site also offers contact information and links to the bank's regional institutions.

Guidebooks, Publications, and Networks (Including Computer Software)

Export.gov, through the U.S. Government Bookstore, distributes, for a charge, guidebooks that include, among others:

- *A Basic Guide to Exporting*
- *Export Programs Guide: A Business Guide to Federal Export Assistance*
- *Export Administration Regulations*
- *Breaking Into the Trade Game: A Small Business Guide to Exporting*

To order, visit http://bookstore.gpo.gov or http://export.gov, or call (866) 512-1800.

High-Tech Exporting Assistance

- *Global Wizard Documents for Export* ($895), Export Internet Trade Systems, Inc., (203) 396-0022 or http://documentsforexports.com.
- *Export Software,* Version 3.1 ($1,600), Unz & Company, (800) 631-3098 or http://www.unzco.com.
- *FedEx Document Preparation Center* (free), Federal Express Corp., use at http://www.fedex.com/GTM.
- *PIERS* provides data processing, commodity trade data, international trade statistics, global trade information for all cargo types, and directories. For prices, visit http://www.piers.com or call (800) 952-3839.

Appendix

Contents

Subscription Agreement

This Subscription Agreement, (the "Agreement") is made this day of_____; by and between Company One, a _____ corporation ("Company1") and_____ (the "Subscriber").

Whereas, Subscriber acknowledges receipt of the executive summary (the "Executive Summary") describing the growth and development plans of Company1 provided in connection with this Agreement;

Whereas, Subscriber understands that the Executive Summary is for informational purposes only, and while believed to be accurate, Company1 can not guarantee that the information contained therein will not be subject to change;

Whereas, Subscriber understands that Company1 has been formed in order to develop, promote, and administer _____; and

Whereas, Subscriber desires to enter into this Agreement with Company1 in order to set forth the terms under which the Subscriber agrees to subscribe for Company1's shares of common stock (the "Common Stock").

Now Therefore, in consideration of the mutual covenants, conditions, promises, and other good and valuable consideration set forth herein, the receipt of which is hereby acknowledged, the parties hereby agree as follows:

1.   SUBSCRIPTION. The undersigned Subscriber, intending to be legally bound, hereby irrevocably subscribes for and agrees to purchase _____ shares ("Shares") of Common Stock of Company1 for consideration of $_____. Subscriber shall deliver herewith a bank check in the amount above, made payable to Company1.

2.   ACCEPTANCE OF SUBSCRIPTION. The execution and delivery of this Subscription Agreement will not constitute an agreement between the undersigned and Company1 until this subscription is accepted on behalf of Company1. The undersigned acknowledges that Company1 may accept or reject, in whole or in part, any tendered subscription for any reason, including, without limitation, any subscription the acceptance of which might in the opinion of counsel for Company1, require the registration of the Stock under any applicable federal or state securities laws. If Company1 rejects this subscription in whole or in part, this Subscription Agreement shall become null and void as to said rejected portion and all sums paid to Company1 by the undersigned shall be returned, and all rights and obligations hereunder shall terminate.

3.   INVESTMENT REPRESENTATION. The Subscriber is acquiring the Common Stock for the Subscriber's own account for investment only and not with a view to resale or distribution of any part thereof. The Subscriber is aware that there currently is no market for the sale of the Common Stock and that it is not anticipated that such a market will develop, and that the Subscriber may not be able to sell or dispose of the Common Stock. The Subscriber understands that the Common Stock have not been registered or qualified for sale under the Securities Act of 1933, as amended (the "Act"), or any state securities or blue sky laws, in reliance upon certain exemptions from registration and qualification thereunder, and that the Subscriber has no right to require Company1 to register the Common Stock under the Act or any such state laws. The Subscriber acknowledges that Company1's reliance upon such exemptions is based on the representations and agreements set forth herein. The Subscriber understands that the Common Stock may not be sold by the Subscriber except pursuant to an effective registration statement under the Act or an exemption from registration thereunder, and that an opinion of counsel satisfactory to Company1 may be required as a condition of any such sale. The Subscriber consents to the placement of a legend on the certificate(s) evidencing the shares of Common Stock referring to their issuance in an exempt transaction and setting forth such restrictions on resale.

4.   REPRESENTATIONS AND WARRANTIES. The Subscriber hereby acknowledges, represents, warrants, covenants, agrees, and understands that (please initial each space provided):

(a) _____ **The Subscriber** has carefully reviewed the risks of, and other considerations relevant to, a purchase of the Common Stock and fully understands all such risks. The Subscriber, either alone or with the Subscriber's purchaser representative(s), has such knowledge and experience in financial and business matters and investments in particular that the Subscriber is or they are capable of evaluating the merits and risks of the Subscriber's purchase of the Common Stock. The Subscriber has adequate means of providing for current needs and personal contingencies, has no need for liquidity in this investment, and can bear the economic risk of this investment (that is, can afford a complete loss of this investment and can hold the Common Stock indefinitely). The Subscriber has obtained, in the Subscriber's judgment, sufficient information relating to Company1 and its proposed business to evaluate the merits and risks of this investment.

(b) _____ **The Subscriber** confirms that, if requested, all documents, records, books, and information pertaining to the Subscriber's proposed purchase of the Common Stock, the offering of the Common Stock, or the business of Company1 have been made available to the Subscriber. The Subscriber has been given access to any additional information necessary to verify the accuracy of any representation made to the Subscriber by Company1's management team.

(c) _____**The Subscriber** has had an adequate opportunity to ask questions of a person or persons acting on behalf of Company1 concerning the proposed business and affairs of Company1 and the terms and conditions of the Subscriber's purchase of the Common Stock, and all such questions have been answered to the satisfaction of the Subscriber.

(d) _____ **The Subscriber** understands that the Executive Summary provided in connection with this Agreement is for informational purposes only, and while believed to be accurate, the information contained therein is subject to change.

(e) _____ **The Subscriber** understands that neither the Securities and Exchange Commission nor any state securities commission or other state regulatory agency has made any finding or determination relating to the fairness of public investment in the Common Stock and that no such commission or agency has recommended or endorsed or will recommend or endorse the purchase of the Common Stock.

(f) _____ **The Subscriber** is an accredited investor within the meaning of Rule 501(a) of Regulation D under the Act because (please check one or both of the following spaces, as appropriate) _____(i) my individual net worth, or joint net worth with my spouse, currently exceeds $1,000,000; or _____(ii) my individual income in each of the two most recent years was in excess of $200,000, or my joint income with my spouse in each of those years was in excess of $300,000, and I have a reasonable expectation of reaching the same income level in the current year.

(g) _____ **The Subscriber** confirms that no representations or promises have been made by neither Company1, nor its principals, to induce the Subscriber to enter into this Agreement, except as specifically included herein.

(h) _____ **The foregoing representations**, acknowledgments, and covenants are made by the Subscriber with the intent that they be relied upon in determining the undersigned's suitability as a purchaser of the Common Stock, and the Subscriber hereby agrees to indemnify Company1, the affiliates of each, and the respective officers, directors, employees, agents, and representatives of each (including their legal counsel) against all losses, claims, costs, expenses, damages, or liabilities that any of them may suffer or incur, caused or arising from their reliance thereon. The Subscriber undertakes to notify Company1 immediately of any change in any representation or warranty or other information relating to the Subscriber set forth herein that takes place prior to issuance of the Common Stock.

5.   LOCK-UP PROVISION. In the event Company1 undertakes to conduct an initial public offering, the Subscriber agrees to abide by any lock-up provision or other restriction of sale of the Common Stock as required under any underwriters or other distribution agreement entered into between Company1 and such underwriter or distributor.

6.   BINDING EFFECT. This Subscription Agreement and the acknowledgments, representations, warranties, agreements, and indemnities contained herein, shall survive and continue after the acceptance of the Subscriber's subscription by Company1, and shall be binding upon the heirs, legal representatives, successors, and assigns of the Subscriber.

7.   ENTIRE AGREEMENT. This Agreement contains the entire agreement between the parties with respect to the subject matter hereunder and no waiver, alteration, or modification of any of the provisions hereof shall be binding unless it is in writing and signed by all of the parties hereto.

8.   ASSIGNMENTS. The Subscriber may not assign this Agreement or the rights arising hereunder without the prior written consent of Company1.

9.   NOTICES. All notices or other communications hereunder shall be in writing and shall be delivered or mailed by registered or certified mail, return receipt requested, postage prepaid, to the undersigned subscriber or Company1 at the addresses set forth below:

If to Company 1: _____

Attn: _____

With a copy to: _____

If to the Subscriber: _____

Attn: _____

With a copy to: _____

10. GOVERNING LAW. This Agreement shall be governed by and enforced in accordance with the laws of the State of _____.

11. COUNTERPARTS. This Agreement may be executed in multiple counterparts, each of which shall be an original but all of which together shall constitute one and the same instrument.

IN WITNESS WHEREOF, the parties have caused this Agreement to be duly executed and effective as of the date first above written.

ATTEST: Company One, Inc.

By: _____

Its: _____

Witness: _____

Subscriber: _____

Type of Subscriber (Check One)

_____ Individual(s)*

_____ Trust**

_____ Company***

_____ Corporation****

* For unmarried individuals, please provide a signed Subscription Agreement for each individual.

** If a custodian, trustee, or agent, please include trust, agency, or other agreement and a certificate authorizing investment and as to legal existence of the trust.

*** If a partnership, please provide a certified copy of the partnership agreement and any amendment thereto. If a limited partnership, please provide, in addition, a certificate of limited partnership as currently in effect.

**** If a corporation, please include articles of incorporation and bylaws, as amended and currently in effect, certified corporate resolution or other document authorizing the investment, certificate of incumbency of officers, and certified or audited financial statements for the preceding three fiscal years.

RESIDENTIAL ADDRESS OF SUBSCRIBER: _____

_____

SUBSCRIBER: _____

_____

_____

(Number and Street)

_____

(City, State, and Zip Code)

_____

(Signature)

_____

(Social Security or Taxpayer Identification Number)

ACCEPTANCE BY COMPANY 1: _____

Accepted this_____ day of _____

By: _____

Title: _____

Confidential Purchaser Questionnaire

GrowCo, Inc.

(a [STATE] Company)

Private Placement of Company Interests ("Shares")

GrowCo, Inc.

[ADDRESS]

Attn: C.E.O.

Gentlemen:

The information contained herein is being furnished to you in order for you to determine whether the undersigned's Subscription Agreement to purchase an interest (one or more Shares) in GrowCo, Inc. (the "Company") may be accepted by you in light of the requirements of Section 4(2) of the Securities Act of 1933, as amended (the "Securities Act") and Rule 504 of Regulation D promulgated thereunder, and an exemption contained in the securities laws of certain states. The undersigned prospective investor (the "Investor") understands that the information is needed in order to satisfy various suitability requirements as provided in the Memorandum and Subscription Agreement provided herewith, and that the Investor and/or his or her financial or other advisor ("Purchaser Representative") has knowledge and experience in financial and business affairs such that the Investor is capable of evaluating the merits and risks of the proposed investment. The Investor understands that (a) you will rely on the information contained herein for purposes of such determination; (b) the Shares will not be registered under the Securities Act in reliance upon the exemption from registration afforded by Section 4(2) of the Securities Act and Rule 504 of Regulation D; (c) the Shares will not be registered under the securities laws of any state in reliance on similar exemptions; and (d) this Questionnaire is not an offer of Shares or any other securities.

The Investor understands that, although this Questionnaire and the responses provided herein will be kept confidential, you may need to present it to such parties as you deem advisable in order to establish the applicability under any federal or state securities laws of an exemption from registration.

In accordance with the foregoing, the following representations and information are hereby made and furnished:

Full Name: _____

Home Address: _____

_____

Home Phone: (   ) _____ – _____ Fax: (   ) _____ – _____

Name of Business: _____

Business Address: _____

_____

Business Phone: (   ) _____ – _____ Fax: (   ) _____ – _____

Occupation or Title: _____

Age: _____ Nature of Business: _____

Previous Business or Employment during past five (5) years:

Social Security or Tax Identification Number: _____

PLEASE ANSWER ALL QUESTIONS.

1. **(a) My individual net income** (not including my spouse) was in excess of $200,000 in 201___ and 201___:

Yes _____ No _____

(b) I anticipate that my individual net income will exceed $200,000 in 2012:

Yes _____ No _____

(c) Our joint income (income of myself and my spouse together) was in excess of $300,000 in 201___ and 201___:

Yes _____ No _____

(d) I anticipate that our joint income will exceed $200,000 in 201___:

Yes _____ No _____

(e) My current total net worth (individual or joint, if married) including real estate, investments, savings, stocks, bonds, pension, and profit sharing (including the total current value of home, autos, furnishings, and personal belongings) is more than $1,000,000:

Yes _____ No _____

2. **My current total net worth** (individual or joint, if married) including real estate, investments, savings, stocks, bonds, pension, and profit sharing (excluding the total current value of home, autos, furnishings, and personal belongings is (check one) less than $250,000 _____ ; $250,000 or more _____ ; or $500,000 or more _____.

3. **I have invested in other private placements of securities:** (If yes, please describe below.)

Yes _____ No _____

A description of my partnership investments and any other substantial experience in business or financial matters that enables me to evaluate the merits and risks of this investment is as follows:

FREQUENCY OF PRIOR INVESTMENTS (Check One in Each Column)

Marketable Securities	Real Estate	Oil and Gas, Leasing, Etc.	Tax Advantaged Investments
Frequently	_____	_____	_____
Occasionally	_____	_____	_____
Never	_____	_____	_____

Method of Investment of Evaluation:

Each prospective Investor is required to retain the services of a Purchaser Representative when such prospective Investor does not have sufficient knowledge and experience in financial and business matters to be capable of evaluating the merits and risks of acquiring Share(s). The following is an indication of my knowledge and experience or, alternatively, the necessity of the services of a Purchaser Representative:

(i) I have such knowledge and experience in financial matters that I am capable of evaluating the merits and risks of an investment in the Share(s) and will not require the services of a Purchaser Representative. I offer as evidence of such knowledge and experience in these matters the information contained in this Questionnaire.

Yes _____ No _____

(ii) I have retained the services of a Purchaser Representative. I acknowledge the following named person(s) to be my Purchaser Representative in connection with evaluating the merits and risks of an investment in the Shares.

Yes _____ No _____

Purchaser Representative Name _____

The above named Purchaser Representative has furnished to me a completed Purchaser Representative Questionnaire, a copy of which I reviewed prior to signing this Questionnaire and which I am delivering to you herewith. I and the above-named Purchaser Representative together have such knowledge and experience in financial matters that we are capable of evaluating the merits and risks of an investment in the Share(s).

IF YOU HAVE CHECKED "YES" UNDER METHOD (ii), THIS QUESTIONNAIRE MUST BE ACCOMPANIED BY ONE COMPLETED AND SIGNED COPY OF THE PURCHASER REPRE-SENTATIVE QUESTIONNAIRE.

I understand that the Company will be relying on the accuracy and completeness of my responses to the foregoing questions and the Investor represents and warrants to the Company as follows:

(i)   The answers to the above questions are complete and correct and may be relied upon by the Company in determining whether the Investor meets the suitability standards for an investment in the Shares;

(ii) I will notify the Company immediately of any material change in any statement made herein occurring prior to the closing of any purchase by me of Shares of the Company; and

(iii) I have sufficient knowledge and experience in financial matters to evaluate the merits and risks of the prospective investment and I am able to bear the economic risk of the investment and currently could afford a complete loss of such investment.

IN WITNESS WHEREOF, the Investor has executed this Confidential Purchaser Questionnaire, this _____ day of _____ , 2012 and declares that it is truthful and correct.

(Check One)

_____ Individual(s)*

_____ Trust**

_____ Company***

_____ Corporation****

_____
Signature of Prospective Investor

_____
Print Investor Name and Title (if applicable)

_____
Signature of Prospective Co-Investor

_____
Print Co-Investor Name and Title (if applicable)

* For unmarried individuals, please provide a signed Subscription Agreement for each individual.

** If a custodian, trustee, or agent, please include trust, agency, or other agreement and a certificate authorizing investment and as to legal existence of the trust.

*** If a partnership, please provide a certified copy of the partnership agreement and any amendments thereto. If a limited partnership, please provide, in addition, a certificate of limited partnership as currently in effect.

**** If a corporation, please include articles of incorporation and bylaws, as amended and currently in effect, certified corporate resolution or other document authorizing the investment, certificate of incumbency of officers, and certified or audited financial statements for the preceding three fiscal years.

Purchaser Representative Questionnaire

GrowCo, Inc.

(a [STATE] Company)

Private Placement of Company Interests ("Shares")

GrowCo, Inc.

[ADDRESS]

Attn: C.E.O.

Gentlemen:

The information contained herein is being furnished to you in order for you to determine whether the sale of shares (the "Shares") representing shareholder interests in GrowCo, Inc. (the "Company"), may be made to the following prospective Investor:

(Insert name of prospective Investor)

in light of the requirements of Section 4(2) of the Securities Act of 1933, as amended (the "Securities Act") and Rule 504 of Regulation D promulgated thereunder. The undersigned understands that (a) you will rely on the information set forth herein for purposes of such determination; (b) the Shares will not be registered under the Securities Act in reliance upon the exemption from registration afforded by Section 4(2) of the Securities Act and Rule 504 of Regulation D; (c) the Shares will not be registered under the securities laws of any state in reliance on similar exemptions; and (d) this Questionnaire is not an offer of Shares or any other securities to the undersigned Purchaser Representative.

I note that you have provided to the above-named prospective Investor a Confidential Private Placement Memorandum, dated [DATE] prepared by the Company in connection with the placement of Shares (the "Memorandum"). It should be noted by you that nothing herein shall be construed as a representation by me that I have attempted to verify the information set forth in the Memorandum; RATHER TO THE CONTRARY, THE SCOPE OF MY ENGAGEMENT BY, AND MY DISCUSSION WITH, THE ABOVE PROSPECTIVE INVESTOR HAVE BEEN LIMITED TO A DETERMINATION OF THE SUITABILITY OF AN INVESTMENT IN THE SHARES BY THE ABOVE-NAMED PROSPECTIVE INVESTOR IN LIGHT OF SUCH INVESTOR'S CURRENT INVESTMENT CIRCUMSTANCES AS SUCH CIRCUMSTANCES HAVE BEEN PRESENTED TO ME. FOR THIS PURPOSE, I HAVE ASSUMED, BUT DO NOT IN ANY WAY REPRESENT OR WARRANT, EITHER TO YOU OR TO THE ABOVE-NAMED PROSPECTIVE INVESTOR, THAT THE INFORMATION SET FORTH IN THE MEMORANDUM IS ACCURATE AND COMPLETE IN ALL MATERIAL RESPECTS. EACH AND EVERY STATEMENT MADE BY ME IN THE FOLLOWING PARAGRAPHS IS QUALIFIED BY THIS PARAGRAPH.

With the above in mind, I herewith furnish to you the following information:

1.   (a) I have reviewed the Memorandum describing the offering; (b) the Company has made available to me all documents relating to an investment in the Company that I have requested and has provided answers to all of my questions concerning the offering; (c) I have discussed the Memorandum with the prospective Investor with a view to determining whether an investment in the Shares by such prospective Investor is appropriate in light of such Investor's financial circumstances, as such circumstances have been disclosed to me by such prospective Investor; and (d) I have advised the above-named prospective

Investor, whom I represent, as to the merits and risks of an investment in the Company. I have not relied upon any representation or other information, whether oral or written, other than as set forth in the Memorandum.

2.   I have such knowledge and experience in financial matters as to be capable of evaluating, alone, or together with other Purchaser Representatives of the prospective Investor, the merits and risks of an investment in the Share(s). I offer as evidence of such knowledge and experience in these matters the following additional information (e.g., investment experience, business experience, profession, education):

3.   I am not "affiliated" with and am not "compensated" by the Company or any affiliate or selling agent of the Company, directly or indirectly (see "Note" below).

4.   There is no material relationship between me or my affiliates and the Company or its other affiliates that now exists or is mutually understood to be contemplated or that has existed at any time during the previous two years. (State below "No Exceptions" or set forth any exceptions and give details. Any such exceptions must not cause you to be affiliated with or compensated by the Company or its affiliates.)

If any exceptions exist and are described above, please confirm that such exceptions were disclosed to the above-named Investor in writing prior to the date hereof by attaching hereto a copy of such disclosure.

NOTE: The relationships that will render a person "affiliated" include (i) a present or intended relationship of employment, either as an employee, employer, independent contractor, or principal, (ii) any relationship within the definition of the term "affiliate" set forth below, or as an officer, director, or general partner of an affiliate, and (iii) the beneficial ownership by the Purchaser Representative of Shares of the Company or any securities of its affiliates or selling agents, unless such ownership is less than 1% of such securities.

Affiliate of the Company shall mean a person controlling, controlled by, or under common control with the Company. A person controls another person within the meaning of this definition through the possession, direct or otherwise, of the power to direct or cause the direction of the management, policies, or actions of the other person.

I agree to notify you promptly of any changes in the information described in this Questionnaire that may occur prior to the completion of the transaction.

Very Truly Yours:

_____

Dated   (Signature of Purchaser Representative)

_____

Print Purchaser Representative Name

_____

Street Address

_____

City   State   Zip Code

_____

Telephone

Form D

FORM D	UNITED STATES SECURITIES AND EXCHANGE COMMISSION Washington, D.C. 20549	OMB APPROVAL

		OMB Number: 3235-0076
		Expires: May 31, 2014
		Estimated average burden hours per response......16.00

FORM D

NOTICE OF SALE OF SECURITIES
PURSUANT TO REGULATION D,
SECTION 4(6), AND/OR
UNIFORM LIMITED OFFERING EXEMPTION

SEC USE ONLY	
Prefix	Serial
DATE RECEIVED	

Name of Offering   (☐ check if this is an amendment and name has changed, and indicate change.)

Filing Under (Check box(es) that apply):   ☐ Rule 504 ☐ Rule 505 ☐ Rule 506 ☐ Section 4(6) ☐ ULOE
Type of Filing: ☐ New Filing ☐ Amendment

A. BASIC IDENTIFICATION DATA

1. Enter the information requested about the issuer

Name of Issuer   (☐ check if this is an amendment and name has changed, and indicate change.)

Address of Executive Offices   (Number and Street, City, State, Zip Code)   Telephone Number (Including Area Code)

Address of Principal Business Operations   (Number and Street, City, State, Zip Code)   Telephone Number (Including Area Code)
(if different from Executive Offices)

Brief Description of Business

Type of Business Organization
☐ corporation   ☐ limited partnership, already formed   ☐ other (please specify):
☐ business trust   ☐ limited partnership, to be formed

	Month	Year		

Actual or Estimated Date of Incorporation or Organization: ☐☐ ☐☐ ☐ Actual ☐ Estimated
Jurisdiction of Incorporation or Organization: (Enter two-letter U.S. Postal Service abbreviation for State:
CN for Canada; FN for other foreign jurisdiction) ☐☐

GENERAL INSTRUCTIONS

Federal:
Who Must File: All issuers making an offering of securities in reliance on an exemption under Regulation D or Section 4(6), 17 CFR 230.501 et seq. or 15 U.S.C. 77d(6).

When To File: A notice must be filed no later than 15 days after the first sale of securities in the offering. A notice is deemed filed with the U.S. Securities and Exchange Commission (SEC) on the earlier of the date it is received by the SEC at the address given below or, if received at that address after the date on which it is due, on the date it was mailed by United States registered or certified mail to that address.

Where To File: U.S. Securities and Exchange Commission, 450 Fifth Street, N.W., Washington, D.C. 20549.

Copies Required: Five (5) copies of this notice must be filed with the SEC, one of which must be manually signed. Any copies not manually signed must be photocopies of the manually signed copy or bear typed or printed signatures.

Information Required: A new filing must contain all information requested. Amendments need only report the name of the issuer and offering, any changes thereto, the information requested in Part C, and any material changes from the information previously supplied in Parts A and B. Part E and the Appendix need not be filed with the SEC.

Filing Fee: There is no federal filing fee.

State:
This notice shall be used to indicate reliance on the Uniform Limited Offering Exemption (ULOE) for sales of securities in those states that have adopted ULOE and that have adopted this form. Issuers relying on ULOE must file a separate notice with the Securities Administrator in each state where sales are to be, or have been made. If a state requires the payment of a fee as a precondition to the claim for the exemption, a fee in the proper amount shall accompany this form. This notice shall be filed in the appropriate states in accordance with state law. The Appendix to the notice constitutes a part of this notice and must be completed.

ATTENTION

Failure to file notice in the appropriate states will not result in a loss of the federal exemption. Conversely, failure to file the appropriate federal notice will not result in a loss of an available state exemption unless such exemption is predictated on the filing of a federal notice.

SEC 1972 (6-02)   Persons who respond to the collection of information contained in this form are not
required to respond unless the form displays a currently valid OMB control number.   1 of 9

A. BASIC IDENTIFICATION DATA

2.   Enter the information requested for the following:

- Each promoter of the issuer, if the issuer has been organized within the past five years;
- Each beneficial owner having the power to vote or dispose, or direct the vote or disposition of, 10% or more of a class of equity securities of the issuer.
- Each executive officer and director of corporate issuers and of corporate general and managing partners of partnership issuers; and
- Each general and managing partner of partnership issuers.

Check Box(es) that Apply: ☐ Promoter   ☐ Beneficial Owner   ☐ Executive Officer   ☐ Director   ☐ General and/or Managing Partner

Full Name (Last name first, if individual)

Business or Residence Address   (Number and Street, City, State, Zip Code)

Check Box(es) that Apply: ☐ Promoter   ☐ Beneficial Owner   ☐ Executive Officer   ☐ Director   ☐ General and/or Managing Partner

Full Name (Last name first, if individual)

Business or Residence Address   (Number and Street, City, State, Zip Code)

Check Box(es) that Apply: ☐ Promoter   ☐ Beneficial Owner   ☐ Executive Officer   ☐ Director   ☐ General and/or Managing Partner

Full Name (Last name first, if individual)

Business or Residence Address   (Number and Street, City, State, Zip Code)

Check Box(es) that Apply: ☐ Promoter   ☐ Beneficial Owner   ☐ Executive Officer   ☐ Director   ☐ General and/or Managing Partner

Full Name (Last name first, if individual)

Business or Residence Address   (Number and Street, City, State, Zip Code)

Check Box(es) that Apply: ☐ Promoter   ☐ Beneficial Owner   ☐ Executive Officer   ☐ Director   ☐ General and/or Managing Partner

Full Name (Last name first, if individual)

Business or Residence Address   (Number and Street, City, State, Zip Code)

Check Box(es) that Apply: ☐ Promoter   ☐ Beneficial Owner   ☐ Executive Officer   ☐ Director   ☐ General and/or Managing Partner

Full Name (Last name first, if individual)

Business or Residence Address   (Number and Street, City, State, Zip Code)

Check Box(es) that Apply: ☐ Promoter   ☐ Beneficial Owner   ☐ Executive Officer   ☐ Director   ☐ General and/or Managing Partner

Full Name (Last name first, if individual)

Business or Residence Address   (Number and Street, City, State, Zip Code)

(Use blank sheet, or copy and use additional copies of this sheet, as necessary)

2 of 9

B. INFORMATION ABOUT OFFERING

		Yes	No
1.	Has the issuer sold, or does the issuer intend to sell, to non-accredited investors in this offering?...............	☐	☐

Answer also in Appendix, Column 2, if filing under ULOE.

2. What is the minimum investment that will be accepted from any individual?... $ _____

		Yes	No
3.	Does the offering permit joint ownership of a single unit?	☐	☐

4. Enter the information requested for each person who has been or will be paid or given, directly or indirectly, any commission or similar remuneration for solicitation of purchasers in connection with sales of securities in the offering. If a person to be listed is an associated person or agent of a broker or dealer registered with the SEC and/or with a state or states, list the name of the broker or dealer. If more than five (5) persons to be listed are associated persons of such a broker or dealer, you may set forth the information for that broker or dealer only.

Full Name (Last name first, if individual)
_____

Business or Residence Address (Number and Street, City, State, Zip Code)
_____

Name of Associated Broker or Dealer
_____

States in Which Person Listed Has Solicited or Intends to Solicit Purchasers

(Check "All States" or check individual States) ....   ☐ All States

AL	AK	AZ	AR	CA	CO	CT	DE	DC	FL	GA	HI	ID
IL	IN	IA	KS	KY	LA	ME	MD	MA	MI	MN	MS	MO
MT	NE	NV	NH	NJ	NM	NY	NC	ND	OH	OK	OR	PA
RI	SC	SD	TN	TX	UT	VT	VA	WA	WV	WI	WY	PR

Full Name (Last name first, if individual)
_____

Business or Residence Address (Number and Street, City, State, Zip Code)
_____

Name of Associated Broker or Dealer
_____

States in Which Person Listed Has Solicited or Intends to Solicit Purchasers

(Check "All States" or check individual States) ....   ☐ All States

AL	AK	AZ	AR	CA	CO	CT	DE	DC	FL	GA	HI	ID
IL	IN	IA	KS	KY	LA	ME	MD	MA	MI	MN	MS	MO
MT	NE	NV	NH	NJ	NM	NY	NC	ND	OH	OK	OR	PA
RI	SC	SD	TN	TX	UT	VT	VA	WA	WV	WI	WY	PR

Full Name (Last name first, if individual)
_____

Business or Residence Address (Number and Street, City, State, Zip Code)
_____

Name of Associated Broker or Dealer
_____

States in Which Person Listed Has Solicited or Intends to Solicit Purchasers

(Check "All States" or check individual States) ....   ☐ All States

AL	AK	AZ	AR	CA	CO	CT	DE	DC	FL	GA	HI	ID
IL	IN	IA	KS	KY	LA	ME	MD	MA	MI	MN	MS	MO
MT	NE	NV	NH	NJ	NM	NY	NC	ND	OH	OK	OR	PA
RI	SC	SD	TN	TX	UT	VT	VA	WA	WV	WI	WY	PR

(Use blank sheet, or copy and use additional copies of this sheet, as necessary.)

C. OFFERING PRICE, NUMBER OF INVESTORS, EXPENSES AND USE OF PROCEEDS

1. Enter the aggregate offering price of securities included in this offering and the total amount already sold. Enter "0" if the answer is "none" or "zero." If the transaction is an exchange offering, check this box ☐ and indicate in the columns below the amounts of the securities offered for exchange and already exchanged.

Type of Security	Aggregate Offering Price	Amount Already Sold
Debt	$	$
Equity	$	$
☐ Common ☐ Preferred		
Convertible Securities (including warrants)	$	$
Partnership Interests	$	$
Other (Specify _____)	$	$
Total	$	$

Answer also in Appendix, Column 3, if filing under ULOE.

2. Enter the number of accredited and non-accredited investors who have purchased securities in this offering and the aggregate dollar amounts of their purchases. For offerings under Rule 504, indicate the number of persons who have purchased securities and the aggregate dollar amount of their purchases on the total lines. Enter "0" if answer is "none" or "zero."

	Number Investors	Aggregate Dollar Amount of Purchases
Accredited Investors		$
Non-accredited Investors		$
Total (for filings under Rule 504 only)		$

Answer also in Appendix, Column 4, if filing under ULOE.

3. If this filing is for an offering under Rule 504 or 505, enter the information requested for all securities sold by the issuer, to date, in offerings of the types indicated, in the twelve (12) months prior to the first sale of securities in this offering. Classify securities by type listed in Part C — Question 1.

Type of Offering	Type of Security	Dollar Amount Sold
Rule 505		$
Regulation A		$
Rule 504		$
Total		$

4 a. Furnish a statement of all expenses in connection with the issuance and distribution of the securities in this offering. Exclude amounts relating solely to organization expenses of the insurer. The information may be given as subject to future contingencies. If the amount of an expenditure is not known, furnish an estimate and check the box to the left of the estimate.

Transfer Agent's Fees	☐	$
Printing and Engraving Costs	☐	$
Legal Fees	☐	$
Accounting Fees	☐	$
Engineering Fees	☐	$
Sales Commissions (specify finders' fees separately)	☐	$
Other Expenses (identify) _____	☐	$
Total	☐	$

C. OFFERING PRICE, NUMBER OF INVESTORS, EXPENSES AND USE OF PROCEEDS

b.   Enter the difference between the aggregate offering price given in response to Part C — Question 1 and total expenses furnished in response to Part C — Question 4.a. This difference is the "adjusted gross proceeds to the issuer." .... $_____

5.   Indicate below the amount of the adjusted gross proceed to the issuer used or proposed to be used for each of the purposes shown. If the amount for any purpose is not known, furnish an estimate and check the box to the left of the estimate. The total of the payments listed must equal the adjusted gross proceeds to the issuer set forth in response to Part C — Question 4.b above.

	Payments to Officers, Directors, & Affiliates	Payments to Others
Salaries and fees	☐ $_____	☐ $_____
Purchase of real estate	☐ $_____	☐ $_____
Purchase, rental or leasing and installation of machinery and equipment	☐ $_____	☐ $_____
Construction or leasing of plant buildings and facilities	☐ $_____	☐ $_____
Acquisition of other businesses (including the value of securities involved in this offering that may be used in exchange for the assets or securities of another issuer pursuant to a merger)	☐ $_____	☐ $_____
Repayment of indebtedness	☐ $_____	☐ $_____
Working capital	☐ $_____	☐ $_____
Other (specify):	☐ $_____	☐ $_____
	☐ $_____	☐ $_____
Column Totals	☐ $_____	☐ $_____
Total Payments Listed (column totals added)	☐ $_____	

D. FEDERAL SIGNATURE

The issuer has duly caused this notice to be signed by the undersigned duly authorized person. If this notice is filed under Rule 505, the following signature constitutes an undertaking by the issuer to furnish to the U.S. Securities and Exchange Commission, upon written request of its staff, the information furnished by the issuer to any non-accredited investor pursuant to paragraph (b)(2) of Rule 502.

Issuer (Print or Type)	Signature	Date
Name of Signer (Print or Type)	Title of Signer (Print or Type)	

─────── **ATTENTION** ───────

Intentional misstatements or omissions of fact constitute federal criminal violations. (See 18 U.S.C. 1001.)

E. STATE SIGNATURE

1. Is any party described in 17 CFR 230.262 presently subject to any of the disqualification
    provisions of such rule? ....

                                                                                      Yes   No
                                                                                      ☐   ☐

See Appendix, Column 5, for state response.

2. The undersigned issuer hereby undertakes to furnish to any state administrator of any state in which this notice is filed a notice on Form
    D (17 CFR 239.500) at such times as required by state law.

3. The undersigned issuer hereby undertakes to furnish to the state administrators, upon written request, information furnished by the
    issuer to offerees.

4. The undersigned issuer represents that the issuer is familiar with the conditions that must be satisfied to be entitled to the Uniform
    limited Offering Exemption (ULOE) of the state in which this notice is filed and understands that the issuer claiming the availability
    of this exemption has the burden of establishing that these conditions have been satisfied.

The issuer has read this notification and knows the contents to be true and has duly caused this notice to be signed on its behalf by the undersigned
duly authorized person.

Issuer (Print or Type)	Signature	Date
Name (Print or Type)	Title (Print or Type)	

Instruction:

Print the name and title of the signing representative under his signature for the state portion of this form. One copy of every notice on Form
D must be manually signed. Any copies not manually signed must be photocopies of the manually signed copy or bear typed or printed
signatures.

				APPENDIX					
1	2		3	4				5	
	Intend to sell to non-accredited investors in State (Part B-Item 1)		Type of security and aggregate offering price offered in state (Part C-Item 1)	Type of investor and amount purchased in State (Part C-Item 2)				Disqualification under State ULOE (if yes, attach explanation of waiver granted) (Part E-Item 1)	
State	Yes	No		Number of Accredited Investors	Amount	Number of Non-Accredited Investors	Amount	Yes	No
AL									
AK									
AZ									
AR									
CA									
CO									
CT									
DE									
DC									
FL									
GA									
HI									
ID									
IL									
IN									
IA									
KS									
KY									
LA									
ME									
MD									
MA									
MI									
MN									
MS									

1	2		3	4					5	
	Intend to sell to non-accredited investors in State (Part B-Item 1)		Type of security and aggregate offering price offered in state (Part C-Item 1)	Type of investor and amount purchased in State (Part C-Item 2)					Disqualification under State ULOE (if yes, attach explanation of waiver granted) (Part E-Item 1)	
State	Yes	No		Number of Accredited Investors	Amount	Number of Non-Accredited Investors	Amount		Yes	No
MO										
MT										
NE										
NV										
NH										
NJ										
NM										
NY										
NC										
ND										
OH										
OK										
OR										
PA										
RI										
SC										
SD										
TN										
TX										
UT										
VT										
VA										
WA										
WV										
WI										

APPENDIX

	APPENDIX								
1	**2**		**3**	**4**				**5**	
	Intend to sell to non-accredited investors in State (Part B-Item 1)		Type of security and aggregate offering price offered in state (Part C-Item 1)	Type of investor and amount purchased in State (Part C-Item 2)				Disqualification under State ULOE (if yes, attach explanation of waiver granted) (Part E-Item 1)	
State	**Yes**	**No**		**Number of Accredited Investors**	**Amount**	**Number of Non-Accredited Investors**	**Amount**	**Yes**	**No**
WY									
PR									

Security Agreement

THIS SECURITY AGREEMENT (the "Security Agreement") is made as of this _____ day of _____, 201___, by and between (i) _____ _____, a _____ corporation located at _____ _____ (hereinafter referred to as the "Borrower") and (ii) _____ _____ (hereinafter referred to as "Secured Party").

Recitals:

1.   **THE BORROWER IS THE MAKER OF A CERTAIN PROMISSORY NOTE** issued the _____ day of _____, 201_____, in the original face amount of $_____, which has been issued to Secured Party by the Borrower ("Note").

2.   **SECURED PARTY HAS REQUIRED**, and the Borrower has agreed, in consideration of issuing the Note pursuant to the terms thereof and the benefits to be derived by the Borrower therefrom, that the Borrower grant Secured Party a security interest in certain of the Borrower's assets as security for the payment of the Note.

3.   **THIS SECURITY AGREEMENT** is executed in order to secure the payment of the Note and for other purposes herein set forth.

Now, Therefore, in consideration of the Note, the mutual promises and covenants herein contained, and other good and valuable consideration, the receipt and sufficiency of which are hereby acknowledged, the parties hereto hereby agree as follows:

1.   **INCORPORATION OF RECITALS.** The foregoing recitals are incorporated herein by reference to the same extent as if fully set forth herein.

2.   **DEFINITIONS.** As herein used:

"Collateral" means (i) the equipment and copyrighted materials used at a Center including, but not limited to,_____ ; (ii) all guarantees thereof; (iii) all insurance on all the foregoing and the proceeds of that insurance; and (iv) all cash and noncash proceeds and products of all of the foregoing and the proceeds and products of other proceeds and products.

"Obligations" means all existing and future liabilities and obligations of the Borrower to Secured Party, whether absolute or contingent of any nature whatsoever, now existing or hereafter incurred arising out of or relating to the Note, or future obligations of the Borrower to Secured Party and all obligations of the Borrower to Secured Party created or referred to herein.

"Person" means an individual, a corporation, a government or governmental subdivision or agency or instrumentality, a business trust, an estate, a trust, a partnership, a cooperative, an association, two or more Persons having a joint or common interest, or any other legal or commercial entity.

"Proceeds" means any proceeds as that term is defined in the U.C.C. and shall include whatever is received upon the sale, exchange, collection, or other disposition of Collateral or proceeds, including without limitation insurance payable by reason of loss or damage to the Collateral.

3.   **SECURITY INTEREST IN COLLATERAL.** The Borrower hereby assigns to Secured Party and grants to Secured Party a lien upon and a security interest in the Collateral of the Borrower as security for the payment and performance of the Obligations.

4.   **SECURITY AGREEMENT AS SECURITY FOR THE NOTE.** This Security Agreement is made to provide security for the payment of, and fulfillment of all covenants and conditions of the Note, this Security Agreement, any other of the Obligations, and any instrument of

the Borrower evidencing and securing the Note or any other of the Obligations and for all renewals, modifications, or extensions of any of the foregoing or any substitutions therefore, together with all costs, expenses, advances, and liabilities, including attorneys' fees, which may be later incurred by Secured Party in collection and enforcement of any of the foregoing, or any enforcement of this Security Agreement.

5.   ALTERATION OR AMENDMENT OF COLLATERAL. Except as otherwise permitted herein (i) the Borrower shall not further alter, amend, or modify any of the Collateral, other than in the ordinary course of business, without the prior written consent of the Secured Party; and (ii) any alteration, modification, amendment, supplement, or change in the Collateral made with or without the prior written consent of the Secured Party shall be deemed a part of the security granted hereby.

6.   WARRANTIES AND COVENANTS OF THE BORROWER. The Borrower hereby warrants and covenants as follows:

(a) Ownership of Collateral. The Borrower is (or will be) the owner of the Collateral and has (or will have when any additional collateral is acquired) the right to make this Security Agreement. The Collateral is (or will be when acquired) free and clear of all liens, security interests, claims, charges, encumbrances, taxes, and assessments, except those of Secured Party.

(b) Payment and Performance. The Borrower shall pay and perform all of the Obligations and liabilities secured by this Security Agreement according to its terms.

(c) Sale of Collateral. Except as otherwise permitted herein, and except as to the sale or other disposition of the Collateral in the ordinary course of the Borrower's business, the Borrower will not sell, lease, transfer, exchange, or otherwise dispose of the Collateral without the prior written consent of Secured Party.

(d) Further Assurances and Title. The Borrower will defend its title to the Collateral against all persons and will, upon request of Secured Party, (i) furnish further assurances of title, and (ii) execute and deliver to Secured Party in form satisfactory to Secured Party, any financing or continuation statement, security agreement, or other document as Secured Party may request in order to perfect, preserve, maintain, or continue perfected the security interest created hereunder or its priority. The description in any financing statement of collateral by general classification shall not be construed to limit the Collateral assigned as described in Section 3 hereof. The Borrower will pay the costs of filing any financing, continuation, or termination statements as well as any recordation or transfer tax with respect thereto and with respect to the Collateral or the security interest created by this Security Agreement.

(e) Location of Collateral. The Collateral is to be located and may not be relocated without the prior written notification of Secured Party.

(f) Insurance. The Borrower agrees to keep the Collateral insured against loss, damage, theft, and other risks in such amounts, with such companies, under such policies, and in such form, all as shall be satisfactory to Secured Party. Such policies shall list Payee as a "Loss Payee" and provide that any loss thereunder shall be payable to Secured Party as his interest may appear (and Secured Party may apply any proceeds of such insurance that may be received by him toward payment of the Note or any other Obligations of the Borrower secured hereunder, whether or not due, in such order of application as Secured Party may determine) and copies of such policies or certificates thereof, shall, if Secured Party requests, be provided to Secured Party.

(g) Performance by Secured Party. Upon failure by the Borrower to perform any of the acts described herein to be performed by the Borrower, Secured Party, at his option and at the Borrower's sole expense, may perform any of said acts in any manner deemed proper by Secured Party.

(h) Advances Secured. All payments, costs, and expenses made or incurred by or on behalf of Secured Party pursuant to subparagraph (d) above or otherwise under this Security Agreement, shall be deemed advanced by Secured Party to the Borrower and secured by this Security Agreement. The Borrower shall pay such costs and expenses to Secured Party on demand and the same shall bear interest from the date incurred or advanced until paid in full at the rate of _____ % per annum.

7.   **SECURED PARTY RIGHT IN THE COLLATERAL.** So long as the Obligations, or any part thereof, shall remain unpaid and this Security Agreement is in effect, upon the occurrence of any event of default under the Note, Secured Party shall have all of the rights of a secured party in the Collateral.

8.   **EVENTS OF DEFAULT.** The Borrower shall be in default hereunder and under the Note upon its breach of any of its Obligations to Secured Party.

9.   **REMEDIES UPON DEFAULT.** If an Event of Default shall occur, the Secured Party may, at his option, (a) declare the unpaid balance of the principal sum of the Note due together with interest accrued thereon and all other sums and indebtedness secured hereby to be immediately due and payable, and may proceed to enforce payment of the same; (b) take, retain, and receive any interest whatsoever of the Borrower in the Collateral and all proceeds of the Collateral until the Obligations are paid and satisfied in full; (c) collect, compromise, or sell at public or private sale, at the option of the Secured Party at any time or times thereafter, without demand, advertisement, or notice (other than as set forth hereinbelow or as specifically required by law), the Collateral, or any one or more or part thereof, or any substitutes therefor or additional thereto, applying the net proceeds thereof, after deduction of all costs and expenses of such collection, compromise, or sale (including trustee's and attorney's fees), to the payment of the Note and/or any other of the Obligations, including interest thereon, and in case such net proceeds shall be insufficient, the Borrower shall immediately pay to the Secured Party the amount of such deficiency, with interest thereon at the rate of _____ % per annum from the date of the receipt in immediately available funds of the proceeds of such collection, compromise, or sale, until paid. Ten (10) days notice of the time and place of such sale shall be sent by certified or registered mail to the Borrower and the Borrower hereby waives all other notice thereof. The Borrower will sign, certify under oath, and/or acknowledge an assignment of its interest in the Collateral and any and all other instruments necessary or appropriate to implement the covenants and agreements of this paragraph immediately after receipt of all such instruments. All rights conferred on Secured Party hereby are in addition to those granted to Secured Party by the U.C.C. and all other laws. Any notices required under the U.C.C. shall be deemed reasonable if mailed by Secured Party to the parties entitled thereto at their last known addresses at least ten (10) days prior to disposition of the Collateral, or any portion thereof, and, in reference to a private sale, need state only that Secured Party intends to negotiate such sale.

10.   **REMEDIES CUMULATIVE.** Each right, power, and remedy as provided for in this Security Agreement and the Note now or hereafter existing at law or in equity or by statute or otherwise shall be cumulative and concurrent and shall be in addition to every other right, power, or remedy provided for in this Security Agreement or in the Note now or hereafter existing at law or in equity or by statute or otherwise, and the exercise or beginning of the exercise of any one or more of such rights, powers, or remedies shall not preclude the simultaneous or later exercise of any or all such other rights, powers, or remedies.

11.   **NO WAIVER.** No failure or delay by the Secured Party to insist upon the strict performance of any term, conditions, covenant, or agreement of this Security Agreement or of the Note, or to exercise any right, power, or remedy consequent upon a breach thereof, shall constitute a waiver of any such term, condition, covenant, or agreement or of any such breach,

or preclude Secured Party from exercising any such right, power, or remedy at any later time or times. No waiver of strict performance in any instance shall be deemed a waiver of such performance at any future time. By accepting payment after the due date of any amount payable under the Note or under this Security Agreement, the Secured Party shall not be deemed to waive the right either to require prompt payment when due of all other amounts payable under the Note or under this Security Agreement or to declare a default for failure to effect such prompt payment of any such other amount.

12. TERMINATION OF SECURITY INTEREST. This Security Agreement and the security interest thereby created shall terminate and a termination statement shall be promptly executed and filed, upon payment in full of the Obligations secured hereby.

13. MISCELLANEOUS. The paragraph headings of this Security Agreement are for convenience only and shall not limit or otherwise affect any of the terms hereof. Neither this Security Agreement nor any term, condition, covenant, or agreement hereof may be changed, waived, discharged, or terminated orally, but only by an instrument in writing signed by the party against whom enforcement of the change, waiver, discharge, or termination is sought. This Security Agreement shall be binding upon the successors and assigns of the Borrower. As used herein the singular shall include the plural as the context may require.

14. NOTICES. All notices, requests, instructions, or other documents required hereunder shall be deemed to have been given or made when delivered by registered mail or certified mail, return receipt requested, postage prepaid to:

If the BORROWER then: _____

_____

If the SECURED PARTY then: _____

_____

Either party may from time to time give the other notice of a change in the address to which notices are to be given and of any successors in interest.

15. COUNTERPARTS. This Security Agreement may be executed in one or more counterpart signature pages which when assembled, shall constitute a fully executed copy hereof.

In Witness Whereof, the Borrower and the Secured Party have caused this Security Agreement to be executed, sealed, and delivered on the date first written above as their free acts and deeds for the uses and purposes herein stated.

ATTEST: _____

THE BORROWER: _____

_____

Secretary   President

By: _____

_____

Secretary   President

THE SECURED PARTY: _____

By: _____

_____

Secretary   President

Promissory Note

THIS NOTE HAS NOT BEEN REGISTERED UNDER THE SECURITIES ACT OF 1933, AS AMENDED (THE "ACT"), OR THE SECURITIES LAWS OF ANY STATE. THIS NOTE MAY NOT BE SOLD, OFFERED FOR SALE, PLEDGED, HYPOTHECATED, OR OTHERWISE TRANS-FERRED IN THE ABSENCE OF REGISTRATION UNDER SAID ACT AND ALL OTHER APPLI-CABLE SECURITIES LAWS UNLESS AN EXEMPTION FROM REGISTRATION IS AVAILABLE.

$ _____,   Date_____

This Note ("Note") is secured by a security agreement ("Security Agreement") of even date herewith.

For Value Received, and subject to the terms and conditions of the Security Agreement, the terms of which are hereby incorporated by reference herein, _____ ("the Company"), a _____ corporation, hereby promises to pay to the order of ("the Holder") the principal sum of $ _____ in installments as herein provided, in law-ful money of the United States and to pay interest on the unpaid balance of principal, from the date of this Note until paid at a rate per annum equal to _____% over the prime rate as charged from time to time by _____ Bank (such interest rate to be adjusted as of the opening of business on the first day following any change in rate).

1.   **THE NOTE.** Interest and principal on this Note shall be payable at the offices of the Company and mailed to the address of the Holder hereof as reflected on the Company's records or at such other address as the Holder from time to time may designate in writing to the Company.

2.   **PAYMENTS OF PRINCIPAL AND INTEREST.** Principal shall be paid in three annual installments of $_____ each on _____ of each year commencing _____, 20_____ and ending _____, 20_____. Interest shall be calculated on an an-nual basis and shall be paid in annual installments along with each principal payment.

3.   **PREPAYMENTS PRIOR TO MATURITY.** The Company may, at any time, prepay this Note in whole or in part. Any prepayments received with respect to this Note shall first be applied to interest then due and owing, with the remainder, if any, applied to the payment of principal.

4.   **EVENTS OF DEFAULT.**

4.1 Events of Default Defined. This Note shall be governed by the terms and conditions defining an Event of Default, which are set forth in Section 8 of the Security Agreement.

4.2 Notification. If an Event of Default shall occur without the Holder's knowledge, the Company will notify the Holder promptly in writing of the Event of Default describing it in reasonable detail, including a statement of the nature and length of existence thereof, and what action the Company proposes to take with respect thereto, and such written notifica-tion will be signed by one of the Company's officers.

5.   **NOTICES.** Any request, demand, authorization, direction, notice, consent, waiver, or other document permitted by this Note to be made upon, given or furnished to, or filed with the Company or the Holder shall be sufficient for every purpose hereunder if in writing and mailed to the Company, addressed to it at _____

_____ (or such subsequent address as the Company shall advise the Holder hereof in writing) and if to the Holder at the address the Holder provides the Company (or at such further address as the Holder hereof shall advise the Company in writing). All notices required hereunder shall be deemed to have been given or made when actually delivered to or received by the party to which the notice is addressed at its respective address.

6. MUTILATION, DESTRUCTION, LOSS OR REISSUANCE.

6.1 Mutilation. This Note, if mutilated, may be surrendered and thereupon the Company shall execute and deliver in exchange therefore a new Note of like tenor and principal amount.

6.2 Destruction, loss, etc. If there is delivered to the Company (i) evidence of the destruction, loss, or theft of this Note and (ii) such security or indemnity as may be required by it to save it harmless, then, in the absence of notice to the Company that this Note has been acquired by a bona fide purchaser, the Company shall execute and deliver in lieu of such destroyed, lost, or stolen Note, a new Note of like tenor and principal amount.

6.3 New Note. Every new Note issued in accordance with this Section in lieu of any mutilated, destroyed, lost, or stolen Note shall constitute an original contractual obligation of the Company, whether or not the mutilated, destroyed, lost, or stolen Note shall be at any time enforceable by anyone, and shall be entitled to all of the benefits of the initial Note issued.

6.4 Reissuance. This Note may be surrendered and thereupon the Company shall execute and deliver in exchange therefore, as the Holder may direct, new Notes in smaller denominations but of like tenor and in exact principal amount in the aggregate and each new Note shall constitute an original contractual obligation of the Company and shall be entitled to all the benefits of the initial Note issued.

6.5 Additional Sums. On the issuance of any new Note under this Section, the Company may require of the Holder payment of a sum sufficient to cover any tax or other governmental charge that may be imposed in relation thereto and any other expenses connected therewith.

7. SUCCESSORS.
All of the covenants, stipulations, promises, and agreements in this Note contained by or on behalf of the Company shall bind and inure to the benefit of its successors whether so expressed or not and also to the benefit of the Holder and its successors.

8. LAWS OF [STATE] TO GOVERN.
This Note shall be deemed to be a contract made under the laws of the State of _____ and for all purposes shall be construed in accordance with the laws of the State of _____.

9. TRANSFERABILITY OF NOTE.
This Note is not transferable except pursuant to an effective registration statement under the Securities Act of 1933, as amended, or unless an exemption from the registration provisions of such Act is applicable.

10. SECTION HEADINGS.
The section headings herein are for convenience only and shall not affect the construction hereof, and the words "hereof" and "hereunder" and other words of similar import refer to this Note as a whole and not to any particular section or subdivision.

In Witness Whereof, the Company has caused this Note to be executed in its corporate name by its duly authorized officer and to be dated as of the day and year first above written.

ATTEST: _____

THE BORROWER: _____

_____   _____
Secretary   President

State Small-Business Loan Programs

Most states have an economic-development office or finance authority that offers assistance to small businesses and those owned by women and minorities. Programs vary from state to state. Here are a few programs from two states. Check with your state authorities to see what's available.

Florida

Enterprise Florida

Office of Minority Business Development
Telephone: (305) 569-2654
Fax: (305) 569-2657

Enterprise Florida's Office of Minority Business Development (OMBD) develops statewide initiatives to help minority- and women-owned businesses prosper in Florida and in the global marketplace. It is an advocate for minority economic development and provides assistance to minority businesses and organizations. OMBD's responsibilities include acting as the state clearinghouse for information, resources, and referrals; developing initiatives for economically depressed urban communities; identifying universal barriers that prevent the growth of minority businesses and defining appropriate solutions; and convening annual minority business conferences. OMBD advocates and assists in the development of statewide strategies for American women, African Americans, Hispanic Americans, Native Americans, and Asian Americans.

Minority Business Development Centers

Miami: (305) 591-7355
Fort Lauderdale: (954) 485-5333
West Palm Beach: (561) 863-0895

Minority Business Development Centers offer existing and potential minority entrepreneurs a wide range of services, from initial counseling on how to start a business to the more complex issues of planning and growth. General business counseling, information dissemination, and referral services are free of charge. Assistance beyond this is considered management and technical assistance, for which the Minority Business Development Agency subsidizes from 65 to 80 percent of the total cost in accordance with the client's annual sales level. For additional information, write or call the Minority Business Development Center nearest you.

Arizona

Self Employment Loan Fund, Inc. (SELF)

Jean Rosenberg, Executive Director
Andrea Madonna, Project Director
201 North Central Avenue
Suite CC10
Phoenix, AZ 85073-1000
Telephone: (602) 340-8834
Fax: (602) 340-8953

E-Mail: self@uswest.net
selfbuseduc@uswest.net

Self Employment Loan Fund, Inc. (SELF) is a private nonprofit organization that provides training, technical assistance, and loan access to low-income individuals, primarily women and minorities, who are starting or expanding small businesses. The training sessions are 10 to 14 weeks in length, with the outcome being a completed business plan. Upon the completion of the business plan, participants are eligible for SELF's peer lending process, called Borrower's Circles. These circles of three to eight individuals provide an avenue for support, debt repayment, and continuing business education. SELF serves all of Maricopa County and will, with the OWBO grant, be providing its services in Graham and Gila counties. The population of Maricopa County is urban and makes up more than half of the state's population; Graham and Gila counties are rural areas with high unemployment and few opportunities for nascent entrepreneurs. In its first three years of operation, SELF served more than 350 individuals through the training program and lent $83,000 to 60 borrowers.

Arizona Minority/Women Owned Business Program
Telephone: (602) 280-1480 or (800) 542-5684
Fax: (602) 280-1339

The Minority/Women Owned Business Program functions include providing coordination and publicity for programs and services that assist minority and women business owners. The office assists state agencies in certification of minority- and women-owned businesses. In addition, this office conducts workshops and seminars to help state agencies and local companies procure goods and services from qualified firms.

Term Sheet

GrowCo, Inc. Term Sheet

Summary of Proposed Terms

Series A Preferred Stock Offering

GENERAL

Security	Series A Preferred Stock
Number of Shares	2,000,000 Shares of Series A Preferred Stock
Price Per Share	$2.00
Total Proceeds	$4.0 million

CAPITALIZATION

After the closing, the capitalization will consist of the following (on a fully diluted basis):

	Shares	Percentage
Series A Preferred	2,000,000	45.00%
Common	2,000,000	45.00%
Employee Stock Option Plan	444,444	10.00%
TOTAL	4,444,444	100.00%

Description of Series A Preferred Stock

DIVIDENDS. The holders of Series A Preferred Stock shall be entitled to receive dividends in preference to any dividend on Common Stock at the rate of 10% per share per annum, whenever funds are legally available and when and as declared by the Board of Directors. The dividends shall be cumulative.

LIQUIDATION PREFERENCE. Upon liquidation, dissolution, or winding up of the company, the holders of Series A Preferred Stock shall first be entitled to receive, in preference to the holders of Common Stock, an amount equal to the price paid by them for their Series A Preferred Stock plus declared and unpaid dividends; thereafter, the holders of Common Stock shall be entitled to all remaining proceeds up to a total amount per share equal to the priority payment per share of Series A Preferred Stock. Then all holders of all classes of stock share equally any remaining proceeds (on an as converted basis). A consolidation, merger, or reorganization of the Company, a sale by the Company of all or substantially all its assets, or a sale of 50% or more of the Company's stock, shall be treated as a liquidation for these purposes.

REDEMPTION. At any time commencing four years after the closing, holders of at least a majority of the Series A Preferred Stock will have the option to have the Series A Preferred Stock redeemed by the Company, which redemption shall be made in no more than two consecutive annual installments commencing on the date redemption is requested at a price per share equal to (i) two times the initial issue price plus declared and unpaid dividends for those shares redeemed on the first annual installment date and (ii) 2.25 times the initial issue price plus declared and unpaid dividends for the balance of shares remaining to be redeemed on the second annual installment date, subject at all times to funds legally available therefore.

CONVERSION. Each share of Series A Preferred Stock shall be convertible at any time, at the option of the holder, one-for-one into Common Stock shares of the Company, subject to adjustment as described below.

Each share of Series A Preferred Stock shall be automatically converted at then applicable conversion price rate, which initially shall be the issuance price per share of Series A Preferred Stock (the "conversion price"), upon consummation of an underwritten public offering of Common Stock by the Company at a price per share of at least four times the initial issue price per share and net cash proceeds to the Company in excess of $7.5 million, provided all declared and unpaid dividends have been paid.

ANTIDILUTION PROVISIONS. The conversion price of the Series A Preferred Stock shall be subject to weighted average adjustment in the event that the Company issues additional shares (other than up to 444,444 shares reserved for employees, consultants, the acquisition of technology, and similar purposes as described below) at a purchase price less than the applicable conversion price. The conversion price of the Series A Preferred Stock shall also be adjusted proportionally upon certain standard events, such as stock splits and stock dividends.

EMPLOYEE STOCK OPTION.

Plan. A pool of 10% of the Company's Common Stock (444,444 shares) on a fully diluted basis, calculated immediately after the closing, shall be reserved at fair market value (calculated at time of issuance) for subsequent incentive grants to employees, consultants, sellers of technology to the Company, etc., under incentive and nonqualified stock option plans and stock purchase agreements; these shares shall be excluded from the antidilution formula. All shares reserved for consultants and employees under these plans shall vest ratably over no less than a three-year period from the date of grant.

VOTING RIGHTS. Series A Preferred Stock shall have the right to that number of votes equal to the number of shares of Common Stock issuable upon conversion of the Series A Preferred Stock.

PROTECTIVE PROVISIONS. Consent of the holders of at least a majority of the Series A Preferred Stock, voting as a separate class, shall be required for any action that (i) alters or changes the rights preferences or privileges of the Series A Preferred Stock, (ii) increases the authorized number of shares of Series A Preferred Stock, (iii) increases the authorized number of shares of Preferred Stock, (iv) creates any new class or series of shares having preference over or being on a parity with the Series A Preferred Stock, (v) involves the merger, consolidation, or reorganization of the Company, sale of all or substantially all of its assets, or sale of more than 50% of the Company's stock, (vi) involves any transaction that would result in a dividend to holders of Series A Preferred Stock, (vii) pays dividends (other than in Common Stock) on the Common Stock, or (viii) causes the Company to repurchase or otherwise acquire shares other than pursuant to any Certificate of Determination filed by the Company. The rights under (v)–(viii) shall remain in effect so long, but only so long, as the number of shares of Series A Preferred Stock outstanding represent voting power that, if fully converted, would be sufficient to elect one member of the Board of Directors.

INFORMATION RIGHTS. So long as any investor continues to hold shares of Series A Preferred Stock or Common Stock issued upon conversion of the Series A Preferred Stock, the Company shall deliver to such investor (i) internally prepared quarterly financial statements and audited annual financial statements prepared by nationally recognized independent public accountants, (ii) an annual budget at least 30 days prior to the beginning of each fiscal year prepared on a monthly basis, and (iii) quarterly financial statements with management's analysis of results and a statement of an executive officer explaining any differences from budget, and the investor shall be entitled to standard inspection rights; provided, however, that all rights under (i)–(iii) above shall terminate upon an underwritten public offering of the Common Stock of the Company.

REGISTRATION RIGHTS DEMAND RIGHTS. At any time after four years from the date of the closing or six months after the Company's initial public offering, whichever is earlier, persons holding at least 50% of the Series A Preferred Stock (or 50% of Common Stock, issuable upon conversion of the Series A Preferred Stock) may request registration by the Company of their shares if the anticipated aggregate offering price, net underwriting discounts and commissions, would exceed $3 million, and the Company will use its best efforts to cause such shares to be registered. The Company shall not be obligated to effect more than one registration under these demand rights provisions.

S-3 REGISTRATION RIGHTS. Holders of the Common Stock issued upon conversion of the Series A Preferred Stock shall be entitled to unlimited registration rights on Form S-3 for an aggregate offering price of at least $500,000.

COMPANY REGISTRATION. Holders of the Common Stock issued upon conversion of the Series A Preferred Stock shall be entitled to three "piggyback" registrations on registrations of the Company's equity, subject to pro rata cutback in the underwriter's discretion, except that the Series A Preferred Stock holders (holding Common Stock issued upon conversion of the Series A Preferred Stock) shall at all times be entitled to have registered at least 50% of any shares to which piggyback rights shall pertain in any offering after the initial public offering.

EXPENSES. The registration expenses (exclusive of underwriting discounts and commissions) of all registrations shall be borne by the Company, except that the Company shall bear the registration expenses of no more than two Form S-3 registrations and two "piggyback" registrations.

OTHER PROVISIONS. Other provisions shall be contained in the Stock Purchase Agreement with respect to registration rights as are reasonable, including cross-indemnification, the Company's ability to delay the filing of the demand registration for a period of 60 days once a year, the period of time in which the registration statement shall be kept effective, underwriting arrangements, and the like.

BOARD REPRESENTATION. The Board of Directors will initially consist of three members. The Series A Preferred Stock shall have the right, in the charter documents of the Company, to elect one Director. All other shareholders shall have the right to elect one Director. The third member shall be derived from the Company's industry and shall be mutually acceptable to both the Series A Preferred Stock as a class and the Common Stock as a class. The Board of Directors shall not be increased above three members without the consent of holders owning a majority of the Series A Preferred Stock.

KEY-PERSON INSURANCE. The Company will obtain and maintain until all Series A Preferred Stock has been redeemed or converted key-man term life insurance in an amount to be agreed upon on the Company's key employees, with proceeds payable to the Company.

PREEMPTIVE RIGHTS. The Articles shall provide for preemptive rights to be held by the holders of Series A Preferred Stock on any future private offerings of equity financing pro rata (based on those Common and Preferred shares then outstanding), to terminate upon the first underwritten public offering.

CO-SALE AGREEMENT. Shares of Common Stock owned by certain of the principal share-holders shall be subject to co-sale provisions.

PROPRIETARY INFORMATION AND INVENTIONS AGREEMENT. Each officer and key employee of the Company with the exception of _____ , _____, and _____ shall have entered into a proprietary information and inventions agreement in a form reasonably acceptable to the Company and the investors.

DUE DILIGENCE. The investors shall have the right to conduct a legal and financial audit prior to closing.

STOCK PURCHASE AGREEMENT. The investment shall be made pursuant to a Stock Purchase Agreement that shall contain, among other things, appropriate representations and warranties of the Company. In addition, such agreement shall require customary officer's certificates and an opinion of counsel by the Company's counsel, satisfactory to counsel for the investors. THE INVESTMENT OF THE INVESTORS IS CONTINGENT UPON, AMONG OTHER THINGS, THE NEGOTIATION AND EXECUTION OF A SATISFACTORY STOCK PURCHASE AGREEMENT AS CONTEMPLATED ABOVE.

EXPENSES. The Company shall bear its own legal fees and other expenses with respect to the transaction and shall pay for the reasonable fees and disbursements of investors' special legal counsel, Dewey, Dilutem, and Howe. Investors' counsel shall draft all agreements.

Representations and Warranties

ORGANIZATION, QUALIFICATIONS, AND CORPORATE POWER

(a) **GrowCo, Inc**, ("the Company") is a corporation duly incorporated, validly existing, and in good standing under the laws of the State of Delaware, and is duly qualified as a foreign corporation in each other jurisdiction in which the failure to be qualified would have a materially adverse effect upon the Company. The Company has the corporate power and authority to own and hold its properties and to carry on its business as currently conducted and as proposed to be conducted, to execute, deliver, and perform this Agreement, and to issue, sell, and deliver the Preferred Stock, to issue the Springing Warrants upon certain redemptions of the Preferred Stock, and, upon conversion of the Preferred Stock and exercise of the Springing Warrants, to issue and deliver the shares of Common Stock required thereunder.

(b) **The Company** does not own of record or beneficially, directly or indirectly, (i) any shares of outstanding capital stock or securities convertible into capital stock of any other corporation; or (ii) any participating interest in any partnership, joint venture, or other noncorporate business enterprise.

AUTHORIZATION OF AGREEMENT, ETC.

(a) **The execution, delivery, and performance by the Company** of this Agreement, the Stockholders Agreement, and the Registration Rights Agreement, the issuance, sale, and delivery of the Preferred Stock, the potential issuance of the Springing Warrants, and the issuance and delivery of the shares of Common Stock upon conversion of the Preferred Stock and exercise of the Springing Warrants have been duly authorized by all requisite corporate action and will not violate any applicable provision of law, any order of any court or other agency of government, the Articles of Incorporation or Bylaws of the Company, or any provision of any indenture, agreement, or other instrument by which the Company or any of its properties or assets is bound or affected, or conflict with, result in a breach of, or constitute (with due notice or lapse of time or both) a default under any such indenture, agreement, or other instrument, or result in the creation or imposition of any lien, charge, or encumbrance of any nature whatsoever upon any of the properties or assets of the Company.

(b) **The Shares**, when issued in accordance with this Agreement and upon proper payment therefore, will be validly issued, fully paid, and nonassessable. Shares of Common Stock have been duly reserved for issuance upon conversion of the Preferred Stock and exercise of the Springing Warrants, and when issued upon conversion of the Preferred Stock and exercise of the Springing Warrant, will be validly issued, fully paid, and nonassessable. Neither the issuance, sale, and delivery of the Preferred Stock, the potential issuance of the Springing Warrants, nor the issuance and delivery of the shares of Common Stock upon conversion of the Shares or exercise of the Springing Warrants is subject to any preemptive right of stockholders of the Company or to any right of first refusal or other similar right in favor of any person.

VALIDITY

This Agreement has been duly executed and delivered by the Company and constitutes the valid and legally binding obligation of the Company, enforceable in accordance with its terms.

CAPITAL STOCK

The authorized capital stock of the Company consists of One Hundred Thousand (100,000) shares of Common Stock, One Dollar ($1.00) par value per share, of which Fifty Thousand

(50,000) shares are, as of the date of this Agreement, validly issued and outstanding, fully paid, and nonassessable, to those stockholders of the Company set forth in Schedule 4.0 hereof and One Hundred Thousand (100,000) shares of Preferred Stock, One Dollar ($1.00) par value per share, of which immediately prior to Closing none will have been issued. Except as set forth in Schedule 4.0 and by virtue of this Agreement: (i) no subscription, warrant, option, convertible security, or other right (contingent or otherwise) to purchase or acquire any shares of any class of capital stock of the Company is authorized or outstanding, (ii) the Company has no commitment to issue any shares, warrants, options, or other such rights or to distribute to holders of any class of its capital stock any evidence of indebtedness or assets, (iii) except as provided under the Stockholders Agreement or the provisions in its Articles of Incorporation authorizing the Preferred Stock, the Company has no obligation (contingent or otherwise) to purchase, redeem, or otherwise acquire any shares of its capital stock or any interest therein or to pay any dividend or make any other distribution in respect thereof, and (iv) the Company has no obligation or commitment to register under the Act any securities issued or to be issued by it.

FINANCIAL STATEMENTS

The Company has furnished to each investor the unaudited balance sheet of the Company as of December 31, 201__, certified by its Chief Financial Officer, and the related unaudited statement of income. Such financial statements are complete and correct, have been prepared in accordance with GAAP, and fairly present the financial position of the Company as of such respective dates, and the results of its operations for the respective periods then ended. Except as set forth in such financial statements, the Company had as of the Closing Date, no material changes in obligations or liabilities, absolute, accrued, or contingent.

ACTIONS PENDING

There is no action, suit, investigation, or proceeding pending or, to the knowledge of the Company, threatened against or affecting the Company or any of its respective properties or rights, before any court or by or before any governmental body or arbitration board or tribunal. There does not exist any basis for any such action, suit, investigation, or proceeding, that will result in any material liability being imposed on the Company. The foregoing includes, without limiting its generality, actions pending or threatened (or any basis therefore known to the Company) involving the prior employment of any employees or prospective employees of the Company or their use, in connection with the Company's business, of any information or techniques that might be alleged to be proprietary to their former employer(s).

TRADE SECRETS

No third party has claimed or has threatened that any person affiliated with the Company has, in respect of his activities with the Company to date, violated any of the terms or conditions of his employment contract with such third party, or disclosed or utilized any trade secrets or proprietary information or documentation of such third party, or interfered in the employment relationship between such third party and any of its employees. No person affiliated with the Company has employed, to the extent that it would have a material adverse effect on the Company, any trade secrets or any information or documentation proprietary to any former employer. No person affiliated with the Company has violated, to the extent that it would have a material adverse effect on the Company, any confidential relationship that such person may have had with any third party in connection with the development, manufacture, and sale of any products of the Company.

GOVERNMENTAL APPROVALS

No registration or filing with, or consent or approval of, or other action by, any Federal, state, or other governmental agency is or will be necessary for the valid execution, delivery, and performance of this Agreement, the issuance, sale, and delivery of the Preferred Stock, the potential issuance of the Springing Warrants, and upon conversion of the Preferred Stock and exercise of the Springing Warrants, the issuance and delivery of the shares of Common Stock issuable thereunder, (other than the requirements of applicable securities laws, all of which requirements will be satisfied).

OFFERING OF THE PREFERRED STOCK

Neither the Company nor any person authorized or employed by the Company as agent, broker, dealer, or otherwise in connection with the offering or sale of the Preferred Stock or any similar security of the Company, has offered the Preferred Stock or any such securities for sale to, or solicited any offers to buy the Preferred Stock or any similar securities of the Company from, or otherwise approached or negotiated with respect thereto any person or persons other than the Purchasers such as to cause the Preferred Stock to have to be registered under the Act. Neither the Company nor any person acting on its behalf has taken or will take any action (including, without limitation, any offer, issuance, or sale of any security of the Company under circumstances that might require the integration of such security with the Preferred Stock under the Act or the rules and regulations of the Commission) which might subject the offering, issuance, or sale of the Preferred Stock to the registration provisions of the Act.

LACK OF DEFAULTS

The Company knows of no default in its performance of any obligation, covenant, or condition contained in any note, debenture, mortgage, or other agreement to which it is a party, nor of any default with respect to any order, writ, injunction, or decree of any court, governmental authority, or arbitration board or tribunal to which it is a party, which would have a material adverse effect on the business of the Company. The Company knows of no material violation of any law, ordinance, governmental rule, or regulation to which it is subject, nor has it failed to obtain any licenses, permits, franchises, or other governmental authorizations necessary for the ownership of its properties or to the conduct of its business where any such violation, breach, default, or failure to obtain would result in a material adverse effect upon the business of the Company. The Company has conducted and will conduct its business and operations in substantial compliance with all federal, state, county, and municipal laws, statutes, ordinances, and regulations and is in substantial compliance with all applicable requirements of all federal, state, county, and municipal regulatory authorities.

VERACITY OF STATEMENTS

No statement in the Preferred Stock Purchase Agreement, any exhibit hereto or any document required to be submitted hereunder or any business plan furnished to any of the investors by the Company in connection with the negotiation or entering into this Agreement contains any untrue statement of a material fact or omits any material fact necessary to make the statement, in light of the circumstances in which it was made, not misleading. There is no fact of which the Company is presently aware which has not been disclosed to the investors and which the Company presently believes to materially and adversely affect or is presently believed to be likely to materially and adversely affect the properties, business, prospects, profits, or condition (financial or otherwise) of the Company or the ability of the Company to perform its obligations under this Agreement.

Venture Capital–Style Series A Preferred Stock Charter Amendments

The following is a statement of the designations and the powers, privileges, and rights, and the qualifications, limitations, or restrictions thereof in respect of each class of capital stock of the Corporation.

A. COMMON STOCK.

1. General. The voting, dividend, and liquidation rights of the holders of the Common Stock are subject to and qualified by the rights of the holders of the Preferred Stock of any series as may be designated by the Board of Directors upon any issuance of the Preferred Stock of any series.

2. Voting. The holders of the Common Stock are entitled to one vote for each share held at all meetings of stockholders (and written actions in lieu of meetings). There shall be no cumulative voting.

The number of authorized shares of Common Stock may be increased or decreased (but not below the number of shares thereof then outstanding) by the affirmative vote of the holders of a majority of the stock of the Corporation entitled to vote, irrespective of the provisions of Section 242(b)(2) of the General Corporation Law of Delaware.

3. Dividends. Dividends may be declared and paid on the Common Stock from funds lawfully available therefore as and when determined by the Board of Directors and subject to any preferential dividend rights of any then outstanding Preferred Stock.

4. Liquidation. Upon the dissolution or liquidation of the Corporation, whether voluntary or involuntary, holders of Common Stock will be entitled to receive all assets of the Corporation available for distribution to its stockholders, subject to any preferential rights of any then outstanding Preferred Stock.

B. PREFERRED STOCK.

Preferred Stock may be issued from time to time in one or more series, each of such series to have such terms as stated or expressed herein and in the resolution or resolutions providing for the issue of such series adopted by the Board of Directors of the Corporation as hereinafter provided. Any shares of Preferred Stock, which may be redeemed, purchased, or acquired by the Corporation, may be reissued except as otherwise provided by law. Different series of Preferred Stock shall not be construed to constitute different classes of shares for the purposes of voting by classes unless expressly provided.

Authority is hereby expressly granted to the Board of Directors from time to time to issue the Preferred Stock in one or more series, and in connection with the creation of any such series, by resolution or resolutions providing for the issue of the shares thereof, to determine and fix such voting powers, full or limited, or no voting powers, and such designations, preferences, and relative participating, optional, or other special rights, and qualifications, limitations, or restrictions thereof, including without limitation thereof, dividend rights, special voting rights, conversion rights, redemption privileges, and liquidation preferences, as shall be stated and expressed in such resolutions, all to the full extent now or hereafter permitted by the General Corporation Law of Delaware. Without limiting the generality of the foregoing, the resolutions providing for issuance of any series of Preferred Stock may provide that such series shall be superior or rank equally or be junior to the Preferred Stock of any other series to the extent permitted by law. Except as otherwise specifically provided in this Certificate of Incorporation, no vote of the holders of the Preferred Stock or Common Stock shall be a prerequisite to the issuance of any shares of any series of the Preferred Stock authorized by and complying with the conditions of this Certificate of Incorporation, the right to have such vote being expressly waived by all present and future holders of the capital stock of the Corporation.

C.   SERIES A CONVERTIBLE PREFERRED STOCK.

Two Million (2,000,000) shares of the authorized and unissued Preferred Stock of the Corporation are hereby designated "Series A Convertible Preferred Stock" (the "Series A Preferred Stock") with the following rights, preferences, powers, privileges, and restrictions, qualifications, and limitations.

1.   Dividends

(a) The holders of shares of Series A Preferred Stock shall be entitled to receive, out of funds legally available therefore, dividends of $____ per share per annum (subject to appropriate adjustment in the event of any stock dividend, stock split, combination, or other similar recapitalization affecting such shares), payable when and as declared by the Board of Directors of the Corporation. Such dividends shall accrue and shall be cumulative from the date of issuance of each share of Series A Preferred Stock, whether or not declared.

(b) The Corporation shall not declare or pay any cash dividends on shares of Common Stock until the holders of the Series A Preferred Stock then outstanding shall have first received a dividend at the rate specified in paragraph (a) of this Section 1.

2.   Liquidation, Dissolution, or Winding Up; Certain Mergers, Consolidations, and Asset Sales.

(a) In the event of any voluntary or involuntary liquidation, dissolution, or winding up of the Corporation, the holders of shares of Series A Preferred Stock then outstanding shall be entitled to be paid out of the assets of the Corporation available for distribution to its stockholders, but before any payment shall be made to the holders of Common Stock or any other class or series of stock ranking on liquidation junior to the Series A Preferred Stock (such Common Stock and other stock being collectively referred to as "Junior Stock") by reason of their ownership thereof, an amount equal to $_____ per share (subject to appropriate adjustment in the event of any stock dividend, stock split, combination, or other similar recapitalization affecting such shares), plus any accrued but unpaid dividends and any dividends declared but unpaid on such shares. If upon any such liquidation, dissolution, or winding up of the Corporation the remaining assets of the Corporation available for distribution to its stockholders shall be insufficient to pay the holders of shares of Series A Preferred Stock the full amount to which they shall be entitled, the holders of shares of Series A Preferred Stock and any class or series of stock ranking on liquidation on a parity with the Series A Preferred Stock shall share ratably in any distribution of the remaining assets and funds of the Corporation in proportion to the respective amounts that would otherwise be payable in respect of the shares held by them upon such distribution if all amounts payable on or with respect to such shares were paid in full.

(b) After the payment of all preferential amounts required to be paid to the holders of Series A Preferred Stock and any other class or series of stock of the Corporation ranking on liquidation on a parity with the Series A Preferred Stock, upon the dissolution, liquidation, or winding up of the Corporation, the remaining assets and funds of the Corporation available for distribution to its stockholders shall be distributed among the holders of shares of Series A Preferred Stock, Common Stock, and any other class or series of stock entitled to participate in liquidation distributions with the holders of Common Stock, pro rata based on the number of shares of Common Stock held by each (assuming conversion into Common Stock of all such shares).

(c) Any merger or consolidation of the Corporation into or with another corporation (except one in which the holders of capital stock of the Corporation immediately prior to such merger or consolidation continue to hold at least 75% by voting power of the capital stock of the surviving corporation), or sale of all or substantially all the assets of the Corporation, shall be deemed to be a liquidation of the Corporation for purposes of this Section 2, and the agreement or plan of merger or consolidation with respect to such merger, consolidation, or sale shall provide that the consideration payable to the stockholders of the Corporation (in the case of a merger or consolidation), or consideration payable to the Corporation, together with all other available assets of the Corporation (in the case of an asset sale), shall be distributed to the holders of capital stock of the Corporation in accordance with Subsections 2(a) and 2(b) above. The amount deemed distributed to the holders of Series A Preferred Stock upon any such merger, consolidation, or sale shall be the cash or the value of the property, rights, or securities distributed to such holders by the Corporation or the acquiring person, firm, or other entity. The value of such property, rights, or other securities shall be determined in good faith by the Board of Directors of the Corporation.

(d) The Corporation may not liquidate, dissolve, or wind up if the assets of the Corporation then available for distribution to its stockholders shall be insufficient to pay the holders of shares of Series A Preferred Stock the full amount to which they shall be entitled upon such liquidation, dissolution, or winding up under this Section 2, without the prior written approval of the holders of a majority of the then outstanding shares of Series A Preferred Stock.

3.   Voting

(a) Each holder of outstanding shares of Series A Preferred Stock shall be entitled to the number of votes equal to the number of whole shares of Common Stock into which the shares of Series A Preferred Stock held by such holder are then convertible (as adjusted from time to time pursuant to Section 4 hereof), at each meeting of stockholders of the Corporation (and written actions of stockholders in lieu of meetings) with respect to any and all matters presented to the stockholders of the Corporation for their action or consideration. Except as provided by law, by the provisions of Subsection 3(b) or 3(c) below or by the provisions establishing any other series of Preferred Stock, holders of Series A Preferred Stock and of any other outstanding series of Preferred Stock shall vote together with the holders of Common Stock as a single class.

(b) GrowCo, Inc., a Delaware corporation, and its designees shall be entitled to elect two directors of the Corporation, and the holders of record of the shares of Common Stock and of any other class or series of voting stock (including the Series A Preferred Stock), exclusively and as a separate class, shall be entitled to elect the balance of the total number of directors of the Corporation. A vacancy in any directorship filled by GrowCo, Inc. shall be filled only by vote or written consent in lieu of a meeting by GrowCo, Inc. or by any remaining director or directors elected by GrowCo, Inc. pursuant to this Subsection 3(b).

(c) The Corporation shall not amend, alter, or repeal the preferences, special rights, or other powers of the Series A Preferred Stock so as to affect adversely the Series A Preferred Stock, without the written consent or affirmative vote of the holders of a majority of the then outstanding shares of Series A Preferred Stock, given in writing or by vote at a meeting, consenting or voting (as the case may be) separately as a class. For this purpose, without limiting the generality of the foregoing, the authorization of any shares of capital stock on a parity with or with preference or priority over the Series A Preferred Stock as to the right to receive either dividends or amounts distributable upon liquidation, dissolution, or winding up of the Corporation shall be deemed to affect adversely the Series A Preferred Stock. The number of authorized shares of Series A Preferred Stock may be increased or decreased (but not below the number of shares then outstanding) by the directors of the Corporation pursuant to Section 151 of the General Corporation Law of Delaware or by the affirmative vote of the holders of a majority of the then outstanding shares of the Common Stock, Series A Preferred Stock, and all other classes or series of stock of the Corporation entitled to vote thereon, voting as a single class, irrespective of the provisions of Section 242(b)(2) of the General Corporation Law of Delaware.

In addition to any other rights provided by law, so long as any shares of Series A Preferred Stock shall be outstanding, the Corporation shall not, without first obtaining the affirmative vote or written consent of the holders of not less than 51% of the then outstanding shares of Series A Preferred Stock:

(a) Amend or repeal any provision of, or add any provision to, the Corporation's Certificate of Incorporation or Bylaws, if such action would adversely affect the preferences, rights, privileges, or powers of, or the restrictions provided for the benefit of, Series A Preferred Stock;

(b) Authorize or issue any new or existing class or classes or series of capital stock having any preference or priority as to dividends or assets superior to or on a parity with any such preference or priority of the Series A Preferred Stock, or authorize or issue shares of stock of any class or any bonds, debentures, notes, or other obligations convertible into or exchangeable for, or having rights to purchase, any shares of stock of the Corporation having any preference or priority as to dividends or assets superior to or on a parity with any such preference or priority of the Series A Preferred Stock;

(c) Reclassify any Common Stock into shares having any preference or priority as to dividends or assets superior to or on a parity with any such preference or priority of the Series A Preferred Stock;

(d) Pay or declare any dividend or distribution on any shares of its capital stock (except dividends payable solely in shares of Common Stock), or apply any of its assets to the redemption, retirement, purchase, or acquisition, directly or indirectly, through subsidiaries or otherwise, of any shares of its capital stock; or

(e) Merge or consolidate into or with any other corporation or other entity or sell all or substantially all of the Corporation's assets.

4.   Optional Conversion

The holders of the Series A Preferred Stock shall have conversion rights as follows (the "Conversion Rights"):

(a) Right to Convert. Each share of Series A Preferred Stock shall be convertible, at the option of the holder thereof, at any time and from time to time, and without the payment of additional consideration by the holder thereof, into such number of fully paid and nonassessable shares of Common Stock as is determined by dividing $_____ by the Series A Conversion Price (as defined below) in effect at the time of conversion. The "Series A Conversion Price" shall initially be $_____. Such initial Series A Conversion Price, and the rate at which shares of Series A Preferred Stock may be converted into shares of Common Stock, shall be subject to adjustment as provided below.

In the event of a notice of redemption of any shares of Series A Preferred Stock pursuant to Section 6 hereof, the Conversion Rights of the shares designated for redemption shall terminate at the close of business on the fifth full day preceding the date fixed for redemption, unless the redemption price is not paid when due, in which case the Conversion Rights for such shares shall continue until such price is paid in full. In the event of a liquidation of the Corporation, the Conversion Rights shall terminate at the close of business on the first full day preceding the date fixed for the payment of any amounts distributable on liquidation to the holders of Series A Preferred Stock.

(b) Fractional Shares. No fractional shares of Common Stock shall be issued upon conversion of the Series A Preferred Stock. In lieu of any fractional shares to which the holder would otherwise be entitled, the Corporation shall pay cash equal to such fraction multiplied by the then effective Series A Conversion Price.

(c) Mechanics of Conversion.

(i) In order for a holder of Series A Preferred Stock to convert shares of Series A Preferred Stock into shares of Common Stock, such holder shall surrender the certificate or certificates for such shares of Series A Preferred Stock, at the office of the transfer agent for the Series A Preferred Stock (or at the principal office of the Corporation if the Corporation serves as its own transfer agent), together with written notice that such holder elects to convert all or any number of the shares of the Series A Preferred Stock represented by such certificate or certificates. Such notice shall state such holder's name or the names of the nominees in which such holder wishes the certificate or certificates for shares of Common Stock to be issued. If required by the Corporation, certificates surrendered for conversion shall be endorsed or accompanied by a written instrument or instruments of transfer, in form satisfactory to the Corporation, duly executed by the registered holder or his or its attorney duly authorized in writing. The date of receipt of such certificates and notice by the transfer agent (or by the Corporation if the Corporation serves as its own transfer agent) shall be the conversion date ("Conversion Date"). The Corporation shall, as soon as practicable after the Conversion Date, issue and deliver at such office to such holder of Series A Preferred Stock, or to his or its nominees, a certificate or certificates for the number of shares of Common Stock to which such holder shall be entitled, together with cash in lieu of any fraction of a share.

(ii) The Corporation shall at all times when the Series A Preferred Stock shall be outstanding, reserve and keep available out of its authorized but unissued stock, for the purpose of effecting the conversion of the Series A Preferred Stock, such number of its duly authorized shares of Common Stock as shall from time to time be sufficient to effect the conversion of all outstanding Series A Preferred Stock. Before taking any action that would cause an adjustment reducing the Series A Conversion Price below the then par value of the shares of Common Stock issuable upon conversion of the Series A Preferred Stock, the Corporation will take any corporate action that may, in the opinion of its counsel, be necessary in order that the Corporation may validly and legally issue fully paid and nonassessable shares of Common Stock at such adjusted Series A Conversion Price.

(iii) Upon any such conversion, no adjustment to the Series A Conversion Price shall be made for any declared but unpaid dividends on the Series A Preferred Stock surrendered for conversion or on the Common Stock delivered upon conversion.

(iv) All shares of Series A Preferred Stock that shall have been surrendered for conversion as herein provided shall no longer be deemed to be outstanding and all rights with respect to such shares, including the rights, if any, to receive notices and to vote, shall immediately cease and terminate on the Conversion Date, except only the right of the holders thereof to receive shares of Common Stock in exchange therefor and payment of any accrued but unpaid dividends and any dividends declared but unpaid thereon. Any shares of Series A Preferred Stock so converted shall be retired and canceled and shall not be reissued, and the Corporation (without the need for stockholder action) may from time to time take such appropriate action as may be necessary to reduce the authorized number of shares of Series A Preferred Stock accordingly.

(v) The Corporation shall pay any and all issue and other taxes that may be payable in respect of any issuance or delivery of shares of Common Stock upon conversion of shares of

Series A Preferred Stock pursuant to this Section 4. The Corporation shall not, however, be required to pay any tax that may be payable in respect of any transfer involved in the issuance and delivery of shares of Common Stock in a name other than that in which the shares of Series A Preferred Stock so converted were registered, and no such issuance or delivery shall be made unless and until the person or entity requesting such issuance has paid to the Corporation the amount of any such tax or has established, to the satisfaction of the Corporation, that such tax has been paid.

(d) Adjustments to Series A Conversion Price for Diluting Issues:

(i) Special Definitions. For purposes of this Subsection 4(d), the following definitions shall apply:

(A) "Option" shall mean rights, options, or warrants to subscribe for, purchase, or otherwise acquire Common Stock or Convertible Securities.

(B) "Series A Original Issue Date" shall mean the date on which a share of Series A Preferred Stock was first issued.

(C) "Convertible Securities" shall mean any evidences of indebtedness, shares, or other securities directly or indirectly convertible into or exchangeable for Common Stock.

(D) "Additional Shares of Common Stock" shall mean all shares of Common Stock issued (or, pursuant to Subsection 4(d)(iii) below, deemed to be issued) by the Corporation after the Series A Original Issue Date, other than:

(I) shares of Common Stock issued or issuable upon conversion of any Convertible Securities or exercise of any warrants outstanding on the Series A Original Issue Date;

(II) shares of Common Stock issued or issuable as a dividend or distribution on Series A Preferred Stock;

(III) shares of Common Stock issued or issuable by reason of a dividend, stock split, split-up, or other distribution on shares of Common Stock that is covered by Subsection 4(e) or 4(f) below; or

(IV) up to 100,000 shares of Common Stock issued or issuable to employees or directors of, or consultants to, the Corporation pursuant to a plan or arrangement approved by the Board of Directors of the Corporation and by a majority of the members of the Board of Directors who are not employees of the Company or any of its subsidiaries (provided that any Options for such shares that expire or terminate unexercised shall not be counted toward such maximum number).

(ii) No Adjustment of Series A Conversion Price. No adjustment in the number of shares of Common Stock into which the Series A Preferred Stock is convertible shall be made, by adjustment in the applicable Series A Conversion Price thereof: (a) unless the consideration per share (determined pursuant to Subsection 4(d)(v)) for an Additional Share of Common Stock issued or deemed to be issued by the Corporation is less than the applicable Series A Conversion Price in effect immediately prior to the issue of such Additional Shares, or (b) if prior to such issuance, the Corporation receives written notice from the holders of at least 75% of the then outstanding shares of Series A Preferred Stock agreeing that no such adjustment shall be made as the result of the issuance of Additional Shares of Common Stock.

(iii) Issue of Securities Deemed Issue of Additional Shares of Common Stock. If the Corporation at any time or from time to time after the Series A Original Issue Date shall issue any Options (excluding Options covered by Subsection 4(d)(i)(D)(IV) above) or Convertible Securities or shall fix a record date for the determination of holders of any class of securities entitled to receive any such Options or Convertible Securities, then the maximum number of shares of Common Stock (as set forth in the instrument relating thereto without regard to any provision contained therein for a subsequent adjustment of such number) issuable upon the exercise of such Options or, in the case of Convertible Securities and Options therefor, the conversion or exchange of such Convertible Securities, shall be deemed to be Additional Shares of Common Stock issued as of the time of such issue or, in case such a record date shall have been fixed, as of the close of business on such record date, provided that Additional Shares of Common Stock shall not be deemed to have been issued unless the consideration per share (determined pursuant to Subsection 4(d)(v) hereof) of such Additional Shares of Common Stock would be less than the applicable Series A Conversion Price in effect on the date of and immediately prior to such issue, or such record date, as the case may be, and provided further that in any such case in which Additional Shares of Common Stock are deemed to be issued:

(A) No further adjustment in the Series A Conversion Price shall be made upon the subsequent issue of Convertible Securities or shares of Common Stock upon the exercise of such Options or conversion or exchange of such Convertible Securities;

(B) If such Options or Convertible Securities by their terms provide, with the passage of time or otherwise, for any increase or decrease in the consideration payable to the Corporation, upon the exercise, conversion, or exchange thereof, the Series A Conversion Price computed upon the original issue thereof (or upon the occurrence of a record date with respect thereto), and any subsequent adjustments based thereon, shall, upon any such increase or decrease becoming effective, be recomputed to reflect such increase or decrease insofar as it affects such Options or the rights of conversion or exchange under such Convertible Securities;

(C) Upon the expiration or termination of any such unexercised Option, the Series A Conversion Price shall not be readjusted, but the Additional Shares of Common Stock deemed issued as the result of the original issue of such Option shall not be deemed issued for the purposes of any subsequent adjustment of the Series A Conversion Price;

(D) In the event of any change in the number of shares of Common Stock issuable upon the exercise, conversion, or exchange of any such Option or Convertible Security, including, but not limited to, a change resulting from the antidilution provisions thereof, the Series A Conversion Price then in effect shall forthwith be readjusted to such Series A Conversion Price as would have obtained had the adjustment that was made upon the issuance of such Option or Convertible Security not exercised or converted prior to such change been made upon the basis of such change; and

(E) No readjustment pursuant to clause (B) or (D) above shall have the effect of increasing the Series A Conversion Price to an amount that exceeds the lower of (i) the Series A Conversion Price on the original adjustment date, or (ii) the Series A Conversion Price that would have resulted from any issuances of Additional Shares of Common Stock between the original adjustment date and such readjustment date.

In the event the Corporation, after the Series A Original Issue Date, amends the terms of any such Options or Convertible Securities (whether such Options or Convertible Securities were outstanding on the Series A Original Issue Date or were issued after the Series A Original Issue Date), then such Options or Convertible Securities, as so amended, shall be deemed to have been issued after the Series A Original Issue Date and the provisions of this Subsection 4(d)(iii) shall apply.

(iv) Adjustment of Series A Conversion Price Upon Issuance of Additional Shares of Common Stock. In the event the Corporation shall at any time after the Series A Original Issue Date issue Additional Shares of Common Stock (including Additional Shares of Common

Stock deemed to be issued pursuant to Subsection 4(d)(iii), but excluding shares issued as a stock split or combination as provided in Subsection 4(e) or upon a dividend or distribution as provided in Subsection 4(f)), without consideration or for a consideration per share less than the applicable Series A Conversion Price in effect immediately prior to such issue, then and in such event, such Series A Conversion Price shall be reduced, concurrently with such issue, to a price (calculated to the nearest cent) determined by multiplying such Series A Conversion Price by a fraction, (A) the numerator of which shall be (1) the number of shares of Common Stock outstanding immediately prior to such issue plus (2) the number of shares of Common Stock which the aggregate consideration received or to be received by the Corporation for the total number of Additional Shares of Common Stock so issued would purchase at such Series A Conversion Price; and (B) the denominator of which shall be the number of shares of Common Stock outstanding immediately prior to such issue plus the number of such Additional Shares of Common Stock so issued; provided that, the number of shares of Common Stock deemed issuable upon exercise or conversion of such outstanding Options and Convertible Securities shall not give effect to any adjustments to the conversion price or conversion rate of such Options or Convertible Securities resulting from the issuance of Additional Shares of Common Stock that is the subject of this calculation.

(v) Determination of Consideration. For purposes of this Subsection 4(d), the consideration received by the Corporation for the issue of any Additional Shares of Common Stock shall be computed as follows:

(A) Cash and Property: Such consideration shall:

(I) insofar as it consists of cash, be computed at the aggregate of cash received by the Corporation, excluding amounts paid or payable for accrued interest and for accrued dividends;

(II) insofar as it consists of property other than cash, be computed at the fair market value thereof at the time of such issue, as determined in good faith by the Board of Directors; and

(III) in the event Additional Shares of Common Stock are issued together with other shares or securities or other assets of the Corporation for consideration which covers both, be the proportion of such consideration so received, computed as provided in clauses (I) and (II) above, as determined in good faith by the Board of Directors.

(B) Options and Convertible Securities. The consideration per share received by the Corporation for Additional Shares of Common Stock deemed to have been issued pursuant to Subsection 4(d)(iii), relating to Options and Convertible Securities, shall be determined by dividing:

(x) the total amount, if any, received or receivable by the Corporation as consideration for the issue of such Options or Convertible Securities, plus the minimum aggregate amount of additional consideration (as set forth in the instruments relating thereto, without regard to any provision contained therein for a subsequent adjustment of such consideration) payable to the Corporation upon the exercise of such Options or the conversion or exchange of such Convertible Securities, or in the case of Options for Convertible Securities, the exercise of such Options for Convertible Securities and the conversion or exchange of such Convertible Securities, by:

(y) the maximum number of shares of Common Stock (as set forth in the instruments relating thereto, without regard to any provision contained therein for a subsequent adjustment of such number) issuable upon the exercise of such Options or the conversion or exchange of such Convertible Securities.

(vi) Multiple Closing Dates. In the event the Corporation shall issue on more than one date Additional Shares of Common Stock which are comprised of shares of the same series or class of Preferred Stock, and such issuance dates occur within a period of no more than 120 days, then, upon the final such issuance, the Series A Conversion Price shall be adjusted to give effect to all such issuances as if they occurred on the date of the final such issuance (and without giving effect to any adjustments as a result of such prior issuances within such period).

(e) Adjustment for Stock Splits and Combinations. If the Corporation shall at any time or from time to time after the Series A Original Issue Date effect a subdivision of the outstanding Common Stock, the Series A Conversion Price then in effect immediately before that subdivision shall be proportionately decreased. If the Corporation shall at any time or from time to time after the Series A Original Issue Date combine the outstanding shares of Common Stock, the Series A Conversion Price then in effect immediately before the combination shall be proportionately increased. Any adjustment under this paragraph shall become effective at the close of business on the date the subdivision or combination becomes effective.

(f) Adjustment for Certain Dividends and Distributions. In the event the Corporation at any time, or from time to time after the Series A Original Issue Date shall make or issue, or fix a record date for the determination of holders of Common Stock entitled to receive, a dividend or other distribution payable in additional shares of Common Stock, then and in each such event the Series A Conversion Price then in effect immediately before such event shall be decreased as of the time of such issuance or, in the event such a record date shall have been fixed, as of the close of business on such record date, by multiplying the Series A Conversion Price for the Series A Preferred Stock then in effect by a fraction:

(1) the numerator of which shall be the total number of shares of Common Stock issued and outstanding immediately prior to the time of such issuance or the close of business on such record date, and

(2) the denominator of which shall be the total number of shares of Common Stock issued and outstanding immediately prior to the time of such issuance or the close of business on such record date plus the number of shares of Common Stock issuable in payment of such dividend or distribution; provided, however, if such record date shall have been fixed and such dividend is not fully paid or if such distribution is not fully made on the date fixed therefore, the Series A Conversion Price shall be recomputed accordingly as of the close of business on such record date and thereafter the Series A Conversion Price shall be adjusted pursuant to this paragraph as of the time of actual payment of such dividends or distributions; and provided further, however, that no such adjustment shall be made if the holders of Series A Preferred Stock simultaneously receive (i) a dividend or other distribution of shares of Common Stock in a number equal to the number of shares of Common Stock as they would have received if all outstanding shares of Series A Preferred Stock had been converted into Common Stock on the date of such event or (ii) a dividend or other distribution of shares of Series A Preferred Stock which are convertible, as of the date of such event, into such number of shares of Common Stock as is equal to the number of additional shares of Common Stock being issued with respect to each share of Common Stock in such dividend or distribution.

(g) Adjustments for Other Dividends and Distributions. In the event the Corporation at any time or from time to time after the Series A Original Issue Date shall make or issue, or fix a record date for the determination of holders of Common Stock entitled to receive, a dividend or other distribution payable in securities of the Corporation other than shares of Common Stock, then and in each such event provision shall be made so that the holders of the Series A Preferred Stock shall receive upon conversion thereof in addition to the number of shares of Common Stock receivable thereupon, the amount of securities of the Corporation that they would have received had the Series A Preferred Stock been converted into Common Stock on the date of such event and had they thereafter, during the period from the date of such event to and including the conversion date, retained such securities receivable by them as aforesaid during such period, giving application to all adjustments called for during such period under this paragraph with respect to the rights of the holders of the Series A Preferred Stock; and provided further, however, that no such adjustment shall be made if the holders of Series A Preferred Stock simultaneously receive a dividend or other distribution of such securities in an amount equal to the amount of such securities as they would have received if all outstanding shares of Series A Preferred Stock had been converted into Common Stock on the date of such event.

(h) Adjustment for Reclassification, Exchange, or Substitution. If the Common Stock issuable upon the conversion of the Series A Preferred Stock shall be changed into the same or a different number of shares of any class or classes of stock, whether by capital reorganization, reclassification, or otherwise (other than a subdivision or combination of shares or stock dividend provided for above, or a reorganization, merger, consolidation, or sale of assets provided for below), then and in each such event the holder of each such share of Series A Preferred Stock shall have the right thereafter to convert such share into the kind and amount of shares of stock and other securities and property receivable, upon such reorganization, reclassification, or other change, by holders of the number of shares of Common Stock into which such shares of Series A Preferred Stock might have been converted immediately prior to such reorganization, reclassification, or change, all subject to further adjustment as provided herein.

(i) Adjustment for Merger or Reorganization, etc. In case of any consolidation or merger of the Corporation with or into another corporation or the sale of all or substantially all of the assets of the Corporation to another corporation (other than a consolidation, merger, or sale which is covered by Subsection 2(c)), each share of Series A Preferred Stock shall thereafter be convertible (or shall be converted into a security which shall be convertible) into the kind and amount of shares of stock or other securities or property to which a holder of the number of shares of Common Stock of the Corporation deliverable upon conversion of such Series A Preferred Stock would have been entitled upon such consolidation, merger, or sale; and, in such case, appropriate adjustment (as determined in good faith by the Board of Directors) shall be made in the application of the provisions in this Section 4 set forth with respect to the rights and interest thereafter of the holders of the Series A Preferred Stock, to the end that the provisions set forth in this Section 4 (including provisions with respect to changes in and other adjustments of the Series A Conversion Price) shall thereafter be applicable, as nearly as reasonably may be, in relation to any shares of stock or other property thereafter deliverable upon the conversion of the Series A Preferred Stock.

(j) No Impairment. The Corporation will not, by amendment of its Certificate of Incorporation or through any reorganization, transfer of assets, consolidation, merger, dissolution, issue or sale of securities, or any other voluntary action, avoid or seek to avoid the observance or performance of any of the terms to be observed or performed hereunder by the Corporation, but will at all times in good faith assist in the carrying out of all the provisions of this Section 4 and in the taking of all such action as may be necessary or appropriate in order to protect the Conversion Rights of the holders of the Series A Preferred Stock against impairment.

(k) Certificate as to Adjustments. Upon the occurrence of each adjustment or readjustment of the Series A Conversion Price pursuant to this Section 4, the Corporation at its expense shall promptly compute such adjustment or readjustment in accordance with the terms hereof and furnish to each holder of Series A Preferred Stock a certificate setting forth such adjustment or readjustment and showing in detail the facts upon which such adjustment or readjustment is based. The Corporation shall, upon the written request at any time of any holder of Series A Preferred Stock, furnish or cause to be furnished to such holder a similar certificate setting forth (i) such adjustments and readjustments, (ii) the Series A Conversion Price then in effect, and (iii) the number of shares of Common Stock and the amount, if any, of other property which then would be received upon the conversion of Series A Preferred Stock.

(l)   Notice of Record Date. In the event:

(i) that the Corporation declares a dividend (or any other distribution) on its Common Stock payable in Common Stock or other securities of the Corporation;

(ii) that the Corporation subdivides or combines its outstanding shares of Common Stock;

(iii) of any reclassification of the Common Stock of the Corporation (other than a subdivision or combination of its outstanding shares of Common Stock or a stock dividend or stock distribution thereon), or of any consolidation or merger of the Corporation into or with another corporation, or of the sale of all or substantially all of the assets of the Corporation; or

(iv) of the involuntary or voluntary dissolution, liquidation, or winding up of the Corporation;

then the Corporation shall cause to be filed at its principal office or at the office of the transfer agent of the Series A Preferred Stock, and shall cause to be mailed to the holders of the Series A Preferred Stock at their last addresses as shown on the records of the Corporation or such transfer agent, at least ten days prior to the date specified in (A) below or twenty days before the date specified in (B) below, a notice stating

(A) the record date of such dividend, distribution, subdivision, or combination, or, if a record is not to be taken, the date as of which the holders of Common Stock of record to be entitled to such dividend, distribution, subdivision, or combination are to be determined, or

(B) the date on which such reclassification, consolidation, merger, sale, dissolution, liquidation, or winding up is expected to become effective, and the date as of which it is expected that holders of Common Stock of record shall be entitled to exchange their shares of Common Stock for securities or other property deliverable upon such reclassification, consolidation, merger, sale, dissolution, or winding up of the Corporation.

5.   MANDATORY CONVERSION.

(a) Upon the closing of the sale of shares of Common Stock, at a price to the public of at least $_____ per share (subject to appropriate adjustment for stock splits, stock dividends, combinations, and other similar recapitalizations affecting such shares), in a public offering pursuant to an effective registration statement under the Securities Act of 1933, as amended, resulting in at least $25,000,000 of gross proceeds to the Corporation (the "Mandatory Conversion Date"), (i) all outstanding shares of Series A Preferred Stock shall automatically be converted into shares of Common Stock, at the then effective conversion rate and (ii) the number of authorized shares of Preferred Stock shall be automatically reduced by the number of shares of Preferred Stock that had been designated as Series A Preferred Stock, and all provisions included under the caption "Series A Convertible Preferred Stock," and all references to the Series A Preferred Stock, shall be deleted and shall be of no further force or effect.

(b) All holders of record of shares of Series A Preferred Stock shall be given written notice of the Mandatory Conversion Date and the place designated for mandatory conversion of all such shares of Series A Preferred Stock pursuant to this Section 5. Such notice need not be given in advance of the occurrence of the Mandatory Conversion Date. Such notice shall be sent by first class or registered mail, postage prepaid, to each record holder of Series A Preferred Stock at such holder's address last shown on the records of the transfer agent for the Series A Preferred Stock (or the records of the Corporation, if it serves as its own transfer agent). Upon receipt of such notice, each holder of shares of Series A Preferred Stock shall surrender his or its certificate or certificates for all such shares to the Corporation at the place designated in such notice, and shall thereafter receive certificates for the number of shares of Common Stock to which such holder is entitled pursuant to this Section 5. On the Mandatory Conversion Date, all rights with respect to the Series A Preferred Stock so converted, including the rights, if any, to receive notices and vote (other than as a holder of Common Stock) will terminate, except only the rights of the holders thereof, upon surrender of their certificate or certificates therefore, to receive certificates for the number of shares of Common Stock into which such Series A Preferred Stock has been converted, and payment of any accrued but unpaid dividends and any declared but unpaid dividends thereon. If so required by the Corporation, certificates surrendered for conversion shall be endorsed or accompanied by written instrument or instruments of transfer, in form satisfactory to the Corporation, duly executed by the registered holder or by his or its attorney duly authorized in writing. As soon as practicable after the Mandatory Conversion Date and the surrender of the certificate or certificates for Series A Preferred Stock, the Corporation shall cause to be issued and delivered to such holder, or on his or its written order, a certificate or certificates for the number of full shares of Common Stock issuable on such conversion in accordance with the provisions hereof and cash as provided in Subsection 4(b) in respect of any fraction of a share of Common Stock otherwise issuable upon such conversion.

(c) **All certificates evidencing shares of Series A Preferred Stock** which are required to be surrendered for conversion in accordance with the provisions hereof shall, from and after the Mandatory Conversion Date, be deemed to have been retired and canceled and the shares of Series A Preferred Stock represented thereby converted into Common Stock for all purposes, notwithstanding the failure of the holder or holders thereof to surrender such certificates on or prior to such date. Such converted Series A Preferred Stock may not be reissued, and the Corporation may thereafter take such appropriate action (without the need for stockholder action) as may be necessary to reduce the authorized number of shares of Series A Preferred Stock accordingly.

6. REDEMPTION.

(a) **The Corporation will, subject to the conditions set forth below**, on September _____, 201____, and on each of the first and second anniversaries thereof (each such date being referred to hereinafter as a "Mandatory Redemption Date"), upon receipt not less than 60 nor more than 120 days prior to the applicable Mandatory Redemption Date of written request(s) for redemption from holders of at least 51% of the shares of Series A Preferred Stock then outstanding (an "Initial Redemption Request"), redeem from each holder of shares of Series A Preferred Stock that requests redemption pursuant to the Initial Redemption Request or pursuant to a subsequent election made in accordance with Section 6(b) below (a "Requesting Holder"), at a price equal to $1.45 per share, plus any accrued but unpaid dividends and any dividends declared but unpaid thereon, subject to appropriate adjustment in the event of any stock dividend, stock split, combination, or other similar recapitalization affecting such shares (the "Mandatory Redemption Price"), the number of shares of Series A Preferred Stock requested to be redeemed by each Requesting Holder, but not more than the following respective portions of the number of shares of Series A Preferred Stock held by such Requesting Holder on the applicable Mandatory Redemption Date.

Mandatory Redemption Date	Maximum Portion of Shares of Series A Preferred Stock to Be Redeemed
September _____, 201____	33%
September _____, 201____	50%
September _____, 201____	All outstanding shares of Series A Preferred Stock

(b) The Corporation shall provide notice of its receipt of an Initial Redemption Request, specifying the time, manner, and place of redemption and the Mandatory Redemption Price (a "Redemption Notice"), by first class or registered mail, postage prepaid, to each holder of record of Series A Preferred Stock at the address for such holder last shown on the records of the transfer agent therefor (or the records of the Corporation, if it serves as its own transfer agent), not less than 45 days prior to the applicable Mandatory Redemption Date. Each holder of Series A Preferred Stock (other than a holder who has made the Initial Redemption Request) may elect to become a Requesting Holder on such Mandatory Redemption Date by so indicating in a written notice mailed to the Company, by first class or registered mail, postage prepaid, at least 30 days prior to the applicable Mandatory Redemption Date. Except as provided in Section 6(c) below, each Requesting Holder shall surrender to the Corporation on the applicable Mandatory Redemption Date the certificate(s) representing the shares to be redeemed on such date, in the manner and at the place designated in the Redemption Notice. Thereupon, the Mandatory Redemption Price shall be paid to the order of each such Requesting Holder and each certificate surrendered for redemption shall be canceled.

(c) If the funds of the Corporation legally available for redemption of Series A Preferred Stock on any Mandatory Redemption Date are insufficient to redeem the number of shares of Series A Preferred Stock required under this Section 6 to be redeemed on such date from Requesting Holders, those funds which are legally available will be used to redeem the maximum possible number of such shares of Series A Preferred Stock ratably on the basis of the number of shares of Series A Preferred Stock which would be redeemed on such date if the funds of the Corporation legally available therefore had been sufficient to redeem all shares of Series A Preferred Stock required to be redeemed on such date. At any time thereafter when additional funds of the Corporation become legally available for the redemption of Series A Preferred Stock, such funds will be used, at the end of the next succeeding fiscal quarter, to redeem the balance of the shares that the Corporation was theretofore obligated to redeem, ratably on the basis set forth in the preceding sentence.

(d) Unless there shall have been a default in payment of the Mandatory Redemption Price, on the Mandatory Redemption Date all rights of the holder of each share redeemed on such date as a stockholder of the Corporation by reason of the ownership of such share will cease, except the right to receive the Mandatory Redemption Price of such share, without interest, upon presentation and surrender of the certificate representing such share, and such share will not from and after such Mandatory Redemption Date be deemed to be outstanding.

(e) Any Series A Preferred Stock redeemed pursuant to this Section 6 will be canceled and will not under any circumstances be reissued, sold, or transferred and the Corporation may from time to time take such appropriate action as may be necessary to reduce the authorized Series A Preferred Stock accordingly.

7.   **WAIVER.** Any of the rights of the holders of Series A Preferred Stock set forth herein may be waived by the affirmative vote of the holders of more than 66 ⅔% of the shares of Series A Preferred Stock then outstanding.

Employment and Confidentiality Agreement

This Agreement (the "Agreement" or "Employment Agreement"), made and entered into this _____ day of _____, 201_____, by and between GrowCo, Inc. (the "Company"), a Delaware corporation, and _____ (the "Employee").

WITNESSETH

Whereas, the Company is duly organized and validly existing as a corporation in good standing under the laws of the State of Delaware; and

Whereas, the Corporation's Board of Directors has offered employment to the Employee subject to certain terms and conditions hereinafter set forth and the Employee has indicated his willingness to accept such employment;

Now, therefore, in consideration of the mutual promises and covenants as hereinafter set forth, the parties hereto intending to be legally bound agree as follows:·

1.   EMPLOYMENT. The Company hereby agrees to employ the Employee and the Employee hereby agrees to accept employment with the Company in accordance with the terms and conditions set forth in this Employment Agreement.

2.   TERM OF THE EMPLOYMENT AGREEMENT. Subject to the provisions for termination as hereinafter provided, the term of this Employment Agreement shall begin on the date hereof and shall be for a term of _____, thereafter renewable at a _____ to _____ basis, unless either party gives to the other notice of its intention to terminate this Agreement.

3.   COMPENSATION. For all services rendered by the Employee pursuant to this Agreement, the Company shall pay the Employee in accordance with the Schedule A affixed hereto and a part hereof, including any subsequent changes.

4.   DUTIES. The Employee is engaged by the Company as the Company's Chief Operations Officer. As such, the Employee shall be expected to manage the affairs of the Company on a day-to-day basis and to assume and perform such executive or managerial duties and responsibilities as are assigned from time to time by the Board of Directors.

5.   EXCLUSIVE SERVICE. The Employee shall devote his full time, attention, energies, and best efforts to rendering services on behalf of the Company and shall not, without the prior written consent of the Company, during the terms of this Agreement, engage in the rendering of such services or in any other business activity (whether or not such business activity is pursued for gain, profit, or other pecuniary advantage). This restriction, however, shall not be construed as preventing the Employee from expending reasonable amounts of time for charitable and professional activities or from investing his assets in such form or manner as will not require any services on the part of the Employee in the operation of the affairs of the companies in which such investments are made.

6.   WORKING FACILITIES. The Company, at its own expense, shall furnish the Employee with supplies, equipment, and such other facilities and services suitable to his position and adequate for the performance of the assigned duties.

7.   TERMINATION. This Employment Agreement shall be terminated and the relationship between the Employee and the Company shall be deemed severed upon the occurrence of any of the following:

(a) Upon the death of the Employee during his employment.

(b) If the Employee shall voluntarily cease to render the services for which he was hired.

(c) Upon the imposition of any governmental authority having jurisdiction over the Employee to such extent that he cannot engage in the duties for which he was employed.

(d) If the Employee fails or refuses to faithfully and diligently perform the usual and customary duties of his employment and adhere to the provisions of this Employment Agreement.

(e) If the Employee fails or refuses to comply with the reasonable policies, standards, and regulations of the Company that from time to time may be established.

(f) If the Employee conducts himself in an unprofessional, unethical, immoral, or fraudulent manner, or the Employee's conduct discredits the Company or is detrimental to the reputation, character and standing of the Company.

If the Employee terminates, in accordance with any of the provisions of this Paragraph 7, the Employee shall be entitled to receive such compensation, if any, accrued under the terms of this Employment Agreement, but unpaid as of the date of actual termination of employment.

8.   NONCOMPETITION AGREEMENT.

(a) Upon termination of this Employment Agreement by Employee pursuant to paragraph 7 (b), Employee will not directly or indirectly solicit, contact, or induce any Pipeline Prospect of the Company to patronize any person, firm, or association rendering products or services similar to those rendered by the Company, hereinafter referred to as the Competitor, for twelve (12) months form his date of termination, nor will the Employee directly or indirectly handle, manage, supervise, render, or perform any service for a Pipeline Prospect of the Company similar to those rendered by the Company on behalf of the Competitor for a twelve (12) month period following termination of the Employment Agreement.

Furthermore upon termination of the Employment Agreement pursuant to paragraph 7(b), Employee is precluded from accepting employment with another multilevel marketing company engaged in the sale of technology-based products for a two (2) year period following the date of termination.

(b) For the purposes of this Agreement, a "Pipeline Prospect" shall be defined as any prospect which in the six months prior to the Employee's termination date:

(i) received a proposal or engagement letter from the Company or

(ii) had a meeting with Employee or any manager of the Company for the purpose of developing a client relationship.

(iii) the Employee will not directly or indirectly solicit, contact, or induce any client of the Company to patronize any person, firm, or association rendering products or services similar to those rendered by the Company, hereinafter referred to as the Competitor, for a two (2) year period following termination of this Employment Agreement, nor will the Employee directly or indirectly handle, manage, supervise, render, or perform any service for a client of the Company similar to those rendered by the Company or on behalf of the Competitor for a two (2) year period following termination of the Employment Agreement.

(iv) In the event of a breach of this Provision, the Employee agrees to pay the Company two times the fees billed to any client serviced by the Competitor firm for the twelve (12) months after obtaining a Pipeline Prospect as a client.

(v) In the event of a breach of this Provision, the Employee agrees to pay the Company an amount equal to the fees billed by the Company to the applicable client during the two (2) year period prior to and ending on the earlier of the date (the "Engagement Date") the Employee or Competitor (i) began providing services to the Company client. Said amount shall be paid in full to the Company within fifteen (15) days after the Engagement Date.

(vi) In the event that the enforcement of the covenant contained in this Provision becomes the subject of any legal action, it is intended that the periods referred to in this Provision shall not begin to run until the entry of a final judicial order granting enforcement of such covenant.

(vii) In the event that a court of competent jurisdiction shall determine in any case that the enforcement of the covenant contained in this Provision would not be reasonable, but that enforcement of a covenant which is more limited in time or geographic area would be reasonable, it is intended that the more limited covenant determined by such court to be reasonable shall be given in such case in lieu of the covenant contained in this Provision.

9.   NONSOLICITATION OF EMPLOYEES. At all times during the period of the Employee's employment and for three (3) years after termination of this Employment Agreement, the Employee will not directly or indirectly, hire or employ any employee of the Company or otherwise encourage or entice any employee of the Company to leave his or her employment; provided, however, if the Company seeks injunctive relief pursuant to Section 11 of this Employment Agreement, said three (3) years period will extend from the date of docketing the injunction or entry of a court order granting injunctive relief, but in no event will such three (3) year period extend beyond four (4) years from the termination date of this Employment Agreement.

10.   PROPRIETARY INFORMATION. All files, workpapers, spreadsheets, records, financial information, database information, and similar items (including any photocopies or electronic media versions of any of the above) relating to the Company as well as any Company client or prospective client, whether prepared by the Employee or otherwise coming into the Employee's possession, will at all times remain the exclusive property of the Company. The Employee agrees not to make or retain copies of such materials in his possession after the date of termination of this Employment Agreement.

11.   INJUNCTIVE RELIEF. The Employee agrees that the breach or threat of breach or attempted breach of any provision of Sections 8, 9, and 10 of this Employment Agreement will cause irreparable harm to the Company for which any remedies at law would be inadequate. Accordingly, in the event of any breach or threatened or attempted breach of any such provision by the Employee, the Company will, in addition to and not to the exclusion of any other rights and remedies at law or in equity, be entitled to:

(a) full temporary and permanent injunctive relief enjoining and restraining the Employee from continuing such volatile acts or a decree for specific performance of the provisions of said Sections of this Employment Agreement, without being required to show actual damage or irreparable harm, or to furnish a bond or other security, or

(b) damages to the Company caused by the Employee. Further, the Employee will not plead in defense thereto that there would be adequate remedy at law.

12.   LEGAL FEES. Employee agrees that if the Employee is found in violation of any provision of Sections 8, 9, or 10 of the Employment Agreement in any legal proceeding (including any appeal thereof) brought by the Company, Employee shall pay to the Company all costs and expenses (including, without limitation, court costs and reasonable attorneys' fees) incurred by the Company with respect to such proceeding.

13.   ALTERATION, AMENDMENT, OR TERMINATION. No change or modification of this Employment Agreement shall be valid unless the same is in writing and signed by all parties thereto. No waiver of any provision of this Employment Agreement shall be valid unless in writing and signed by the person against whom it is sought to be enforced. The failure of any party at any time to insist upon strict performance of any condition, promise, agreement, or understanding set forth herein shall not be construed as a waiver or relinquishment of the right to insist upon strict performance of the same condition, promise, agreement, or understanding at a future time. The invalidity or unenforceability of any particular provision of this Employment Agreement shall be construed in all respects as if such invalid or unenforceable provisions were omitted.

14. INTEGRATION. This Employment Agreement sets forth (and is intended to be an integration of) all promises, agreements, conditions, warranties, understandings, and representations, oral or written, express or implied, among them with respect to the terms of employment other than as set forth herein.

15. CONFLICTS OF LAW. This Employment Agreement shall be subject to and governed by the laws of the State of Delaware irrespective of the fact that one or more of the parties now is or may become a resident of another state.

16. BENEFIT AND BURDEN. This Employment Agreement shall inure to the benefit of, and shall be binding upon, the parties hereto and their respective successors, heirs, and personal representatives. This Employment Agreement shall not be assignable.

In Witness Whereof, the Company has caused this Employment Agreement to be signed by its duly authorized officers and its corporate seal to be affixed hereto, and each of the parties hereto has executed this Agreement on the date and year above written.

ATTEST: GrowCo, Inc.

_____

Secretary   President

WITNESS: _____

EMPLOYEE: _____

Lock-Up and Registration Rights Agreement

This **Registration Rights Agreement** (the "Agreement") is made by and among GrowCo, Inc. (the "Company"), and _____ (the "Holder").

Recitals

A.   This Agreement is entered into in connection with the Stock Purchase Agreement ("Stock Purchase Agreement"), dated as of _____, 201___, by and among the Company, the Holder, and certain affiliates thereof, relating to the sale by the Holder of all of the issued and outstanding capital stock of GrowCo, Inc.

B.   In order to induce the Holder to enter into the Stock Purchase Agreement, the Company has agreed to grant the Holder one-time demand registration rights and limited follow-on registration rights as set forth below for the benefit of the Holder and certain direct transferees.

C.   In order to induce the Company to enter into the Stock Purchase Agreement and related agreements and to issue _____ shares (the "Shares") of common stock of the Company, par value $.01 (the "Common Stock"), the Holder has agreed to be bound by certain restrictions on the transfers of the Shares as set forth below for the benefit of the Company, its affiliates, successors, and assigns.

Agreements

The Company and the Holder covenant and agree as follows:

1.   CERTAIN DEFINITIONS. For purposes of this Agreement:

a. The terms **"register," "registered"** and **"registration"** refer to a registration effected by preparing and filing a registration statement or statements or similar documents in compliance with the Securities Act of 1933, as amended (the "Securities Act") and pursuant to Rule 415 under the Securities Act or any successor rule providing for offering securities on a continuous basis ("Rule 415") and the declaration or ordering of effectiveness of such registration statement or document by the Securities and Exchange Commission (the "SEC").

b. The term "Registrable Securities" means (i) the Shares, and (ii) any Common Stock of the Company issued as (or issuable upon the conversion or exercise of any convertible security, warrant, right, or other security which is issued as) a dividend or other distribution with respect to, or in exchange for, or in replacement of, the Shares.

c. The term "Permitted Transferee" means any member of Holder's immediate family to whom a transfer of Registrable Securities is made solely for estate planning purposes.

d. Any capitalized terms not defined herein have the meanings set forth in the Stock Purchase Agreement.

2.   REGISTRATION.

a. (i) **Subject to the restrictions set forth in Section 8 below**, in the event that the Company proposes, at any time during the two-year period following the date of this Agreement, to file a registration statement on a general form of registration under the Securities Act and relating to shares of Common Stock issued or to be issued by it, then the Company shall give written notice of such proposal to the Holder and to Permitted Transferees, if any. If, within 10 days after the giving of such notice, the Holder or any Permitted Transferee shall request in writing that all or a portion of the Registrable Securities be included in such proposed registration, the Company will, at its own expense (except as set forth in Section 2(c) hereof), also register such securities as shall have been so requested in writing; provided, however, that the Holder and any Permitted Transferee shall cooperate with the Company in the preparation of such registration statement to the extent required to furnish information concerning the Holder and any Permitted Transferee as the Securities and Exchange Commission or its rules and regulations may require.

(ii) Other than as provided in Section 2(a)(i) and subject to the restrictions set forth in Section 8 below, the Holder may request that the Company register the Registrable Securities by filing a registration statement on a general form of registration under the Securities Act, in which case the Company shall use its best efforts to (A) effect the registration under the Securities Act of all Registrable Securities, and (B) register and qualify the Registrable Securities under such securities or Blue Sky laws of such states as shall be reasonably requested by the Holder and to take all other actions necessary or advisable to enable the disposition of such Registrable Securities in such states, provided that the Company shall not be required in connection therewith or as a condition thereto to qualify to do business or to file a general consent to service of process in any such states. The Holder shall be entitled to make and the Company shall be obligated to respond to only one request under this Section 2(a)(ii).

b. In connection with the filing of a registration statement pursuant to Section 2(a)(i) or (ii) hereof, the Company shall:

(i) notify the Holder and any Permitted Transferee as to the filing thereof and of all amendments thereto filed prior to the effective date of said registration statement;

(ii) notify the Holder and any Permitted Transferee promptly after it shall have received notice thereof, of the time when the registration statement becomes effective or any supplement to any prospectus forming a part of the registration statement has been filed;

(iii) prepare and file without expense to the Holder or any Permitted Transferee any necessary amendment or supplement to such registration statement or prospectus as may be necessary to comply with Section 10(a)(3) of the Securities Act or advisable in connection with the proposed distribution of the Registrable Securities by the Holder or any Permitted Transferee; unless the provisions of Section 2(c) are applicable;

(iv) take all reasonable steps to qualify the Registrable Securities being so registered for sale under the securities or Blue Sky laws in such reasonable number of states as Holder or any Permitted Transferee may designate in writing and to register or obtain the approval of any federal or state authority which may be required in connection with the proposed distribution, except, in each case, in jurisdictions in which the Company must either qualify to do business or file a general consent to service of process as a condition to the qualification of such securities;

(v) notify the Holder and any Permitted Transferee of any stop order suspending the effectiveness of the registration statement and use its reasonable best efforts to remove such stop order; and

(vi) furnish to the Holder and any Permitted Transferee, as soon as available, copies of any such registration statement and each preliminary or final prospectus and any supplement or amendment required to be prepared pursuant to the foregoing provisions of this Section 2, all in such quantities as such owners may from time to time reasonably request. Upon written request, the Company shall also furnish to each owner, without cost, one set of the exhibits to such registration statement.

c. If the Company gives notice pursuant to this Section 2(a)(i) for the purpose of permitting registration (whether involving an underwritten or other offering) of Registrable Securities, the Company shall have the right to determine the aggregate size of the offering and to limit the number of shares to be registered at the request of Holder or any Permitted Transferee pursuant to Section 2(a), including the right to exclude all shares to be registered at the request of Holder or any Permitted Transferee, if the Company's underwriters or financial advisors provide Holder with written notice of their determination that such limitation or exclusion is necessary or advisable to ensure a successful offering of the Company securities. If the Company limits the number of (but does not exclude) such Registrable Securities, the maximum number of shares to be registered on behalf of Holder or any Permitted Transferee shall be determined by multiplying the number of shares of Registrable Securities such holder has properly requested be registered by a fraction, the numerator of which shall be the number of shares of Common Stock to be included in such registration by all selling shareholders, and the denominator of which is the number of shares of Common Stock validly requested to be included in such registration by all holders of Common Stock having registration rights.

d. The Holder and any Permitted Transferee agree to pay all of the underwriting discounts and commissions and their own counsel fees with respect to the Registrable Securities owned by them and being registered.

e. The Company agrees to use reasonable efforts to negotiate and enter into a usual and customary appropriate cross-indemnity agreement with any underwriter (as defined in the Securities Act) for the Holder and any Permitted Transferee in connection with the filing of a registration statement pursuant to Section 2 hereof.

f. The Company agrees to use reasonable efforts to negotiate and enter into a usual and customary appropriate cross-indemnity agreement with the Holder and such registered owners.

3.   REGISTRATION STATEMENT. When required under this Agreement to effect the registration of the Registrable Securities under Section 2(a)(ii), the Company shall, as soon as practicable, prepare and file with the SEC a registration statement (the "Registration Statement") with respect to all Registrable Securities, use its best efforts to cause the Registration Statement to become effective not later than on the earliest practicable date, and to keep the Registration Statement effective at all times until all of the Securities shall have been publicly sold or are capable of public sale without registration under the Securities Act (whether or not subject to any volume limitations under Rule 144), which Registration Statement (including any amendments or supplements thereto and prospectuses contained therein) shall not contain any untrue statement of a material fact or omit to state a material fact required to be stated therein or necessary to make the statements therein not misleading. The holders of a majority in interest of the Registrable Securities shall have the right to select underwriters, if any, from time to time in connection with the sale of Registrable Securities (although no Holder shall be obligated to make any such sale at such time), subject to the approval of the Company, which shall not be unreasonably withheld.

4.   FURNISH INFORMATION. It shall be a condition precedent to the obligations of the Company to take any action pursuant to this Agreement with respect to Holder or any Permitted Transferee that Holder and any Permitted Transferee shall furnish to the Company such information regarding itself, the Registrable Securities held by it, and the intended method of disposition of such securities as shall be reasonably required to effect the registration of the Registrable Securities and shall execute such documents in connection with such registration as the Company may reasonably request.

5.   EXPENSES OF REGISTRATION. All expenses, other than underwriting discounts and commissions, incurred by the Company or any Holder in connection with the transactions contemplated by this Agreement, including, without limitation, the registration, filing, or qualification of the Registrable Securities and all registration, listing, filing, and qualification fees, printers fees, accounting fees (including the expenses of any "cold comfort" letters), the fees and disbursements of counsel for the Company shall be borne by the Company; provided, however, the Company shall not be required to pay for expenses of any registration begun pursuant to Section 2(a)(ii), the request for which has been subsequently withdrawn by any Holder, in which case, such expenses shall be borne by the Holder requesting such withdrawal.

6.   INDEMNIFICATION.

a. The Company will indemnify and hold harmless Holder, Permitted Transferees, and any underwriter (as defined in the Securities Act and the Securities Exchange Act of 1934, as amended (the "Exchange Act")) with respect to any Registrable Securities sold by the Holder and each person, if any, who controls any such underwriter within the meaning of the Securities Act or the Exchange Act (collectively, the "Holder Indemnified Parties"), against any losses, claims, damages, expenses, or liabilities (joint or several) to which any of them may become subject under the Securities Act, the Exchange Act, or otherwise, insofar as such losses, claims, damages, expenses, or liabilities (or actions or proceedings, whether commenced or threatened, in respect thereof) arise out of or are based upon any of the following statements, omissions, or violations (collectively, a "Violation"): (i) any untrue statement or alleged untrue statement of a material fact contained in the Registration Statement, including any preliminary prospectus or final prospectus contained therein or any amendments or supplements thereto, (ii) the omission or alleged omission to state therein information required to be stated therein, or necessary to make the statements therein not misleading, or (iii) any violation or alleged violation by the Company of the Securities Act, the Exchange Act, or any state securities or Blue Sky law; and the Company will reimburse each Holder Indemnified Party, promptly as such expenses are incurred, for any legal or other expenses reasonably incurred by any of them in connection with investigating or defending any such loss, claim, damage, liability, action, or proceeding; provided, however, that the indemnity agreement contained in this Section 6(a) shall not apply to amounts paid in settlement of any such loss, claim, damage, expense, liability, action, or proceeding if such settlement is effected without the consent of the Company, which consent shall not be unreasonably withheld, nor shall the Company be liable in any such case for any such loss, claim, damage, expense, liability, action, or proceeding to the extent that it arises out of or is based upon a Violation which occurs in reliance upon and in conformity with written information furnished expressly for use in the Registration Statement by the Holder, Permitted Transferee, or any such underwriter, as the case may be. Such indemnity shall remain in full force and effect regardless of any investigation made by or on behalf of the Holder Indemnified Parties and shall survive the transfer of the Registrable Securities by Holder to a Permitted Transferee.

b. Each Holder and Permitted Transferee, jointly and severally, will indemnify and hold harmless the Company, each of its directors, each of its officers who has signed the Registration Statement, each person, if any, who controls the Company within the meaning of the Securities Act or the Exchange Act (collectively, the "Company Indemnified Parties") against any losses, claims, damages, expenses, or liabilities (joint or several) to which any of them may become subject, under the Securities Act, the Exchange Act, or other federal or state law, insofar as such losses, claims, damages, expenses, or liabilities (or actions in respect thereof) arise out of or are based upon: (i) any untrue statement or alleged untrue statement of a material fact contained in the Registration Statement, including any preliminary prospectus or final prospectus contained therein or any amendments or supplements thereto, and (ii) the omission or alleged omission to state therein information required to be stated therein, or necessary to make the statements therein not misleading, in each case to the extent (and only to the extent) that such losses, claims, damages, expenses, or liabilities are caused by statements made in the Registration Statement in reliance upon and in conformity with written information furnished by such Holder expressly for use therein; and such Holder and Permitted Transferee will reimburse any legal or other expenses reasonably incurred by any of them in connection with investigating or defending any such loss, claim, damage, liability, action, or proceeding; provided, however, that the indemnity agreement contained in this Section 6(b) shall not apply to amounts paid in settlement of any such loss, claim, damage, expense, liability, action, or proceeding if such settlement is effected without the consent of such Holder, which consent shall not be reasonably withheld; provided, further, that no Holder or Permitted Transferee shall be liable under this Section 6(b) for any amount of losses, claims, damages, expenses, or liabilities in excess of the net proceeds to such Holder or Permitted Transferee from the sale of Registrable Securities that are the subject of the loss, claim, damage, expense, liability, action, or proceeding giving rise to the request for indemnification under this Section 6.

c. Promptly after receipt by an indemnified party under this Section 6 of notice of the commencement of any action (including any governmental action), such indemnified party shall, if a claim in respect thereof is to be made against any indemnifying party under this Section 6, deliver to the indemnifying party a written notice of the commencement thereof and the indemnifying party shall have the right to participate in and, to the extent the indemnifying party so desires, jointly with any other indemnifying party similarly notified, to assume control of the defense thereof with counsel mutually satisfactory to the indemnifying and indemnified parties; provided, however, that an indemnified party shall have the right to retain its own counsel, with the fees and expenses to be paid by the indemnifying party, if, in the reasonable opinion of counsel for the indemnified party, representation of such indemnified party by the counsel retained by the indemnifying party would be inappropriate due to actual or potential differing interests between such indemnified party and any other party represented by such counsel in such proceeding. The failure to deliver written notice to the indemnifying party within a reasonable time of the commencement of any such action shall relieve such indemnifying party of any liability to the indemnified party under this Section 6 only to the extent prejudicial to its ability to defend such action, but the omission so to deliver written notice to the indemnifying party shall not relieve it of any liability that it may have to any indemnified party otherwise than under this Section 6. The indemnification required by this Section 6 shall be made by periodic payments of the amount thereof during the course of the investigation or defense; promptly as such expense, loss, damage, or liability is incurred.

d. To the extent any indemnification by an indemnifying party is prohibited or limited by law, or is otherwise unavailable to or insufficient to hold harmless an indemnified party, the indemnifying party agrees to make the maximum contribution with respect to any amounts for which it would otherwise be liable under this Section 6, provided that (i) no person guilty of fraudulent misrepresentation (within the meaning of Section 11(f) of the Securities Act) shall be entitled to contribution from any person who was not guilty of such fraudulent misrepresentation and (ii) the maximum amount of any contribution by any Holder or Permitted Transferee shall be limited in amount to the net proceeds received by such Holder or Permitted Transferee from the sale of Registrable Securities that are the subject of the loss, claim, damage, expense, liability, action, or proceeding giving rise to the request for indemnification or contribution under this Section 6.

7.   REPORTS UNDER THE EXCHANGE ACT. With a view to making available to Holder and any Permitted Transferee the benefits of Rule 144 ("Rule 144") under the Securities Act and any other rule or regulation of the SEC that may at any time permit Holder or a Permitted Transferee to sell securities of the Company to the public without registration, the Company agrees to use its best efforts to:

a. make and keep public information available, as those terms are understood and defined in Rule 144, at all times after 90 days after the effective date of a registration statement filed by the Company for the initial offering of its securities to the general public;

b. file with the SEC in a timely manner all reports and other documents required of the Company under the Securities Act and the Exchange Act; and

c. furnish to each Holder and Permitted Transferee, so long as such Holder or Permitted Transferee owns any Registrable Securities, forthwith upon request (i) a written statement by the Company that it has complied with the reporting requirements of Rule 144 (at any time after 90 days after the effective date of the first registration statement filed by the Company with the SEC), (ii) a copy of the most recent annual or quarterly report of the Company and such other reports and documents so filed by the Company and (iii) such other publicly available information as may be reasonably requested in availing the Holder of any rule or regulation of the SEC which permits the selling of any such securities without registration.

8.   TRANSFER RESTRICTIONS. The Holder hereby agrees that, without the prior written consent of the Company, he will not, during the period commencing on the date hereof and ending on the first anniversary of the date of this Agreement, offer, pledge, sell, contract to sell, sell any option or contract to purchase, purchase any option or contract to sell, grant any option, right or warrant to purchase, or otherwise transfer or dispose of, directly or indirectly, any Registrable Securities or any securities convertible into or exercisable or exchangeable for, directly or indirectly, or (2) enter into any swap or other arrangement that transfers to another, in whole or in part, any of the economic consequences of ownership of the Registrable Securities, whether any such transaction described in clause (1) or (2) above is to be settled by delivery of Common Stock or such other securities, in cash or otherwise. In addition, the Holder agrees that, without prior written consent of the Company, it will not, during the period commencing on the date hereof and ending on the first anniversary of the date of this Agreement, make any demand for or exercise any right with respect to, the registration of any Registrable Securities or any security convertible into or exercisable or exchangeable for Common Stock. Notwithstanding any of the foregoing restrictions to the contrary, Holder may, with the consent of the Company, which consent shall not be unreasonably withheld, transfer all or a portion of the Registrable Securities to one or more Permitted Transferee(s); provided, however, that such Permitted Transferee shall be subject all the transfer restrictions applicable to Holder without the Permitted Transferee exception (which shall be available only to Holder).

9.   ASSIGNMENT OF REGISTRATION RIGHTS. Rights under this Agreement may be assigned by Holder only to Permitted Transferees of such Holder's Registrable Securities; provided, however, that the Company is, within a reasonable time after such transfer or assignment, furnished with written notice of the name and address of such transferee or assignee and the Registrable Securities with respect to which such registration rights are being assigned; provided, further, that such assignment shall be effective only if, immediately following such transfer or assignment, the further disposition of such securities by the transferee or assignee is restricted under the Securities Act. This Agreement shall be binding upon and inure to the benefit of the respective heirs, successors, and assigns of the parties hereto.

10. MISCELLANEOUS.

a. Notices required or permitted to be given hereunder shall be in writing and shall be deemed to be sufficiently given when personally delivered or sent by registered mail, return receipt requested, addressed (i) if to the Company, to GrowCo, Inc., 1234 Main Street, Anytown, USA 12345, Attention: Chief Financial Officer, and (ii) if to a Holder, at the address set forth in the Stock Purchase Agreement entered into with the Company or at such other address as each such party furnishes by notice given in accordance with this Section 10(a). This Agreement may be executed in any number of counterparts, each of which shall be an original, but all of which together shall constitute one instrument.

b. Failure of any party to exercise any right or remedy under this Agreement or otherwise, or delay by a party in exercising such right or remedy, will not operate as a waiver thereof. No waiver will be effective unless and until it is in writing and signed by the party giving the waiver.

c. This Agreement shall be enforced, governed by, and construed in all respects in accordance with the laws of the State of _____, as such laws are applied by _____ courts to agreements entered into and to be performed in _____ by and between residents of _____. In the event that any provision of this Agreement is invalid or unenforceable under any applicable statute or rule of law, then such provision shall be deemed inoperative to the extent that it may conflict therewith and shall be deemed modified to conform with such statute or rule of law. Any provision hereof which may prove invalid or unenforceable under any law shall not affect the validity or enforceability of any other provision hereof.

d. This Agreement constitutes the entire agreement between the parties hereto with respect to the subject matter hereof and may be amended only by a writing executed by the Company and the Holder and any Permitted Transferees.

Dated this _____ day of _____, 201_____.

ATTEST: GrowCo, Inc.

_____

Secretary   President

WITNESS: _____

EMPLOYEE: _____

Checklist for a Typical Underwriter's Due Diligence Request

Below is a list of subjects and documents to be covered in connection with the corporate review/due diligence investigation of _____ (the "Company") for the proposed initial public offering. Please make available all documents relevant to the subjects listed below. If no documents are available with respect to a particular subject, we would appreciate the opportunity to interview management employees familiar with the subject matter.

Please provide a response in connection with each item described below, stating which documents are delivered in response to which inquiry and noting the extent to which any request is inapplicable. If there are any questions do not hesitate to contact _____ at _____.

I.   General Corporate Matters

A.   CHARTER DOCUMENTS/CORPORATE STRUCTURE

1. Certificate of Incorporation and Bylaws (including any amendments) of the Company and any subsidiaries or other entities, if any, in which the Company has a controlling equity or other ownership interest. The term "subsidiary" as used in this checklist covers all such entities.

2. List of Subsidiaries, including an organizational chart showing ownership of such entities and any agreements relating to the Company's interest.

3. List of states and other jurisdictions (including other countries) in which the Company or any of its subsidiaries are qualified to do business as foreign corporations, or in which its or their trade names are registered, and description of Company (or subsidiary) operations in such states or other jurisdictions.

4. List of each state in which the Company or any subsidiary maintains an office or an agent who resides in such state and in which the Company or the subsidiary is not qualified to do business and/or does not file tax returns.

B.   CAPITAL STOCK

1. Description of the classes of authorized capital stock of the Company and any subsidiaries, and a statement of the number of issued and outstanding shares of each class and any conversion rights associated therewith.

2. Access to the stock books and stock transfer ledgers of the Company and each of its subsidiaries.

3. All documents creating restrictions with respect to any class of capital stock.

4. All agreements, warrants, options, or other rights to purchase or acquire any shares of capital stock or other securities of the Company or any of its subsidiaries, and any commitments, including stock option plans, with respect to the foregoing. Indicate for each agreement, warrant, option, or other rights, the date issued or granted, the number of shares presently exercisable or convertible into, the consideration received or to be received by the Company, and a copy of the form of such option, warrant, agreement, or right.

5. All agreements among stockholders of the Company with respect to the voting and/or sale or other disposition of shares of the Company's capital stock and all agreements to which the Company is a party with respect to the voting and/or sale or other disposition of the stock of other companies owned by the Company.

6. List of all family and other relationships known to the Company among stockholders that might indicate beneficial ownership of stock other than as shown on the stock record books of the Company.

7. List of the names of all stockholders of the Company and the number of shares of each class held by each such stockholder.

8. Documents relating to all offerings and issuances of securities by the Company and any of its subsidiaries.

9. An analysis of the dilution that would result from the exercise of all outstanding warrants, options, and other rights to purchase stock by conversion or otherwise and a computation of any antidilution adjustments applicable to any securities resulting from the contemplated transaction.

10. List of and records relating to all dividends paid since the Company's inception, indicating preferred and common dividends separately, if applicable, and stating whether paid in cash or stock. List of the amount(s) of any dividends in arrears.

11. Documents relating to all inquiries and/or indications of interest with respect to investments in the Company.

C.   MINUTES

1. Minutes of all meetings of, and all actions in lieu of a meeting by, the Board of Directors (and of all committees thereof) of the Company and any subsidiaries since the Company's inception.

2. Minutes of all meetings of, and all actions without a meeting by, the stockholders of the Company and each of its subsidiaries since the Company's inception.

D.   ORGANIZATION

1. Description of the management structure of the Company and each of its subsidiaries, including any organizational charts.

2. List of the names and addresses of officers and directors of the Company and each of its subsidiaries.

3. List of all family relationships among the officers, directors, principal stockholders, and/or key employees of the Company and each of its subsidiaries.

4. List of all of the Company's promoters and any consideration they have received or may receive.

5. List of all agreements or other instruments pursuant to which capital stock has been issued to promoters or otherwise.

II.   Claims, Litigation, and Arbitration

A. Description of the status of each presently threatened or pending claim, litigation, or arbitration, and of each claim, litigation, or arbitration concluded or settled since the Company's inception, as to which the Company or any subsidiary is a party (whether as plaintiff or defendant, and including specifically claims or proceedings before any state commission or agency).

B. Description of any outstanding judgments against the Company or any subsidiary.

C. Description of any bankruptcy, criminal, or other judicial proceeding pending, expected, or completed within the past five years involving the Company, any of its subsidiaries, or any of the Company's officers, directors, or principal stockholders.

III. Compliance with Laws

A. List of all governmental agencies to which the Company reports and a brief description of significant laws or regulations, existing or proposed, affecting the industry or operations of the Company.

B. Description of all recent, current, and/or threatened claims or citations for failure by the Company or any subsidiary to comply with applicable laws, including environmental laws, consumer laws, occupational health and safety laws, labor and equal employment opportunity laws, etc., and measures presently being taken to ensure compliance.

C. Description of current status of any federal and state regulatory audits and inspections, including environmental, occupational health and safety, etc.

IV. Personal and Employee Benefits

A.   CONTRACTS WITH EMPLOYEES

1. All employment and/or consulting contracts with any officers, directors, and/or employees of, or consultants to, the Company or its subsidiaries, including a description of any oral agreements.

2. All other contracts with any officers, directors, and/or employees of, or consultants to, the Company or its subsidiaries, including confidentiality agreements, noncompetition agreements, etc.

B.   EMPLOYEE BENEFITS

1. Description of all pension and profit-sharing plans and other employee benefit plans, including bonus plans, stock purchase or bonus plans or arrangements, stock option plans, group or key-man life insurance plans, salary continuation plans, supplemental unemployment benefit plans, medical insurance or reimbursement plans, etc., and any amendments or proposed amendments to any such plans, and copies of each (including those specified below).

2. (a) For each pension plan (including any terminated plan):

(i) Plan documents (including related trust documents) with all amendments;

(ii) Directors' resolutions adopting plan and all amendments;

(iii) Summary Plan Description;

(iv) All IRS determination letters;

(v) Applications for IRS determination letters (Form 5300 or 5301 and attachments);

(vi) Annual Returns/Reports (Forms 5500) for past five years; and

(vii) All correspondence regarding the plan with/from IRS, Department of Labor, and/or Pension Benefit Guaranty Corporation during past five years.

(b) For each welfare benefit plan:

(i) Plan document (including any related trust documents or insurance contract) and all amendments;

(ii) Summary Plan Description; and

(iii) Annual Returns/Reports (Forms 5500) for past five years.

(c) For each stock option or similar plan involving capital stock of the Company:

(i) The number of options, rights, shares, units, etc., granted to each director, officer, employee, and stockholder under any such plans;

(ii) the dates on which any such options, rights, shares, units, etc., were granted, and the dates on which they are exercisable (if applicable); and

(iii) the terms of such options.

3. A description of any other benefits given to any officer, director, employee, or principal stockholder, including benefits such as club memberships, automobiles, housing, etc.

C. CONTRACTS WITH UNIONS. All contracts, agreements, or side letters with unions to which the Company or any subsidiary is a party.

D. EMPLOYMENT POLICIES. Any statement, handbook, or manual of employment policies, including working hours, overtime pay, workers compensation, unemployment compensation, vacation and sick pay, emergency leave, etc.

E. INTERNAL LOANS BY THE COMPANY. A list of all loans or guaranties that the Company or any subsidiary has made since its inception to any officer, director, employee, or stockholder.

F. DIRECTORS AND OFFICERS. Biographies, résumés, and copies of all Directors and Officers questionnaires.

V.   Intellectual Property Rights

A.   SOFTWARE AGREEMENTS

1. Schedule and copies of all Research and Development Agreements, licensing agreements, and confidentiality agreements.

B.   TRADE AND SERVICE MARKS

1. Schedule and description of all trade names and trade and service marks to which the Company and its subsidiaries have (or had) title or other rights.

2. Evidence of registration of all trade or service marks that have been registered with the U.S. Patent and Trademark Office (the "PTO") and correspondence with the PTO with respect thereto.

3. Any royalty and similar agreements relating to the use of such trademarks or service marks.

C.   PATENTS, COPYRIGHTS, AND OTHER RIGHTS. Schedule and description of all patents, copyrights, and other intellectual property rights owned by or assigned to the Company and its subsidiaries (to the extent not covered elsewhere on this list) showing for each: nature of patent, patent number, date of issue, date acquired, cost, reserve or amortization, present book value, and intrinsic value.

D.   GENERALLY

1. All royalty or other agreements relating to software, trade names, trade or service marks, patents, copyrights, licenses, or other similar rights.

2. All pending or proposed applications for trade or service marks, patents, copyrights, or other similar rights, or pending or proposed license agreements therefor, owned or used (or proposed to be owned or used) in the business of the Company or its subsidiaries.

3. Description of any actual or threatened disputes or claims of infringement, invalidity, etc., of (or relating to) trade or service marks, trade names, patents, copyrights, or other similar rights owned or used by the Company and its subsidiaries.

4. Description of and any policy statements of the Company and its subsidiaries with respect to research and development by employees and consultants of the Company and its subsidiaries, including copies of any assignment agreements and employee trade secret and nondisclosure agreements.

VI. Real Property

A.   SCHEDULE AND DESCRIPTION of all real property owned by the Company and its subsidiaries, including the following:

1. Location

2. Description

3. Date of Purchase

4. Description of any liens or mortgages

B. Evidence of title to real estate, including land, buildings, and fixtures (e.g., copy of deed into the Company).

C. Copies of leases or assignments of lease agreements of real property in which the Company or any subsidiary is (i) a lessee or assignee of a lessee, or (ii) a lessor.

D. Title insurance policy covering each parcel of real property issued in connection with the acquisition of such property by the Company or any subsidiary and any endorsements thereto or other subsequent title reports.

E. All documents referred to in each of the foregoing title insurance policies, and all documents relating to any subsequent liens, easements, restrictions, or other encumbrances.

F. Value reports or appraisals of any real property owned by the Company or any subsidiary.

G. Evidence of payment of all real estate and personal property taxes and other governmental fees, assessments, or charges levied on any real property owned by the Company or any subsidiary.

H. Environmental audits, engineering studies, soil tests, and similar evaluations or reports with respect to any property owned by the Company or any subsidiary.

VII. Other Property and Rights

A. Sale and Leaseback Agreements. Any sale and leaseback agreements or arrangements or financing leases of the Company or its subsidiaries relating to the acquisition of capital assets, through leases.

B. Conditional Sale Agreements. Any conditional sale agreements, mortgages, etc., relating to the acquisition of assets on an installment basis.

C. Equipment and Other Nonrealty Leases. All leases on equipment (including computers), long distance transmission facilities, and other material personal property.

D. Other Property. Schedule and description, including manner of ownership or holding, of other significant personal property.

E. Permits, Licenses, Etc. Schedule of all governmental permits, licenses, and approvals (including specifically permits, licenses, and approvals issued by any state commission or agency) held by the Company or any subsidiary and of all tariffs and similar filings made by the Company or any subsidiary thereof with any federal or state government, commission, or agency.

VIII. Insurance

A. Schedule of insurance coverage summarizing all policies, including information as to the carrier, effective dates, coverage amount, and premium amount with respect to each policy.

B. All insurance policies covering the Company or any subsidiary (complete policies with all current premium information), including:

1. Title insurance

2. Property insurance

3. Corporate liability insurance

4. Directors and officers liability insurance

5. Stop-loss, catastrophic, and similar insurance

6. Other forms of insurance.

C. CLAIMS EXPERIENCE FOR THE LAST FIVE YEARS under each of the above policies.

IX.   Financing and Banking

A.   CREDIT AGREEMENTS AND LOANS TO THE COMPANY

1. **All agreements of the Company or its subsidiaries** relating to the borrowing of money, including term loan and revolving credit agreements and debt instruments and any other agreements issued thereunder, and the current balance of each such source of indebtedness.

2. **All guaranties of any of the Company's borrowings,** including without limitation, letters of credit and guaranties by other entities or persons (including specifically any of the Company's promoters, officers, directors, employees, or stockholders).

3. **All documents evidencing security interests** against real property, personal property, or other tangible or intangible property of the Company or any subsidiary and an indication of where such documents are filed.

B.   LOANS OR GUARANTIES MADE BY THE COMPANY

1. **All agreements of the Company or its subsidiaries** relating to loans by the Company or its subsidiaries to, or guaranties of the obligations of, other entities or persons (including specifically the Company's promoters, officers, directors, employees, or stockholders).

2. **All documents evidencing security interests taken by the Company** in real or personal property of others and an indication of where such documents and/or financing statements are filed.

C. OTHER INDEBTEDNESS. Any other information or documents evidencing indebtedness of the Company or any subsidiary.

D. BANKING RELATIONSHIPS. Schedule of banking relationships of the Company and its subsidiaries.

X.   Other Agreements

To the extent not covered elsewhere in this list:

A. Agreements relating to any significant acquisition or disposition of assets or business by the Company or any subsidiary since inception.

B. All documents relating to any transactions or contracts between or among the Company or any subsidiary and any officers, directors, employees, stockholders, or entities that are controlled by such parties.

C. Present or pending joint venture or partnership agreements and other such arrangements in which the Company or any subsidiary is a party or is otherwise involved.

D. Significant license agreements of the Company or any subsidiary.

E. Contracts and agreements for construction of facilities for the Company or any subsidiary.

F. Secrecy and nondisclosure agreements with third parties relating to technical and other proprietary information.

G. Contracts pertaining to Company research and development activities.

H. Engagement letters with financial advisors, investment bankers, finders, business brokers, or similar advisors or service providers relating to any transaction of the type referred to in Sections IX. A, B, C, and D above.

I. Any other significant contracts of the Company or any subsidiary, including copies of forms or standard agreements used in the ordinary course of the Company's business.

XI. Financial Accounting and Expenditures

A. Financial statements for all completed fiscal years since the Company's inception and most recent interim periods for the Company and its subsidiaries. Such statements should disclose changes in accounting methods from one period to another.

B. Capital expenditures since the Company's inception, commitments for future expenditures, and program for planned future capital expenditures, if any. Include a summary of expenses for repairs and maintenance, advertising and promotion, and research and development.

C. Current revenue, expense, and capital expenditure budget of the Company and its subsidiaries.

D. Cash flow projections for future years for the Company and its subsidiaries.

E. Accounts receivable aging analysis of the Company and its subsidiaries.

F. Correspondence with accountants relating to audits, reviews, or examinations of the Company and any subsidiaries since the relevant company's inception, including accountants' letters to management and attorneys' letters delivered in connection with audits, reviews, or examinations.

G. Assets and liabilities not recorded on the most current balance sheets of the Company and its subsidiaries.

XII. Reports and Planning

A.   MANAGEMENT REPORTS

1. The Company's current business or strategic plan and any long-range business plans, including any industry projections, or Company-specific projections for FY 201_____ and FY 201_____.

2. Copies of reports or studies (including any projections or other forecasts) relating to the Company's financial condition, business operations, marketing programs, etc.

3. Periodic and other reports or memoranda prepared by management or consultants for the Board of Directors or any committee thereof.

B.   CUSTOMERS AND COMPETITORS

1. Schedule of sales of each product of the Company and its subsidiaries in each state and country for the last three years.

2. Schedule of top 13 customers with contact name for reference check.

3. List of major competitors and description of Company's competitive position in the industry.

4. List of potential entrants to market and description of the ease/burdens of market entry.

C.   NEWS REPORTS. Copies of any press releases or magazine articles or reports on the Company or its subsidiaries published, distributed, or released during the past year.

D.   REPORTS TO GOVERNMENT AGENCIES. Copies of significant reports to or correspondence with any federal, state, or local governmental agency since the Company's inception.

XIII. Tax Matters

A. Federal, state, and local tax returns and IRS audit reports of the Company and any subsidiaries since the relevant company's inception and any agreements between the Company or any subsidiary and the IRS extending the statute of limitations for any action establishing liability or any claim related to the above-referenced returns and reports.

B. Audit adjustments proposed by the IRS.

C. Any memoranda prepared in connection with any material tax problems affecting the Company or any of its subsidiaries or affiliates during the past five years or which may arise in the future.

D. Any settlement documents or deficiency assessments.

XIV. Industry, Business, and Strategy

A. List of all products in the order of their current dollar sales volume, stating whether any products are subject to any unusual governmental restriction on sale or are subject to any unusual number of consumer complaints.

B. A sample package of documents used by the Company or its subsidiaries in marketing the services of the Company or any of its subsidiaries.

C. Description of the marketplace to which the Company or any subsidiary's business activities are directed, including an analysis of the competition within that marketplace.

D. Description of the Company's facilities, location of any operations, and number of employees

E. Any YAK compliance plan and minutes of any YAK committee meeting.

F. Number of employees by functional area, projected growth, timing, and composition of growth.

G. Project introduction schedule, market penetration, and capital expenditure information.

H. Any other documents, agreements, or information material to the Company or its operations.

Topics Covered in the Legal Audit Questionnaire

A company that is planning an IPO should work with its legal advisors and management team to conduct its own legal audit before the underwriter performs its due diligence. Following are some questions the company should ask as part of that legal audit.

CORPORATE MATTERS

- Under what form of ownership is the company operated? When was this decision made? Does it still make sense? Why or why not?
- Have all annual filings and related actions, such as state corporate annual reports or required directors' and shareholders' meetings, been satisfied?
- What are the company's capital requirements in the next 12 months? How will this money be raised?
- What alternatives are being considered? What issues are triggered by these strategies?
- Have applicable federal and state securities laws been considered in connection with these proposed offerings?
- Will key employees be offered equity in the enterprise as an incentive for performance and loyalty? Is such equity available? Has the adoption of such plans been properly authorized? Will the plan be qualified or nonqualified? Up to what point?
- Has anyone met with the key employees to ascertain their goals and preferences?
- Have all necessary stock option plans and employment agreements been prepared and approved by the shareholders and directors of the corporation?
- Will any of the founders of the company be retiring or moving on to other projects? How will this affect the current structure?
- If the company is a corporation, was an election under Subchapter S ever made? Why or why not? If the entity is an S corporation, does it still qualify? Will such a choice be unduly restrictive as the company grows (e.g., ability to attract foreign investment, taxation of undistributed earnings, etc.)?
- If the entity is not a Subchapter S corporation, could it still qualify? Is this a more sensible entity under the applicable tax laws? Or should a limited liability company (LLC) be considered as an alternative?
- Have bylaws been prepared and carefully followed in the operation and management of the corporation? Have annual meetings of shareholders and directors been properly held and conducted? Have the minutes of these meetings been properly and promptly entered into the corporate record book.
- Have transactions "outside the regular course of business" been approved or ratified by directors (or, where required, by shareholder agreements or bylaws) and resolutions been recorded and entered into the corporate records?
- Are there any "insider" transactions or other matters that might constitute a conflict of interest? What "checks and balances" are in place to ensure that these transactions are properly handled?
- Have quorum, notice, proxy, and voting requirements been met in each case under applicable state laws?
- To what extent does the company's organizational and management chart reflect reality?
- Are customers and suppliers properly informed of the limits of authority of the employees, officers, or other agents of the company?

BUSINESS-PLANNING MATTERS

- Has a business and management plan been prepared? Does it include information about the company's key personnel; strategic objectives; realistic and well-documented financial statements; current and planned products and services; market data, strategy, and evaluation of competition; capital structure and allocation of proceeds; capital formation needs; customer base; distribution network; sales and advertising strategies; facility and labor needs; risk factors; and realistic milestones and strategies for the achievement of these plans and objectives?
- How and when was the business plan prepared? Has it been reviewed and revised on a periodic basis, or is it merely collecting dust on a manager's bookshelf?
- Has it been changed or supplemented to reflect any changes in the company's strategies, plans, or objectives?
- To whom has the plan been shown? For what purposes? Have steps been taken to preserve the confidential nature of the document?
- To what extent have federal and state securities laws been reviewed to prevent violations due to the misuse of the business plan as a disclosure document?

COMPLIANCE WITH GOVERNMENTAL AND EMPLOYMENT LAW REGULATIONS

- Have all required federal and state tax forms been filed (i.e., employer's quarterly and annual returns, federal and state unemployment tax contributions, etc.)?
- Are federal and state record-keeping requirements being met for tax purposes?
- Have all payroll and unemployment tax accounts been established? Has the company been qualified to "do business" in each state where such filing is required?
- Have all required local business permits and licenses been obtained?
- Are the company's operational policies in compliance with OSHA, EEOC, NLRB, and zoning requirements? Has the company ever had an external environmental law compliance audit performed?
- Has the company developed policies and programs related to smoking, substance-abuse testing, child labor laws, family leave, or child care? Are they in compliance with federal, state, and local laws?
- Have modifications been made to the workplace in compliance with the Americans with Disabilities Act? Have steps been taken to ensure compliance with applicable equal employment opportunity, affirmative action, equal pay, wage and hour, immigration, employee benefit, and workers compensation laws?
- When did the company last consult these statutes to ensure that its current practices are consistent with applicable laws?
- Has an employment manual been prepared? When is the last time that it was reviewed by qualified counsel?

EMPLOYEE BENEFIT PLANS

- Has the company adopted a medical reimbursement plan? Group life insurance? Retirement plans? Disability plans? If no, should they be adopted? If yes, have all amendments to the structure and ongoing management of these plans been made to maintain qualification?
- Have annual reports been filed with the U.S. Department of Treasury and U.S. Department of Labor for pension and profit-sharing plans?
- Have there been any changes in the administration of these plans? Have there been any recent transactions between the plan and the company, its trustees, or its officers and directors?

CONTRACTUAL MATTERS

- On which material contracts is the company directly or indirectly bound? Were these agreements drafted in compliance with applicable laws, such as your state's version of the Uniform Commercial Code?
- Is your company still able to meet its obligations under these agreements? Is any party to these agreements in default? Why? What steps have been taken to enforce the company's rights and/or mitigate damages?
- To what extent are contractual forms used when selling company products and services? When was the last time these forms were updated? What problems have these forms triggered? What steps have been taken to resolve these problems?
- Are employees who possess special skills and experience under an employment agreement with the company? When was the last time the agreement was reviewed and revised? What about sales representatives of the company? Are they under some form of a written agreement and commission schedule? Has the scope of their authority been clearly defined and communicated to the third parties with whom they deal?
- To what extent does the company hire independent contractors? Have agreements been prepared with these parties? Have the intellectual-property law issues, such as "work for hire" provisions, been included in these agreements?

PROTECTION OF INTELLECTUAL PROPERTY

- To what extent are trademarks, patents, copyrights, and trade secrets among the intangible assets of the business? What are the internal company procedures for dealing with these key assets?
- What agreements (such as ownership of inventions, nondisclosure, and noncompete) have been struck with key employees who are exposed to the company's intellectual property?
- What procedures are in place for receiving new ideas and proposals from employees and other parties? What steps have been taken to protect the company's "trade dress," where applicable?
- Have trademarks, patents, and copyrights been registered? What monitoring programs are in place to detect infringement and ensure proper usage by third parties?
- Are documents properly stamped with copyright and confidentiality notices?
- Has counsel been contacted to determine whether a new discovery is eligible for registration?
- Does the company license any of its intellectual property to third parties? Has experienced licensing and franchising counsel prepared the agreements and disclosure documents?

RELATIONSHIPS WITH COMPETITORS

- How competitive is your industry? How aggressive is the company's approach to its markets and its competitors?
- What incentives are offered for attracting and retaining customers?
- To what professional and trade associations does the company belong? What types of information are exchanged?
- Does the company engage in any type of communication or have any cooperative agreement with a competitor regarding price, geographic territories, or distribution channels that might constitute an antitrust violation or an act of unfair competition?

- Has the company established an in-house program to educate employees on the mechanics and pitfalls of antitrust violations?
- Has an antitrust action ever been brought or threatened by or against the company? What were the surrounding facts? What was the outcome?
- Have you recently hired a former employee of a competitor? How was he or she recruited? Does this employee use skills or knowledge gained from the prior employer? To what extent has the prior employer been notified?
- What steps are being taken to avoid a lawsuit involving misappropriation of trade secrets and/or interference with contractual regulations?
- Does the company engage in comparative advertising? How are the products and services of the competitor generally treated?
- Are any of your trademarks or trade names similar to those of competitors? Have you been involved in any prior litigation with a competitor? Threatened litigation?

FINANCING MATTERS

- What equity and debt financing have been obtained in the past three years?
- What continuing reporting obligations or other affirmative/negative covenants remain in place? What triggers a default, and what new rights are created to the investors or lenders upon default?
- What security interests remain outstanding?

MARKETING AND DISTRIBUTION ISSUES

- Has the company clearly defined the market for its products and services?
- Who are the key competitors? What are their respective market shares, strengths, weaknesses, strategies, and objectives?
- What new players are entering this market? What barriers exist to new entry?
- What is the saturation point of this market?
- What are the key distribution channels for bringing these products to the market? Have all necessary agreements and regulations affecting these channels been adequately addressed (i.e., labeling and warranty laws, consumer protection laws, pricing laws, distributorship agreements, etc.)?
- If the company is doing business abroad, have all import/export regulations been carefully reviewed?
- Has a system been established to ensure compliance with the Foreign Corrupt Practices Act?
- Is the company considering franchising as a method of marketing and distribution to expand market share? To what extent can all key aspects of the company's proven success be reduced to an operations manual and taught to others in a training program?
- To what extent are competitors engaged in franchising?
- If franchising is appropriate for distribution of the company's products or business, have all necessary offering documents and agreements been prepared by experienced franchise legal counsel?
- What initial franchise fee will be charged? Ongoing royalties? Are these fees competitive?
- What ongoing programs and support are provided to franchisees?
- What products and services must the franchisee buy from your company?
- Under what conditions may a franchise be terminated or transferred?
- Are any alternatives to franchising being considered? Has the company looked at dealer termination; multilevel marketing, or pyramid laws?

Confidential Questionnaire for Directors and Officers

To: CEO of Grow Co.

This questionnaire is being furnished to all directors, nominees for directors, and officers of Grow Co. ("the Company"). The purpose of the questionnaire is to obtain information required to be disclosed in the Company's Proxy Statement, Annual Report to Stockholders, Annual Report on Form 10-K, and other disclosure documents. The disclosure documents are required to be prepared in accordance with the Securities Exchange Act of 1934, as amended (the "Exchange Act").

The length and complexity of this questionnaire is the unfortunate result of the many rules and regulations of the Securities and Exchange Commission relating to the preparation of a publicly held company's annual disclosure documents. Your patience in completing this questionnaire is much appreciated. If you should have any questions, please feel free to contact the Company's counsel or _____, respectively.

Before completing this questionnaire, please read carefully the definitions, which are included in the Glossary. Unless otherwise directed, please answer every question and state your answers as of the date this questionnaire is completed. If you have any doubt as to whether any matter should be reported, please give the relevant facts so that those responsible for preparing the appropriate disclosure documents can make the decision whether such information should be included in such documents. If additional space is required for you to fully answer any of the questions, please complete your answer on a separate sheet and attach it to the questionnaire.

Please bear in mind that the Proxy Statement, Annual Report to Stockholders, and Annual Report on Form 10-K prepared from this completed questionnaire will be understood to be accurate as of their dates. Therefore, it is necessary to update your answers if you learn of additional material information between the date of completion of this questionnaire and the date of the Proxy Statement, Annual Report to Stockholders, or Annual Report on Form 10-K.

After you have completed this questionnaire, please date and sign one copy and return it as soon as possible, but not later than _____,

to _____

_____

_____

_____

Questions

BIOGRAPHICAL INFORMATION

WHERE APPLICABLE, THE TERM "COMPANY" INCLUDES SUBSIDIARIES OF GROW CO., UNLESS THE QUESTION EXPRESSLY STATES OTHERWISE.

1. NAME AND DATE OF BIRTH. Please state your full name, address, and date of birth.

Name: _____

Address: _____

Date of birth: _____

2. POSITION WITH COMPANY. Please indicate all positions (including as a director) and offices you presently hold with the Company. Please also indicate the term or length of time held.

LIST OF POSITIONS	COMPANY	TERM

3.   ARRANGEMENTS FOR SELECTION OF DIRECTORS OR EXECUTIVE OFFICERS.
Were you selected to serve as a director, nominated to become a director, or selected to serve as an executive officer, of the Company, pursuant to any arrangement or understanding between yourself and any other person (except the directors and executive officers of the Company acting in such capacity)? If so, name such person and describe the arrangement or understanding.

_____ was not selected to serve in my present capacity pursuant to an arrangement.

_____ was selected to serve in my present capacity according to the following arrangement:_____

4.   FAMILY RELATIONSHIPS.   Are you related by blood, marriage, or adoption to any director, officer, or nominee to become a director of the Company? If so, state the identity of the director, officer, or nominee and the nature of the relationship. Relationships more remote than first cousin need not be mentioned.

_____ I am not related to a director, officer, etc.

_____ I am related to a director, officer, etc.

Describe: _____

_____

IDENTITY OF OFFICER, DIRECTOR, OR NOMINEE	NATURE OF RELATIONSHIP

5.   BUSINESS EXPERIENCE. Please give a brief account of your business experience during the past five years (together with applicable dates); include your principal occupations and employment during that period and the name and principal business of any corporation or other organization in which such occupations and employment were carried on and state whether such corporation or organization is a parent, subsidiary, or other affiliate of the Company. If you are an executive officer of the Company and have been employed by the Company for less than five years, include a brief explanation of the nature of your responsibilities in prior positions. What is required is information relating to the level of your professional competence, which may include, depending upon the circumstances, such specific information as the size of the operation supervised.

DATES	POSITION/ RESPONSIBILITIES	CORPORATION NAME AND ADDRESS	COMPANY SUBSIDIARY OR AFFILIATE	BUSINESS RELATIONSHIPS

6.1 DIRECTORSHIPS. Please list all directorships you presently hold in publicly held companies or companies registered under the Investment Company Act of 1940, as amended (the "Investment Company Act").

_____ I do not presently hold any such directorship.

_____ I hold the following directorships:

COMPANY NAME	TERM

6.2 OTHER POSITIONS. Since January 1, 201____, were you (i) an officer of another entity (includes corporations, partnerships, etc.), (ii) a member of the compensation committee of another entity or other committee performing equivalent functions, or (iii) a member of the board of directors of another entity? Do not include any tax-exempt entity under Section 501(c)(3) of the Internal Revenue Code.

_____ I have not held any such positions.

_____ I have held the following positions:

ENTITY'S NAME*	POSITION	TERM

* Please circle the name of any entity for which the entire board performed compensation committee functions.

7.   LEGAL PROCEEDINGS. Have any of the following events occurred during the past five years?

If so, please describe._____

7.1 BANKRUPTCY PETITION. Was a petition under the Bankruptcy Act or any state insolvency law filed by or against, or a receiver, fiscal agent, or similar officer appointed by a court for the business or property of, (i) you, (ii) any partnership in which you were a general partner at or within two years before such event, or (iii) any corporation or business association of which you were an executive officer at or within two years before such event?

_____ No such petition has been filed.

_____ A petition has been filed.

Describe. _____

_____

_____

_____

7.2 CRIMINAL PROCEEDINGS. Were you convicted in a criminal proceeding, or are you the named subject of a pending criminal proceeding? Omit traffic violations and other minor offenses.

_____ I have not been convicted in a, or named in a pending, criminal proceeding.

_____ I have been convicted in a, or named in a pending, criminal proceeding.

Describe._____

_____

_____

7.3 INJUNCTIONS. Were you the subject of any court order, judgment, or decree, not subsequently reversed, suspended, or vacated, of any court of competent jurisdiction, permanently or temporarily enjoining or otherwise limiting you from any of the following activities:

_____

_____

7.3.1 Acting as a futures commission merchant, introducing broker, commodity trading advisor, commodity pool operator, floor broker, leverage transaction merchant, any other person regulated by the Commodity Futures Trading Commission, or an associated person of any of the foregoing, or as an investment advisor, underwriter, broker, or dealer in securities, or as an affiliated person, director, or employee of any investment company, bank, savings and loan association, or insurance company, or engaging in or continuing any conduct or practice in connection with such activity?

_____ I have not been the subject of any such court order, judgment, or decree.

_____ I have been the subject of such a court order, judgment, or decree.

Describe. _____

_____

_____

7.3.2 Engaging in any type of business practice?

_____ I have not been the subject of any such court order, judgment, or decree.

_____ I have been the subject of such a court order, judgment, or decree.

Describe. _____

_____

_____

_____

_____

7.3.3 Engaging in any activity in connection with the purchase or sale of any security or commodity or in connection with any violation of federal or state securities laws or federal commodities laws?

_____ I have not been the subject of any such court order, judgment, or decree.

_____ I have been the subject of such a court order, judgment, or decree.

Describe. _____

_____

_____

_____

7.4 SUSPENSIONS. Were you the subject of any order, judgment, or decree, not subsequently reversed, suspended, or vacated, of any federal or state authority barring, suspending, or otherwise limiting for more than 60 days your right to engage in any of the activities described in question 7.3.1 above or your right to be associated with persons engaged in any such activity?

_____ I have not been the subject of any such judgment, order, or decree.

_____ I have been the subject of such a judgment, order, or decree.

Describe. _____

_____

_____

_____

7.5 SECURITIES AND COMMODITIES LAW VIOLATIONS. Were you found by a court of competent jurisdiction in a civil action or by the Securities and Exchange Commission or the Commodities Futures Trading Commission to have violated any federal or state securities or commodities law, where such judgment has not subsequently been reversed, suspended, or vacated?

_____ I have not been found in violation of federal or state securities or commodities law.

_____ I have been found in violation of federal or state securities or commodities law.

Describe. _____

_____

_____

_____

8. LEGAL PROCEEDINGS ADVERSE TO THE COMPANY

8.1 GENERAL. Describe briefly any material pending legal proceeding known to you to which the Company is a party or of which any of the Company's property is the subject. If the business ordinarily results in actions for negligence or other claims, no such action or claim need be described unless it departs from the normal kind of such actions.

_____ I know of no pending legal proceedings to which the Company is a party.

_____ I know of such legal proceedings.

Describe, including the name of the court or agency in which the proceedings are pending, the date initiated, the principal parties thereto, the factual basis alleged to underlie the proceeding, and the relief sought: _____

_____

_____

_____

8.2 PERSONAL. Do you know of any pending or contemplated legal proceedings (including administrative proceedings and investigations by governmental authorities) in which either you or any associate of yours is a party adverse to the Company, or in which either you or any associate has an interest adverse to the Company?

_____ I know of no pending or contemplated legal proceedings in which either I or an associate has an interest adverse to the Company.

_____ I know of legal proceedings in which either I or an associate has an interest adverse to the Company.

Describe, including the name of the court or agency in which the proceedings are pending, the date initiated, the principal parties thereto, the factual basis alleged to underlie the proceeding, and the relief sought: _____

_____

_____

8.3 OTHER DIRECTORS, OFFICERS, SECURITY HOLDERS, AND AFFILIATES. Do you know of any pending or threatened legal proceeding in which any other director or officer or any affiliate of the Company, or any security holder who owns of record or is the beneficial owner of more than 5% of any class of voting securities of the Company, or any associate of any such director, officer, affiliate, or security holder, is a party adverse to the Company or in which such director, officer, affiliate, security holder, or associate has any interest adverse to the Company or any of its subsidiaries?

_____ I know of no such pending or threatened legal proceeding involving such parties.

_____ I know of legal proceedings in which such parties have an interest adverse to the Company.

Describe, including the name of the court or agency in which the proceedings are pending, the date initiated, the principal parties thereto, the factual basis alleged to underlie the proceeding, and the relief sought: _____

_____

_____

8.4 GOVERNMENTAL PROCEEDING. Do you know of any legal, regulatory, or administrative proceeding brought or contemplated by any governmental authority (including but not limited to antitrust, price-fixing, tax, environmental, copyright, or patent litigation) to which the Company is or may be a party or of which the property of the Company or its subsidiaries is the subject?

_____ I know of no such pending or threatened governmental proceeding.

_____ I know of a governmental proceeding to which the Company or its properties is subject.

Describe, including the name of the court or agency in which the proceedings are pending, the date initiated, the principal parties thereto, the factual basis alleged to underlie the proceeding, and the relief sought: _____

_____

_____

Executive Compensation

9. OTHER ANNUAL COMPENSATION. Note: Most information concerning compensation paid to you during the fiscal year ended December 31, 201____, will be obtained directly from the Company. Please describe any payment or other personal compensation or benefit of or similar to the type described below received by you or any member of your family from any party (including parties other than the Company, such as banks or suppliers) for services rendered to the Company, during the fiscal year ended December 31, 201____. These personal benefits should be valued on the basis of the provider's cost of providing such benefits. Among the benefits that should be reported are the following:

(1) Payments for home repairs and improvements;

(2) Payments for housing and other living expenses (including domestic service) incurred at your principal and/or vacation residence;

(3) The personal use of Company property, such as automobiles or apartments;

(4) Payment of personal travel expenses, entertainment, and related expenses (such as club membership);

(5) Payment of legal, accounting, or other professional fees for matters unrelated to the business of the Company;

(6) Personal use of the Company's staff; and

(7) Benefits which you have obtained from third parties, such as cash payments, favorable bank loans, and benefits from suppliers, if the Company directly or indirectly compensates the third party for providing the benefits to you.

Please note that the examples given above are not meant to be exhaustive. Also note that the personal benefits to be described should not be limited to those items that you have reported, or plan to report, on your income tax return. You need not describe personal benefits that are directly related to your job performance, such as parking spaces, meals at Company facilities, and office space and furnishings at Company-maintained offices.

_____ I have received no such payments.

_____ I have received the following payments.

DESCRIPTION	VALUE

10. TERMINATION OF EMPLOYMENT AND CHANGE-IN-CONTROL ARRANGEMENTS. Please describe any compensatory plan or arrangement, including payments to be received from the Company, if such plan or arrangement results or will result from the resignation, retirement, or any other termination of your employment with the Company, or from a change in control of the Company or a change in your responsibilities following a change in control and the amount involved (including all periodic payments or installments) exceeds $100,000.

_____ No such compensatory plans or arrangements exist.

_____ The following compensatory plans or arrangements exist.

Describe. _____.

_____

_____

_____

Security Ownership of Certain Beneficial Owners and Management

11. PLEASE STATE BELOW THE NAME OF ANY INDIVIDUAL, CORPORATION, GROUP, OR OTHER ENTITY personally known by you to be the beneficial owner of more than 5% of any class of voting or equity securities of the Company. A "group" for this purpose is any general partnership, limited partnership, syndicate, or other group formed for the purpose of acquiring voting or equity securities of the Company.

_____ I know of no such securities holder.

_____ I know of such securities holder.

Describe. _____

_____

_____

_____

12. PLEASE STATE IN THE TABLE BELOW THE AMOUNT OF VOTING OR EQUITY SE-CURITIES OF THE COMPANY of which you are the beneficial owner on the date hereof. Please review at this time the definition for "beneficial ownership" in the attached Glossary. Even though you may not actually have or share voting or investment power with respect to securities owned by persons in your family or living in your home, out of an abundance of caution, you may wish to include such shares in your beneficial ownership disclosure in the table on the next page and then disclaim such ownership in your answer to question 13. If any of the securities listed have been pledged, have been otherwise deposited as collateral, are the subject matter of any voting trust or other similar agreement, or are the subject of any contract providing for the sale or other disposition of securities, please describe the details on a separate sheet and attach it to this questionnaire.

_____ I hold no voting or equity securities of the Company.

_____ I hold voting or equity securities of the Company as listed below:

AMOUNT BENEFICIALLY OWNED	NUMBER OF SHARES OF COMMON STOCK
Shares owned beneficially by you	_____
Of such shares:	_____
Shares as to which you have sole voting power	_____
Shares as to which you have shared voting power	_____

Shares as to which you have sole investment power   _____

Shares as to which you have shared investment power   _____

Shares which you have a right to acquire within 60 days after the date
hereof (e.g., pursuant to the exercise of an option, warrant, or other   _____
right, etc.)

Shares the beneficial ownership of which you disclaim (see question 13)   _____

Shares pledged, deposited as collateral, subject to a voting trust, or
subject to a contract for sale or other disposition   _____

13. IF YOU WISH TO DISCLAIM BENEFICIAL OWNERSHIP OF ANY OF THE SHARES REPORTED ABOVE, please furnish the following information with respect to the person or persons who should be shown as the beneficial owners of the shares in question:

NAME OF BENEFICIAL OWNER	RELATIONSHIP OF SUCH PERSON TO YOU	NUMBER OF SHARES BENEFICIALLY OWNED

14. IF YOU HOLD MORE THAN 5 PERCENT OF ANY CLASS OF VOTING SECURITIES OF THE COMPANY pursuant to any voting trust or similar agreement, state the title of such securities, the amount held or to be held pursuant to the trust or agreement, and the duration of the agreement. If you are a voting trustee, please also outline your voting rights and other powers under the trust or agreement.

_____ I do not hold more than 5% of any class of voting securities of the Company pursuant to a voting trust agreement.

_____ I hold more than 5% of the following class(es) of voting securities of the Company pursuant to a voting trust agreement.

Describe. _____

_____

_____

_____

15. PLEASE DESCRIBE ANY ARRANGEMENTS, including the pledge of voting securities, the operation of which may at a subsequent date result in a change of control of the Company.

_____ I know of no such arrangements.

_____ I know of such an arrangement or arrangements.

Describe. _____

_____

_____

_____

Certain Relationships and Related Transactions

16. DESCRIBE BRIEFLY IF YOU OR ANY MEMBER OF YOUR IMMEDIATE FAMILY had or will have any direct or indirect material interest in any transaction, or series of similar transactions, which took place since January 1, 201_____, or any currently proposed transaction, or series of similar transactions, to which the Company or any of its subsidiaries was or is to be a party, in which the amount involved exceeds $60,000. Describe the nature of your or your family member's interest in the transaction(s), the amount of such transaction(s), and, if possible, the amount of interest in dollars that you or your family member has in the transaction(s).

_____ There is not nor will there be any such material interest in any transaction.

_____ There is or will be a material interest in the following transaction(s).

Describe. _____

_____

_____

_____

17. DID YOU OR YOUR ASSOCIATES HAVE ANY TRANSACTIONS at any time since January 1, 201____, or do you or your associates have any presently proposed transactions, to which a pension, retirement, savings, or similar plan provided by the Company or any subsidiary was or is proposed to be a party? If so, please describe.

_____ I know of no such transaction.

_____ I know of such a transaction.

Describe. _____

_____

_____

_____

18. ARE YOU NOW, OR HAVE YOU SINCE JANUARY 1, 201___, been an executive officer or do you now own, or have you owned, of record or beneficially, since January 1, 201____, in excess of a 10% equity interest in any firm, corporation, or other business or professional entity:

18.1 that made at any time during the fiscal year ended December 31, 201____, or has made or proposes to make during the Company's current fiscal year, payments to the Company or its subsidiaries for property or services in excess of 5% of (i) the Company's consolidated gross revenues for the fiscal year ended December 31, 201____ or (ii) the other entity's consolidated gross revenues for its most recent full fiscal year;

_____ I have no such interest.

_____ I have such an interest. See Question 22.

18.2 to which the Company or its subsidiaries made at any time during the fiscal year ended December 31, 201____, or has made or proposes to make during the Company's current fiscal year, payments for property or services in excess of 5% of (i) the Company's consolidated gross revenues for the fiscal year ended December 31, 201____ or (ii) the other entity's consolidated gross revenues for its most recent full fiscal year; or

_____ I have no such interest.

_____ I have such an interest. See Question 22.

18.3 to which the Company or its subsidiaries was indebted at December 31, 201____, in an aggregate amount in excess of 5% of the Company's total consolidated assets at December 31, 201____ ?

_____ I have no such interest.

_____ I have such an interest. See Question 22.

19. ARE YOU, OR DURING THE FISCAL YEAR ENDED DECEMBER 31, 201____, were you, a member of, or of counsel to, a law firm that the Company retained during the fiscal year ended December 31, 201____, or has retained or proposes to retain during the current fiscal year? If so, state the fees paid to your firm by the Company if the amount exceeds 5% of the firm's gross revenues for its last full fiscal year.

_____ I have no such relationship.

_____ I have such a relationship. See Question 22.

20. ARE YOU, OR DURING THE FISCAL YEAR ENDED DECEMBER 31, 201____, were you, a partner or executive officer of any investment banking firm that performed services for the Company, other than as a participating underwriter in a syndicate, during the fiscal year ended December 31, 201____, or that the Company has or proposes to have perform services during the current year? If so, state the compensation received by such firm if the amount exceeds 5% of the investment banking firm's consolidated gross revenues for its last full fiscal year.

_____ I have no such relationship.

_____ I have such a relationship. See Question 22.

21. IS THERE ANY OTHER PERSONAL OR BUSINESS RELATIONSHIP(S) that exists between you and the Company that is substantially similar in nature and scope to those relationships listed above in questions 18–20?

_____ No such other relationship exists.

_____ Another relationship exists. See Question 22.

22. IF YOU ANSWERED YES TO ANY OF QUESTIONS 18–21 ABOVE, describe each such relationship, including in your description the identity of each entity, the amount of business done with the Company during the fiscal year ended December 31, 201____, and the amount of business proposed to be done during the current fiscal year.

NAME OF ENTITY	NATURE OF MY AFFILIATION WITH ENTITY	RELATIONSHIP OF COMPANY AND ENTITY	AMOUNT OF PAYMENTS PROPOSED

23. IF YOU, ANY OF YOUR ASSOCIATES, OR ANY MEMBER OF YOUR IMMEDIATE FAMILY were indebted to the Company or any of its subsidiaries at any time since January 1, 201____, in an amount in excess of $60,000, state (i) the largest aggregate amount of indebtedness outstanding at any time during such period, (ii) the nature of the indebtedness and of the transaction(s) in which it was incurred (if such indebtedness arose under Section 16(b) of the Exchange Act and has not been discharged by payment, state the amount of any profit realized and describe the transaction), (iii) the amount of indebtedness outstanding as of the date hereof, and (iv) the rate of interest paid or charged. If indebtedness of an associate or immediate family member is described, name the associate or immediate family member and explain your relationship with the associate.

_____ I know of no such indebtedness.

_____ Such indebtedness exists or has existed.

Describe. _____

_____

_____

_____

24. PLEASE LIST THE FULL NAME, FORM (E.G., PARTNERSHIP, CORPORATION, ETC.), nature of business done by, and principal place of business of each of your associates (see the definition of associate in the Glossary on the next page) referred to in the answers to this questionnaire and your relationship with such associates as follows, if applicable:

NAME	FORM	NATURE OF BUSINESS DONE	PRINCIPAL PLACE OF BUSINESS	RELATIONSHIP

I understand that the information that I am furnishing herein will be used by the Company in connection with the preparation of its Proxy Statement, Annual Report to Stockholders, and Annual Report on Form 10-K. I will advise the Company as soon as possible if any events occur between now and the date of filing of the Company's definitive Proxy Statement that would change my answer to any question asked above.

Signature: _____

Print Name: _____

Dated: _____

Glossary

AFFILIATE. The term "affiliate" means any person who directly, or indirectly through one or more intermediaries, controls, or is controlled by, or is under common control with, the Company.

ARRANGEMENT. The term "arrangement" means any agreement, plan, contract, authorization, or understanding, whether or not set forth in a formal document.

ASSOCIATE. The term "associate" means:

(a) any corporation or organization, other than the Company or any of its subsidiaries, of which you are an officer or partner or are, directly or indirectly, the beneficial owner of 10% or more of any class of equity securities;

(b) any trust or other estate in which you have a beneficial interest or as to which you serve as trustee or in a similar fiduciary capacity; or

(c) your spouse, or any relative of yours, or relative of your spouse living in your home or who is a director or officer of the Company or any of its subsidiaries.

BENEFICIAL OWNERSHIP. You are the beneficial owner of a security if you, directly or indirectly, through any contract, arrangement, understanding, relationship, or otherwise have or share:

(a) voting power, which includes the power to vote, or to direct the voting of, such security, or

(b) investment power, which includes the power to dispose, or to direct the disposition, of such security.

You are also the beneficial owner of a security if you, directly or indirectly, create or use a trust, proxy, power of attorney, pooling arrangement, or any other contract, arrangement, or device with the purpose or effect of divesting yourself of beneficial ownership of a security or preventing the vesting of such beneficial ownership. Therefore, whether or not you are the record holder of securities, you may be the beneficial owner of securities held by you for your own benefit (regardless of how registered) and securities held by others for your benefit (regardless of how registered), such as by custodians, brokers, nominees, pledgees, etc., and including securities held by an estate or trust in which you have an interest as legatee or beneficiary, securities owned by a partnership of which you are a partner, securities held by a personal holding company of which you are a stockholder, etc., and securities held in the name of your spouse, minor children, and any relative (sharing the same home).

Finally, you are deemed to be the beneficial owner of a security if you have the right to acquire beneficial ownership of such security at any time within sixty days, including but not limited to, (a) through the exercise of any option, warrant, or right or (b) through the conversion of a security or (c) pursuant to the power to revoke a trust, discretionary account, or similar arrangement or (d) pursuant to the automatic termination of a trust, discretionary account, or similar arrangement.

Note that the same security may be beneficially owned by more than one person. For example, several co-trustees may share the power to vote or dispose of shares.

CONTROL. The term "control" means the possession, directly or indirectly, of the power to direct or cause the direction of the management and policies of any person, whether through the ownership of voting securities, by contract, or otherwise.

EXECUTIVE OFFICER. The term "executive officer" means the president, secretary, treasurer, any vice president in charge of a principal business function (such as sales, administration, or finance), and any other person who performs similar policy-making functions for the Company. Executive officers of subsidiaries may be deemed executive officers of the Company if they perform such policy-making functions for the Company.

FAMILY RELATIONSHIP. The term "family relationship" means any relationship by blood, marriage, or adoption, not more remote than first cousin.

IMMEDIATE FAMILY. The term "immediate family" includes your spouse, parents, children, siblings, mothers- and fathers-in-law, sons- and daughters-in-law, and brothers- and sisters-in-law, and includes any person to whom you directly or indirectly contribute financial support.

MATERIAL TRANSACTION. The term "transaction" is to be understood in its broadest sense, and includes the direct or indirect receipt of anything of value. To be "material," the amount involved in the transaction or series of similar transactions, including all periodic installments in the case of any lease or other agreement providing for periodic installments, must exceed $10,000.

PLAN. The term "plan" includes, but is not limited to, the following: any plan, contract, authorization, or arrangement, whether or not set forth in any formal documents, pursuant to which the following may be received: cash, stock, restricted stock, phantom stock, stock options, stock appreciation rights, stock options in tandem with stock appreciation rights, warrants, convertible securities, performance units, and performance shares. A plan may be applicable to one person.

Please note that your answers in this questionnaire should disclose indirect as well as direct interests in material transactions. Transactions in which you would have a direct interest would include your purchasing or leasing anything of value (e.g., stock in a business acquired by the Company, office space, plants, Company apartments, computers, raw materials, finished goods, etc.) from or selling or leasing anything of value to, or borrowing or lending cash or other property from or to, the Company or any subsidiary. Transactions in which you would have an indirect interest are similar transactions with the Company by any corporation or organization described in clause (a) of the definition for "associate."

Please note that the examples given above are not meant to be exhaustive.

Data to Gather When Implementing a Franchising Program

The FTC and the Registration States have adopted regulations that dictate the contents of the franchise offering circular. The disclosure requirements range from the history of the company and its principals (including litigation and bankruptcies) to a detailed description of the terms of the franchise agreement to be executed by the franchisee. The mandatory contents of the franchise offering circular will, therefore, provide an appropriate starting point for a new franchisor in developing its franchising program.

‡   **INFORMATION REGARDING THE COMPANY AND ITS PRINCIPALS.** The following information should be provided with respect to the Company and its principals:

a. History of the Company's operations and business. Identify any predecessors and/or affiliated companies.

b. Describe the market to be serviced by franchisees. The description will include information about general or specific markets to be targeted, whether the market is developed or developing, and whether the business is seasonal. In addition, general information about industry-specific laws and regulations must be included, along with a description of the competition.

c. Identify all of the Company's directors, principal officers, and other executives who have management responsibility in connection with the operation of the Company's business. As to each, provide a summary of their job history for at least the past five (5) years.

d. Identify and describe all litigation in which the Company, its officers, and its directors are involved or have previously been involved.

e. Identify and describe any and all bankruptcy proceedings involving the Company, its officers, and its directors.

‡   **INITIAL FEES.** The offering circular must disclose all payments a franchisee is required to make to the franchisor before opening the franchised business. This will include the initial franchise fee and any other preopening purchases/leases from the franchisor. Before determining the initial franchise fee, you may want to compare the fees charged by competitors. The fee may be expressed as a single amount for all franchisees, or it may be a range of amounts, based on criteria you specify. In addition, we will need to know if you have any plans for allowing the fee to be paid in installments, and whether the fee will be refundable under certain conditions. The disclosure should also discuss the allocation of the initial franchise fees collected by the franchisor. For example, fees are often used to cover administrative and legal costs associated with the franchise offer, as well as to fund initial training programs and other preopening assistance provided by the franchisor.

‡   **ROYALTY.** The royalty rate and method of payment must be determined. Again, a comparison of competitors' royalty structures may be helpful. The royalty formula (e.g., percentage of gross sales), payment frequency, and refundability must be disclosed.

‡   **ADVERTISING FUND.** Will you require franchisees to contribute to a regional or national advertising fund? Typically advertising fund contributions are based on the same formula, and made with the same frequency, as royalty payments. If such a fund is contemplated, you will need to discuss the fund's objectives, administration, and participants (company-owned stores?). Note: All fees collected for the advertising fund must be used for that purpose.

‡   **OTHER FEES PAID TO FRANCHISOR.** The offering circular must identify all other fees that a franchisee is required to pay to the franchisor, or to the franchisor's affiliate,

including fees collected on behalf of third parties. Typically, these fees include ongoing training/consultant fees and expenses, real property and equipment leases, required supply purchases, transfer fees, renewal fees, and audit fees.

‡   **INITIAL INVESTMENT.** The offering circular must include à chart detailing all costs necessary to begin operation of the franchised business and to operate the business during the first three months (or some other initial phase more appropriate for the industry), including the costs of furniture, equipment, supplies, inventory, leasehold improvements, rent security, utilities, advertising, insurance, licenses, and permits. (Please note that the "initial phase" is not the equivalent of a "break-even point.") Many of the cost items will be stated in a low-high range, rather than a specific amount.

‡   **SOURCES FOR PRODUCTS AND SERVICES.** What products and services must franchisees purchase: (a) only from the franchisor or its affiliates? (b) only from approved suppliers? (c) only in accordance with the franchisor's specifications? Will the franchisor derive any revenue from these purchases? For example, if there are proprietary items that must be purchased from you or a particular designated supplier, then this needs to be disclosed in the offering circular.

‡   **FRANCHISEE'S OBLIGATIONS.** The franchisee's principal obligations under the franchise agreement are disclosed in a chart referencing 24 specific obligations. The chart also serves as a cross-reference for franchisees between the offering circular and the franchise agreement.

‡   **FINANCING.** Will the franchisor or its affiliates offer any direct or indirect financing arrangements to franchisees? Indirect financing includes guarantying franchisee loans and facilitating arrangements with lenders. If so, then the terms of the loan must be disclosed.

‡   **FRANCHISOR'S OBLIGATIONS.** These obligations are broken down into two categories: obligations performed before the franchised business opens and ongoing obligations.

a. Preopening Obligations. How will the franchisor assist franchisees (if at all) in locating a site for the business, or in developing the site so that it is suitable for the operation of the franchised business? Will the franchisor hire and/or train franchisees' employees?

b. Ongoing Obligations. What assistance (if any) will the franchisor provide with: (i) developing/improving the franchised business, (ii) operating problems encountered by franchisees, (iii) administrative, bookkeeping, and inventory control procedures? Specific details about the franchisor's advertising program and any computer systems or cash registers required to be used in the business must be provided.

In addition, a training program must be developed that will be offered to franchisees and/or the franchisees' manager. The training program should encompass instruction in the operation and management of a franchised business as well as instruction in the areas of advertising, marketing, personnel management, bookkeeping, inventory control, and any other issues unique to the operation of the franchised business. In connection with the training program, the following must also be determined:

a. Who will bear the costs for said training?

b. Who will pay the transportation, lodging, and other miscellaneous expenses associated with training?

c. How many people will be required to attend training, and who will be required to attend (i.e., the franchisee, the franchisee's manager, or the franchisee's employees)?

d. If additional designees of the franchisee attend, will there be a charge?

e. Where will training be held and what is the length of said training?

f. When will the franchisee and its managers or employees be required to complete the training program (i.e., how many weeks prior to the opening of the franchise)?

The franchisor's training program must be described in detail, including information regarding the location, duration, and a general outline of the training program. What topics will be covered? What materials will be used? Who are the instructors? Is training mandatory?

‡   **TERRITORY.** Will franchisees be granted an exclusive territory? Will there be conditions on exclusivity? Will franchisees be subject to performance standards?

‡   **FRANCHISEE PARTICIPATION.** Are franchisees required to participate personally in the direct operation of the franchised business?

‡   **RESTRICTIONS ON GOODS AND SERVICES.** Are there any restrictions or conditions on the products that the franchisee may sell? For example, is the franchisee obligated to sell only those products approved by the franchisor?

‡   **RENEWAL; TERMINATION; TRANSFER; DISPUTE RESOLUTION.**

a. Term and Renewal. What will be the term of the franchise agreement? Will the franchisee be able to renew the agreement, and, if so, under what conditions? Will a fee be charged? Under what conditions may the franchisor terminate the agreement? Under what conditions (if any) may the franchisee terminate the agreement?

b. Termination. What obligations are imposed on franchisees after the franchise agreement is terminated or expires? Will the franchisee be bound by a noncompete agreement? Will the noncompete restrict the franchisees' activities during and after the term of the agreement? What obligations (if any) are imposed on the franchisor after termination or expiration of the agreement?

c. Transfer. May franchisees assign or transfer the franchise agreement? If so, under what conditions? Will a fee be charged? Will the franchisor have a right of first refusal to purchase the franchised business before it can be transferred or sold to a third party?

d. Dispute Resolution. How and where will disputes be settled? (For example, must disputes be arbitrated? Will the arbitration or litigation take place in _____ ?)

Please note that some state laws limit the franchisor's ability to enforce these provisions of the franchise agreement.

‡   **PUBLIC FIGURES.** Will any public figure be involved in promoting or managing the franchise system?

‡   **EARNINGS CLAIMS.** Do you intend to include an earnings claim in the offering circular?

‡   **LIST OF OUTLETS.** Although there are currently no franchisees, information about any company-owned stores must be disclosed, including the locations of these stores over the last three years and projections about the number of additional stores to be opened in the next fiscal year and their locations.

Index